铁道机车运用与维护专业群丛书

直线电机与磁浮驱动（汉英双语）

Linear Motor and Maglev Drive（Chinese-English Bilingual）

主编　李益民
主审　郭育华

西南交通大学出版社
·成　都·

图书在版编目（CIP）数据

直线电机与磁浮驱动 ＝ Linear Motor and Maglev Drive（Chinese-English Bilingual）：汉、英 / 李益民主编. -- 成都：西南交通大学出版社，2025. 3.
ISBN 978-7-5774-0365-6

Ⅰ.U260.4；U237

中国国家版本馆 CIP 数据核字第 20257QB329 号

Zhixian Dianji yu Cifu Qudong（Han-Ying Shuangyu）
直线电机与磁浮驱动（汉英双语）
Linear Motor and Maglev Drive（Chinese-English Bilingual）

主　编／李益民	策划编辑／李　伟
	责任编辑／李　伟
	封面设计／何东琳设计工作室

西南交通大学出版社出版发行
（四川省成都市金牛区二环路北一段 111 号西南交通大学创新大厦 21 楼　610031）
营销部电话：028-87600564　　028-87600533
网址：https://www.xnjdcbs.com
印刷：四川森林印务有限责任公司

成品尺寸　185 mm×260 mm
印张　20.25　　字数　442 千
版次　2025 年 3 月第 1 版　　印次　2025 年 3 月第 1 次

书号　ISBN 978-7-5774-0365-6
定价　58.00 元

课件咨询电话：028-81435775
图书如有印装质量问题　本社负责退换
版权所有　盗版必究　举报电话：028-87600562

前　言

随着社会经济的发展和人民生活水平的日益提高，人们的出行次数迅速增加，同时人们对旅行质量的要求也在逐步提高，这要求社会提供更加快捷、安全、舒适及符合环保要求的交通运输工具。磁浮铁路符合这些要求，它有可能成为21世纪主要的交通运输工具之一。我国国土辽阔，人口众多，尤其适合发展磁浮铁路。

世界上已有十几个国家开展过磁浮铁路的研究探索工作，目前比较成熟并具有代表性的磁浮铁路技术有三大类型：日本的高速地面运输系统（HSST）（实际为中低速磁浮铁路系统）、德国的常导超高速磁浮铁路技术（TR）及日本的超导超高速磁浮铁路技术（ML）。它们的共同之处都是依靠磁浮技术将列车悬浮起来并利用直线电机（或称线性电机）驱动列车行驶。

日本的高速地面运输系统（High Speed Surface Transport，HSST）采用常导、短定子直线电机及列车驱动的磁浮铁路技术，目前最高速度为130 km/h，适合于城市轨道交通、机场旅客运输等中短距离的旅客运输，其技术已经达到实用化程度。

德国的磁浮铁路技术（Trans Rapid，TR，简称"运捷"）采用常导、长定子直线同步电机及路轨驱动的磁浮铁路技术，最高试验速度为450 km/h（1993年），适用于中长距离的超高速旅客运输，其技术基本成熟，目前已经建成的上海浦东机场磁浮示范线采用的就是该项技术。

日本的超导磁浮铁路技术（Magnetic Levitation，ML，或称Maglev），采用低温超导、长定子直线同步电机及路轨驱动的磁浮铁路技术，最高试验速度已达552 km/h（1999年），适用于中长距离的超高速旅客运输，其技术也基本成熟。

上述三种磁浮铁路技术各有特点，究竟采用哪种形式，各个国家及各位专家有不同的看法。日本的超导磁浮铁路技术先进，运行速度高，得到大家的普遍认可，它在未来的中长途旅客运输中具有良好的发展前景。

截止到2024年10月，世界上磁浮商业营运线路共有9条（1条已停运，系1984年建成长620 m连接英国伯明翰机场和火车站的低速磁浮系统，最高速度50 km/h，属世界上首条商业运营的公共运输低速磁浮系统，1996年由于磁浮车故障率太高，维护频繁，磁浮系统停运），其中5条商业营运线路就在中国。中国第一条商业运营线——上海浦东机场磁浮示范线，是引进德国技术于2002年年底建成的国内首条高速常导磁浮线路，至今已22年，仍是全球唯一商业运营的高速磁浮线路；第二条商业运营线——长沙机场线，全长 18.55 km，是世界上最长的中低速磁浮运营线，设计最高速度为 100 km/h；第三条商业运营线——北京首条磁浮线路中低速磁浮交通示范线 S1 线，全长 10.236 km，属于中低速磁浮线路，设计最高速度为 100 km/h；第四条商业运营线是湖南凤凰磁浮文化旅游观光线，设计速度 100 km/h，线路全长 9.121 km，该线路于 2022 年 7 月 1 日正式运营；第五条商业运营线是广东清远磁浮旅游专线，设计速度 100 km/h（磁浮列车设计速度 120 km/h），线路全长 38 km，首期线路长 8.1 km。另外 3 条商业运营的中低速磁浮线路在日本、美国和韩国，一条是 2005 年 3 月开通的日本名古屋中低速磁浮线路，连接名古屋到爱知世博会举办地——丰田市，全长约 9 km；一条是 2010 年完工的华盛顿杜勒斯机场磁浮主航站楼地铁，采用德国 TR 技术，采用长定子直线同步电机驱动，由地面控制中心予以控制；另一条是 2014 年 7 月开通的韩国仁川国际机场至龙游站磁浮线路，全长 6.1 km。

磁浮技术沉寂多年后，近年来以长沙磁浮和北京磁浮为代表的国产中低速磁浮另辟蹊径，呈现燎原之势。应该说，长沙机场线和北京 S1 线示范着磁浮的性能优势与应用场景，也折射出磁浮技术发展与应用的曲折进程。我国在未来还将建设新的高速磁浮和中低速磁浮线路。

本书介绍的主要内容有绪论、直线电机、日本超导超高速磁浮铁路技术、德国常导超高速磁浮铁路技术、中国上海磁浮示范线、日本中低速磁浮 HSST 系统和我国磁浮铁路研究、发展及实践。

本书由西安铁路职业技术学院牵引动力学院李益民教授主编（编写第一章、第五章、第六章和第七章第一、二节），西南交通大学电气工程学院郭育华副教授主审。参加编写的还有西安铁路职业技术学院机电工程学院李晴工程师（编写第二章）、西安铁路职业技术学院牵引动力学院刘芳璇副教授（编写第三章）和朱慧勇讲师（编写第四章）、西安市轨道交通集团运营分公司王永卿高级工程师（编写第七章第三、四节）。西安铁路职业技术学院基础部周亚婷讲师（翻译第三章、第四章和第七章）、基础部张瑞珏讲师（翻译第五章和第六章）、机电工程学院李晴工程师（翻译第二章）、牵引动力学院朱慧勇讲师（翻译第一章）等负责翻译。全书由李益民负责统稿。

非常感谢西南交通大学电气工程学院卢国涛和刘国清二位老师，他们为本书编写提供了不少实用资料。

由于编者手中缺少综合介绍磁浮铁路技术的书籍，尤其缺少介绍中国国内磁浮铁路的书籍，因此书中疏漏和不足难免存在，敬请大家批评指正。

编 者

2024 年 8 月 28 日

PREFACE

With the development of social economy and the improvement of people's living standards, the number of people's trips is increasing rapidly, and people's requirements for the quality of travel are also gradually improving, which requires the society to provide more efficient, safe, comfortable and environmentally friendly means of transportation. The maglev railway meets these requirements, and it will probably become one of the main means of transportation in the 21st century. China has a vast territory and a large population, which is especially suitable for the development of maglev railway.

More than a dozen countries in the world have carried out research and exploration of maglev railway. At present, there are three types of maglev railway technology which are relatively mature and representative: Japan's high speed surface transport system (HSST) (actually a medium-low speed maglev railway system), Germany's normal conductor ultra-high speed maglev technology (TR) and Japan's superconducting ultra-high speed maglev technology (ML). What they have in common is that they rely on maglev technology to suspend the train and use linear motor to drive the train.

The High Speed Surface Transport System (HSST) in Japan adopts the maglev railway technology of normal conductor, short-stator linear motor and train drive, with the highest speed of 130 km/h at present, which is suitable for medium and short distance passenger transport such as urban rail transit and airport passenger transport. Its technology has reached a practical level.

The maglev railway technology in Germany (Trans Rapid, TR) adopts the maglev railway technology driven by normal conductor, long stator linear synchronous motor and rail, with the maximum test speed of 450 km/h (1993), which is suitable for medium and long distance ultra-high speed passenger transportation, and its technology is basically mature. At present, the maglev demonstration line of Shanghai Pudong Airport has been built using this technology.

Magnetic Levitation (ML, or Maglev) technology in Japan adopts low-temperature superconducting, long-stator linear synchronous motor and rail-driven maglev railway technology, with a maximum test speed of 552 km/h (1999), which is suitable for medium and long distance ultra-high speed passenger transport. Its technology is also basically mature.

The above three kinds of maglev railway technologies have their own characteristics, and various countries and experts have different views on which form to adopt. Japan's superconducting maglev railway has advanced technology and high running speed, which is generally recognized by everyone. It has a good development prospect in the future medium and long distance passenger transport.

As of October 2024, there are nine maglev commercial lines in the world (one has been suspended, which is a 620 m long low-speed maglev system built in 1984 connecting Birmingham Airport and Railway Station in the United Kingdom, with a maximum speed of 50 km/h, which is the first commercial public transport low-speed maglev system in the world. Due to the high failure rate and frequent maintenance of the maglev vehicles, the maglev system is out of service in 1996), of which five commercial lines are in China. Shanghai Pudong Airport Maglev Demonstration Line, the first commercial operation line in China, is the first high-speed normally conducting maglev line in China built at the end of 2002 by introducing German technology. It has been 22 years since then and is still the only high-speed maglev line in commercial operation in the world; The second commercial operation line, Changsha Airport Line, with a total length of 18.55 km, is the longest medium and low speed maglev operation line in the world, with a designed maximum speed of 100 km/h. The third commercial operation line is the first medium-low speed maglev traffic demonstration line S1 in Beijing, with a total length of 10.236 km, belonging to the medium-low speed maglev line, with a designed maximum speed of 100 km/h. The fourth commercial operation line is the Hunan Phoenix Maglev Cultural Tourism Line, with a designed speed of 100 km/h and a total line length of 9.121 kilometers. This line officially began operations on July 1, 2022. The fifth commercial operation line is the Guangdong Qingyuan Maglev Tourism Line, with a designed speed of 100 km/h (the maglev train has a designed speed of 120 km/h). The total line length is 38 kilometers, with the first phase of the line being 8.1 kilometers. The other three commercial medium and low speed maglev lines are in Japan, the United States and the Republic of Korea (ROK). One is the Nagoya medium and low speed maglev line opened in March 2005, which connects Nagoya to Toyota City, the host city of the Aichi World Expo, with a total length of about 9 km; One is the Washington Dulles Airport Maglev Main Terminal Subway completed in 2010, which adopts German TR technology and is driven by long stator linear synchronous motor and controlled by the ground control center; the other is the maglev line from Incheon International Airport to Yongyow Station in ROK, which was opened in July 2014, with a total length of 6.1 km.

After years of silence in maglev technology, in recent years, the domestic medium and low speed maglev represented by Changsha Maglev and Beijing Maglev has opened up a new path, showing a prairie fire. It should be said that Changsha Airport Line and Beijing S1 Line demonstrate the performance advantages and application scenarios of maglev, and also reflect the tortuous process of the development and application of maglev technology. China will also build new high-speed maglev and medium-low speed maglev lines in the future.

The main contents of this book include introduction, linear motor, Japan's superconducting ultra-high speed maglev railway technology, Germany's normal conducting ultra-high speed maglev railway technology, China's Shanghai maglev demonstration line, Japan's medium-low speed maglev HSST system and China's maglev railway research, development and practice.

This book is edited by Professor Li Yimin of the Traction Power Institute at Xi'an Railway Vocational and Technical College (author of Chapters 1, 5, 6, and Sections 1 and 2 of Chapter 7), with Associate Professor Guo Yuhua of the School of Electrical Engineering at Southwest Jiaotong University serving as the chief reviewer. Other contributors include Engineer Li Qing of the Mechanical and Electrical Engineering Institute at Xi'an Railway Vocational and Technical College (author of Chapter 2), Associate Professor Liu Fangxuan of the Traction Power Institute (author of Chapter 3), and Lecturer Zhu Huiyong of the same institute (author of Chapter 4). Senior Engineer Wang Yongqing of the Xi'an Urban Rail Transit Group Operation Branch contributed by writing Sections 3 and 4 of Chapter 7. For translations, Lecturer Zhou Yating of the Basic Courses Department (translator of Chapter 3, 4, and 7), Lecturer Zhang Ruijue (translator of Chapter 5 and 6), Engineer Li Qing (translator of Chapter 2), and Lecturer Zhu Huiyong (translator of Chapter 1) were responsible. The entire book was compiled and finalized by Professor Li Yimin.

We are very grateful to Lu Guotao and Liu Guoqing, two teachers from the School of Electrical Engineering of Southwest Jiaotong University, for providing a lot of practical information for the compilation of this book.

Due to the lack of books on comprehensive introduction of maglev railway technology in the hands of editors, especially the lack of books on maglev railway in China, omissions and shortcomings in the book are unavoidable. Please criticize and correct them.

Compiler
August 28, 2024

目 录

CONTENTS

第一章 绪 论 ·· 1
Chapter 1　Introduction of Maglev Train ································ 1

　第一节　铁路分类 ·· 2
　Section 1.1　Classification of Railway ······································ 2

　第二节　磁浮铁路分类 ··· 9
　Section 1.2　Classification of Maglev Railway ····························· 9

　第三节　磁浮列车的工作原理 ··· 25
　Section 1.3　Working Principle of Maglev Train ························· 25

　第四节　磁浮列车的分类 ··· 30
　Section 1.4　Classification of Maglev Train ······························· 30

　第五节　国外磁浮交通技术的应用发展概况 ································ 34
　Section1. 5　Overview of Application and Development of Maglev
　　　　　　　Transportation Technology in Foreign Countries ······· 34

　第六节　磁浮轴承 ··· 49
　Section 1.6　Magnetic Bearing ··· 49

　复习思考题 ··· 49
　Questions for Revision ·· 49

第二章　直线电机 ·· 51
Chapter 2　Linear Motor ·· 51

　第一节　直线电机的基本结构 ··· 51
　Section 2.1　Basic structure of linear motor ······························ 51

　第二节　直线电机的工作原理 ··· 56
　Section 2.2　Working Principle of Linear Motor ························· 56

　第三节　直线电机的分类 ··· 62
　Section 2.3　Classification of Linear Motor ······························· 62

　第四节　有关直线电机的标准 ··· 67
　Section 2.4　Standards for Linear Motors ································ 67

　复习思考题 ··· 71
　Questions for Revision ·· 71

第三章　日本超导超高速磁浮铁路技术 ································ 72
Chapter 3　Superconducting Ultra-high-speed Maglev Railway Technology in Japan ································ 72

第一节　日本磁浮铁路技术的发展过程 ···················· 72
Section 3.1　Development Process of Maglev Railway Technology in Japan ······· 72

第二节　山梨试验线概况 ·· 77
Section 3.2　Overview of Yamanashi Test Line ·············· 77

第三节　基本原理 ·· 82
Section 3.3　Basic Principles ··· 82

第四节　车辆及列车编组 ·· 90
Section 3.4　Vehicle and Train Formation ······················ 90

第五节　供电及控制 ·· 105
Section 3.5　Power Supply and Control ························· 105

复习思考题 ·· 111
Questions for Revision ·· 111

第四章　德国常导超高速磁浮铁路技术 ···································· 112
Chapter 4　Technology of Normal Conducting Ultra-high-speed Maglev Railway in Germany ································ 112

第一节　概　述 ·· 112
Section 4.1　Overview ·· 112

第二节　基本原理 ·· 122
Section 4.2　Basic Principle ··· 122

第三节　列车与车辆 ·· 128
Section 4.3　Train and Vehicle ·· 128

第四节　线　路 ·· 135
Section 4.4　Line ·· 135

第五节　供电与运行控制 ·· 144
Section 4.5　Power Supply and Operation Control ········· 144

第六节　安全性能 ·· 151
Section 4.6　Safety Performance ···································· 151

第七节　环保性能 ·· 157
Section 4.7　Environmental Protection Performance ······ 157

第八节　德国、日本超高速磁浮铁路技术经济比较 ······ 165
Section 4.8　Technical and Economic Comparison of Ultra-high-speed Maglev Railway in Germany and Japan ···················· 165

复习思考题 ·· 183
   Questions for Revision ··· 183

第五章　中国上海磁浮示范线 ··· 184
Chapter 5　China Shanghai Maglev Demonstration Line ············· 184

   第一节　概　述 ·· 185
   Section 5.1　Overview ··· 185
   第二节　线路设计 ·· 200
   Section 5.2　Line Design ··· 200
   第三节　轨道结构 ·· 207
   Section 5.3　Track Structure ·· 207
   第四节　车站与维修基地 ··· 220
   Section 5.4　Station and Maintenance Base ································· 220
   复习思考题 ·· 223
   Questions for Revision ··· 223

第六章　日本中低速磁浮 HSST 系统 ·· 224
Chapter 6　Japan Medium and Low Speed Maglev HSST System ··· 224

   第一节　概　述 ·· 224
   Section 6.1　Overview ··· 224
   第二节　工作原理 ·· 235
   Section 6.2　Operating Principle ·· 235
   第三节　HSST 试验线 ·· 240
   Section 6.3　HSST Test Line ·· 240
   第四节　车　辆 ·· 242
   Section 6.4　Vehicles ·· 242
   第五节　轨　道 ·· 248
   Section 6.5　Track ·· 248
   第六节　供电系统 ·· 250
   Section 6.6　Power Supply System ·· 250
   第七节　安全与救援措施 ··· 251
   Section 6.7　Safety and Rescue Measures ··································· 251
   第八节　HSST 与 TR 系统的比较 ··· 253
   Section 6.8　Comparison of HSST and TR System ························ 253
   复习思考题 ·· 259
   Questions for Revision ··· 259

第七章　我国磁浮铁路研究、发展及实践 ······················· 261
Chapter 7　Research, Development and Practice of Maglev Railway
　　　　　　in China ·· 261

    第一节　磁浮技术在中国的研究及发展概况 ················· 262
    Section 7.1　Research and Development of Maglev Technology in China ······ 262
    第二节　我国已建成的磁浮铁路线 ································ 280
    Section 7.2　Maglev Railway Lines Built in China ························ 280
    第三节　我国在建或拟建的磁浮铁路线 ························ 300
    Section 7.3　Maglev Railway Lines Under Construction or Proposed
　　　　　　　　in China ··· 300
    第四节　新型磁浮交通方式的探索 ································ 304
    Section 7.4　Exploration of New Maglev Transportation Mode ·········· 304
    复习思考题 ·· 309
    Questions for Revision ·· 309

参考文献 ·· 310
References ·· 310
附录　学习资源 ·· 311
Appendix　Learning Resources ·· 311

第一章 绪 论

Chapter 1　Introduction of Maglev Train

　　磁浮列车（Maglev Train）是一种现代高科技轨道交通工具，它通过电磁力实现列车与轨道之间的无接触悬浮和导向，再利用直线电机产生的电磁力牵引列车运行。

　　Maglev Train is a modern high-tech rail transit tool, which realizes the non-contact suspension and guidance between the train and the track through the electromagnetic force, and then uses the electromagnetic force generated by the linear motor to pull the train to run.

　　1922 年，德国工程师赫尔曼·肯佩尔（Hermann Kemper）提出了电磁悬浮原理，继而申请了专利。20 世纪 70 年代以后，随着工业化国家经济实力不断增强，为提高交通运输能力以适应其经济发展和民生的需要，德国、日本、美国等国家相继开展了磁浮运输系统的研发。

　　In 1922, the German engineer Hermann Kemper proposed the principle of electric maglev, and then applied for a patent. After the 1970s, with the continuous economic strength of of industrialized countries, in order to improve the transportation capacity to meet the needs of their economic development and people's livelihood, Germany, Japan, the United States and other countries have carried out the research and development of maglev transportation system.

　　目前有三种典型的磁浮技术：第一种是德国发明的常导电磁悬浮技术，我国上海磁浮列车、长沙磁浮列车和北京磁浮列车均采用该技术；第二种是日本发明的低温超导磁浮技术，如日本在建的中央新干线磁浮线路；第三种是高温超导磁浮技术，与低温超导磁浮技术的液氦冷却（－269 ℃）不同，高温超导磁浮技术采用液氮冷却（－196 ℃），工作温度得到了提高。日本的超导磁浮（ML）、德国的常导磁浮（TR）和日本航空的常导磁浮（HSST）都是典型磁浮技术的代表。

　　At present, there are three typical maglev technologies: the first is the normal conducting magnetic levitation technology invented in Germany, which is used in Shanghai Maglev train, Changsha Maglev train and Beijing Maglev train. The second is the low temperature superconducting magnetic levitation technology invented in Japan, such as the central Shinkansen maglev line under construction in Japan. The third is the high temperature superconducting magnetic levitation technology, which is different from the liquid helium cooling of the low temperature superconducting magnetic levitation technology (−269 °C), the high temperature superconducting magnetic levitation technology uses liquid nitrogen cooling (−196 °C), and the working temperature is improved. Japan's superconducting maglev (ML), Germany's constant conducting maglev (TR) and Japan Airlines' constant conducting maglev (HSST) are all representatives of the typical maglev technology.

  本章主要介绍磁浮铁路的分类、作用以及上述磁浮铁路的发展。为此先定义铁路的类型和磁浮铁路的类型。

  This chapter mainly introduces the classification, function and development of the maglev railway. The type of railway and maglev railway will be defined firstly.

第一节 铁路分类

Section 1.1 Classification of Railway

  日本的超导磁浮线路和德国的常导磁浮线路属于超高速铁路。超高速铁路是相对高速铁路而言的，是由列车的最高运行速度决定的。根据列车的最高运行速度的不同，铁路可以划分为低速、快速、高速和超高速铁路等类型。

  The superconducting magnetic levitation lines in Japan and the normal magneticlevitation lines in Germany belong to ultra-high-speed railway. Ultra-high-speed railway is relative to high-speed railway, which is determined by the maximum running speed of trains. According to the different maximum running speeds of trains, the railway can be divided into low-speed, fast-speed, high-speed, and ultra-high-speed railway.

一、低速铁路

1.1.1 Low-speed Railway

  列车最高运行速度不大于 120 km/h 的铁路称为低速铁路，即通常意义上的铁路，也称普速铁路、普通铁路、常速铁路或简称为铁路。这种铁路大部分为客货混线运输的铁路，目前世界上绝大部分铁路都属于这种铁路。

  The railway with the maximum running speed of no more than 120 km/h is called low speed railway, which is also known as the common speed railway, ordinary railway, constant speed railway or simply called railway. Most of these railways are for the passenger and freight mixed line transportation, and most of the railways in the world belong to this kind of railway at present.

根据《铁路主要技术政策》的划分，低速铁路一般包括特别繁忙干线、繁忙干线、干线、支线及城际铁路。

According to the classification of "*Main Technical Policies for Railways*", low-speed railway generally include extremely busy trunk lines, busy trunk lines, trunk lines, branch lines and intercity railway.

（一）特别繁忙干线

1.1.1.1　Extremely Busy Trunk Lines

在国家重要的交通运输大通道中担当客货运输主力，在路网中起极重要的骨干作用，且客货行车量达到或超过 100 对的线路称为特别繁忙干线。

As the main force of passenger and freight transportation in the national important transportation corridor, and playing an extremely important backbone role in the road network, the lines with passenger and freight traffic reaching or exceeding 100 pairs are called particularly busy trunk lines.

（二）繁忙干线

1.1.1.2　Busy Trunk Lines

连接经济发达地区或经济大区，在路网中起重要的骨干作用，且客货行车量单线达到或超过 30 对和双线达到或超过 60 对的线路称为繁忙干线。

Busy trunk lines connect economically developed regions or large economic areas, play an important role in the road network, and the single line passenger and freight traffic volume reaches or exceeds 30 pairs and the double line passenger and freight traffic volume reaches or exceeds 60 pairs.

（三）干　线

1.1.1.3　Trunk Lines

连接大中城市，在路网中起骨干作用，且客货行车量超过 15 对的线路称为干线。

Connecting large and medium-sized cities, playing a backbone role in the road network, and the passenger and freight traffic volume exceeds 15 pairs are called trunk lines.

（四）支　线

1.1.1.4　Branch Lines

连接中小城市，在路网中起辅助、联络作用，或为地区经济交通运输服务，或客货行车量不超过 15 对的线路称为支线。

The lines that connect small and medium-sized cities, play an auxiliary and liaison role in the road network, or serve the regional economic transportation, or the passenger and freight traffic volume does not exceed 15 pairs are called branch lines.

（五）城际铁路

1.1.1.5　Intercity Railway

长度在 500 km 以下、客货运输繁忙、相邻两大城市间的铁路称为城际铁路。

A railway with a length of less than 500 km and heavy passenger and freight transport between two adjacent big cities is called an intercity railway.

二、快速铁路

1.1.2　Fast-speed Railway

列车最高运行速度为 120～200 km/h 的铁路称为快速铁路，其中以客运为主的铁路，列车的最高运行速度不低于 160 km/h。快速铁路有时也称为中速铁路。我国铁路大提速的速度目标值大部分都是由低速铁路的速度范围提高到快速铁路的速度范围。目前，我国的主要干线铁路已由低速铁路升级为快速铁路。未来的铁路大提速将在规定范围内将低速铁路改造为快速铁路。

The railway with the maximum running speed of 120-200 km/h is called the fast-speed railway, among which the maximum running speed of the train is not less than 160 km/h for passenger transport. Fast-speed railway is sometimes called medium-speed railway. The speed target value of China's railway acceleration is mostly raised from the speed range of low-speed railway to the speed range of fast-speed railway. At present, the main trunk railway has been upgraded from low-speed railway to fast-speed railway. In the future railway acceleration, High-speed railway will be transformed from low-speed railway within the specified scope.

原先曾经将列车最高运行速度为 160～200 km/h 的铁路称为准高速铁路。2000 年，铁道部颁布的《铁路主要技术政策》已将准高速铁路归为快速铁路。

Previously, the railway with the maximum running speed of 160-200 km/h was called quasi high-speed railway. In 2000, Ministry of Railways issued the "Main Technical Policies for Railways", which classified quasi high-speed railway as fast-speed railway.

三、高速铁路

1.1.3 High-speed Railway

高速铁路，简称高铁，在不同国家、不同时代有不同规定。一般将列车最高运行速度为 200～350 km/h 的铁路称为高速铁路。日本 1970 年在《全国新干线铁路整备法》中规定：在主要区间能以 200 km/h 以上速度运行的干线铁路为新干线（即最高速度）。在欧洲，新建铁路的列车最高运行速度为 250～300 km/h，既有线达到 200 km/h 的铁路称为高速铁路。目前，国际上一般认为列车最高运行速度达到 200 km/h 及以上的铁路才能称为高速铁路。中国国家铁路局将高速铁路定义为：新建设计开行 250 km/h（含预留）及以上动车组列车、初期运营速度不小于 200 km/h 的客运专线铁路。

High-speed Railway, has different regulations in different countries and times. Generally, the railway with the maximum running speed of 200-350 km/h is called high-speed railway. In 1970, Japan stipulated in the National Shinkansen Railway Servicing Law that Shinkansen (the highest speed) is the trunk railway that can run at a speed of more than 200 km/h in the main section. In Europe, the maximum running speed of trains on new railway is 250-300 km/h, and the railway with existing lines up to 200 km/h are called high-speed railway. At present, it is generally believed that only the railway with a maximum train speed of 200 km/h and above can be called a high-speed railway. China National Railway Administration defines high-speed railway as a new passenger dedicated railway designed to operate 250 km/h (including reserved) and above EMU trains, and the initial operating speed is not less than 200 km/h.

世界上第一条高速铁路是日本的东海道新干线，于 1964 年 10 月建成通车。

The world's first high-speed railway was the Tokaido Shinkansen in Japan, which put into use in October 1964.

我国第一条客运专线——秦沈客运专线已于 2003 年 10 月 12 日开通运营，其最高速度为 200～250 km/h。

China's first dedicated passenger line, Qinhuang-Shenyang dedicated passenger line, was put into operation on October 12, 2003, with a maximum speed of 200-250 km/h.

低速、快速、高速铁路有一个共同的特点：列车依靠轮轨接触方式驱动，即列车车轮紧贴钢轨运行，钢轨为车轮提供支承、牵引及导向三大功能。

Low-speed, fast-speed and high-speed railway have a common feature: trains are driven by wheel-rail contact, that is, the wheel runs against the rail, which provides support, traction and guidance for the wheel.

四、超高速铁路——磁浮铁路

1.1.4 Ultra-high-speed Railway—Maglev Railway

为了与轮轨接触的高速铁路相区别,我们建议将列车最高运行速度超过 350 km/h 的铁路称为超高速铁路。

In order to distinguish from the high-speed railway with wheel rail contact, we suggest that the railway with the maximum running speed of more than 350 km/h be called Ultra-high-speed railway.

目前,一般认为轮轨接触型铁路的实用最高速度为 350 km/h 左右,故欲使列车达到更高的运行速度,难以依靠传统的轮轨接触方式,而要依靠其他的牵引方式来降低列车的运行阻力,尤其是轮轨摩擦阻力。为此国际上曾研制过气垫列车、磁浮列车等新型的铁路运输工具,但目前比较成熟的超高速铁路技术仍然为磁浮铁路技术。

At present, it is generally believed that the maximum practical speed of wheel-rail contact railway is about 350 km/h, so it is difficult to rely on the traditional wheel-rail contact mode to make the train reach a higher running speed, and it is necessary to rely on other traction modes to reduce the train running resistance, especially the wheel-rail friction resistance. For this reason, new means of railway transport such as air cushion train and maglev train have been developed in the world, but maglev railway technology is still the most mature ultra-high-speed railway technology at present.

磁浮铁路目前分为低速、中速、高速和超高速几种类型,列车最高运行速度超过 350 km/h 的磁浮铁路为超高速磁浮铁路。目前,中美两国正在准备研制磁浮飞机,其最高运行速度为 500 km/h,这种磁浮飞机也应归入超高速磁浮铁路的范畴。

Currently, maglev railway can be divided into low-speed, medium-speed, high-speed and ultra-high-speed. Ultra-high-speed maglev railways are those with the highest train speed exceeding 350 km/h. Currently, China and the US are preparing to develop maglev aircraft with a maximum operating speed of 500 km/h, which should also fall under the category of ultra-high-speed maglev railway.

五、高速、超高速铁路的发展阶段

1.1.5 Development Stage of High-speed and Ultra-high-speed Railway

高速铁路和超高速铁路一般统称为高速铁路,可以将其按最高运行速度及其发展阶段进一步分类。考虑到将来的发展,高速及超高速铁路可以划分为五代。

High-speed railway and ultra-high-speed railway are generally referred to as high-speed railway, which can be further classified according to the highest operating speed and development stage. Considering the future development, high-speed and ultra-high-speed railway can be divided into five generations.

（一）第一代

1.1.5.1 The First Generation

第一代属于高速铁路的范畴，列车最高运行速度为 200～250 km/h。它采用传统的轮轨接触形式。这一代高速铁路的典型代表是世界上第一条高速铁路——日本东海道新干线，1964年10月1日建成通车，当时列车最高运行速度为 210 km/h。我国的秦沈客运专线全线设计速度达到 200 km/h 或以上，基础设施预留 250 km/h 的提速条件，故该条线路应属于第一代高速铁路。

The first generation belongs to the category of high-speed railway, with the maximum running speed of trains at 200-250 km/h. It uses the traditional wheel-rail contact form. The typical representative of this generation of high-speed railway is the world's first high-speed railway, Japan's Tokaido Shinkansen, which was completed on October 1, 1964, with a maximum running speed of 210 km/h. The designed speed of Qinhuangdao-Shenyang passenger dedicated line has reached 200 km/h or above, and the infrastructure has reserved 250 km/h for speed increase. Therefore, this line should belong to the first generation of high-speed railway.

（二）第二代

1.1.5.2 The Second Generation

第二代属于高速铁路的范畴，列车最高运行速度为 250～350 km/h。它也采用传统的轮轨接触方式。目前新建的高速铁路大多属于这种类型。日本后来建设的北陆新干线（最高运行速度 260 km/h）、法国的东南线（最高运行速度 270 km/h）及大西洋线（最高运行速度 300 km/h）、中国的京沪高速铁路（设计最高运行速度 350～380 km/h，运营速度 350 km/h）均属于第二代高速铁路。

The second generation belongs to the category of high-speed railway, with the maximum running speed of trains at 250-350 km/h. It also adopts the traditional wheel-rail contact mode. Most of the new high-speed railways are of this type. The Japan's later built Hokuriku Shinkansen (maximum operating speed 260 km/h), France's Southeast Line (maximum operating speed 270 km/h) and Atlantic Line (maximum operating speed 300 km/h), China's Beijing-Shanghai high-speed railway (design maximum operating speed 350-380 km/h, Operating speed of 350 km/h) are the second generation of high-speed railway.

（三）第三代

1.1.5.3　The Third Generation

第三代属于超高速铁路的范畴，列车最高运行速度为 350～550 km/h，主要依靠磁浮方式实现线路与列车之间的无接触运行。其主要特点是线路修建在地面上并且列车在普通的大气环境中运行。目前能实现这一运行速度的磁浮方式只有日本的 ML 方式（最高运行速度 500 km/h，超导磁浮）和德国的运捷（最高运行速度 440 km/h，常导磁浮 TR）。我国于 2002 年 12 月开始试运营的上海磁浮示范线（最高运行速度 430 km/h）和青岛开发的速度 600 km/h 高速磁浮试验样车也属于第三代高速铁路范畴。

The third generation belongs to the category of ultra-high-speed railway, the maximum running speed of trains is 350-550 km/h, mainly relying on maglev mode to realize the non-contact operation between the line and train. Its main feature is that the line is built on the ground and trains run in ordinary atmospheric environment. At present, the only maglev modes that can achieve this operating speed are Japan's ML mode (maximum operating speed 500 km/h, superconducting maglev) and Germany's TR (maximum operating speed 440 km/h, permanent maglev TR). China's Shanghai Maglev Demonstration Line (maximum operating speed 430 km/h) began trial operation in December 2002 and the 600 km/h high-speed maglev test model developed in Qingdao also belong to the category of third generation high-speed railway.

（四）第四代

1.1.5.4　The Fourth Generation

第四代属于超高速铁路的范畴，其主要特点是线路采用高架低真空管道形式。管道内保留 10%～20%的空气，即将常温时的空气密度（1.2 kg/m³）降为低真空密度（0.12～0.24 kg/m³）。列车最高运行速度可达 2 000～3 000 km/h，大约为两倍的音速。目前这种交通方式只是处于前期构想和试验阶段，预计 10 年左右时间，这种超高速铁路可能成为现实。

The fourth generation belongs to the category of ultra-high-speed railway, its main feature is that the line adopts the form of elevated low vacuum pipe. 10%-20% air is retained in the pipe, that is, the air density at normal temperature (1.2 kg/m³) is reduced to low vacuum density (0.12-0.24 kg/m³). The maximum running speed of the train can reach 2 000-3 000 km/h, which is about twice the speed of sound. At present, this mode of transportation is only in the preliminary conception and experimental stage, and it is expected that in 10 years or so, the ultra-high speed rail line may become a reality.

（五）第五代

1.1.5.5　The Fifth Generation

第五代属于超高速铁路的范畴，其主要特点是线路采用地下真空管道磁浮形式。20 世纪 70 年代末，美国一家咨询公司设计了一种"行星号"的未来地下铁道，理论速度可达 22 500 km/h，纽约至洛杉矶只需半小时即可到达。这种超高速列车不但可以获得极高的运行速度，而且其运营费比普通铁路便宜 90%，比飞机便宜 95%。这是一种理想型、科幻型的超高速铁路。限于现代科技水平及经济方面的原因，这种高速铁路目前还难以实现。

The fifth generation belongs to the category of ultra-high-speed railway, its main feature is that the line uses the maglev form of underground vacuum pipe. In the late 1970s, an American consulting firm designed a future underground train called "Planet" that could theoretically reach speeds of 22 500 km/h and travel from New York to Los Angeles in just half an hour. This super-fast train can not only achieve extremely high speed, but also operate 90% cheaper than normal railway and 95% cheaper than airplane. This is an ideal, sci-fitype of super-fast railway. Limited to the level of modern science and technology and economic reasons, this kind of high-speed railway is still difficult to achieve.

从上面的分析可以看出，将来高速、超高速铁路的发展方向是磁浮铁路。

From the above analysis, it can be seen that the development direction of high-speed and ultra-high -speed railway in the future is magnetic levitation railway.

第二节　磁浮铁路分类

Section 1.2　Classification of Maglev Railway

根据不同的划分方式，磁浮铁路可以划分为多种类型。

Maglev railway can be divided into various types according to different ways of classification.

一、按应用范围划分

1.2.1　According to the Application Range

应用范围主要体现在线路长度、在路网中的作用、最高运行速度及所属管理部门等方面。据此磁浮铁路可以划分为干线磁浮、城际磁浮和城市磁浮。

The application range is mainly reflected in the line length, the role in the road network, the highest running speed and the subordinate management department. Accordingly, maglev railway can be divided into trunk maglev, intercity maglev and urban maglev.

（一）干线磁浮

1.2.1.1 Trunk Maglev

这里的干线包括前述的特别繁忙干线、繁忙干线和干线，线路长度一般超过500 km，在国家重要的交通运输大通道担当客运主力，连接经济发达地区、经济大区或大中城市，在路网中起重要的骨干作用。该铁路的最高运行速度一般要达到高速或超高速铁路的速度范围，一般归铁路部门或交通部门经营管理。

The trunk lines here include the aforementioned particularly busy trunk lines, busy trunk lines and trunk lines. The length of the line is generally more than 500 km. It acts as the main passenger transport force in the country's important transportation corridors, connecting economically developed areas, economic regions or large and medium-sized cities, and plays an important backbone role in the road network. The maximum operating speed of the railway should generally reach the speed range of high-speed or ultra-high-speed railway, which is generally operated and managed by the railway department or the transportation department.

（二）城际磁浮

1.2.1.2 Intercity Maglev

其线路长度在500 km以下，连接客运繁忙的相邻两大城市。运行速度一般达到中高速铁路的速度范围，一般归铁路部门或交通部门经营管理。

Its line length is less than 500 km, connecting two neighboring cities with heavy passenger traffic. The running speed generally reaches the speed range of medium and high speed railway, which is generally operated and managed by the railway departments or the transportation departments.

（三）城市磁浮

1.2.1.3 Urban Maglev

其线路长度不超过100 km，承担市内交通、机场内交通或机场与市区间交通的任务。由于运行距离较短，列车的运行速度一般是在中低速的速度范围内，一般归市政部门或民航部门管理。

Its line length is not more than 100 km, and it is responsible for urban traffic, intra-airport traffic or traffic between airports and urban areas. Due to the short running distance, the running speed of trains is generally in the range of medium and low speed, which is generally managed by municipal authorities or civil aviation authorities.

二、按运行速度划分

1.2.2 According to the Running Speed

根据前述划分标准，按照列车的最高运行速度，磁浮铁路可分为低速（常速）磁浮、中速磁浮、高速磁浮和超高速磁浮铁路。一般将低速和中速磁浮统称为中低速磁浮，而将高速和超高速磁浮统称为高速磁浮。中低速磁浮主要适用于城市轨道交通（含机场内交通），高速磁浮主要适用于干线和城际交通。

According to the above classification standards and the highest running speed of trains, maglev railway can be divided into low-speed (normal speed) maglev railway, medium-speed maglev railway, high-speed maglev railway and ultra-high-speed maglev railway. Generally, low-speed and medium-speed maglev railway are collectively referred to as medium-low-speed maglev railway, while high-speed and ultra-high-speed maglev railway are called as high-speed maglev railway. Medium-low-speed maglev railway is mainly applicable to urban rail transit (including intra-airport traffic), while high-speed maglev railway is mainly applicable to trunk lines and intercity traffic.

三、按导体材料划分

1.2.3 According to the Conductor Material

根据直线电机线圈绕组是否使用超导体材料，磁浮铁路可以划分为超导磁浮和常导磁浮。

Maglev railway can be divided into superconducting maglev railway and normal maglev railway according to whether the coil winding of linear motor is made of superconducting material or not.

（一）超导磁浮

1.2.3.1 Superconducting Maglev

超导磁浮的线圈使用超导材料。超导材料在周围环境温度低于其临界温度后就处于超导状态，即超导绕组内的电阻几乎为零。超导电磁铁能产生强大的磁场，具有极高的工作效率，因此可以使列车获得较大的悬浮高度和更快的运行速度。其缺点主要为超导磁铁结构复杂，体积庞大，并且为了使超导绕组始终处于超导状态，在列车上还要配备制冷装置。日本的 ML 技术属于超导磁浮技术。

The coil of superconducting magnetic levitation uses superconducting materials. Superconducting materials are in a superconducting state when the ambient temperature is lower than its critical temperature, that is, the resistance in the superconducting winding is almost zero. Superconducting electromagnet can produce strong magnetic field and has high working efficiency, so it can make the train obtain larger suspension height and faster running speed. Its main disadvantages are that the superconducting magnet has complex structure and huge volume. In order to keep the superconducting winding in superconducting state, the train is also equipped with a refrigeration device. Japan's ML technology belongs to superconducting magnetic levitation technology.

（二）常导磁浮

1.2.3.2　Normal Maglev

常导磁浮使用普通材料制成线圈绕组，采用普通导体通电励磁，产生电磁悬浮力和导向力。这种直线电机具有结构简单、养护维修方便等优点。其主要缺点是线圈绕组中电阻较大。因此这种直线电机的功率损失较大，并且线圈绕组容易发热，列车的运行速度也会受到一定限制。德国的运捷（TR）、日本的 HSST 及我国的大部分磁浮研究都属于常导磁浮技术。

The normal maglev uses coil windings made of common materials, and ordinary conductor is used for energizing excitation to generate electromagnetic suspension force and guiding force. The linear motor has the advantages of simple structure, convenient maintenance and so on. The main disadvantage is that the resistance in the coil winding group is larger. Therefore, the power loss of the linear motor is large, and the winding is easy to heat, and the running speed of the train will be limited to a certain extent. Germany's TR, Japan's HSST, and most of China's maglev research belong to normal maglev technology.

四、按制冷剂及工作温度划分

1.2.4　According to Refrigerant and Working Temperature

超导磁浮铁路依靠制冷剂使超导绕组维持在超导状态。目前，超导磁浮常用的制冷剂为液氮和液氦。根据两者工作温度的不同，磁浮铁路又可划分为高温超导磁浮和低温超导磁浮两类。

Superconducting magnetic levitation railway relies on refrigerant to maintain superconducting winding in superconducting state. At present, the commonly used refrigerants for superconducting magnetic levitation are liquid nitrogen and liquid helium. According to the different operating temperatures, the maglev railway can be divided into two categories: high-temperature superconducting maglev and low-temperature superconducting maglev.

（一）高温超导磁浮

1.2.4.1　High-temperature Superconducting Maglev

液氮的工作温度为 77 K（－196 °C）。采用适合于该工作温度的超导材料制作的磁浮绕组的磁浮称为高温超导磁浮，目前一般采用液氮作为高温超导线圈绕组制冷剂。我国西南交通大学研制出了高温超导磁浮系统，超导材料使用以钇（Y）为主的钇钡铜氧（YBaCuO）高温超导体块材。

The operating temperature of liquid nitrogen is 77 K (－196 °C). The maglev winding made of superconducting material suitable for the working temperature is called high-temperature superconducting maglev. Currently liquid nitrogen is generally used as the refrigerant for high temperature superconducting coil winding. The high-temperature superconducting maglev system has been developed in Southwest Jiaotong University. The superconducting material is YBaCuO bulk superconductor with yttrium (Y) as the main component.

值得注意的是，高温超导磁浮的工作温度未必是固定的。随着超导技术的发展，磁浮铁路所使用的高温超导工作温度可能升高。将来也有可能使用常温超导磁浮材料，到那时还可能出现常温超导磁浮铁路。

It is worth noting that the working temperature of the high-temperature superconducting maglev is not necessarily fixed. With the development of superconductivity, the working temperature used by maglev railway may increase. In the future, normal temperature superconducting maglev materials may be used, and then normal temperature superconducting maglev railway may appear.

（二）低温超导磁浮

1.2.4.2　Low-temperature Superconducting Maglev

液氦的工作温度为 4.2 K（－269 °C）。采用适合该工作温度的超导材料制作绕组并且采用液氦作为超导绕组制冷剂的磁浮称为低温超导磁浮，简称超导磁浮。日本的 ML 磁浮系统是低温超导磁浮系统，超导绕组使用铌钛合金制造。

The operating temperature of liquid helium is 4.2 K (－269 °C). The maglev, which uses the superconducting material suitable for the working temperature to make the winding and uses liquid as the refrigerant for the superconducting winding, is called low-temperature superconducting maglev, or superconducting magnetic levitation for short. Japan's ML maglev system is a low-temperature superconducting maglev system, and the superconducting winding is made of niobium titanium alloy.

【拓展：超导磁浮】

Expansion: Superconducting Maglev

超导磁浮，利用超导体的抗磁性实现磁浮。人们把在实现超导的过程中处于超导状态的导体称为"超导体"。超导体的直流电阻率在一定的低温下突然消失，称作零电阻效应。导体没有了电阻，电流流经超导体时就不发生热损耗，电流可以毫无阻力地在导线中形成强大的电流，从而产生超强磁场。

Superconducting maglev uses the diamagnetism of superconductors to achieve maglev. The conductor in the superconducting state in the process of realizing superconductivity is called the "superconductor". The DC resistivity of superconductor suddenly disappears at a certain low temperature, which is called zero resistivity effect. Without the resistance of the conductor, there is no heat loss when the current flows through the superconductor, and the current can form a strong current in the wire without resistance, thus generating a super strong magnetic field.

超导磁浮是主要利用低温超导材料和高温超导材料实现悬浮的一种方式。低温超导技术采用在列车车轮旁边安装小型超导磁体，在列车向前行驶时，超导磁体则向轨道产生强大的磁场，并和安装在轨道两旁的铝环相互作用，产生一种向上的浮力，消除车轮与钢轨的摩擦力，起到加快车速的作用。高温超导磁浮是一项利用高温超导块材磁通钉扎特性，而不需要主动控制就能实现稳定悬浮的技术。超导在运载上的其他应用还有用作轮船动力的超导电机、电磁空间发射工具及飞机悬浮跑道。

Superconducting maglev is a way of levitation mainly using low-temperature superconducting materials and high-temperature superconducting materials. Low-temperature superconductivity technology uses a small superconducting magnet installed next to the train wheel. When the train moves forward, the superconducting magnet generates a strong magnetic field towards the rail, and interacts with the aluminum rings installed on both sides of the track to produce an upward buoyancy force, eliminating the friction between the wheel and the rail, thus accelerating the speed. High-temperature superconducting maglev is a technology that utilizes the magnetic flux nailing characteristics of high-temperature superconducting blocks to achieve stable suspension without active control. Other applications of superconductivity in transport include superconducting motors for ship power, electromagnetic space launch vehicles, and floating runways for aircraft.

超导磁浮原理：把一块磁铁放在超导盘上，由于超导盘把磁感应线排斥出去，超导盘与磁铁之间有排斥力，结果磁铁悬浮在超导盘的上方。这种超导悬浮在工程技术中可以被大大利用，超导悬浮列车就是一例。使列车悬浮起来，与轨道脱离接触，这样列车在运行时的阻力降低很多，沿轨道"飞行"的速度可达 500 km/h。

Principle of superconducting maglev: Put a magnet on the superconducting disk. Because the superconducting disk repels the magnetic induction line, there is a repulsive force between the superguide disk and the magnet. As a result, the magnet is suspended above the superconducting disk. This kind of superconducting suspension can be greatly utilized in engineering technology, such as superconducting suspension train. The train is suspended and out of contact with the track, and the resistance during operation is much reduced, and the speed along the track can be up to 500 km/h.

日本所研制的低温超导磁浮在 2015 年 4 月 21 日创造了地面轨道交通工具载人速度的世界新纪录（603 km/h），并计划于 2027 年修建中央新干线磁浮线。这条低温超导磁浮商业运营线旨在连接东京、名古屋和大阪三大城市，全程 498 km，运行速度为 505 km/h。

The low-temperature superconducting maglev developed by Japan set a new world record for the manned speed of ground rail transit (603 km/h) on April 21, 2015, and the Central Shinkansen Maglev line is scheduled to be built in 2027. The low-temperature superconducting maglev commercial operation line aims to connect the three cities of Tokyo, Nagoya and Osaka, covering a distance of 498 km at a speed of 505 km/h.

与普通磁浮相比，利用超导磁体实现磁浮具有以下优点：悬浮的间隙大，一般可大于 100 mm；速度高，可达到 500 km/h 以上；可同时实现悬浮、导向和推进；推进直线同步电机效率高达 80%；低能耗的客运和货运；不需要铁心，因为是永久电流工作，不需要车上供电系统，所以质量轻，耗电少。当然这些优点是相对需要复杂的低温系统的低温超导而言的，若高温超导能实现工程运用，则磁浮系统各方面的性能将大为提高。

Compared with ordinary maglev, maglev using superconducting magnets has the following advantages: The suspension gap is large, generally larger than 100 mm; The speed can reach 500 km/h above; It can realize suspension, guidance and propulsion at the same time; Promote linear synchronous motor efficiency up to 80%; Low-energy passenger and freight transport; There is no need for an iron core, because it is a permanent current work, no need for on-board power supply system, so it is light in weight and consumes less power. Of course, these advantages are relative to the low-temperature superconductors that need complex low-temperature systems. If high-temperature superconductors can be used in engineering, performance of the maglev system in all aspects will be greatly improved.

高温超导体被发现后，超导态可以在液氮温区（$-196\ ℃$ 以上）出现，超导悬浮的装置更为简单，成本也大为降低。2000 年，我国西南交通大学超导技术研究所研制成功了世界首辆载人高温超导磁浮实验车"世纪号",证明了高温超导磁浮车在原理上的可行性。

After the discovery of high-temperature superconductors, superconducting states can be found in the liquid nitrogen temperature region (−196 °C). Superconducting suspension devices are much simpler and much cheaper. In 2000, the Superconducting Technology Research Institute of Southwest Jiaotong University successfully developed the world's first manned high temperature superconducting maglev experiment vehicle "Century", which proved the feasibility of high temperature superconducting maglev in principle.

五、按直线电机的定子长度划分

1.2.5　According to the Stator Length of Linear Motor Division

根据直线电机的定子长度不同,直线电机可以划分为长定子直线电机和短定子直线电机。据此,磁浮也分为长定子直线电机磁浮和短定子直线电机磁浮。

Linear motors can be divided into long stator linear motors and short stator linear motors according to their different stator lengths. Accordingly, maglev is also divided into long stator linear motor maglev and short stator linear motor maglev.

(一) 长定子直线电机

1.2.5.1　Long Stator Linear Motor

长定子直线电机的定子设置在导轨上,其定子绕组可以在导轨上无限长地铺设,故称为长定子。长定子磁浮一般采用导轨驱动技术,列车的运行速度和运行工况由地面控制中心直接控制。长定子直线电机通常用在高速及超高速磁浮铁路中,应用于干线及城轨铁路领域。

The stator of long stator linear motor is arranged on the guide rail, and its stator windings can be laid on the guide rail indefinitely, so it is called long stator. The long stator maglev generally adopts the guide rail drive technology, and the train running speed and operating conditions are directly controlled by the ground control center. Long stator linear motor is usually used in high-speed and ultra-high-speed maglev railway, in the field of dry line and urban rail.

(二) 短定子直线电机

1.2.5.2　Short Stator Linear Motor

短定子直线电机的定子设置在车辆上。由于长度受列车长度的限制,故称为短定子。短定子磁浮一般采用列车驱动技术,列车的运行速度和运行工况由司机直接控制。短定子直线电机通常用在中低速磁浮铁路中,应用于城市轨道交通领域。长沙磁浮列车就是采用短定子直线电机。

The stator of short stator linear motor is set on the vehicle. Because the length is limited by the length of the train, so it is called short stator. Short stator maglev generally adopts train driving technology, the train speed and operating conditions are directly controlled by the driver. Short stator linear motor is usually used in medium and low-speed maglev railway, and applied in urban rail transit. Changsha maglev train adopts short stator linear motor.

六、按直线电机的磁场是否同步运行划分

1.2.6　According to Whether the Magnetic Field of Linear Motor Runs Synchronously

按直线电机的磁场是否同步运行,直线电机可以划分为直线同步电机和直线感应电机两种类型。

According to whether the magnetic field of linear motor runs synchronously, linear motor can be divided into linear synchronous motor and linear induction motor.

(一) 直线同步电机 (LSM)

1.2.6.1　Linear Synchronous Motor(LSM)

直线同步电机一般采用长定子技术,转子磁场与定子磁场同步运行,控制定子(初级线圈,导轨侧)磁场的移动速度就可以准确控制列车的运行速度。高速、超速、超高速磁浮铁路一般使用这种长定子直线同步电机。该电机技术复杂,一般用于长大干线交通或城际交通系统中。德国的运捷(TR)和日本的ML系统均使用这种直线同步电机。

Linear synchronous motor generally uses the long stator technology, the rotor magnetic field and the stator magnetic field operate synchronously. The train speed can be accurately controlled by controlling the moving speed of the stator (primary coil, guide rail side) magnetic field. High-speed, overspeed and ultra-high-speed maglev railway generally uses this kind of long stator linear synchronous motor. The motor technology is complex, and it is generally used in long trunk line traffic or intercity traffic system. The linear synchronous motor is used in Germany's TR and Japan's ML systems.

(二) 直线感应电机 (LIM)

1.2.6.2　Linear Induction Motor(LIM)

直线感应电机的转子磁场与定子磁场不同步运行,故也称直线异步电机。次级线

圈（导轨侧）的磁场移动速度低于初级线圈磁场的移动速度。

The rotor magnetic field and stator magnetic field of linear induction motor do not operate synchronously, so it is also called linear asynchronous motor. The magnetic field movement speed of the secondary coil (rail side) is lower than that of the primary coil.

短定子直线感应电机结构比较简单，制造成本较低；其缺点是效率和功率因数相对较低，运行中需要地面供电装置对磁浮列车接触供电，不能实现车辆、线路之间完全无接触地运行，所以该电机更适合中低速磁浮铁路使用，一般用于城市轨道交通。日本的HSST系统及我国目前自行研制的磁浮系统大部分使用这种直线感应电机。

The short stator linear induction motor has simple structure and low manufacturing cost. Its disadvantage is that the efficiency and power factor are relatively low, and the ground power supply device is required to supply the maglev train with contact power during operation, which cannot realize the complete non-contact operation between vehicles and lines. Therefore, the motor is more suitable for medium and low-speed maglev railway, and is generally used for urban rail transit. The HSST system in Japan and the magnetic levitation system developed by China at present mostly use this linear induction motor.

七、按驱动方式划分

1.2.7　Accoding to the Driving Way

列车的运行工况（牵引、惰行、制动）及运行速度完全由定子绕组中的移动磁场控制。按照直线电机的初级线圈（定子线圈）的安设位置不同，磁浮铁路可以划分为导轨驱动和列车驱动两种类型。

The running condition (traction, inert running, braking) and running speed of the train are completely controlled by the moving magnetic field in the stator winding. According to the different installation position of the primary coil (stator coil) of the linear motor, maglev railway can be divided into two types: guide rail drive and train drive.

（一）导轨驱动磁浮

1.2.7.1　Guide Rail Drive Maglev

导轨驱动也称为路轨驱动。直线电机的初级线圈（定子线圈）设置在导轨上，采用长定子同步技术。该列车的运行工况及运行速度由地面控制中心控制，列车司机不能直接控制。导轨驱动磁浮一般用于干线或城际交通。德国的运捷（TR）和日本的ML系统均使用这种导轨驱动技术。

Guide rail drive is also known as rail drive. The primary coil (stator coil) of linear motor is arranged on the guide rail, and long stator synchronization technology is adopted.

The running condition and speed of the train are controlled by the ground control center, and the train driver can not directly control. Guide rail drive maglev is generally used for trunk line or intercity traffic. Germany's Trans Rapid (TR) and Japan's ML systems both use this guide rail drive technology.

（二）列车驱动磁浮

1.2.7.2　Train Drive Maglev

中低速磁浮直线电机的初级线圈（定子线圈）设置在车辆上，故这种磁浮铁路也称为列车驱动的磁浮铁路。该列车的运行工况及运行速度由列车司机控制。列车驱动磁浮一般用于城市轨道交通。目前，我国自行研制的磁浮系统大都使用这种列车驱动技术。

The primary coil (stator coil) of medium-low speed maglev linear motor is arranged on the vehicle, so this kind of maglev railway is also called train-driven maglev railway. The running condition and speed of the train are controlled by the train driver. Train drive maglev is generally used for urban rail transit. At present, most of the self-developed maglev system in China uses this kind of train drive technology.

八、按导轨形式划分

1.2.8　According to the Guide Rail Structure

磁浮铁路所使用的导轨结构有多种形式，常用的有"T"形、"⊥"形、"U"形和"一"形导轨。

The guide rail structure used by maglev railway has a variety of forms, such as "T" "⊥" "U" and "一" guides.

（一）"T"形导轨

1.2.8.1　"T" shaped guide rail

这种导轨梁的横断面为"T"形。直线电机的驱动绕组及悬浮绕组均安装在导轨梁两侧翼的下方，导向绕组安装在两侧翼的外端，导轨梁直接安装在桥墩上。德国高速磁浮运捷和日本中低速 HSST 系统采用这种导轨结构形式。

The cross section of this guide beam is in a "T" shape. The drive winding and suspension winding of the linear motor are installed under the two flanks of the guide beam, the guide winding is installed on the outer end of the two flanks, and the guide beam is directly installed on the pier. Germany's high speed maglev railway and Japan's medium and low speed HSST system adopt this form of guide rail structure.

由于这种磁浮列车"抱"着导轨运行，故遇突发事故时的安全性更好，并且线路设计中的最小曲线半径更小。但它对轨道梁的加工精度、列车的悬浮及导向的控制要求很高。

Because the maglev train "holds" the guideway, it is safer in the event of an emergency, and the minimum curve radius in the route design is smaller. But it has high requirements on the machining precision of the track beam, the control of the train suspension and guidance.

（二）"⊥"形导轨

1.2.8.2 "⊥" shaped guide rail

这种导轨结构类似于城市轨道交通中的跨座式独轨交通。日本早期磁浮试验线曾经采用过这种结构形式。由于这种导轨的凸出部分侵占车辆的底部空间，影响车厢的载客率，所以目前一般不再采用这种导轨结构形式。

This structure is similar to the straddle monorail in urban rail transit. This structure was used in the early maglev test line in Japan. Because the protruding part of this kind of guide rails encroaches on the bottom space of the vehicle, affecting the passenger capacity of the carriage, this guide rail structure form is generally no longer used at present.

（三）"U"形导轨

1.2.8.3 "U" shaped guide rail

这种导轨梁的横断面为"U"形，列车在 U 形槽中运行。地面的驱动、悬浮及导向绕组均安装在 U 形槽的内侧壁。这种导轨梁可以采用高架结构架设在桥墩上，也可以采用无碴轨道形式铺设在路基上。与 T 形导轨的要求相比，U 形轨道梁的加工精度及对列车的悬浮控制、导向控制的要求较低，但对最小曲线半径的要求更高（即要求最小曲线半径更大）。日本的 ML 系统目前采用这种导轨结构形式。

The cross section of the rail beam is in a "U" shape, and the train runs in a U-shaped groove. The ground drive, suspension and guide windings are installed on the inner side wall of the U-shaped groove. This kind of guideway beam can be erected on the pier by elevated structure, and can also be laid on the roadbed by ballastless track. Compared with the requirements of T-shaped guide rail, U-shaped track beam has lower requirements for machining accuracy, suspension control and steering control of trains, but the requirements of the minimum curve radius are higher (that is, the minimum curve radius is required to be larger). The Japanese ML system currently adopts this form of guide rail structure.

（四）"一"形导轨

1.2.8.4 "一" Shaped Guide Rail

这种导轨梁的横断面为"一"形，地面绕组均安装在导轨梁的正上方，车辆绕组均安装在车辆的下方，列车在导轨梁上方运行。这种导轨梁一般架设在桥墩上，采用高架结构，结构简单，但导向功能稍差，因此主要适用于中低速磁浮。我国西南交通大学研制的"世纪号"高温超导磁浮采用这种导轨结构形式。

The cross section of the guide rail beam is "一" shape. The ground windings are installed above the guide rail beam, the vehicle windings are installed below the vehicle, and the train runs above the guide rail beam. This kind of guide rail beam is generally set up on the pier, using the elevated structure, The structure is simple, but the guiding function is slightly poor, so it is mainly applicable to medium and low speed maglev. The "Century" high temperature superconducting magnetic levitation developed by Southwest Jiaotong University in China adopts this guide rail structure.

九、按悬浮方式划分

1.2.9 According to the Suspension Way

按照将车辆悬浮起来的原理及方式不同，磁浮铁路可以划分为电磁悬浮、电动悬浮两种类型。

According to the different principle and methods of vehicle suspension, maglev railway can be divided into two types: Electromagnetic suspension and Electrodynamic suspension.

（一）电磁悬浮

1.2.9.1 Electromagnetic Suspension

电磁悬浮（Electromagnetic suspension, EMS）也称为磁吸式悬浮或常导吸引型磁浮，一般采用"T"形导轨，车辆环抱导轨运行。导轨上的驱动、悬浮绕组安装在导轨侧翼底部，车辆上的驱动、悬浮绕组安装在车辆下翼的上缘，通过电磁作用将列车向上吸起悬浮于轨道上。磁铁和铁磁轨道之间的悬浮气隙一般为 8～12 mm。列车通过控制悬浮磁铁的励磁电流来保证稳定的悬浮气隙。

The Electromagnetic suspension (EMS), also known as magnetic suspension or normal magnetic levitation, generally uses a T-shaped guide rail in which vehicles orbit. The driving and suspension windings on the guide rail are installed at the bottom of the flank of the guide rail, and the driving and suspension windings on the vehicle are installed on the upper edge of the lower wing of the vehicle, so that the train is sucked up and suspended on the track through electromagnetic action. The levitation air gap between the magnet and the ferromagnetic track is typically 8-12 mm. The train ensures a stable suspension air gap by controlling the excitation current of the suspension magnet.

德国的运捷（TR）系统及日本的 HSST 系统均采用这种悬浮方式。这种悬浮方式由于采用磁铁异性相吸的原理，磁场在直线电机的初级、次级线圈之间基本上可以形成闭合回路，磁场向外界扩散较少，电磁污染程度很低，磁场对人的影响可以忽略不计。

The TR system in Germany and the HSST system in Japan both use this suspension mode. Due to the adoption of the principle that opposite magnets attract each other, the magnetic field can basically form a closed loop between the primary coil and the secondary coil of the linear motor, the diffusion of the magnetic field to the outside is less, the degree of electromagnetic pollution is very low, and the influence of the magnetic field on people can be ignored.

【拓展：电磁悬浮技术】

Expansion: Electromagnetic Levitation Technology

电磁悬浮技术的主要原理是利用高频电磁场在金属表面产生的涡流来实现对金属球或金属样品的悬浮。将一个金属样品放置在通有高频电流的线圈上时，高频电磁场会在金属材料表面产生一高频涡流，这一高频涡流与外磁场相互作用，使金属样品受到一个洛伦兹力的作用。在合适的空间配置下，可使洛伦兹力的方向与重力方向相反，通过改变高频源的功率使电磁力与重力相等，即可实现电磁悬浮。

The main principle of electromagnetic levitation technology is to realize the suspension of metal ball or metal sample by the eddy current generated by high frequency electromagnetic field on the metal surface. When a metal sample is placed on a coil with a high frequency current, the high frequency electromagnetic field will generate a high frequency eddy current on the surface of the metal material. This high frequency eddy current interacts with the external magnetic field and causes a Lorentz force to be exerted on the metal sample. The direction of Lorentz force can be made opposite to the direction of gravity under the appropriate spatial configuration. By changing the power of the high frequency source to make the electromagnetic force equal to gravity, electromagnetic maglev can be realized.

（二）电动悬浮

1.2.9.2　Electrodynamic Suspension

电动悬浮（EDS），也称为磁斥式磁浮或超导排斥型磁浮。当列车运动时，车载磁体（一般为低温超导线圈或永久磁铁）的运动磁场在安装于线路上的悬浮线圈中产生感应电流，两者互相作用，地面绕组产生的磁场同性相斥将车辆悬浮起来。电动悬浮的悬浮高度一般为 100～150 mm。

Electrodynamic suspension (EDS) is also known as magnetic repulsion maglev or superconducting repulsion maglev. When the train moves, the moving magnetic field of the on-board magnet (usually low-temperature superconducting coil or permanent magnet) generates induced current in the suspension coil installed on the line. The two interact with each other, and the magnetic field generated by the ground winding repels each other to suspend the vehicle. The suspension height of electric suspension is generally 100-150 mm.

与电磁悬浮相比，电动悬浮系统在静止时不能悬浮，必须达到一定的运行速度（120～150 km/h）后才能悬浮。电动悬浮系统在应用速度下，悬浮间隙较大，不需要进行主动控制。

Compared with electromaglev, Electrodynamic suspension system can not be suspended when it is stationary and must reach a certain running speed (120-150 km/h) before suspension. At the application speed, the suspension gap of Electrodynamic suspension system is large, so it does not need active control.

电动悬浮可以采用"⊥"形导轨，车辆跨在导轨上运行。日本早期的 ML 系统采用这种悬浮方式。磁斥式磁浮还可以采用另一种导轨结构形式，即"一"形导轨。速度比较低的磁浮铁路可以采用这种悬浮方式。我国西南交通大学研制的高温超导磁浮采用这种悬浮方式。

Electrodynamic suspension can use a "⊥" shaped guide rail, vehicles straddle the guide rail. Early ML systems in Japan used this suspension method. Magnetic repulsion maglev can also adopt another form of guide rail structure, namely "一" shaped guide rail. Maglev railway with low speed can use this suspension mode. The high temperature superconducting maglev developed by Southwest Jiaotong University adopts this suspension mode.

日本的 ML 系统采用磁吸、磁斥混合并且以磁斥式为主的悬浮系统。在"U"形导轨侧壁内侧的地面悬浮绕组产生上下极性不同的一组磁场，若车辆侧的磁场与地面侧的磁场相适应，则导轨侧壁的磁场会对车辆磁场产生上吸下斥的混合作用，使车辆悬浮起来。这种悬浮方式也可以称为混合式悬浮方式。

Japan's ML system adopts a suspension system with magnetic attraction and magnetic repulsion mixed and dominated by magnetic repulsion. The ground suspension winding on the inside of the sidewall of the "U" shaped guide rail produces a group of magnetic fields with different upper and lower polarities. If the magnetic field of the vehicle side is compatible with the magnetic field of the ground side, the magnetic field of the side wall of the guide rail will produce a mixed effect of up attraction and down repulsion on the magnetic field of the vehicle, so that the vehicle will be suspended. This type of suspension can also be called mixed suspension.

磁斥式磁浮由于采用磁铁同性相斥的原理，初、次级线圈所产生的磁场在直线电机内部不能闭合，故其电磁污染比磁吸式磁浮要大得多。

Because Magnetic repulsion maglev adopts the priciple that like magenets repel each other, the magnetic field generated by the primary and secondary coils can not be closed in the linear motor, so its electromagnetic pollution is much larger than the magnetic attraction maglev.

十、几种典型磁浮系统的分类特征

1.2.10 Classification Characteristics of Several Typical Maglev Systems

前面总结了磁浮铁路常见的几种分类方法。从不同的角度考虑，还有其他多种分类方法。前面只是选择了几种与本书内容有关的分类方法进行介绍。

Several common classification methods of maglev railway are summarized above. There are many other classification methods from different perspectives. In the front, only a few classification methods related to the content of this book are selected for introduction.

与前述众多分类方法类似，由于磁浮铁路技术目前正处在蓬勃发展、百花齐放的阶段，目前在世界范围内也有众多形式的磁浮系统，本书将在后面几章陆续进行介绍。其中几种具有代表性的磁悬浮系统如下：

Similar to many of the aforementioned classification methods, as maglev railway technology is currently in the stage of vigorous development and flourishing, there are many forms of maglev systems in the world, which will be introduced in the following chapters of this book. Several representative maglev systems are as follows:

（1）ML：日本低温超导超高速磁浮系统。

（1）ML: Japanese cryogenic superconducting ultra-high speed maglev system.

（2）TR：德国常导超高速磁浮铁路系统。

（2）TR: German conventional ultra-high speed maglev railway system.

（3）HSST：日本中低速磁浮系统。

（3）HSST: medium and low speed maglev system in Japan.

（4）世纪号：中国高温超导中低速磁浮系统。

（4）Century: China High Temperature Superconducting Medium and Low Speed Maglev System.

上述磁浮系统的分类特征见表 1-1。

The classification characteristics of the above maglev systems are shown in the table 1-1.

表 1-1 几种典型磁悬浮系统的分类特征

Table 1-1 Classification Characteristics of Several Typical Maglev Systems

项目 Project	日本 ML Japan's ML	德国 TR German's TR	日本 HSST Japan's HSST	中国世纪号 China's Century
应用范围 Application Scope	干线、城际 Trunk Line, Intercity	干线、城际 Trunk Line, Intercity	城际、市内 Intercity, Intracity	市内 Intracity
速度范围 Speed Range	超高速 Ultra-High-Speed	超高速 Ultra-High Speed	中低速、高速 Medium and Low Speed, High Speed	中低速 Medium and Low Speed
线圈导体 Coil Conductor	低温超导 Low Temperature Superconductivity	常导 Normal Conductivity	常导 Normal Conductivity	高温超导 High Temperature Superconductivity
直线电机 Linear Motor	长电子、同步 Long Stator, Synchronous	长电子、同步 Long Stator, Synchronous	短定子 Short Stator	短定子 Short Stator
驱动方式 Drive Mode	导轨驱动 Guide Rail Drive	导轨驱动 Guide Rail Drive	列车驱动 Train Drive	列车驱动 Train Drive
悬浮方式 Suspension Mode	电动悬浮（EDS）磁斥式 EDS Magnetic Repulsion	电磁悬浮（EMS）磁吸式 EMS Magnetic Attraction	磁吸式 Magnetic Attraction	磁斥式 Magnetic Repulsion
导轨结构 Guide Rail Structure	"U"形 "U" Shape	"T"形 "T" Shape	"⊥"形 "⊥" Shape	"一"形 "一"Shape

第三节 磁浮列车的工作原理

Section 1.3 Working Principle of Maglev Train

磁浮列车是一种采用电磁力实现无接触悬浮、导向和驱动的轨道车辆系统。系统依靠电磁吸力或电动斥力将车辆悬浮于轨道上方一定的距离，实现列车与地面轨道间的无机械接触，利用线性电机驱动列车运行。虽然磁浮列车仍然属于陆上有轨交通运输系统，并保留了轨道、道岔和车辆转向架及悬挂系统等许多传统机车车辆的特点，但由于列车在牵引运行时与轨道之间无机械接触，其速度可以达到500 km/h，是当今世界最快的地面交通工具。磁浮列车具有速度快、爬坡能力强、能耗低、运行时噪声小、安全舒适、不燃油、污染小和占地少等明显的优点。磁浮列车从根本上克服了传统列车轮轨黏着限制、机械噪声和磨损等问题，将成为理想的陆上交通工具。磁浮列车的工作原理与传统轮轨列车的工作原理不同，现以电磁悬浮列车为例予以说明，见图1-1。

Maglev train is a kind of rail vehicle system which uses electromagnetic force to achieve non-contact suspension, guidance and drive. The system depends on electromagnetic attraction or electric repulsion to suspend the vehicle above the track for a certain distance, so that there is no mechanical contact between the train and the ground track, and the train is driven by linear motor. Although the maglev train still belongs to the land rail transportation system, and retains many characteristics of traditional locomotives and vehicles, such as track, turnout, vehicle bogie and suspension system, its speed can reach 500 km/h because there is no mechanical contact between the train and the track during traction operation, which is the fastest ground transportation tool in the world today. Maglev train has many obvious advantages, such as high speed, strong climbing ability, low energy consumption, low noise, safety and comfort, no fuel, low pollution and less land occupation. Maglev train will become an ideal means of land transportation because it fundamentally overcomes the problems of wheel-rail adhesion, mechanical noise and wear of traditional trains. The working principle of the maglev train is different from that of the traditional wheel-rail train. The electromagnetic levitation train is taken as an example for illustration, as shown in Figure 1-1.

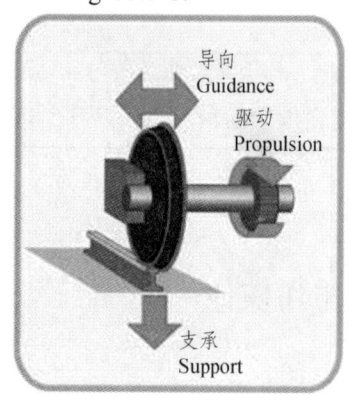

（a）传统轮轨列车
(a) Traditional wheel-rail train

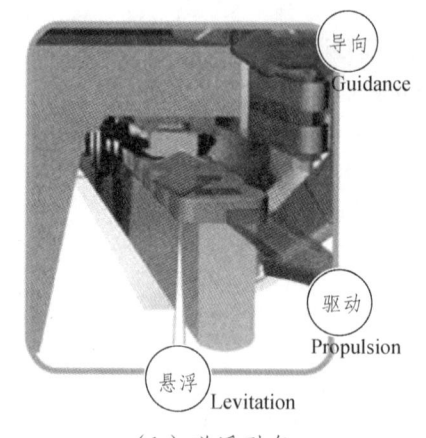

（b）磁浮列车
(b) Maglev train

图1-1 传统轮轨列车与磁浮列车工作原理图

Figure 1-1 Working principle of traditional wheel-rail train and maglv train

磁浮铁路系统由线路、车辆、供电、运行控制系统 4 个主要部分构成。车辆的悬浮、导向和驱动系统是磁浮铁路的核心和关键。

The maglev railway system consists of four main parts: line, vehicle, power supply and operation control system. The suspension, guidance and drive system of the vehicle is the core and key of the maglev railway.

磁浮系统：从目前来看，有应用价值的磁浮系统有两种，分别是电磁吸力悬浮系统（EMS）和电动斥力悬浮系统（EDS）。

Maglev system: At present, there are two kinds of maglev systems with application value, namely, electromagnetic attraction suspension system (EMS) and electromagnetic repulsion suspension system (EDS).

导向系统：用导向力保证磁浮列车沿着导轨的方向运动。导向力可以分为吸力和斥力。磁浮列车的悬浮电磁铁可以同时为导向系统和悬浮系统提供吸力或斥力，导向力也可以由独立的导向电磁铁提供。

Guidance system: The guidance force is used to ensure that the maglev train moves along the direction of the guideway. The guide force can be divided into a suction force and a repulsion force. The suspension electromagnet of the maglev train can provide attraction or repulsion for the guidance system and the suspension system at the same time, and the guidance force can also be provided by an independent guidance electromagnet.

驱动系统：磁浮列车的驱动可采用同步直线电机和异步直线电机。采用同步直线电机时，磁浮列车的支撑电磁铁及悬浮电磁铁一般被用作同步直线电机的励磁磁极，轨道的驱动绕组起到电枢的作用，也就是同步直线电机的长定子绕组。采用异步直线电机驱动时，电机的作用与悬浮磁铁的作用完全分开，电机定子绕组安装在磁浮列车上，轨道上仅安装了异步直线电机的反应板。

Drive system: The maglev train can be driven by synchronous linear motor and asynchronous linear motor. When the synchronous linear motor is used, the supporting electromagnet and the suspension electromagnet of the maglev train are generally used as the excitation magnetic pole of the synchronous linear motor, and the driving winding of the rail plays the role of an armature, that is, the long stator winding of the synchronous linear machine. When the asynchronous linear motor is used for driving, the function of the motor is completely separated from the function of the suspension magnet, the stator winding of the motor is installed on the maglev train, and only the reaction plate of the asynchronous linear motor is installed on the track.

下面以德国 TR-07 磁浮列车为例说明磁浮列车的工作原理。

The German TR-07 maglev train is taken as an example to illustrate the working principle of the maglev train.

1. 悬浮原理

1. Suspension Principle

T 形梁翼底部为同步直线电机的定子,下方为安装在车体上的悬浮电磁铁,即同步直线电机的转子。

A stator of the synchronous linear motor is arranged at the bottom of the T-shaped beam wing, and a suspension electromagnet, namely a rotor of the synchronous linear motor, is arranged below the T-shaped beam wing.

悬浮电磁铁通电产生磁场,与定子的铁心产生吸引力,使磁浮车往上吸向定子,利用位移传感器控制悬浮气隙,使悬浮气隙保持在 10 mm 左右。

The magnetic field generated by the suspension electromagnet is attracted by the iron core of the stator, so that the maglev vehicle is attracted to the stator. The suspension air gap is controlled by the displacement sensor, so that the suspension air gap is maintained at about 10 mm.

2. 导向原理

2. Guiding Principle

磁浮列车的车体从两侧将 T 形梁的翼缘抱住,T 形梁的翼缘两侧面为导向轨,安装在车体上的导向电磁铁通电后与之产生吸引力,通过测量两侧导向电磁铁与导轨的间隙,并调节导向电磁铁的电流,就可控制列车位于对中位置。

The vehicle body of the maglev train holds the flange of the T-shaped beam from two sides, the two side surfaces of the flange of the T-shaped beam are guide rails, the guide electromagnets installed on the vehicle body generate attractive force with the guide electromagnets after being electrified, and the train can be controlled to be positioned at the centering position by measuring the gap between the guide electromagnet on two sides and the guide rail and adjusting the current of the guide electromagnet.

3. 牵引原理

3. Traction Principle

相当于将旋转电机的定子切开,沿路轨展开,车体上的悬浮电磁铁,为电机的转子,定子中三相绕组产生的移动行波磁场作用于转子,从而产生电磁牵引力。

It is equivalent to cutting the stator of the rotating motor and spreading it along the rail. The suspension electromagnet on the car body is the rotor of the motor. The moving traveling wave magnetic field generated by the three-phase winding in the stator acts on the rotor, thus generating electromagnetic traction.

调节定子的供电频率与电压,即可改变磁浮列车的运行速度。

The running speed of the maglev train can be changed by adjusting the power supply frequency and voltage of the stator.

4. 同步直线电机定子的供电原理

4. Power Supply Principle of Linear Synchronous Motor Stator

定子分段铺设于线路上，每段长度不等，视列车长度、该段速度、加速度、坡度、弯道等情况而定，一般为 300～2 000 m。

The stator is laid on the line in sections, and the length of each section is different, depending on the length of the train, the speed, acceleration, slope and curve of the section, which is generally 300-2,000 m.

定子线圈供电来自沿线的变电站，一般变电站间距 25～40 km。两变电站间只允许一列车运行，仅对列车所在的那段定子供电。直线同步电机控制，采用 VVVF 变频变压调速方式。

The power supply of the stator coil comes from the substations along the line. Generally, only one train is allowed to run between the two substations with a distance of 25-40 km, and only the stator where the train is located is supplied with power. The linear synchronous motor is controlled by VVVF variable frequency and variable voltage speed regulation.

5. 制动原理

5. Braking principle

常导磁浮列车的正常制动均利用同步直线电机作为发电机进行控制。高速运行时采用再生制动，将列车动能转化为电能回馈给电网；列车速度较低时，再生制动改为电阻制动；列车速度很低时，直线电机改为反接制动，即电机的牵引方向与列车的运行方向相反，直到列车停止。当直线电机制动失灵或需要紧急制动时，采用涡流制动，即车上的涡流制动电磁铁励磁，使侧向导轨产生涡流形成制动力。

The linear synchronous motor is used as the generator to control the normal braking of the EMS maglev train. During high-speed operation, regenerative braking is used to convert the train kinetic energy into electric energy and feed it back to the power grid; when the train speed is low, the regenerative braking is changed to resistance braking; when the train speed is very low, the linear motor is changed to reverse braking, that is, the traction direction of the motor is opposite to the running direction of the train until the train stops. When the linear motor fails to brake or emergency braking is required, eddy current braking is used, that is, the eddy current braking electromagnet on the vehicle is excited to make the lateral guide rail generate eddy current to form braking force.

第四节　磁浮列车的分类

Section 1.4　Classification of Maglev Train

一、电磁吸力型和电动斥力型

1.4.1　Electromagnetic Attraction Type and Electromagnetic Repulsion Type

磁浮列车从悬浮力的特征上可分为电磁悬浮（EMS）和电动悬浮（EDS）两种，前者以德国的 TR 型和日本的 HSST 型磁浮列车为代表，后者以日本的 ML 型超导磁浮列车为代表。

Maglev train can be divided into electromagnetic suspension (EMS) and electrodynamic suspension (EDS) according to the characteristics of levitation force. The former is represented by TR type maglev train in Germany and HSST type maglev train in Japan, and the latter is represented by ML type superconducting maglev train in Japan.

电磁悬浮也称电磁吸力悬浮（Attractive Levitation），一般采用车辆环抱导轨运行。对车载的、置于导轨下方的悬浮电磁铁通电励磁而产生磁场，磁铁与轨道上的长定子直线电机定子铁心或悬浮轨道相互吸引，将列车向上吸起悬浮于轨道上。磁铁和铁磁轨道之间的悬浮间隙一般为 8～12 mm，故对线路精度的要求相当高。列车通过控制悬浮磁铁的励磁电流来保证稳定的悬浮间隙，通过直线电机来驱动列车行走。这种悬浮方式由于采用磁铁相吸的原理，磁场在磁铁和铁磁轨道间或直线电机的初级、次级线圈之间基本上可以形成闭合回路，磁场向外界扩散较少，电磁污染程度很低，磁场对人的影响可以忽略不计。

Electromagnetic suspension, also known as Attractive Levitation, generally uses vehicles to run around the guide rail. A magnetic field is generated by electrifying and exciting a vehicle-mounted suspension electromagnet arranged below a guide rail, and the magnet and a stator iron core of a long stator linear motor on the rail or the suspension rail are mutually attracted to attract the train to be suspended on the rail. The levitation gap between the magnet and the ferromagnetic rail is generally 8-12 mm, so the requirement for the accuracy of the line is quite high. The train ensures a stable suspension gap by controlling the excitation current of the suspension magnet, and the train is driven by the linear motor. Due to the adoption of the principle of magnet attraction, the magnetic field can basically form a closed loop between the magnet and the ferromagnetic track or between the primary coil and the secondary coil of the linear motor, the diffusion of the magnetic field to the outside is less, the electromagnetic pollution degree is very low, and the influence of the magnetic field on people can be ignored.

电动悬浮也称电动斥力悬浮（Repulsive），当列车运动时，车载磁体（一般为超导线圈或永久磁铁）与其运动磁场在安装于线路上的闭合线圈或导体板中产生感应电流并相互作用，闭合线圈或导体板产生的磁场与车载磁体的磁场同性相斥将车辆悬浮起来，悬浮高度一般可达 100~150 mm。列车运行靠直线电机牵引。与电磁吸力悬浮相比，电动斥力悬浮在静止时不能实现悬浮，必须达到一定速度后才能浮起。电动斥力悬浮系统在应用速度下，悬浮间距较大，不需要进行主动控制。但电磁斥力悬浮由于采用磁铁同性相斥的原理，车载磁铁磁场与轨道上的闭合线圈或导线板产生的磁场不能闭合，故其电磁污染比电磁吸力悬浮要大许多。

Electrodynamic suspension is also called electric Repulsive suspension. When the train moves, the on-board magnet (generally superconducting coil or permanent magnet) and its moving magnetic field generate induced current and interact in the closed coil or conductor plate installed on the line. The magnetic field generated by the closed coil or conductor plate and the magnetic field of the vehicle-mounted magnet repel each other to suspend the vehicle, and the suspension height can generally reach 100-150 mm. The train is driven by linear motor. Compared with electromagnetic force levitation, electrodynamic repulsion levitation can not achieve levitation when it is still and it must reach a certain speed before it can float. The electrodynamic repulsion levitation system has a large levitation distance at the application speed, so it does not need active control. However, due to the principle that magnets repel each other, the magnetic field of the vehicle-mounted magnet and the magnetic field generated by the closed coil or conductor plate on the track can not be closed, so the electromagnetic pollution of electromagnetic repulsion levitation is much greater than that of electromagnetic attraction levitation.

电动悬浮可以采用倒"T"形导轨，车辆跨在导轨上运行，日本早期的 ML 系统采用这种悬浮方式。电动悬浮还可以采用"U"形轨道，如日本后期的超导磁浮列车均采用这种结构。

An inverted "T" shaped guide rail can be used for electrodynamic levitation, and the vehicle runs across the guideway, which was used in the early ML system in Japan. Electrodynamic suspension can also use "U" shaped track, such as the superconducting maglev train in Japan in the later period.

二、常导型磁浮列车与超导型磁浮列车

1.4.2　Normal Conducting Maglev Train and Superconducting Maglev Train

磁浮列车的核心是悬浮系统，根据悬浮电磁铁所用材料不同，磁浮列车划分为常导型磁浮列车与超导型磁浮列车。

The core of the maglev train is the suspension system. According to the different materials used in the suspension electromagnet, the maglev train is divided into the normal conductive maglev train and the superconducting maglev train.

德国 TR 型磁浮列车和日本 HSST 型磁浮列车采用常温导体制成线圈通电励磁，产生电磁悬浮力和导向力，因而称为常导型磁浮列车。常导悬浮电磁铁由于线圈电阻的存在将产生能量消耗，也会使线圈温度增加。超导型悬浮列车利用安装在车辆上的超导线圈，通上电流后产生磁场，磁体的 N 极和 S 极沿列车的运行方向交替分布，用于驱动的定子线圈及用于悬浮和导向的 8 字形短路线圈都设置在 U 形槽的侧壁上，车辆侧的超导磁体与线路侧的 8 字形线圈和无铁心的长定子同步电机线圈共同作用，实现车辆的驱动、悬浮和导向。由于超导线圈的电阻为零，故能量消耗小。超导悬浮又分为高温超导（−196 ℃ 以下）磁浮和低温超导（−269 ℃ 以下）磁浮两类。

TR maglev train in Germany and HSST maglev train in Japan use coils made of normal temperature conductor to excit and generate electromagnetic levitation force and guidance force, so they are called normal conducting maglev trains. Due to the existence of coil resistance, the normal conducting suspension electromagnet will produce energy consumption and increase the temperature of the coil. The superconducting suspension train utilizes superconducting coils installed on the vehicle to generate a magnetic field after current is switched on, the N pole and the S pole of the magnet are alternately distributed along the running direction of the train, stator coils used for driving and 8-shaped short circuit coils used for suspension and guidance are arranged on the side wall of a U-shaped groove, The superconducting magnet on the vehicle side, the 8-shaped coil on the line side and the coreless long stator synchronous motor coil work together to realize the driving, suspension and guidance of the vehicle. Since the resistance of the superconducting coil is zero, the energy consumption is small. Superconducting levitation is divided into high-temperature superconducting (below − 196 ℃) maglev and low-temperature superconducting (below − 269 ℃) maglev.

三、长定子同步驱动型与短定子异步电机驱动型

1.4.3　Long Stator Synchronous Drive Type and Short Stator Asynchronous Motor Drive Type

磁浮列车的牵引电机都是直线电机，一般可分为两种形式，即长定子同步驱动型

与短定子异步电机驱动型。采用长定子同步直线电机时,电机的定子沿整个线路铺设,电机的转子安装在车上,列车的运行速度和运行工况由地面控制中心直接控制。采用短定子异步电机时,电机的定子安装在车上而转子安装在轨道上,其长度受列车长度的限制,列车的运行速度和运行工况由司机直接控制。

The traction motor of maglev train is linear motor, which can be generally divided into two types, namely, long stator synchronous drive type and short stator asynchronous motor drive type. When the long stator synchronous linear motor is used, the stator of the motor is laid along the whole line, the rotor of the motor is installed on the train, and the running speed and working conditions of the train are directly controlled by the ground control center. When the short stator asynchronous motor is used, the stator of the motor is installed on the vehicle and the rotor is installed on the rail, its length is limited by the length of the train, and the running speed and working conditions of the train are directly controlled by the driver.

长定子同步直线电机适合于较高速度(400~500 km/h)的磁浮列车驱动,德国的 TR 型常导磁浮列车和日本的 MLX 型超导磁浮列车都采用了长定子同步直线电机驱动。长定子同步直线电机驱动的列车运行时,车内的照明用电和空调用电是利用车载绕组产生的感应电流供电,能量使用效率非常高;停车时则使用车载蓄电池供电,车载蓄电池可以在列车运行过程中进行充电,实现了车与轨的完全无接触受流,电力使用效率特别好。

Long-stator linear synchronous motor is suitable for high-speed (400-500 km/h) maglev train drive. The TR maglev train in Germany and the MLX maglev train in Japan both use long-stator linear synchronous motor drive. When the train driven by the long stator synchronous linear motor runs, the lighting power and the air conditioning power in the train are supplied by the induced current generated by the on-board winding, and the energy utilization efficiency is very high; when the the train stops, the on-board storage battery is used for power supply, and the on-board storage battery can be charged in the running process of the train, so that the complete non-contact current collection between the train and a rail is realized, so that the power utilization efficiency is particularly high.

日本的 HSST 型低速(50~100 km/h)磁浮列车则采用短定子异步直线电机驱动。短定子异步直线电机结构比较简单,制造成本较低,但效率和功率因数相对较低,运行中需要地面供电装置对磁浮列车接触供电,不能实现车与轨的完全无接触运行,所以更适用于中低速磁浮列车。

The HSST low-speed (50-100 km/h) maglev train in Japan is driven by short-stator asynchronous linear motor. The short-stator asynchronous linear motor is simple in structure and low in manufacturing cost, but the efficiency and the power factor are relatively low, a ground power supply device is required to contact and supply power to a maglev train in operation, and the complete non-contact operation of the train and a rail cannot be realized, so that the short-stator asynchronous linear motor is more suitable for a medium-low speed maglev train.

四、高速磁浮列车和低速磁浮列车

1.4.4 High-speed and Low-speed Maglev Trains

按运行速度来分，德国的 TR 型悬浮列车最大运行速度大致为 500 km/h，日本的 HSST 型悬浮列车最大运行速度为 100 km/h 左右，日本的 MLX 型超导磁浮列车最大运行速度为 500 km/h。所以，德国磁浮列车和日本的超导磁浮列车又称为高速磁浮列车；日本的 HSST 型磁浮列车用于城市或市郊交通，以及连接机场与市区等，称为中低速磁浮列车。

According to the running speed, the maximum running speed of TR type maglev train in Germany is about 500 km/h, the maximum running speed of HSST type maglev train in Japan is about 100 km/h, and the maximum operating speed of MLX type superconducting magnetic levitation train in Japan is 500 km/h. German maglev train and Japanese superconducting maglev train are also called high-speed maglev trains; Japanese HSST maglev trains are used for urban or suburban traffic, as well as connecting airports and urban areas, and are called medium and low speed maglev trains.

第五节 国外磁浮交通技术的应用发展概况

Section 1.5 Overview of Application and Development of Maglev Transportation Technology in Foreign Countries

本节重点介绍国外磁浮交通技术的应用发展概况。
This section focuses on the application and development of maglev transportation technology abroad.

一、磁浮技术在德国的发展状况

1.5.1 Development of Maglev Technology in Germany

（一）早期开发过程

1.5.1.1 Early Development Process

德国是世界上最早研究磁浮列车的国家。1922 年，德国人赫尔曼·肯佩尔

（Hermann Kemper）提出了磁浮原理，并在 1934 年获得世界上第一项有关磁浮技术的专利。由于当时技术和工艺条件限制，在此后 30 多年的时间里，磁浮技术没有得到明显的发展。

Germany is the first country in the world to study the maglev train. In 1922, Hermann Kemper, a German, put forward the principle of maglev and obtained the first patent on maglev technology in the world in 1934. Due to the limitation of technology and process conditions at that time, maglev technology has not been significantly developed in the following 30 years.

自 20 世纪 60 年代末开始，德国因环境和能源问题迫切要求开发新的高速交通体系。1969 年，德国联邦交通部、联邦铁路公司和德国工业界参与了关于"高速与快速铁路的研究"，所研究的高速交通涉及轮轨高速铁路和磁浮高速铁路。在此基础上，在联邦政府的资助下，工业界开始了磁浮铁路的开发工作。

Since the late 1960s, Germany has been pressing for the development of a new high-speed transportation system due to environmental and energy problems. In 1969, the German Federal Ministry of Transport, the Federal Railway Company and the German industry participated in the "High Speed and Fast Speed Railway research", the high-speed traffic studied involves wheel-rail high-speed railway and maglev high-speed railway. On this basis, with federal funding, the maglev railway was developed in Industry.

1971 年 2 月，德国第一辆磁浮原理车 MBB 和一段 660 m 长的试验线路投入试验运行，原理车采用车辆侧的短定子直线电机驱动。1975 年，Thyssen Henschel 公司在卡塞尔（Kassel）工厂的 HMB 试验线上率先实现了线路侧长定子直线同步电机驱动的磁浮车运行，这一试验系统，将直线驱动和磁浮支承结合起来，奠定了今天 TR 磁浮高速铁路发展的基础。1976 年研制的"彗星"号试验车，首次证明磁浮车可以以 400 km/h 以上的速度运行。1977 年，德国研究与技术部决定集中力量发展长定子直线同步电机驱动的常导磁浮交通系统。

In February 1971, the first German maglev principle vehicle MBB and a 660 m long test line were put into test operation. The principle vehicle was driven by a short stator linear motor on the vehicle side. In 1975, Thyssen Henschel Company took the lead in realizing the operation of maglev vehicle driven by linear synchronous motor with long stator on the line side on the HMB test line of Kassel factory. This test system, which combines linear drive with maglev support, laid the foundation for the development of TR maglev high-speed railway today. The "Comet" test vehicle developed in 1976 proved for the first time that the maglev vehicle could run at a speed of more than 400 km/h. In 1977, the German Ministry of Research and Technology decided to concentrate on the development of a permanent magnetic levitation transportation system driven by a long stator linear synchronous motor.

（二）汉堡国际交通博览会磁浮示范线

1.5.1.2　Maglev Demonstration Line of Hamburg International Transport Expo

在 1979 年汉堡国际交通博览会上，一段 900 m 长的 TR 磁浮铁路示范线顺利展出，并按时刻表送出了 5 万名参观者，汉堡市民对以 75 km/h 速度运行的磁浮车产生了极大的兴趣。

At the Hamburg International Transport Fair in 1979, a 900 m long demonstration line of the TR Maglev Railway was successfully exhibited and 50,000 visitors were sent out according to the timetable. Hamburg citizens showed great interest in the maglev train running at a speed of 75 km/h.

（三）埃姆斯兰的 TR 试验设施（TVE）

1.5.1.3　TR Test Facility (TVE) at Emsland

汉堡取得的成功，促成了德国在埃姆斯兰地区的拉滕建造大型试验设施的决定。为了建造第一段线路，德国工业界组成了磁浮铁路联合体（KMT），第一期工程包括 21.5 km 长的试验线路、试验中心和试验车 TR06，该线路于 1983 年 6 月 30 日投入试验运行。

The success of Hamburg led to the German decision to build a large test facility at Ratten in the Emsland region. For the construction of the first section of the line, the German industry formed the Maglev Railway Consortium (KMT). The first phase of the project included a 21.5 km long test line, a test center and a test car TR06. The line was put into test operation on June 30, 1983.

为了提高试验速度，1984 年决定扩建南环线，并于 1987 年建成。至此，TVE 的试验线总长达到 31.5 km。1988 年，TR06 的试验速度达到了 412.6 km/h。1986—1989 年，Thyssen Henschel 公司牵头，研制了面向应用的磁浮列车 TR07。

In order to increase the speed of the test, it was decided to expand the South Link in 1984 and completed in 1987. So far, the total length of the test line of TVE has reached 31.5 km. In 1988, the test speed of TR06 reached 412.6 km/h. From 1986 to 1989, Thyssen Henschel Company took the lead in developing the application-oriented maglev train TR07.

（四）TR 走向应用

1.5.1.4　Application of TR

经过近两年的评价和鉴定，1991 年年底，德国得出 TR 磁浮高速铁路系统技术已成熟的结论。1993 年，TR07 型磁浮列车在 TVE 试验的最高速度达 450 km/h。

After nearly two years of evaluation and appraisal, at the end of 1991, Germany concluded that the technology of TR maglev high-speed railway system was mature. In 1993, TR07 maglev train was tested in TVE with a maximum speed of 450 km/h.

1997年4月,德国决定建造柏林和汉堡之间的磁浮铁路。该线全长292 km,原计划1998年下半年动工,2005年投入商业运行,为此开发了拟用于柏林至汉堡线的TR08型磁浮列车,该车于1999年10月开始在TVE上进行了试验。后来因原来预测的客流量偏大,新的预测表明建设新线将面临亏损的危险,遂于2000年2月取消建设计划。

In April 1997, Germany decided to build a maglev railway between Berlin and Hamburg. The line, with a total length of 292 km, was originally planned to start construction in the second half of 1998 and put into commercial operation in 2005. For this purpose, the TR08 maglev train was developed for the Berlin-Hamburg line, which was tested on TVE in October 1999. Later, because the original forecast of passenger flow was too large, the new forecast indicated that the construction of the new line would face the danger of loss, so the construction plan was cancelled in February 2000.

2000年6月,中国上海市与德国磁浮国际公司合作进行中国高速磁浮列车示范运营线可行性研究。同年12月,中国决定建设上海浦东龙阳路地铁车站至浦东国际机场高速磁浮交通运营示范线。2001年3月,总投资为89亿元人民币的上海磁浮快速列车干线正式开工建设,西起上海地铁2号线的龙阳站,东至浦东国际机场,正线长约30 km,上下行折返运行,全线设两个车站、两个牵引变电站、1个运行控制中心(设在龙阳路车站内部)和1个维修中心,设计运营最高速度430 km/h,单向行驶时间为8 min,发车间隔为10 min。按设计水平,9节车厢可坐乘客959人,每小时发车12列,按每天运行18 h计,年客运量可达1.5亿人次。2002年12月31日,上海磁浮列车示范运营线建成通车。

In June 2000, Shanghai, China cooperated with German Maglev International Company to carry out the feasibility study of China's high-speed maglev train demonstration operation line. In December of the same year, China decided to build a high-speed maglev transportation demonstration line from Longyang Road Metro Station in Pudong, Shanghai, to Pudong International Airport. In March 2001, the construction of Shanghai Maglev Express Train Line, with a total investment of 8.9 billion yuan, was officially started. It starts from Longyang Station of Shanghai Metro Line 2 in the west and ends at Pudong International Airport in the east. The main line is about 30 km long and runs back and forth. The whole line is provided with two stations, two traction substations, one operation control center (set inside the Longyang Road Station) and one maintenance center. The maximum design operating speed is 430 km/h, the one-way running time is 8 minutes, and the departure interval is 10 minutes. According to the design level, 9 carriages can seat 959 passengers, and 12 trains depart every hour. Based on 18 hours of operation per day, the annual passenger volume can reach 150 million person-times. In December 31, 2002, Shanghai Maglev Train Demonstration Line was completed and opened to traffic.

之后德国又建了一条试验线，但 2006 年 9 月 22 日，德国拉滕—德尔彭的磁浮试验线发生了脱轨事故，造成了 25 人死亡，4 人重伤。这影响了磁浮列车技术在德国的推广。德国目前仍没有一条商业运营的磁浮线路，甚至德国媒体界把磁浮列车技术称为"昂贵的高科技玩具"。

A test line was later built in Germany, but on September 22, 2006, a derailment accident occurred on the maglev test line in Ratten-Delpen, Germany, resulting in 25 deaths and 4 serious injuries. This has affected the promotion of maglev train technology in Germany. There is still no commercial maglev line in Germany, and even the German media call maglev train technology an "expensive high-tech toy".

二、磁浮技术在日本的发展状况

1.5.2 Development of Maglev Technology in Japan

（一）采用低温超导磁体的电动悬浮高速列车系统

1.5.2.1 Electrodynamic Suspension High-speed Train System Using Cryogenic Superconducting Magnet

1962 年，日本开始磁浮交通的研究工作。1972 年，在庆祝日本第一条铁路建成 100 周年之际，第一辆由日本国铁开发研制的电动磁浮原理车 ML100 向公众展示，该车在 480 m 长的试验线路上速度达到了 60 km/h。

In 1962, Japan began the research work of maglev transportation. In 1972, on the occasion of the celebration of the 100th anniversary of the first railway in Japan, the first electric maglev train ML100 developed by Japan National Railway was presented to the public, which reached a speed of 60 km/h on a 480 m long test line.

1975 年，日本开始在九州半岛上的宫崎附近建造试验设施，从 1977 年至 1979 年，7 km 长的试验线分段投入使用。1979 年，低温超导的 ML500 型磁浮列车不载人运行速度达到 517 km/h，证明有可能将长定子直线同步电机驱动的磁浮系统用于高速有轨交通。

In 1975, Japan began to build a test facility near Miyazaki on the Kyushu Peninsula, and from 1977 to 1979, a 7 km long test line was put into operation in sections. In 1979, the speed of ML500 maglev train with low temperature superconducting reached 517 km/h without passengers, which proved that it was possible to use the maglev system driven by long stator linear synchronous motor for high-speed rail transit.

1980年研制成的MLU001型磁浮列车，在新建的U形线路上进行了9年试验运行，总共进行了9 000次试验运行，累计行驶了约40 000 km。

The MLU001 maglev train, which was developed in 1980, has been tested for 9 years on the newly built U-shaped line, with a total of 9,000 test runs and a total of about 40,000 km.

1987年3月，日本新的电动悬浮系统试验车MLU002开始在宫崎试验线路上运行。该车长22 m，重17 t，可载44名乘客，设计速度为420 km/h。1989年，MLU002型磁浮列车不载人试验速度达到了494 km/h，但1991年该车在试验运行中发生了火灾事故被烧毁。日本随后又制造了MLU002N型磁浮车，在宫崎试验线进行试验。1994年，MLU002N型磁浮列车不载人运行最高速度达到了431 km/h，载人运行最高速度达到了411 km/h，1996年10月，宫崎试验线关闭。

In March 1987, Japan's new electrodynamic suspension system test vehicle MLU002 began to operate on the Miyazaki test line. The vehicle is 22 m long, weighs 17 t, can carry 44 passengers, and has a design speed of 420 km/h. In 1989, the unmanned test speed of MLU002 maglev train reached 494 km/h, but in 1991, the train was burned down in a fire accident during the test operation. Japan subsequently manufactured the MLU002N maglev vehicle, which was tested on the Miyazaki test line. In 1994, the MLU002N maglev train reached a maximum speed of 431 km/h for unmanned operation and 411 km/h for manned operation. In October 1996, the Miyazaki test line was closed.

由于宫崎试验线没有坡道和隧道，不能满足接近应用条件的试验需要，因此日本运输省决定建设超导磁浮山梨试验线。1991年，山梨试验线开始建设，1997年4月投入试验运行。山梨试验线主要包括18.4 km长的试验线路、变电站、试验中心和两列磁浮车（分别为MLX01和MLX02）。1997年12月24日，三辆编组的MLX01型磁浮列车不载人试验运行速度达到550 km/h，创下当时新的世界纪录。1999年4月，5辆编组的MLX01型磁浮车实现了552 km/h的载人运行速度。1999年12月，日本山梨磁浮列车试验线进行了磁浮列车高速会车试验，创造了会车时相对速度为1 003 km/h的世界最高纪录，当时两车的速度分别为546 km/h和457 km/h。

Because the Miyazaki test line has no ramp and tunnel, it can not meet the test needs close to the application conditions, so the Ministry of Transport of Japan decided to build the superconducting maglev Yamanashi test line. In 1991, the Yamanashi Test Line was constructed and put into trial operation in April 1997. The Yamanashi test line mainly includes 18.4 km long test line, substation, test center and two maglev trains (MLX01 and MLX02 respectively). In December 24, 1997, the unmanned speed of MLX01 maglev train with three trains reached 550 km/h, which set a new world record at that time. In April 1999, the five-car MLX01 maglev train achieved a manned running speed of 552 km/h. In

December 1999, the Yamanashi Maglev Train Test Line in Japan carried out a high-speed passing test of maglev trains, creating the world's highest relative speed of 1,003 km/h when the two trains passed each other. At that time, the speeds of the two trains were 546 km/h and 457 km/h, respectively.

2002年6月，新型试验车辆驶入车辆基地。新型车辆的最大特点是车头流线部分的长高比例显著增大，大大改善了列车头部的空气动力性能。

In June 2002, the new test vehicle entered the vehicle base. The biggest feature of the new vehicle is that the length and height ratio of the front streamline part is significantly increased, which greatly improves the aerodynamic performance of the train head.

2003年12月2日，日本JR磁浮试验最高速度达到581 km/h，在2015年更创下了603 km/h的速度，创下有车厢车辆的陆地极速。日本研发的JR超导磁浮列车由东海旅客铁道（JR东海）和铁道总合技术研究所（JR总研）主导，首列实验列车JR-Maglev MLX01从1970年代开始研发，并且在山梨县建造了5节车厢的实验车和轨道。

In December 2, 2003, the maximum speed of JR maglev test in Japan reached 581 km/h, and in 2015, it set a speed of 603 km/h, setting a land speed for vehicles with carriages. The JR superconducting maglev train developed in Japan is led by the Tokai Railway (JR Tokai) and the Railway General Research Institute (JR General Research Institute). The first experimental train, JR-Maglev MLX01, has been developed since the 1970s, and a five-car experimental train and track have been built in Yamanashi Prefecture.

（二）HSST 磁浮铁路系统

1.5.2.2　HSST Maglev Railway System

日本是世界上第一个拥有中低速磁浮技术的国家。

Japan is the first country in the world with medium and low speed maglev technology.

20世纪70年代中期，为了开发一种联系机场和市区的速度快、噪声低、乘坐舒适的交通工具，日本航空公司开始组织专家对磁浮技术进行研究。1974年4月，小型磁浮试验装置的浮起试验成功；1975年，试制成电磁支承和导向的第一辆试验车HSST-01，电磁浮和直线电机驱动的磁浮车运行试验取得了成功，借助火箭和直线电机驱动，试验车HSST-01在11.6 km长的试验线路上达到了308 km/h的试验速度。

In the mid-1970s, in order to develop a fast, low-noise and comfortable means of transportation linking airports and urban areas, Japan Airlines began to organize experts to study maglev technology. In April 1974, the floating test of the small maglev test device was successful; In 1975, the first test vehicle HSST-01 with electromagnetic support and guidance was trial-produced. The operation test of the maglev vehicle with electromagnetic suspension and linear motor drive was successful. With the help of rocket and linear motor drive, the test vehicle HSST-01 reached a test speed of 308 km/h on a test line with a length of 11.6 km.

1978年，日本向公众展出了 HSST-02 号车，最高速度约为 100 km/h，共有 9 个座位。为了改善舒适性，在车厢和悬浮框架之间采用了二系弹簧悬挂系统。

In 1978, Japan exhibited the HSST-02 to the public, with a top speed of about 100 km/h and a total of nine seats. In order to improve the comfortability, the secondary spring suspension system is used between the carriage and the suspension frame.

为了向公众展示新的磁浮交通技术，并在接近应用的条件下试验新的磁浮交通技术最重要部分的功能，日本从 1983 年开始建造试验和展览车 HSST-03。该车于 1985 年在筑波国际工艺博览会上展出。试验和展览设施由一条 300 m 长的线路、一个进出站、一套供电设备和一个维修站组成。该车有 48 个座位，车速限制在 30 km/h。展览会期间，共有 60 万人次乘坐了磁浮车。1986 年，HSST-03 号车被送到温哥华国际博览会展出，速度达到 40 km/h。

In order to demonstrate the new maglev transportation technology to the public and test the function of the most important part of the new maglev transportation technology under conditions close to application, Japan began to build the test and exhibition vehicle HSST-03 in 1983, which was displayed at the Tsukuba International Craft Fair in 1985. The test and exhibition facility consists of a 300 m long line, an access station, a power supply unit and a maintenance station. With 48 seats and a speed limit of 30 km/h, 600,000 people rode the maglev during the show. In 1986, HSST-03 was sent to the Vancouver International Exposition, where it reached a speed of 40 km/h.

1987年，日本研制成 HSST-04 磁浮车，车重 24 t，长 19.4 m，可容纳约 70 名乘客，设计速度为 200 km/h。它与 HSST-03 一样，也采用了负荷支承、导向和驱动模块化技术，不同的是新车结构中，车辆走行模块从外侧包住线路。

In 1987, Japan developed the HSST-04 maglev vehicle, which weighs 24 t, is 19.4 m long, can accommodate about 70 passengers, and has a design speed of 200 km/h. Like HSST-03, it also adopts the modular technology of load support, guidance and drive, but the difference is that in the new vehicle structure, the vehicle running module wraps the line from the outside.

1990年，日本 HSST 磁浮铁路系统与德国磁浮铁路系统进行了比较和评估，得出 HSST 和 TR 接近实用的结论，并计划研制 HSST100S 型磁浮列车。

In 1990, the Japanese HSST maglev railway system was compared and evaluated with the German maglev railway system, and it was concluded that the HSST and TR were close to practical use, and the HSST100S maglev train was planned to be developed.

1991年，日本在名古屋附近的大江，建成了一条新的面向应用试验的试验线。试验线总长 1 530 m，最小平曲线半径 100 m（主线）和 25 m（分支线）。从 1991 年开始到 1995 年，对 HSST100S 型磁浮车进行了 100 多项面向应用要求的试验，其最高运行速度可达 130 km/h。测试结果表明，HSST100S 型磁浮列车是成功的。1993 年 3 月，以东京大学技术系正田英介教授为主席，日本运输省、建设省和其他单位的专家学者组成的可行性研究委员会对试验结果进行了最后论证，考察了噪声、振动和磁场影响等。结论是 HSST 磁浮铁路系统是舒适的低污染系统，能够应对紧急情况，长期的运行试验证明它是可靠的，并且由于其悬浮的优点使得它的维修量降低。作为城市交通系统，HSST 磁浮铁路系统已进入实用阶段。

In 1991, Japan completed a new test line for application tests in Oe, near Nagoya. The total length of the test line is 1,530 m, and the minimum horizontal curve radius is 100 m (main line) and 25 m (branch line). From 1991 to 1995, more than 100 application-oriented tests were carried out on the HSST100S maglev train. The maximum running speed of the HSST100S maglev train can reach 130 km/h. The test results show that the HSST100 maglev train is successful. In March 1993, a feasibility study committee composed of experts and scholars from the Ministry of Transport, the Ministry of Construction and other units of Japan, chaired by Professor Hidesuke Masada of the Department of Technology of the University of Tokyo, made a final demonstration of the test results and investigated the effects of noise, vibration and magnetic field. The conclusion is that the HSST maglev rail system is a comfortable, low-pollution system, capable of dealing with emergencies, reliable in long-term operational tests, and requires less maintenance due to its levitation advantages. As an urban transportation system, the HSST maglev railway system has entered the practical stage.

1995 年，在 HSST100S 型的基础上，日本又研制了一台新的样车，称为 HSST100L，其模块由 6 个增加到 10 个，长度由 8.5 m/辆增加到 14.4 m/辆，一些器件在 HSST100S 型试验结果的基础上进行了改进。HSST100L 是一列两辆编组的、商业运营车的样车，从 1995 年开始，在大江的试验线路上进行了运行试验。

In 1995, on the basis of HSST100S, a new prototype called HSST100L was developed in Japan. Its modules were increased from 6 to 10, and its length was increased from 8.5 m to 14.4 m per vehicle. Some devices were improved on the basis of the test results of HSST100S. The HSST100L is a two-car, commercially operated train prototype that has been tested on the Oe test line since 1995.

从 2002 年开始，日本建造了一条长 8.9 km 名古屋市区通向爱知世博会会场的磁浮线路——HSST 型低速磁浮线，2005 年 3 月 6 日建成并运营，全程无人驾驶，最高速度为 100 km/h。

Since 2002, Japan has built an 8.9 km long maglev line from Nagoya downtown to Aichi World Expo site, HSST type low-speed maglev line, which was completed and put into operation in March 6, 2005. The whole journey is driverless, and the maximum speed is 100 km/h.

三、磁浮铁路在其他国家的发展状况

1.5.3 Development of Maglev Railway in Other Countries

（一）磁浮铁路在英国的发展

1.5.3.1 Development of Maglev Railway in Britain

在英国，电磁浮系统是被英国铁路协会（BR）认同的，其目的是解决市内短程运输的问题。磁浮系统的研究是在关注经济和运输能力的要求下，考虑能量需求、可用度和安全性，以及噪声、辐射和乘坐舒适性之后进行的。

In the United Kingdom, the electromagnetic levitation system is approved by the British Railway Association (BR), and its purpose is to solve the problem of short-distance transportation in the city. The research of maglev system is based on the requirements of economy and transportation capacity, considering energy demand, availability and safety, as well as noise, radiation and riding comfortableness.

1974 年，英国在德比进行了磁浮列车运行试验，试验车长 3.5 m，重 3 t，线路长 100 m。

In 1974, a maglev train was tested in Derby, England, with a length of 3.5 m, a weight of 3 t, and a line length of 100 m.

为了将新建的伯明翰机场终端与国际博览会展区及火车站连接起来，英国建造了一条 620 m 长的磁浮铁路线，该线路于 1984 年投入载客运行。这条线路是复线，轨道架在 6 m 高的钢结构线路上，来往运行 3 辆由电磁支承、导向系统和直线电机驱动的小型磁浮车，速度可达 50 km/h，磁浮车辆重约 5 t，具有铝焊接底架和玻璃纤维强化塑料制成的车厢结构。一辆车有 6 个座位和 26 个站位，电气设备均布置在车厢地板下面。

In order to connect the new Birmingham Airport Terminal with the international exhibition area and railway station, a 620 m long maglev railway line was built in the UK, which was put into operation in 1984. The line is a double-track line, and the track is erected on a steel structure line with a height of 6 m. Three small maglev vehicles driven by electromagnetic support, guidance system and linear motor in operation, and the speed can reach 50 km/h. The maglev vehicles weigh about 5 t and have an aluminum welded underframe and a carriage structure made of glass fiber reinforced plastic. A car has 6 seats and 26 stations, and the electrical equipment is arranged under the floor of the carriage.

伯明翰磁浮铁路是第一个用在公共旅客运输上的磁浮铁路系统。1996 年，由于该铁路系统故障率高，维护困难，伯明翰磁浮铁路关闭。

The Birmingham Maglev was the first maglev rail system to be used for public passenger transportation. In 1996, the Birmingham Maglev was closed due to the high failure rate and maintenance difficulties of the railway system.

（二）磁浮铁路在苏联的发展

1.5.3.2　Development of Maglev Railway in the Soviet Union

根据苏联交通专家的看法，到 21 世纪，苏联多数城市的直径都将达到 100 km，包括郊区将扩大到 150 km。为了减少乘客在大城市交通中浪费的时间，必须明显地提高当时 30 km/h 的中等旅行速度。除了要有较高的速度外，新的交通系统应该是污染少、经济性好、投资少和运量大。此外交通规划还应包括近郊机场、工业区和疗养区。

According to Soviet transport experts, by the 21st century, the diameter of most Soviet cities will reach 100 km, including 150 km in the suburbs. In order to reduce the time wasted by passengers in metropolitan traffic, then the moderate travel speed of 30 km/h had to be significantly increased. In addition to higher speeds, the new transportation system should be less polluting, more economical, less costly and more powerful. Besides, traffic planning should also include suburban airports, industrial areas and convalescent areas.

大约从 20 世纪 70 年代中期，苏联就已经从理论和实践方面研究了电磁浮和永磁浮技术。由于机动车辆的废气造成严重的环境负担，20 世纪 80 年代初开始在阿拉木图城区制订磁浮铁路设计方案。研究表明，磁浮铁路相对地铁来说，建造费用较低，但是当时苏联在悬浮和导向技术方面还存在问题，发展计划未能实现。

Since the mid-1970s, the Soviet Union has studied electromagnetic levitation and permanent magnetic levitation technology from the theoretical and practical aspects. Due to the serious environmental burden caused by the exhaust gas of motor vehicles, the design scheme of maglev railway in Almaty urban area began to be formulated in the early 1980s. Studies have shown that the construction cost of maglev railway is lower than that of subway, but there were still problems in suspension and guidance technology in the Soviet Union at that time, and the development plan was not realized.

20 世纪 80 年代，在莫斯科附近的拉绵斯卡娅的磁浮铁路试验设施中，一辆重 18 t 的磁浮车在一条 600 m 长的试验线上进行了试验运行。随着苏联的解体，未有面向应用的磁浮铁路的后续研究和开发。

In the 1980s, an 18 t maglev train was put into test operation on a 600 m long test line at the Maglev Railway Test Facility in Lamenskaya, near Moscow. With the disintegration of the Soviet Union, there is no follow-up research and development of application-oriented maglev railway.

（三）磁浮铁路在美国的发展

1.5.3.3 Development of Maglev Railway in the United States

美国从 20 世纪 60 年代初开始磁浮铁路的研究，1975 年停止研究。1989 年起又重新开始评估磁浮列车的实用价值，由铁道总署、陆军工兵总部、能源部牵头，数家公司和大学参加，历时 4 年，定出 4 个磁浮车设计速度均为 500 km/h 的方案，其中 3 个方案为电动型。美国还对大城市间的 16 条线进行了技术经济评估，认为只有纽约—波士顿线能在短期内回收投资并实现盈利。也曾有计划在佛罗里达州修建第一条由德国制造的磁浮铁路线；在宾夕法尼亚州建造 30 km 的磁浮铁路，但这些计划均未实现。

The United States began to study the maglev railway in the early 1960s and stopped in 1975. Since 1989, the practical value of the maglev train has been evaluated again, led by the Railway Administration, the Army Corps of Engineers Headquarters and the Ministry of Energy, with the participation of several companies and universities. After four years, four schemes with a design speed of 500 km/h have been worked out, three of which are electric. The United States also conducted a technical and economic evaluation of 16 lines between large cities, and concluded that only the New York-Boston line could recover its investment and achieve profitability in the short term. There were also plans to build the first maglev railway line made in Germany in Florida and to build a 30 km maglev railway in Pennsylvania, but these plans were not realized.

美国政府在 1998 年预算投入 10 亿美元用于规划和建造一条磁浮铁路，由美国联邦铁路部门支持，寄希望于德国 TR 技术的推广应用。经过前期研究，从最初的 7 条线路选出两条线路进入法定的规划程序。这两条线是：巴尔的摩—华盛顿特区和匹兹堡机场—匹兹堡绿堡。2010 年，华盛顿杜勒斯机场磁浮主航站楼完工，随后磁浮列车投入使用。

In 1998, the U.S. government budgeted $1 billion for the planning and construction of a maglev railway, supported by the Federal Railway Department of the United States, building their hopes on the application the TR technology in Germany. After preliminary study, two lines were selected from the first seven lines to enter the statutory planning process. The two lines are: Baltimore-Washington, D.C. and Pittsburgh Airport-Pittsburgh Green Fort. In 2010, the Maglev Main Terminal at Washington Dulles Airport was completed, and then the maglev train was put into use.

另外一些非联邦政府资助，由地方及公司开发的项目也在积极开展，如 American Maglev Technology 公司在多米尼大学建设校园载客系统，正建造试验线和试验车。美国 Magplane（磁浮飞机）技术公司正开展磁浮飞机的开发，目前正在进行样车、试验线设计。佛罗里达磁浮 2000 公司也在研发高速超导磁浮技术，采用超导磁体电动悬浮，直线同步电机驱动，速度 480 km/h，并已完成概念设计、经济分析，正进行部件研制。General Atomics 公司则研究开发城市磁浮计划，采用永磁电动式悬浮，直线同步电机驱动，正进入1∶1系统试验阶段。

Other projects that are not funded by the federal government and are developed by local governments and companies are also being carried out, such as the American Maglev Technology Company's construction of a campus passenger system at the University of Domini, which is building a test line and a test car. Magplane (Magnetic Levitation Aircraft) Technology Company of the United States is developing the magnetic levitation aircraft, and is currently designing the prototype and test line. Florida Maglev 2000 is also developing high-speed superconducting maglev technology, using superconducting magnet electric suspension, linear synchronous motor drive, speed 480 km/h, and has completed conceptual design, economic analysis, and is developing components. General Atomics is researching and developing the urban maglev project, which uses permanent magnet electric suspension and linear synchronous motor drive, and is entering the 1:1 system test stage.

美国麻省理工学院（MIT）从20世纪70年代开始Magplane概念的研究，在国家科学基金资助下，完成了一个1/25的试验模型，在100 m的试验轨道上进行过5代车的数百次试验，建立了全尺寸的6维仿真模型，对列车的各种性能进行仿真。

The Massachusetts Institute of Technology (MIT) in the United States began to study the Magplane concept in the 1970s. Under the support of the National Science Foundation, a 1/25 test model was completed, hundreds of tests of five generations of trains were carried out on a 100 m test track, and a full-scale six-dimensional simulation model was established to simulate various performances of the train.

（四）磁浮铁路在加拿大的发展

1.5.3.4　Development of Maglev Railway in Canada

考虑到燃料的短缺和昂贵，以及因此而需要限制私家汽车的情况，加拿大交通规划者认识到，未来数年内铁路运输将显著增长，采用轮轨系统已经不能满足要求。这种认识促使加拿大在电动悬浮技术领域内进行研究和开发工作。有关研究于1972年在金士顿大学开展起来。

Given the scarcity and high cost of fuel, and the resulting need to restrict private cars, Canadian transportation planners recognize that rail transportation will grow significantly in the coming years, and that the use of wheel-rail systems is no longer adequate. This recognition has led to Canadian research and development efforts in the area of electrodynamic levitation technology. Research began at Kingston University in 1972.

最初，加拿大研究了电动支承、导向和驱动技术的基本性能和电动悬浮车辆的动力学问题。20世纪70年代末期，建造了旋转试验台，用来对电动悬浮系统和无铁心长定子直线同步电机进行试验。理论和试验研究促成了在电动悬浮技术领域内制定研制接近应用的磁浮车的规划，但后来未见研制接近实用的样车和试验线路。

Initially, Canada studied the basic performance of electric support, guidance and drive technology and the dynamics of electric suspension vehicles. In the late 1970s, rotating test rigs were built to test electrodynamic levitation systems and coreless long-stator linear synchronous motors. Theoretical and experimental studies have contributed to the formulation of a plan to develop a maglev vehicle close to application in the field of electrodynamic levitation technology, but no prototype vehicle and test line close to application have been developed since then.

（五）磁浮铁路在法国的发展

1.5.3.5　Development of Maglev Railway in France

法国交通部和德国联邦研究与技术部的合作协定条款中，规定法国和德国的铁路管理部门、公司和研究所要从事磁浮技术的合作开发工作。法国曾研究过一种用于城市交通的磁浮铁路方案。它的特点是：采用电磁式的支承、导向系统和所谓的 U 形线性电动机驱动，用于市郊运输，车速可达 150 km/h。1983 年至 1984 年间，在 Grenoble 附近，通过旋转的直线电机试验台，对直线感应电机进行了试验，速度可达 300 km/h。20 世纪 80 年代中期以来，法国没有进行过有组织、有影响的磁浮铁路技术研究。

The cooperation agreement between the Ministry of Transport of France and the Federal Ministry of Research and Technology of Germany stipulates that the railway management departments, companies and research institutes of France and Germany should engage in the cooperative development of maglev technology. France has studied a maglev railway scheme for urban transportation. It is characterized by an electromagnetic supporting and guiding system and a so-called U-shaped linear motor drive for suburban transportation at speeds up to 150 km/h. Between 1983 and 1984, a linear induction motor was tested near Grenoble by means of a rotating linear motor test stand. The speed can reach 300 km/h. Since the mid-1980s, France has not carried out organized and influential research on maglev railway technology.

（六）磁浮铁路在韩国的发展

1.5.3.6　Development of Maglev Railway in ROK

韩国是世界上第三个拥有中低速磁浮技术的国家。韩国磁浮的发展过程经历了独立研发（1985—1993 年）、对外合作（1994—1998 年）和商业化尝试（1999 年至今）3 个阶段。

ROK is the third country in the world with medium and low speed maglev technology. The development of maglev in Korea has gone through three stages: independent research and development (1985-1993), foreign cooperation (1994-1998) and commercialization attempt (1999-present).

韩国于 1988 年至 1994 年进行过低速常导磁浮铁路的研究，曾于大田科技展览会展出一辆磁浮车和一段长度约 500 m 的线路，磁浮车试验运行速度达到 60 km/h。韩国磁浮车的结构和尺寸都与日本的 HSST100 型磁浮车相近。韩国还对首尔至釜山的高速交通选用轮轨和磁浮技术进行过经济技术论证，最后决定引进法国的 TGV 高速铁路。

From 1988 to 1994, ROK carried out research on low-speed EMS maglev railway. A maglev train and a section of line with a length of about 500 m were exhibited at the Daejeon Science and Technology Exhibition. The test running speed of the maglev train reached 60 km/h. The structure and size of the Korean maglev vehicle are similar to those of the HSST100 maglev vehicle in Japan. ROK has also conducted economic and technical demonstrations on the selection of wheel-rail and maglev technology for high-speed transportation from Seoul to Busan, and finally decided to introduce the French TGV high-speed railway.

2014 年 7 月，韩国仁川国际机场至仁川龙游站磁浮线路投入运营，全长 6.1 km，列车由韩国自主研发，无人驾驶，最高速度可达 110 km/h。

In July 2014, the maglev line from Incheon International Airport to Ryongyo Station in Incheon, ROK, was put into operation, with a total length of 6.1 km. The train was independently developed by ROK, driverless, with a maximum speed of 110 km/h.

（七）磁浮铁路在瑞士的发展

1.5.3.7　Development of Maglev Railway in Switzerland

瑞士在 20 世纪 70 年代提出瑞士地铁的概念。瑞士地铁是一地下管道旅客运输系统，在管道内可减小空气压力，高速高频地连接瑞士主要城市和地区。车辆采用磁浮系统，由同步直线电机驱动，速度达到 500 km/h。在 1989 年至 1993 年，瑞士进行了技术和经济初步可行性研究，20 世纪 90 年代得到瑞士政府和工业界的支持，主要研究由瑞士联邦工学院（洛桑）和 90 家私人公司进行，目前正进行实验室研究和进一步论证。

Switzerland put forward the concept of Swiss Metro in the 1970s. Swiss Metro is an underground pipeline passenger transport system, which can reduce air pressure in the pipeline and connect major cities and regions of Switzerland at high speed and high frequency. The vehicle uses a maglev system and is driven by a synchronous linear motor with a speed of 500 km/h. From 1989 to 1993, Switzerland carried out a technical and economic preliminary feasibility study. In the 1990s, it was supported by the Swiss government and industry. The main study was carried out by the Swiss Federal Institute of Technology (Lausanne) and 90 private companies. At present, laboratory research and further demonstration are being carried out.

第六节　磁浮轴承

Section 1.6　Magnetic Bearing

在磁浮领域中，磁浮轴承的应用非常广泛。磁浮轴承也称为电磁轴承或磁力轴承。它是利用磁场力将转轴悬浮在磁场中，使转轴在空间无机械接触、无磨损地旋转的一种新型高性能轴承。由于不存在机械接触，转子可在超临界转速（每分钟数十万转）的工况下运行并且可以降低能耗和噪声，具有无须润滑、无油污染、寿命长以及适用于许多应用环境等优点，因而具有一般传统轴承和支承技术所无法比拟的优越性。近年来，国内外对其研究都非常重视。有关磁浮轴承的介绍在此不再赘述，可参见相关资料。

In the field of magnetic levitation, magnetic bearings are widely used. Magnetic bearings are also known as electromagnetic bearings or magnetic bearings. It is a new type of high-performance bearing, which uses magnetic field force to suspend the shaft in the magnetic field, so that the shaft can rotate without mechanical contact and wear in space. Because of the absence of mechanical contact, the rotor can operate at supercritical speed (hundreds of thousands of revolutions per minute) and can reduce energy consumption and noise. It has the advantages of no lubrication, no oil pollution, long life and being suitable for many application environments. Therefore, it has incomparable advantages over traditional bearings and supporting technologies. In recent years, great attention has been paid to its research at home and abroad. The introduction of magnetic bearings will not be repeated here, please refer to the relevant information.

复习思考题

Questions for Revision

1. 根据列车最高运行速度的不同，铁路可以分为哪些类型？

1. What types of railway can be classified according to the maximum running speed of trains?

2. 磁浮铁路按应用范围划分，可以划分为哪些类型？

2. What types of maglev railway can be divided into according to the application scope?

3. 磁浮铁路按运行速度划分，可以划分为哪些类型？

3. According to the operating speed, what types of maglev railway can be divided into?

4. 磁浮铁路按制冷剂及工作温度划分，可以划分为哪些类型？

4. What types of maglev railway can be classified according to refrigerant and working temperature?

5. 磁浮铁路按导体材料划分，可以划分为哪些类型？

5. According to the conductor material, what types of maglev railway can be divided into?

6. 磁浮铁路按直线电机定子长度、直流电机磁场是否同步运行、驱动方式、导轨结构形式、悬浮方式等，可以划分为哪些类型？

6. What types of maglev railway can be divided into according to the length of stator of linear motor, whether the magnetic field of DC motor runs synchronically, the driving mode, the structure of guide rail, the suspension mode, etc.?

7. 简要介绍磁浮列车的工作原理。

7. Briefly introduce the working principle of maglev train.

8. 磁浮列车是如何进行分类的？

8. How are maglev trains classified?

9. 简要介绍国外磁浮交通技术应用发展概况。

9. Briefly introduce the development of maglev transportation technology application abroad.

第二章　直线电机

Chapter 2　Linear Motor

本章主要介绍直线电机的基本结构、基本原理、分类及标准。

This chapter mainly introduces the basic structure, basic principle, classification and standard of linear motor.

第一节　直线电机的基本结构

Section 2.1　Basic structure of linear motor

图 2-1 分别表示了一台旋转电机和一台直线电机。

Figure 2-1 shows a rotary motor and a linear motor respectively.

（a）旋转电机　　　　　　　　　　　（b）直线电机

（a）Rotary Motor　　　　　　　　　（b）Linear Motor

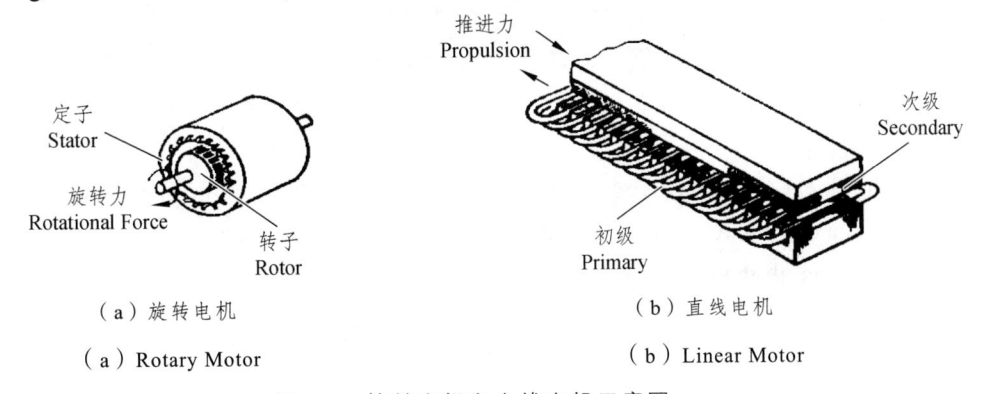

图 2-1　旋转电机和直线电机示意图

Figure 2-1　Schematic Diagram of Rotary Motor and Linear Motor

直线电机可以认为是旋转电机在结构方面的一种演变，它可看作将一台旋转电机沿径向剖开，然后将电机的圆周展成直线，如图 2-2 所示。这样就得到了由旋转电机演变而来的最原始的直线电机。由定子演变而来的一侧称为初级，由转子演变而来的一侧称为次级。

Linear motor can be considered as a structural evolution of rotary motor. It can be regarded as a rotating motor that is cut radially, and then the circumference of the motor is stretched into a straight line, as shown in Fig. 2-2. In this way, the most primitive linear motor evolved from the rotary motor was obtained. The side that evolved from the stator is called primary and the side that evolved from the rotor is called secondary.

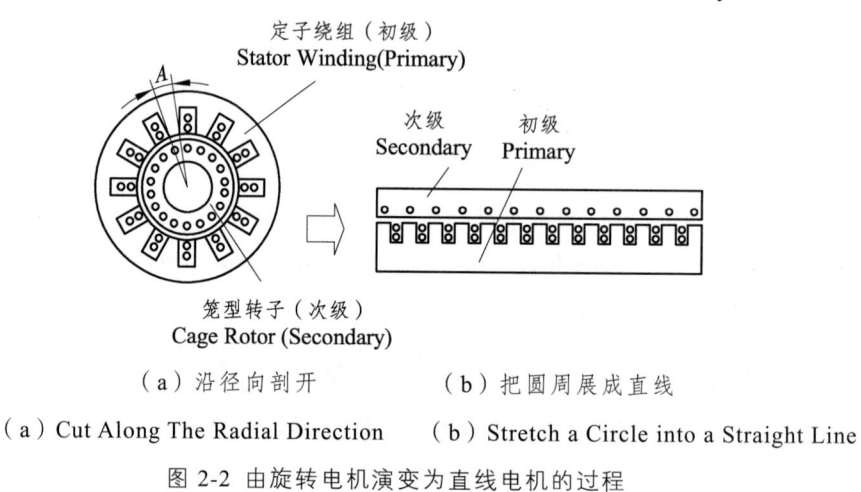

（a）沿径向剖开　　　　（b）把圆周展成直线

（a）Cut Along The Radial Direction　　（b）Stretch a Circle into a Straight Line

图 2-2 由旋转电机演变为直线电机的过程

Figure 2-2 Evolution Process From Rotary Motor to Linear Motor

图 2-2 中演变而来的直线电机，其初级和次级长度是相等的，由于在运行时初级和次级之间要做相对运动，如果在运动开始时，初级与次级正巧对齐，那么在运动中，初级与次级之间互相耦合的部分越来越少，而不能正常运动。为了保证在所需的行程范围内，初级与次级之间的耦合能保持不变，因此实际应用时，是将初级与次级制造成不同的长度。在制造直线电机时，既可以是初级短、次级长，也可以是初级长、次级短。前者称为短初级长次级，后者称为长初级短次级。但是由于短初级在制造成本上、运行费用上均比短次级低得多，因此，目前除特殊场合外，一般均采用短初级、长次级，如图 2-3 所示。

For the linear motor evolved from Figure 2-2, the length of the primary and secondary is equal. Since there is relative motion between the primary and secondary during operation, if the primary is aligned with the secondary at the beginning of the motion, there will be less and less mutual coupling between the primary and the secondary during the motion, and they will not be able to move normally. In order to ensure that the coupling between the primary and the secondary remains constant over the required range of travel, the primary and the secondary are manufactured to different degrees of K in practice. When the linear motor is manufactured, the linear motor can be primary short and secondary long, or primary long and secondary short. The former is called short primary and long secondary, and the latter is called long primary and short secondary. However, since the short primary is much lower than the short secondary in terms of manufacturing cost and operating cost, short primary and long secondary are generally used at present except for special occasions, as shown in Figure 2-3.

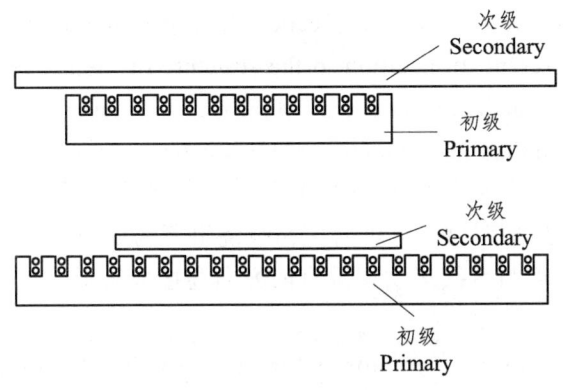

图 2-3 单边型直线电机

Figure 2-3　Single-Sided Linear Motor

图 2-3 所示的直线电机仅在一边安放初级，这种结构形式称为单边型直线电机。该结构的电机，一个最大的特点是在初级与次级之间存在一个很大的法向吸力，一般这个法向吸力在钢次级时约为推力的 10 倍，在大多数场合下，这种法向吸力是不希望存在的。如果在次级的两边都装上初级，那么这个法向吸力可以相互抵消，这种结构形式称为双边型，如图 2-4 所示。

The linear motor shown in Fig. 2-3 has a primary on only one side, which is called a single-sided linear motor. One of the most important characteristics of the motor with this structure is that there is a large normal suction force between the primary and the secondary. Generally, this normal suction force is about 10 times of the thrust force in the steel secondary. In most cases, this normal suction force is undesirable. If the primary is mounted on both sides of the secondary, this normal suction force can be cancelled out. This type of structure is called the double-sided type, as shown in Fig. 2-4.

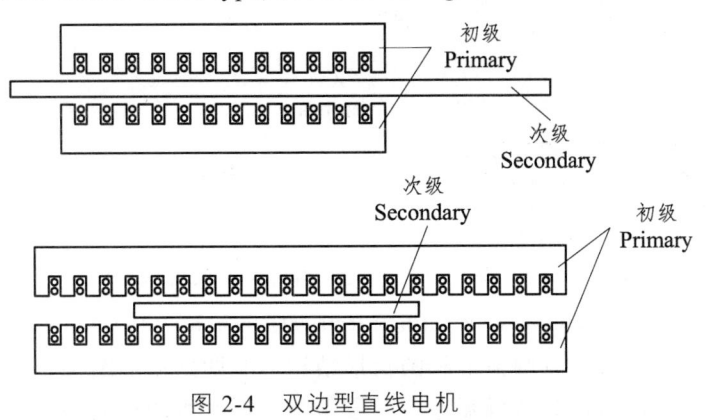

图 2-4 双边型直线电机

Figure 2-4　Double-Sided Linear Motor

上述介绍的直线电机称为扁平型直线电机，是目前应用最广泛的直线电机。除了上述扁平型直线电机的结构形式外，直线电机还可以做成圆筒形（也称管形）结构，它也可以看作是由旋转电机演变过来的，其演变过程如图 2-5 所示。

The linear motor introduced above is called flat linear motor, which is the most widely used linear motor at present. In addition to the structure of the above flat linear motor, the linear motor can also be made into a cylindrical (also called tubular) structure, which can also be seen as evolved from the rotating motor, and its evolution process is shown in Fig. 2-5.

图 2-5（a）表示一台旋转电机以及由定子绕组所构成的磁场极性分布情况。图 2-5（b）表示转变为扁平型直线电机后，初级绕组所构成的磁场极性分布情况。然后将扁平形直线电机沿着与直线运动相垂直的方向卷接成筒形，这样就构成图 2-5（c）所示的圆筒形直线电机。

Fig. 2-5 (a) shows a rotating motor and the polarity distribution of the magnetic field formed by the stator windings. Fig. 2-5 (b) shows the polarity distribution of the magnetic field formed by the primary winding after conversion to a flat linear motor. The flat linear motor is then rolled into a cylindrical shape in a direction perpendicular to the linear motion, thereby forming the cylindrical linear motor shown in fig. 2-5 (c).

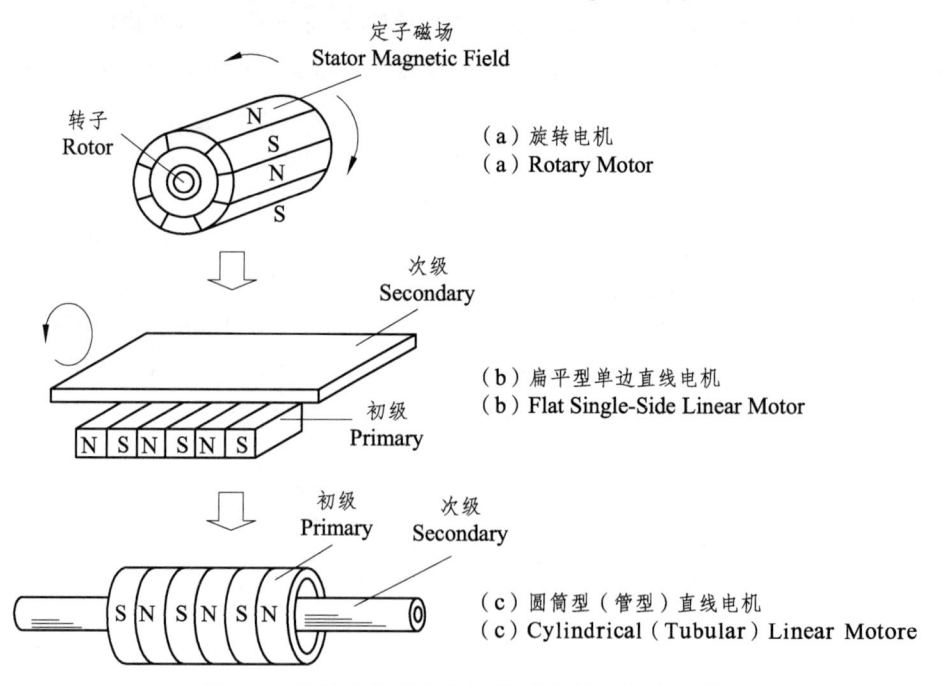

图 2-5　旋转电机演变为圆筒型直线电机的过程

Figure 2-5　The Evolution of Rotating Electrical Machines into Cylindrical Linear Motor

此外，直线电机还有圆弧形和圆盘形结构。所谓圆弧形结构，就是将平板形直线电机的初级沿运动方向改成圆弧形，并放于圆柱形次级的柱面外侧，如图 2-6 所示。

In addition, the linear motor has an arc type and a disc type structure. The so-called arc structure is to change the primary of the flat linear motor into an arc shape along the motion direction and place it outside the cylindrical surface of the cylindrical secondary, as shown in Fig. 2-6.

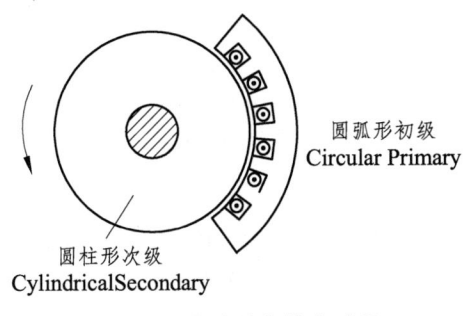

图 2-6 圆弧形直线电动机

Figure 2-6　Arc Linear

图 2-7 是圆盘形直线电机，该电机把次级做成一片圆盘（铜或铝，或铜、铝与铁复合），将初级放在次级圆盘靠近外缘的平面上。圆盘形直线电机的初级可以是双面的，也可以是单面的。圆弧形和圆盘形直线电机的运动实际上是一个圆周运动，如图 2-6 和图 2-7 中的箭头所示，然而由于它们的运动原理和设计方法与扁平形直线电机结构相似，故仍归入直线电机的范畴。

Fig. 2-7 shows a disk-type linear motor in which, the secondary is made into a disk (copper or aluminum, or copper, aluminum and iron composite), and the primary is placed on the plane of the secondary disk near the outer edge. The primary of the disc-type linearmotor can be double-sided or single-sided. The motion of arc-type and disk-type linear motors is actually a circular motion, as shown by the arrows in Fig. 2-6 and Fig. 2-7. However, their motion principle and design method are similar to the structure of flat-type linear motors, so they are still classified as linear motors.

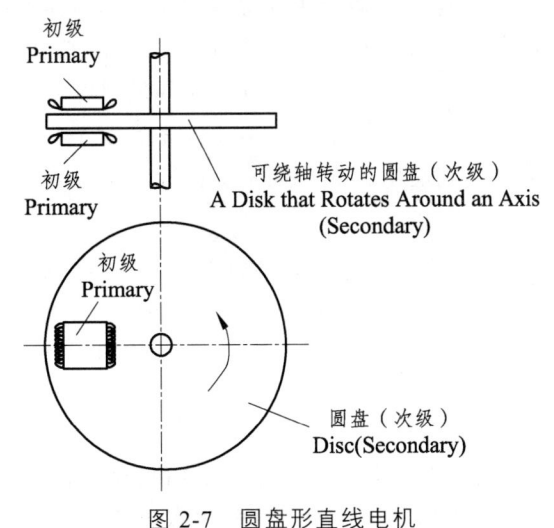

图 2-7 圆盘形直线电机

Figure 2-7　Disc-type Linear Motor

第二节 直线电机的工作原理

Section 2.2　Working Principle of Linear Motor

直线电机不仅在结构上相当于是从旋转电机演变而来的，而且其工作原理也与旋转电机相似。从电机学的一些基本工作原理出发，引申出直线电机的基本工作原理。

The linear motor is not only evolved from the rotary motor in structure, but also its working principle is similar to the rotary motor. Starting from some basic working principles of electrical machinery, the basic working principles of linear motor are derived.

一、旋转电机的基本工作原理

2.2.1　Basic Working Principle of Rotating Motor

图 2-8 表示一台简单的两级旋转电机。图中线圈 AX、BY、CZ 为定子 A、B、C 的三相绕组。当在其中通入三相对称正弦电流后，便在气隙中产生了一个磁场，这个磁场可看成沿气隙圆周呈正弦分布。当 A 相电流达到最大值时，B 和 C 相电流都为负的最大值的 1/2，这时磁场波幅处于 A 相绕组轴线上，如图 2-8（a）所示。经过 $t=2\pi/(3\omega)$ 时间（其中 ω 为电流的角频率）后，B 相电流达到最大值，这时 C 和 A 相都为负的最大值的 1/2，而磁场波幅转到 B 相绕组轴线上，如图 2-8（b）所示。经过 $t=4\pi/(3\omega)$ 时间后，C 相电流达到最大值，A 和 B 相电流都为负的最大值的 1/2，磁场波幅又转到 C 相绕组轴线上，如图 2-8（c）所示。由此可见，电流随时间变化，磁场波幅就按 A、B、C 相序沿圆周旋转。电流变化一个周期，磁场转过一对极。这种磁场称为旋转磁场，它的旋转速度称为同步转速，用 n_s（r/min）表示，它与电流的频率 f（Hz）成正比，而与电机的极对数 p 成反比，如下式所示：

$$n_s = 60f/p$$

Figure 2-8 shows a simple two-stage rotary motor. Coils AX, BY and CZ in the figure are three-phase windings of stators A, B and C. When three-phase symmetrical sinusoidal current is applied to the air gap, a magnetic field is generated in the air gap, and the magnetic field can be regarded as a sinusoidal distribution along the circumference of the air gap. When the current of phase A reaches the maximum value, the current of phase B and C is 1/2 of the maximum negative value, and the magnetic field amplitude is on the axis of phase A winding, as shown in Fig. 2-8 (a). After $t = 2\pi/(3\omega)$ (where is the angular frequency of the current), the current of phase B reaches the maximum value. At this time, both phase C and phase A are 1/2 of the negative maximum value, and the magnetic field amplitude is transferred to the axis of phase B winding, as shown in Fig. 2-8 (b). After $t = 4\pi/(3\omega)$, the current of phase C reaches the maximum value, the current of phase A and B are both 1/2 of the negative maximum value, and the magnetic field amplitude is transferred to the axis of phase C winding, as shown in Fig. 2-8 (c). It can be seen that when the current changes with time, the amplitude of the magnetic field rotates along the circle according to the phase sequence of A, B and C. When the current changes for one cycle, the magnetic field rotates through a pair of poles. This magnetic field is called the rotating magnetic field, and its rotating speed is called the synchronous speed, expressed by n_s (r/min), which is proportional to the frequency f (Hz) of the current and inversely proportional to the number of pole pairs p of the motor, as shown in the following formula:

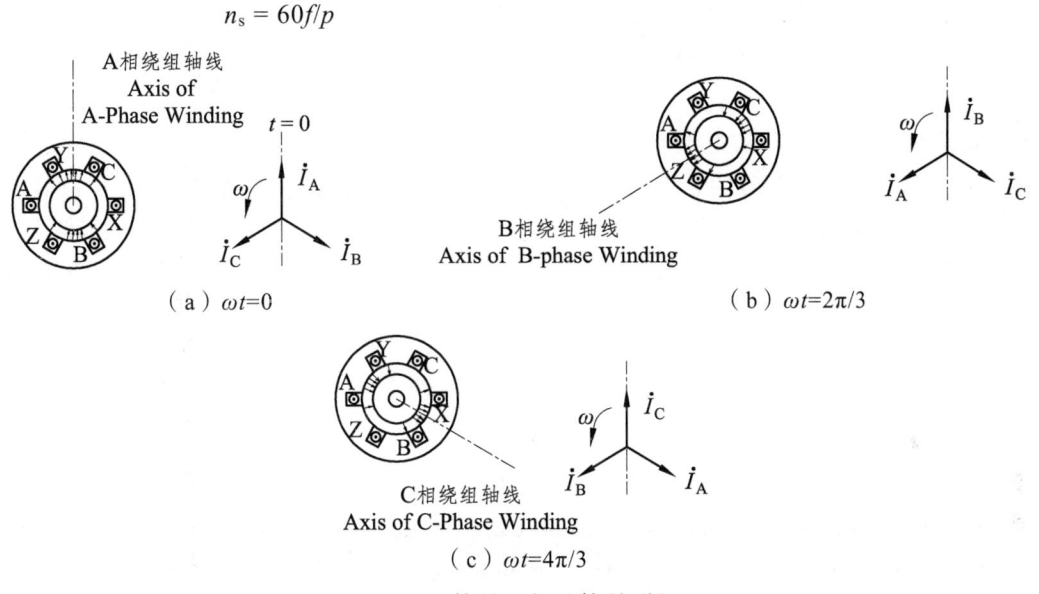

$$n_s = 60f/p$$

图 2-8 旋转电机的旋转磁场

Figure 2-8 Figure 2-8 Rotating Magnetic Field of a Rotary Motor

如果用 v_s（m/s）表示在定子内圆表面上磁场运动的线速度，则有

$$v_s = 2p\tau n_s/60 = 2\tau f$$

式中　　τ——极距（m）。

If v_s (m/s) is used to represent the linear velocity of the magnetic field motion on the inner circumferential surface of the stator, then

$$v_s = 2p\tau n_s/60 = 2\tau f$$

In the formula, τ—polar distance (m).

通过图 2-9 可说明旋转磁场对转子的作用，为了简单起见，图中笼型转子只画出了两根导条。

The effect of rotating magnetic field on the rotor can be illustrated in Fig. 2-9. For simplicity, only two guide bars are drawn for the cage rotor in the figure.

当气隙中旋转磁场以 n_s 同步速度旋转时，该磁场就会切割转子导条，而在其中感应出电动势。电动势的方向可按右手定则确定，示于图中转子导条上。由于转子导条是通过端环短接的，因此在感应电动势的作用下，便在转子导条中产生电流。当不考虑电动势和电流的相位差时，电流的方向即为电动势的方向。这个转子电流与气隙磁场相互作用便产生切向电磁力 F。电磁力的方向可按左手定则确定。由于转子是圆柱体，故转子上每根导条的切向电磁力乘上转子半径，全部加起来即为促使转子旋转的电磁转矩。

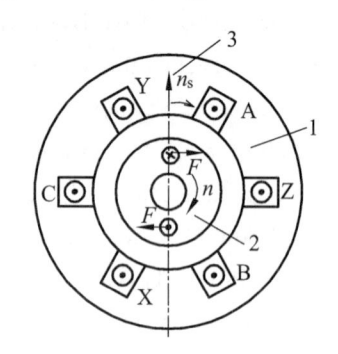

1—定子；2—转子；3—磁场方向。

1—Stator; 2—Rotor; 3—Magnetic Field Direction.

图 2-9　旋转电机的基本工作原理图

Figure 2-9　Basic Working Principle Diagram of Rotary Motor

由此可以看出，转子旋转的方向与旋转磁场的转向是一致的。转子的转速用 n 表示。在电动机运动状态下，转子转速 n 总要比同步转速 n_s 低一些，因为一旦 $n=n_s$，转子就和旋转磁场相对静止，转子导条不切割磁场，于是感应电动势为零，不能产生电流和电磁转矩。转子转速 n 与同步转速 n_s 的差值经常用转差率 s 来表示，即

$$s = \frac{n_s - n}{n_s}$$

$$n_s - n = s n_s$$

$$n = (1-s)\, n_s$$

When the rotating magnetic field rotates at n_s synchronous speed in the air gap, the magnetic field will cut the rotor guide bar and induce electromotive force in it. The direction of the electromotive force can be determined according to the right hand rule, as shown on the rotor guide bar in the figure. Because the rotor guide bar is short connected through the end ring, so under the action of induced electromotive force, the current is generated in the rotor guide bar. When the phase difference between electromotive force and current is not considered, the direction of the current is the direction of the electromotive force. This rotor current interacts with the air-gap magnetic field to generate tangential electromagnetic force F. The direction of the electromagnetic force can be determined by the left hand rule. Because the rotor is a cylinder, the tangential electromagnetic force of each guide bar on the rotor multiplied by the radius of the rotor, all added up to the electromagnetic torque that causes the rotor to rotate. It can be seen that the direction of rotation of the rotor is consistent with the direction of rotation of the rotating magnetic field. The rotor speed is denoted by "n". In the motor motion state, rotor speed "n" is always lower than synchronous speed n_s, because once $n = n_s$, the rotor and rotating magnetic field is relatively static, the rotor guide bar does not cut the magnetic field, so the induced electromotive force is zero, and the current and electromagnetic torque cannot be generated. The difference between the rotor speed "n" and the synchronous speed "n_s" is often expressed by the slip ratio "s".

$$s = \frac{n_s - n}{n_s}$$
$$n_s - n = sn_s$$
$$n = (1-s)\ n_s$$

以上就是一般旋转电机的基本工作原理。

The above is the basic working principle of the general rotating motor.

二、直线电机的基本工作原理

2.2.2　Basic Working Principle of Linear Motor

将图 2-9 所示的旋转电机在顶上沿径向剖开，并将圆周拉直，变成了图 2-10 所示的直线电机。在这台直线电机的三相绕组中通入三相对称正弦电流后，也会产生气隙磁场。当不考虑由于铁心两端开断而引起纵向边端效应时，这个气隙磁场的分布情况与旋转电机的相似，即可看成沿展开的直线方向呈正弦分布。当三相电流随时间变化时，气隙磁场将按 A、B、C 相序沿直线移动。这个原理与旋转电机相似，两者的差异是：这个磁场是平移的，而不是旋转的，因此称为行波磁场。显然，行波磁场的移动速度与旋转磁场在定子内圆表面上的线速度是一样的，即 v_s（m/s），称之为同步速度，且 $v_s=2p\tau n_s/60=2\tau f$。

The rotary motor shown in figure 2-9 is cut radially at the top and the circumference is straightened to become the linear motor shown in Fig. 2-10. When the three-phase symmetrical sinusoidal current is applied to the three-phase windings of the linear motor, the air-gap magnetic field will also be generated. When the longitudinal end effect caused by the breaking of the two ends of the core is not taken into account, the distribution of the air-gap magnetic field is similar to that of a rotary motor, which can be regarded as a sinusoidal distribution along the expanded straight line. When the three-phase current changes with time, the air gap magnetic field will move in a straight line according to the phase sequence of A, B and C. This principle is similar to that of a rotary motor, but the difference is that the magnetic field is translational rather than rotational, so it is called a traveling wave magnetic field. Obviously, the moving speed of the traveling wave magnetic field is the same as the linear speed of the rotating magnetic field on the inner circular surface of the stator, that is, v_s (m/s), which is called synchronous speed, and $v_s=2p\tau n_s/60=2\tau f$.

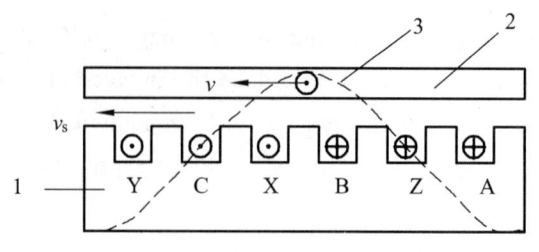

1—初级；2—次级；3—行波磁场。
1—Primary; 2—Secondary; 3—Traveling Wave Magnetic Field.

图 2-10 直线电机的基本工作原理图

Figure 2-10 Basic Working Principle of Linear Motor

再来看行波磁场对次级的作用。假定次级为栅形次级，图 2-10 中仅画出其中的一根导条。次级导条在行波磁场切割下，将产生感应电动势并产生电流。而所有导条的电流和气隙磁场相互作用便产生电磁推力。在这个电磁推力的作用下，如果初级是固定不动的，那么次级就顺着行波磁场运动的方向做直线运动。若次级移动的速度用 v 表示，转差率用 s 表示，则有

$$s = \frac{v_s - v}{v_s}$$

$$v_s - v = sv_s$$

$$v = (1-s)\,v_s$$

Let's look at the effect of the traveling magnetic field on the secondary. The secondary is assumed to be a grid-shaped secondary, only one of which is shown in Figure 2-10. When the secondary conducting bar is cut by the traveling wave magnetic field, the induced electromotive force will be generated and the current will be generated. The interaction between the current of all the conducting bars and the air gap magnetic field produces electromagnetic thrust. Under the action of this electromagnetic thrust, if the primary is fixed, the secondary will move in a straight line along the direction of the traveling wave magnetic field. If the speed of the secondary movement is represented by v and the slip is represented by s, then

$$s = \frac{v_s - v}{v_s}$$

$$v_s - v = sv_s$$

$$v = (1-s)\,v_s$$

在电动机运动状态下，s 在 0 与 1 之间。上述就是直线电机的基本工作原理。

In motor motion, s is between 0 and 1. The above is the basic working principle of linear motor.

应该指出，直线电机的次级大多数采用整块金属板或复合金属板，因此并不存在明显的导条。但在分析时，不妨把整块看成是无限多的导条并列安置，这样仍可以应

用上述原理进行讨论。在图 2-11 中，分别画出了假想导条中的感应电流及金属板内电流的分布，图中 l_δ 为初级铁心的叠片厚度，c 为次级在 l_δ 长度方向伸出初级铁心的宽度，它用来作为次级感应电流的断部通路，c 的大小将影响次级的电阻。

It should be noted that the secondary of the linear motor is mostly made of a single metal plate or a composite metal plate, so there is no obvious conducting bar. However, in the analysis, it is advisable to regard the whole block as an infinite number of conducting bars arranged in parallel, so that the above principle can still be applied for discussion. In Fig. 2-11, the induced current in the imaginary conductor bar and the current distribution in the metal plate are shown respectively. In the figure, l_δ is the lamination thickness of the primary core, and c is the width of the secondary extending out of the primary core in the length direction of l_δ, which is used as the interrupted path of the secondary induced current. The size of c will affect the resistance of the secondary.

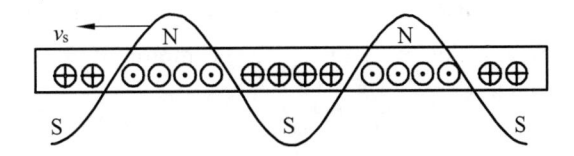

（a）假想导条中的感应电流

(a) Induced Current in an Imaginary Conducting Bar

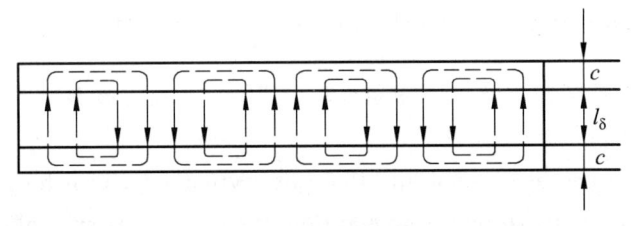

（b）金属板内电流分布

(b) Current Distribution in Metal Plate

图 2-11 次级导体板中的电流

Figure 2-11 Current in Secondary Conductor Plate

我们知道，旋转电机通过对换任意两相的电源线，可以实现反向旋转。这是因为三相绕组的相序相反了，旋转磁场的转向也随之反了。同样，直线电机对换任意两相的电源线后，运动方向也会反过来，根据这一原理，可使直线电机做往复直线运动。

As we know, a rotary motor can rotate in the opposite direction by interchanging the power lines of any two phases. This is because the phase sequence of the three-phase windings is reversed, and the direction of rotation of the rotating magnetic field is also reversed. Similarly, after the linear motor exchanges the power lines of any two phases, the direction of motion will be reversed. According to this principle, the linear motor can do reciprocating linear motion.

第三节 直线电机的分类

Section 2.3　Classification of Linear Motor

直线电机的分类在不同的场合下有不同的分类形式。例如，在考虑外形结构时，往往以结构形式进行分类；当考虑其功能用途时，则又以其功能用途进行分类；而在分析或阐述电机的性能或机理时，则是以其工作原理进行分类。

The classification of linear motor has different forms in different occasions. when considering the shape structure, it is often classified in the form of structure; When considering its functional use, it is classified by its functional use; When analyzing or describing the performance or mechanism of the motor, it is classified according to its working principle.

一、按结构形式分

2.3.1　Classification According to Structural Form

直线电机按其结构形式可分为扁平形、圆筒形（或管形）、圆盘形和圆弧形四种。此外，还有一些特殊结构。

Linear motor can be divided into flat type, cylinder type (or tube type), disc type and arc type according to its structure. In addition, there are some special structures.

所谓扁平形直线电机，顾名思义，即为一种扁平的矩形结构的直线电机，它有单边型和双边型之分。每种形式下又分别有短初级长次级或长初级短次级。

The so-called flat linear motor, as its name implies, is a flat rectangular linear motor, which can be divided into single-sided type and double-sided type. Under each form, there are short primary and long secondary or long primary and short secondary respectively.

所谓圆筒形直线电机，即为一种外形如旋转电机的圆柱形的直线电机。这种直线电机一般均为短初级长次级形式，在需要的场合，还将这种电机做成既有旋转运动又有直线运动的旋转直线电机，旋转直线的运动体既可以是初级，也可以是次级。

The so-called cylindrical linear motor is a cylindrical linear motor with a shape similar to that of a rotary motor. The linear motor is generally in the form of a short primary and a long secondary, and if necessary, the motor is made into a rotary linear motor with both rotary motion and linear motion, and the rotary linear motion body can be either a primary or a secondary.

所谓圆盘形直线电机，即该电机的次级是一个圆盘，不同形式的初级驱动圆盘次级做圆周运动。其初级可以是单边型，也可以是双边型。直线圆盘电机虽然也做旋转运动，但它与普通旋转电机相比，具有如下一些优点：

The so-called disk-type linear motor means that the secondary of the motor is a disk, and the primary of different forms drives the secondary of the disk to do circular motion. Its primary type can be unilateral or bilateral. Although the linear disk motor also rotates, it has the following advantages compared with the ordinary rotary motor:

（1）力矩与旋转速度可以通过多台初级组合的方式或通过初级在圆盘上的径向位置来调节。

（1）The torque and rotational speed can be adjusted by the combination of multiple primaries or by the radial position of the primaries on the disk.

（2）无须通过齿轮减速箱就能得到较低的转速，因而电机噪声和振动很小。

（2）The lower speed can be obtained without the gear reduction box, so the noise and vibration of the motor are very small.

所谓圆弧形电机，它的运动形式是旋转运动，且与普通旋转电机非常接近，然而它与旋转电机相比也是具有如圆盘形直线电机的优点。圆弧形与圆盘形的主要区别，在于次级的形式和初级对次级的驱动点有所不同。

The motion form of the arc type motor is rotary motion, which is very close to that of a common rotary motor. However, compared with the rotary motor, the arc type motor also has the advantages of a disk type linear motor. The main difference between the arc type and the disc type lies in the form of the secondary and the driving point of the primary to the secondary.

按以上结构形式分类的直线电机的相互关系可用图 2-12 所示的形式表示。

The relationship between the linear motors classified according to the above structural forms can be represented in the form shown in Fig. 2-12.

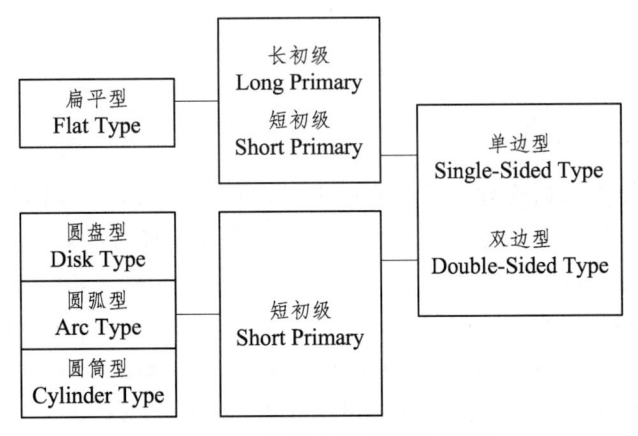

图 2-12　直线电机的结构类型

Figure 2-12　Structure Type of Linear Motor

二、按功能用途分类

2.3.2　Classification According to Function

直线电机，特别是直线感应电动机，按其功能用途可分为力电机、功电机和能电机。

Linear motors, especially linear induction motors, can be divided into force motors, power motors and energy motors according to their functions and uses.

（一）力电机

2.3.2.1　Force Motor

力电机是指单位输入功率所能产生的推力，或单位体积所能产生的推力，主要用于在静止物体上或低速的设备上施加一定的推力的直线电机。它以短时运行、低速运行为主，如阀门的开闭、门窗的移动、机械手的操作、推车等。这种电机效率较低，甚至为零（如对静止物体上施加推力时，效率为零），因此，对这类电机不能用效率这个指标去衡量它，而是用推力与功率的比来衡量，即在一定的电磁推力下，其输入的功率越小，则说明其性能越好。

Force motor refers to the thrust that can be generated by unit input power, or the thrust that can be generated by unit volume, which is mainly used to exert a certain thrust on static objects or low-speed equipment. It mainly runs for a short time and at a low speed, such as the opening and closing of valves, the movement of doors and windows, the operation of manipulators, carts, etc. The efficiency of this kind of motor is low, even zero (for example, the efficiency is zero when the thrust is exerted on a static object). Therefore, this kind of motor can not be measured by the index of efficiency, but by the ratio of thrust to power, that is, under a certain electromagnetic thrust, the smaller the input power is, the better its performance is.

（二）功电机

2.3.2.2　Power Motor

功电机主要作为长期连续运行的直线电机，它的性能衡量指标与旋转电机基本一样，即可用效率、功率因数等指标来衡量其电机性能的优劣，如高速磁浮列车的直线电机、各种高速运行的输送线等。

The power motor is mainly used as a linear motor running continuously for a long time, and its performance measurement index is basically the same as that of the rotary motor, that is, the efficiency, power factor and other indexes can be used to measure the performance of the motor, such as the linear motor of the high-speed maglev train, various high-speed transmission lines, etc.

（三）能电机

2.3.2.3　Energy Motor

能电机是指运动构件在短时间内所能产生的极高能量的驱动电机，它主要是在短时间、短距离内提供巨大的直线运动能，如导弹和鱼雷的发射、飞机的起飞以及冲击、碰撞等试验机的驱动等。这类直线电机的主要性能指标是能效率（能效率=输出的功能/电源所提供的电能）。

Energy motor refers to the driving motor with extremely high energy that can be generated by moving components in a short time. It mainly provides huge linear motion energy in a short time and short distance, such as the launching of missiles and torpedoes, the take-off of aircraft, and the driving of impact and collision test machines. The main performance index of this kind of linear motor is energy efficiency (energy efficiency = output function/electric energy provided by power supply).

三、按工作原理分类

2.3.3　Classification According to Working Principle

从原理上讲，每种旋转电机都有与之相对应的直线电机，然而从使用角度来看，直线电机得到了更广泛的应用。直线电机按其工作原理可分为两个大的方面，即直线电动机和直线驱动器。直线电动机包括交流直线感应电动机（Linear Induction Motors, LIM）、交流直线同步电动机（Linear Synchronous Motors, LSM）、直线直流电动机（Linear DC Motors, LDM）、直线步进（脉冲）电动机［Linear Stepper（Pulse）Motors, LPM］和混合式直线电动机（Linear Hybrid Motors, LHM）等。直线驱动器包括直线振荡电动机（Linear Oscillating Motors, LOM）、直线电磁螺线管电动机（Linear Electric Solenoi, LES）、直线电磁泵（Linear Electromagnetic Pump, LEP）、直线超声波电动机（Linear Ultrasonic Motors, LUM）等。以上这些直线电机又可分成许多不同的种类。图 2-13 表示了直线电机的分类。

In principle, each type of rotary motor has a corresponding linear motor, but from the point of view of use, the linear motor has been more widely used. According to its working principle, linear motor can be divided into two major aspects, namely, linear motor and linear driver. Linear motors include AC linear induction motors (LIM)、AC linear synchronous motors (LSM)、 linear DC motors (LDM)、Linear Stepper (Pulse) Motors (LPM) and Linear Hybrid Motors (LHM). The linear actuator includes linear oscillation motor (LOM)、linear electromagnetic solenoid motor (LES)、linear electromagnetic pump (LEP)、linear ultrasonic motors (LUM), etc. These linear motors can be divided into many different types. Fig. 2-13 shows the classification of linear motors.

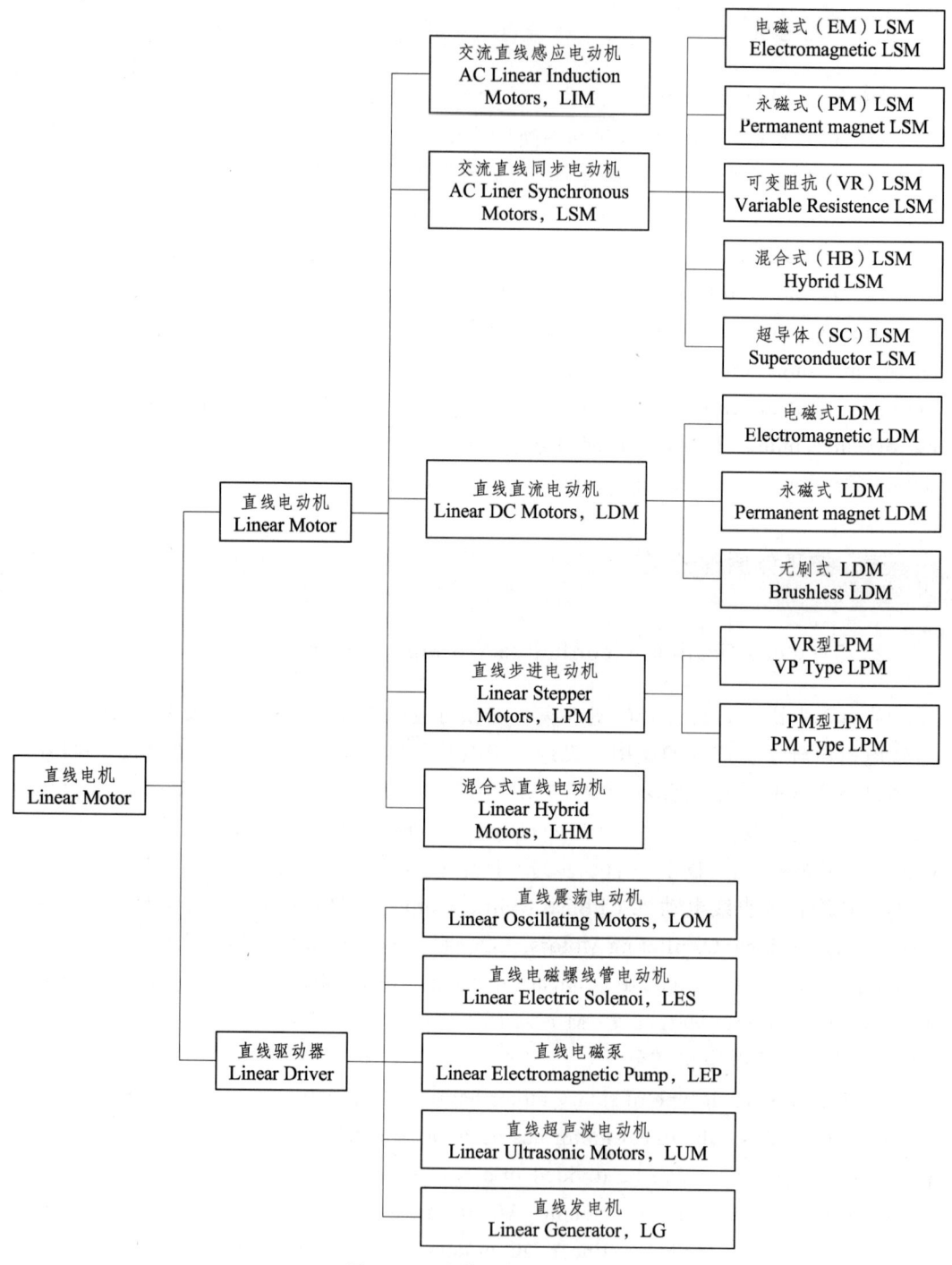

```
直线电机              ┌── 交流直线感应电动机                    ┌── 电磁式（EM）LSM
Linear Motor         │   AC Linear Induction Motors, LIM      │   Electromagnetic LSM
                     │                                         │
                     │                                         ├── 永磁式（PM）LSM
                     │                                         │   Permanent magnet LSM
                     │── 交流直线同步电动机                    │
                     │   AC Liner Synchronous Motors, LSM ────┼── 可变阻抗（VR）LSM
                     │                                         │   Variable Resistance LSM
  直线电动机         │                                         │
  Linear Motor ──────┤                                         ├── 混合式（HB）LSM
                     │                                         │   Hybrid LSM
                     │                                         │
                     │                                         └── 超导体（SC）LSM
                     │                                             Superconductor LSM
                     │                                         ┌── 电磁式 LDM
                     │                                         │   Electromagnetic LDM
                     │── 直线直流电动机                        │
                     │   Linear DC Motors, LDM ────────────────┼── 永磁式 LDM
                     │                                         │   Permanent magnet LDM
                     │                                         │
                     │                                         └── 无刷式 LDM
                     │                                             Brushless LDM
                     │                                         ┌── VR型 LPM
                     │── 直线步进电动机                        │   VP Type LPM
                     │   Linear Stepper Motors, LPM ───────────┤
                     │                                         └── PM型 LPM
                     │                                             PM Type LPM
                     │
                     └── 混合式直线电动机
                         Linear Hybrid Motors, LHM

                         ┌── 直线震荡电动机
                         │   Linear Oscillating Motors, LOM
                         │
                         ├── 直线电磁螺线管电动机
                         │   Linear Electric Solenoi, LES
  直线驱动器          │
  Linear Driver ──────┼── 直线电磁泵
                         │   Linear Electromagnetic Pump, LEP
                         │
                         ├── 直线超声波电动机
                         │   Linear Ultrasonic Motors, LUM
                         │
                         └── 直线发电机
                             Linear Generator, LG
```

图 2-13 直线电机的分类

Figure 2-13 Classification of Linear Motor

第四节　有关直线电机的标准

Section 2.4　Standards for Linear Motors

我国在直线电机方面有一个部颁的 JB/T 7823—2007《三相扁平型直线异步电动机》标准，有些企业制定了一些企业标准。例如，浙江大学直线电机与电器研究所与有关企业制定的《直线电机驱动的窗帘机》标准、《直线电机驱动的冲压机》标准等。编者曾参加过《三相扁平型直线异步电动机》标准的审定，现将该标准的主要内容做简单介绍。

There is a a ministerial standard JB/T 7823—2007 "Three-phase Flat Linear Asynchronous Motor" in China, and some enterprises have formulated some enterprise standards. For example, "The Standard of Curtain Machine Driven by Linear Motor" and "The Standard of Punching Machine Driven by Linear Motor" formulated by the Institute of Linear Motor and Electrical Appliances of Zhejiang University and relevant enterprises. The editor has participated in the examination and approval of "The Standard of Three-phase Flat Linear Asynchronous Motor", and now the main contents of the standard are briefly introduced.

《三相扁平型直线异步电动机》标准规定了单边扁平形结构的低速三相直线异步电动机的形式、基本参数、技术要求、试验方法、检测标准及标志、包装和保用期要求。

"The standard of Three-phase Flat Linear Asynchronous Motor" specifies the form, basic parameters, technical requirements, test methods, inspection standards, marking, packaging and warranty requirements of low-speed three-phase linear asynchronous motors with single-sided flat structure.

一、直线电机的基本形式及基本参数

2.4.1　Basic Form and Basic Parameters of Linear Motor

（一）基本形式

2.4.1.1　Basic Form

该标准将直线电机的名称代号用"XY"表示，X 表示直线形，Y 表示异步。

In this standard, the name code of linear motor is represented by "XY", X represents linear type and Y represents asynchronous type.

直线电机的型号由名称代号、规格代号及次级结构代号组成，如下所示：

The model of linear motor consists of name code, specification code and secondary structure code, as shown below:

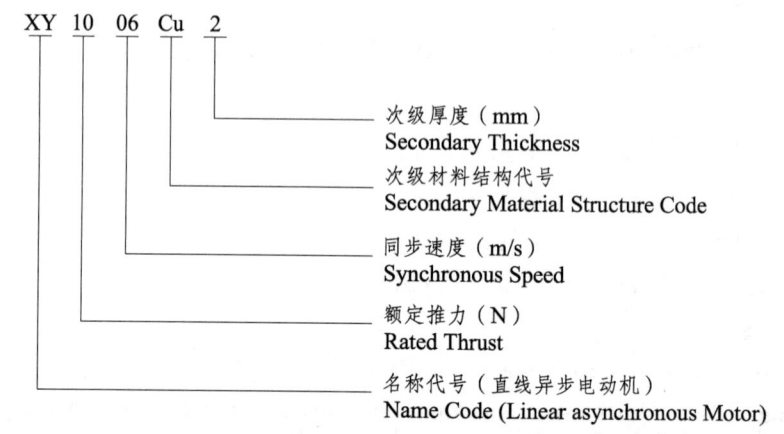

```
XY 10 06 Cu 2
            │
            └── 次级厚度（mm）
                Secondary Thickness
         └───── 次级材料结构代号
                Secondary Material Structure Code
      └──────── 同步速度（m/s）
                Synchronous Speed
   └─────────── 额定推力（N）
                Rated Thrust
└────────────── 名称代号（直线异步电动机）
                Name Code (Linear asynchronous Motor)
```

其中，次级材料结构有钢次级和复合次级，Fe 表示钢次级，复合次级中 Cu 表示铜复合次级，Al 表示铝复合次级。

Among them, the secondary material structure comprises a steel secondary and a composite secondary, Fe represents the steel secondary, Cu in the composite secondary represents the copper composite secondary, and Al represents the aluminum composite secondary.

（二）基本参数

2.4.1.2　Basic Parameters

该标准确定的基本参数主要有以下几点：

The basic parameters determined by this standard are mainly as follows:

（1）额定频率为 50 Hz，额定电压为 380 V，初级绕组为 Y 连接。

(1) The rated frequency is 50 Hz, the rated voltage is 380 V, and the primary winding is Y-connected.

（2）直线电机额定推力（转差率为 1 时）分别为 10，20，30，50，100，200，500，750，1 000，1 500，2 500，3 000，4 000，5 000，6 000，8 000 N。

(2) The rated thrust of linear motor (when the slip is 1) is 10, 20, 30, 50, 100, 200, 500, 750, 1 000, 1 500, 2 500, 3 000, 4 000, 5 000, 6 000, 8 000 N respectively.

（3）直线电机额定同步速度为 3，4.5，6，9，12 m/s。

(3) Rated synchronous speed of linear motor is 3, 4.5, 6, 9, 12 m/s.

（4）直线电机的工作制为断续周期工作，其负载持续率分别为 15%，25%，40%，60%。

（4）The working system of the linear motor is intermittent periodic work, and its duty cycle is 15%, 25%, 40% and 60% respectively.

（5）直线电机的额定气隙分别为 2，3，4 mm。

（5）The rated air gap of linear motor is 2, 3 and 4 mm respectively.

另外，该标准对直线电机的平直度也做了规定，但对安装尺寸和外形尺寸则未做具体要求，可由厂家或用户自行确定。

In addition, the standard also specifies the straightness of the linear motor, but there is no specific requirement for the installation size and shape size, which can be determined by the manufacturer or user.

二、技术要求

2.4.2　Technical Requirements

该标准对直线电机提出了如下一些技术要求：

This standard puts forward the following technical requirements for linear motors:

（1）环境空气的温度和湿度要求；

（1）Ambient air temperature and humidity requirements;

（2）电源电压和频率与额定值的偏差规定；

（2）Deviation provisions of power supply voltage and frequency from rated value;

（3）直线电机推力的容许误差；

（3）Allowable error of linear motor thrust;

（4）直线电机在不同级次结构下的功率因数保证值；

（4）Power factor guarantee value of linear motor under different stage structures;

（5）直线电机的绝缘等级及应能承受的耐压值；

（5）Insulation grade and withstand voltage of linear motor;

（6）直线电机三相电流的允许不平衡值；

（6）Allowable unbalance value of three-phase current of linear motor;

（7）直线电机的表面要求及接线盒要求等。

（7）Surface requirements and junction box requirements of linear motor.

三、试验方法

2.4.3　Test Method

在该标准中，根据国家有关标准并结合直线电机的特点提出和规定了直线电机在推力、电压特性、气隙特性以及温升方面的试验方法。

In this standard, according to the relevant national standards and the characteristics of linear motors, the test methods of thrust, voltage characteristics, air gap characteristics and temperature rise of linear motors are proposed and specified.

四、检验规范

2.4.4 Inspection Specification

在该标准中，对直线电机的出厂试验和型式试验的内容和要求，做出了明确和较详细的规定。

In this standard, the contents and requirements of the factory test and type test of linear motors are clearly and detailedly specified.

五、标志、包装和保用期

2.4.5 Marking, Packaging and Warranty Period

该标准对直线电机出厂的标志、包装均提出了要求，对出厂的铭牌规定了如下必须具备的内容：

The standard puts forward requirements for the marking and packaging of the linear motor when leaving the factory, and specifies the following necessary contents for the nameplate when leaving the factory:

（1）制造厂名；
（1）Name of the manufacturer;
（2）直线电机名称和型号；
（2）Name and model of linear motor;
（3）额定推力、同步速度；
（3）Rated thrust and synchronous speed;
（4）额定电压、堵转电流、额定频率；
（4）Rated voltage, locked-rotor current and rated frequency;
（5）绝缘等级；
（5）Insulation grade;
（6）额定气隙；
（6）Rated air gap;
（7）质量；
（7）Quality;
（8）制造年月和编号；

（8）Date of manufacture and serial number;

（9）标准编号。

（9）Standard No.

复习思考题

Questions for Revision

1. 何为单边型直线电机和双边型直线电机？

1. What are single-sided linear motor and double-sided linear motor?

2. 简要总结直线电机的基本结构。

2. Briefly summarize the basic structure of linear motor.

3. 简要总结直线电机的工作原理。

3. Briefly summarize the working principle of linear motor.

4. 总结直线电机按结构形式不同的分类方法。

4. Summarize the classification methods of linear motors according to different structural forms.

5. 总结直线电机按功能用途不同的分类方法。

5. Summarize the classification methods of linear motors according to different functional uses.

6. 总结直线电机按工作原理不同的分类方法。

6. Summarize the different classification methods of linear motors according to their working principles.

7. 简要叙述直线电机的基本形式。

7. Briefly describe the basic form of linear motor.

8. 简要叙述直线电机型号 XY 10 06 Cu 2 的含义。

8. Briefly describe the meaning of linear motor model XY 10 06 Cu 2.

9. 简要叙述直线电机的基本参数。

9. Briefly describe the basic parameters of linear motor.

第三章 日本超导超高速磁浮铁路技术

Chapter 3 Superconducting Ultra-high-speed Maglev Railway Technology in Japan

从本章开始，将逐项介绍目前比较成熟的几种磁浮铁路技术。德国常导超高速磁浮铁路（TR）技术将在第四章进行介绍，日本的高速地面运输系统（HSST）技术（实际为中低速磁浮铁路技术）将在第六章进行介绍，我国磁浮铁路的研究、发展及有关技术将在第五、七章进行介绍。

From the beginning of this chapter, we will introduce several mature maglev railway technologies one by one. The TR technology of Germany will be introduced in the fourth chapter, the HSST technology of Japan (actually, it is medium and low speed maglev railway technology) will be introduced in the sixth chapter, and the research, development and related technology of maglev railway in China will be described in the fifth and seventh chapters.

本章主要介绍日本超导超高速磁浮铁路（ML）技术。本章先介绍日本磁浮铁路技术的基本原理和发展过程，之后主要介绍日本山梨磁浮铁路试验线的关键技术、相应设备及在山梨试验线所进行的主要试验和试验结果评价。

This chapter mainly introduces the superconductive ultra-high speed maglev railway (ML) technology in Japan. This chapter first introduces the basic principle and development process of maglev railway technology in Japan, and then mainly introduces the key technology and corresponding equipment of the Yamanashi maglev railway test line in Japan, as well as the main tests and test results evaluation conducted on the Yamanashi test line.

第一节 日本磁浮铁路技术的发展过程

Section 3.1 Development Process of Maglev Railway Technology in Japan

日本对磁浮铁路的研究开始于1962年。日本磁浮铁路技术发展经过4个发展阶段。

The study of maglev railway in Japan began in 1962. The development of maglev railway technology in Japan has gone through four stages.

一、起步阶段

3.1.1　Initial Stage

日本在世界上第一条高速铁路——东海道新干线开通的前两年（1962年）就开始进行了磁浮铁路的开发研究。当时经过广泛深入的研究，决定采用超导磁斥式悬浮系统。之后经过十年的努力，于1972年在庆祝日本第一条铁路建成100周年之际，第一辆由日本国铁开发研制的电动磁浮原理车ML100向公众展示。该车在480 m的试验线上实现了60 km/h的悬浮速度。接着日本又研制和试验了LSM200、ML100A试验车。

Japan began developing maglev railway in 1962, two years before the opening of the Tokaido Shinken Line, the world's first high-speed railway. At that time, after extensive and in-depth research, it was decided to adopt the superconducting magnetic repulsion suspension system. After ten years of efforts, in 1972, on the occasion of celebrating the 100th anniversary of the construction of Japan's first railway, the first electric maglev train ML100 developed by Japan National Railway was presented to the public. The vehicle achieved a suspension speed of 60 km/h on a test line of 480 m. Then Japan developed and tested the LSM200, ML100A test vechile.

二、宫崎试验线（倒"T"形导轨、地面悬浮方式）

3.1.2　Miyazaki Test Line (Inverted "T" Guide Rail, Ground Suspension Mode)

1975年，日本开始在九州半岛上修建宫崎试验线。1977—1999年，全长7 km的试验线分段投入使用。试验线全部采用高架结构，线路横断面采用"⊥"形导轨形式，最小曲线半径10 000 m，大部分为平直地段。

In 1975, Japan began to build the Miyazaki Test Line on the Kyushu Peninsula. From 1977 to 1999, the test line with a total length of 7 km was put into use in sections. All test lines are of elevated structure, and the cross section of the line is in the form of "⊥" shaped guide rail, with a minimum curve radius of 10,000 m, and most of them are flat and straight sections.

1977年7月，日本开始对ML500试验车进行试验。1979年5月还专门在ML500车上进行车载液体氦制冷机试验。上述试验工作进行得很顺利，于1979年12月实现517 km/h的当时世界列车运行最高速度。这证明长定子直线同步电机驱动的磁浮系统可用于高速、超高速有轨交通。

In July 1977, Japan began testing the ML500 test vehicle. In May 1979, the on-board liquid helium refrigerator test was specially carried out on the ML500 vehicle. The above test work was carried out smoothly, and the highest speed of 517 km/h in the world at that time was achieved in December 1979. This proves that the maglev system driven by long-stator linear synchronous motor can be used in high-speed and ultra-high-speed rail transit.

三、"U"形导轨、地面悬浮方式

3.1.3　U-shaped Guide Rail and Ground Suspension Mode

日本在已取得研究成果的基础上，为使磁浮铁路向更实用化的阶段迈进，从 1980 年起，将线路的基本形状由原先的"⊥"形断面改进成"U"形断面，但仍为地面悬浮方式。

On the basis of the research results already obtained, in order to make the maglev railway move towards a more practical stage, Japan has improved the basic shape of the line from the original "⊥" shaped section to the "U" shaped section since 1980, but it is still a ground suspension mode.

1980 年，新开发的箱形试验车 MLU001 开始进行行走试验。1987 年，两辆编组的磁浮列车的载人试验速度达到 400.8 km/h。MLU001 在新建的"U"形线路上进行了 9 年的试验运行，总共进行了 9 000 次试验运行，累计行驶约 40 000 km。

In 1980, the newly developed box test vehicle MLU001 began to carry out walking tests. In 1987, the manned test speed of the a two-car maglev train reached 400.8 km/h. MLU001 was operated on the newly built "U" shaped line for nine years, with a total of 9,000 test runs and a cumulative travel of about 40,000 km.

1987 年，日本新的电动悬浮系统试验车 MLU002 开始在宫崎试验线路上运行。该车长 22 m，重 17 t，可载 44 人，设计车速 420 km/h。1989 年，MLU002 型磁浮车不载人试验速度达到 394 km/h。

In 1987, Japan's new electric suspension system test vehicle, MLU002, began operating on the Miyazaki test line. The vehicle is 22 m long, weighs 17 t, can carry 44 people, and has a design speed of 420 km/h. In 1989, the MLU002 maglev vehicle reached a test speed of 394 km/h without people.

1989 年，MLU002 磁浮车在运行试验中发生火灾事故被烧毁。日本随后又制造了 MLU002N 型磁浮车，1993 年 1 月开始在宫崎试验线进行试验，并于 1994 年 2 月达到 431 km/h 的试验速度，载人运行最高速度达到 411 km/h。1996 年 10 月，宫崎试验线关闭。

In 1989, the MLU002 maglev vehicle was burned down in a fire accident during the operation test. The MLU002N maglev vehicle was subsequently manufactured in Japan, which was tested on the Miyazaki test line in January 1993 and reached a test speed of 431 km/h in February 1994, with a maximum manned speed of 411 km/h. In October 1996, the Miyazaki Test Line was closed.

四、山梨试验线（"U"形导轨、侧壁悬浮方式）

3.1.4　Yamanashi Test Line ("U" Guide Rail, Side Wall Suspension Mode)

由于宫崎试验线没有坡道和隧道，曲线地段也不多，不能满足接近应用条件的试验需要，因此日本运输省决定建设山梨磁浮试验线。山梨试验线目前包括 18.4 km 长的试验线路、变电站、实验中心和两列试验车辆。

Because the Miyazaki test line has no ramps and tunnels, and there are not many curve sections, it can not meet the test needs close to the application conditions, so the Ministry of Transport of Japan decided to build the Yamanashi Maglev Test Line. The Yamanashi Test Line currently consists of an 18.4km long test line, substation, test center and two test trains.

1990 年 11 月，日本开始修建山梨试验线；1991 年 6 月开始进行侧壁悬浮方式的走行试验；1995 年开发出山梨试验线车辆 MLX01；1996 年超导磁浮山梨试验中心建成；1997 年 4 月 3 日进行 3 辆 MLX01 编组的试验；1997 年 12 月 24 日不载人试验速度达 500 km/h，创下了新的世界纪录；1999 年 4 月，5 辆编组的 MLX-01 型车的载人试验速度达 552 km/h，这是当时最高的试验速度；1999 年 12 月进行磁浮双向列车试验，创造了会车相对速度超过 1 003 km/h 的最高世界纪录，当时两车运行速度分别为 546 km/h 和 457 km/h。

In November 1990, Japan began to build the Yamanashi test line; in June 1991, it began to carry out the running test of the side wall suspension mode; in 1995, it developed the Yamanashi test line vehicle MLX01; in 1996, the superconducting maglev Yamanashi Test Center was built; on April 3, 1997, it carried out the marshalling test of three MLX01 vehicles; In December 24, 1997, the unmanned test speed reached 500 km/h, setting a new world record, and in April 1999, the manned test speed of the five-car MLX-01 reached 552 km/h, which was the highest test speed at that time; In December 1999, the two-way maglev train was tested, and the highest world record of meeting relative speed exceeding 1,003 km/h was set. At that time, the running speeds of the two trains were 546 km/h and 457 km/h, respectively.

2002 年 6 月，新型试验车辆驶入车辆基地。新型车辆的最大特点是车头流线部分的长高比例显著增大，大大改善了列车头部的空气动力性能。

In June 2002, the new test vehicle entered the vehicle base. The biggest feature of the new vehicle is that the length and height ratio of the front streamline part is significantly increased, which greatly improves the aerodynamic performance of the train head.

五、试验研究的特点

3.1.5　Characteristics of the Experimental Study

日本磁浮铁路在试验研究方面有以下几个特点:

The Japanese maglev railway has the following characteristics in terms of experimental research:

（一）坚持不懈

3.1.5.1　Be Persistent

日本的高速铁路 60 年来在世界范围内一直处于领先水平。其原因是在于持续不断地进行研究和开发，60 年来没有出现过大起大落的现象。

Japan's high-speed railway has been in the leading position in the world for 60 years. The reason for this is that research and development have been carried out continuously, and there have been no major ups and downs in the past 60 years.

（二）勇于创新

3.1.5.2　Be Bold in Innovation

日本的高速铁路是在不断创新中发展起来的，日本的磁浮铁路技术也是在不断创新中发展起来的。在一种形式的导轨车辆系统达到理想的试验结果之前，就已开始新的更好形式的导轨车辆系统的研究。由"⊥"形导轨改成"U"形导轨，由底面悬浮方式改为侧壁悬浮方式，每次创新都使得技术更为先进、实用。

Japan's high-speed railway is developed in continuous innovation, and Japan's maglev railway technology is also developed in continuous innovation. The development of a new and better form of guideway vehicle system begins before one form of guideway vehicle system achieves the desired test results. The "⊥" shaped guide rail is changed into a "U" shaped guide rail, and the bottom suspension mode is changed into a side wall suspension mode, and each innovation makes the technology more advanced and practical.

（三）重视试验

3.1.5.3　Focus on Experimentation

在进行新型导轨、车辆系统的试验研究前，一般先修建相应的试验线，在试验线上验证、发现问题，再进行改进。由室内试验到宫崎试验线再到山梨试验线，在不同的试验场地验证了磁浮铁路相应的理论和技术，同时又发现了许多新问题，这些新问题再在下一次试验或新的试验线上进行试验并研究解决。

Before the test and research of the new guideway and vehicle system, the corresponding test line is generally built first, and then the problems are verified and found on the test line, and then the improvement is made. From the indoor test to the Miyazaki test line and then to the Yamanashi test line, the corresponding theory and technology of maglev railway have been verified in different test sites, and many new problems have been found, which will be tested and solved in the next test or new test line.

（四）确保安全

3.1.5.4　Ensure Safety

新型系统一般先进行无载人试验，再进行载人试验。这就保证了试验人员的人身安全，同时可以使新技术达到实用化程度。

The new system generally carries out unmanned test first, and then carries out manned test. This ensures the personal safety of the test personnel, and at the same time, it can make the new technology practical.

这些特点对于我国高速铁路的研究和建设具有直接的参考作用。

These characteristics have a direct reference for the research and construction of high-speed railway in China.

第二节　山梨试验线概况

Section 3.2　Overview of Yamanashi Test Line

磁浮铁路在 1987 年是个热门话题。山梨县预见到位于甲府附近的新试验线如果成功，将来会作为中央新干线的一部分使用，因此新设立了"磁浮铁路推进局"，开展试验线的申请活动。1991 年甚至为还在设想阶段的"甲府磁浮列车站"的战前广场以及相关道路、基础设施的建设设立了 1 000 亿日元（1 日元约 0.06 元人民币）的基金。

Maglev was a hot topic in 1987. Yamanashi Prefecture foresaw that the new test line near Kofu, if successful, would be used as part of the Central Shinkansen in the future, so a new "Maglev Railway Propulsion Bureau" was set up to carry out the application activities for the test line. In 1991, a fund of 100 billion yen (1 yen about 0.06 yuan) was even set up for the construction of the pre-war square and related roads and infrastructure of the "Kofu Maglev Train Station"which was still in the conceptual stage.

现在的"境川村—八千代町—御坂町—大月市—都留市—秋山村"路线在被选择作为试验线路之前，候选路线还有"大月—河口湖—甲府"南部路线、"大月—胜沼—甲府"南部路线、"大月—胜沼—甲府"北部路线等。最后，因为目前的线路满足运输省的选择标准故被选用。

Before the current route of "Sakaigawa Village-Yachiyo Town-Misaka Town-Otsuki City-Tsuru City-Akiyama Village" was selected as a test route, the candidate routes included the southern route of "Otsuki-Kawaguchiko-Kofu", the southern route of "Otsuki-Katsunuma-Kofu" and the northern route of "Otsuki-Katsunuma-Kofu". Finally, the current route was selected because it met the selection criteria of the Ministry of Transport.

一、新试验线拟建总长 42.8 km

3.2.1　The Proposed Total Length of the New Test Line is 42.8 km

山梨试验线位于日本首都东京西偏南方向的山梨县。试验线总长 42.8 km，其中中间部分为 12.8 km 的复线区间。复线区间由地面段和隧道段构成，进行列车会车、加速、制动等试验。复线区间的两端设有高速道岔、两个变电站及车站，此外还设有车辆基地用的低速道岔。试验线的 80% 为隧道（共 13 座），其中有 40‰的大坡度段、半径为 8 000 m 的全线最小半径的曲线段以及高架桥段等。隧道断面与现在的新干线相比约大 30%，有的高速路段竟达 7.7 m，总体上都是大断面。这是为了缓解车辆超高速通过隧道时产生的空气动力效应。

The Yamanashi Test Line is located in Yamanashi Prefecture, southwest of Tokyo, the capital of Japan. The total length of the test line is 42.8 km, of which the middle part is a 12.8 km double-track section. The double-track section is composed of the ground section and the tunnel section, and the train meeting, acceleration, braking and other tests are carried out. There are high-speed turnouts, two substations and stations at both ends of the double-track section, and there are also low-speed turnouts for the vehicle base. 80% of the test line consists of tunnels (13 in total), of which 40‰ are steep sections, Curve section with the minimum radius of the whole line with a radius of 8,000 m and viaduct sections. Compared with the current Shinkansen, the tunnel section is about 30% larger, and some highway sections are up to 7.7 m, which are generally large sections. This is to mitigate the aerodynamic effects of vehicles passing through the tunnel at a very high speed.

山梨试验线的导轨为"U"字形，导轨的功能与通常的铁路轨道一样。导轨支承车辆的质量（支承功能），防止车辆横向滑动及水平方向摆动（导向功能），提供列车前进及制动时的纵向力（驱动功能）。在"U"字形导轨的垂直部分（两侧）设置有驱动绕组、悬浮绕组及导向绕组，这些绕组与装在车辆连接处的超导磁铁之间产生引力和斥力，因此列车可以沿着导轨悬浮行驶。

The guideway of the Yamanashi Test Line is in the shape of a "U", and the function of the guideway is the same as that of a normal railway track. The guideway supports the mass of the vehicle (supporting function), prevents the vehicle from sliding in the lateral direction and swinging in the horizontal direction (guiding function), and provides the longitudinal force when the train moves forward and brakes (driving function). The vertical parts (both sides) of the U-shaped guide rail are provided with a driving winding, a suspension winding and a guide winding, and attractive force and repulsive force are generated between the windings and a superconducting magnet arranged at the joint of the train, so that the train can run along the guide rail in a suspension manner.

导轨除"U"字形之外，还有车体跨在轨道之上的跨座形、双"L"形及箱体导轨。JR 滨松町—羽田机场间的单轨铁路就是跨座形。全长 7 km 的宫崎试验线开始选用了跨座形，但由于车辆的横断面面积小，乘客座位减少，不适合大量运输的要求。因此，在 1979 年 11 月之后的运行试验中，改为座位空间大的"U"字形导轨。与宫崎试验线（单线）约 3 万个导轨绕组相比，全长 42.8 km 的山梨试验线共使用了 19 万个驱动、悬浮及导向绕组，平均每千米 4 400 个。那么 500 km 长的中央新干线权限按复线计算，需要设置 440 万个地上绕组。因为绕组可实现批量生产，今后不但造价会降低，而且因不需要架线铺轨，因此超导磁浮铁路的地上设备费用与通常的铁路不会有很大区别。

In addition to the "U" shaped guide rails, there are also straddle shaped, double "L" shaped and box shaped guide rails for the car body straddling the rails. The monorail between JR Hamamatsucho and Haneda Airport is straddle-shaped. The 7 km long Miyazaki test line began to use the straddle type, but because of the small cross-sectional area of the vehicle and the reduction of passenger seats, it is not suitable for the requirements of mass transportation. Therefore, in the operation test after November 1979, the "U" shaped guide rail with large seat space was adopted. Compared with the Miyazaki test line (single line) with about 30,000 guideway windings, the Yamanashi test line with a total length of 42.8 km uses 190,000 drive, suspension and guide windings, with an average of 4,400 per kilometer. Then the 500 km long Central Shinkansen is calculated as a double-track line, and 4.4 million overground windings are required. Because the winding can be produced in batches, not only the cost will be reduced in the future, but also the cost of ground equipment of superconducting maglev railway will not be much different from that of ordinary railway because there is no need to lay tracks.

二、18.4 km 的先行区间

3.2.2　18.4 km Leading Section

1997年秋，山梨试验线 18.4 km 长的先行区间（复线）基本完工，加上第一、第二编组的试验车辆费，共耗资 2 000 亿日元。先行区间以山梨县大月市为起点，隧道穿过 JR 中央线、中央高速公路南侧的山岭地带，到达终点都留市的地面区段。其中隧道区段长 16 km，地面区段长 2.4 km。

In the autumn of 1997, the 18.4 km long advance section (double track) of the Yamanashi test line was basically completed, and the cost of the first and second groups of test vehicles was 200 billion yen. The first section starts from Otsuki City, Yamanashi Prefecture, and the tunnel passes through JR Central Line and the mountains on the south side of the Central Expressway, reaching the ground section of Tsuru City. The tunnel section is 16 km long and the ground section is 2.4 km long.

试验线的线间距为 5.8 m，限制坡度 40‰，最小曲线半径 8 000 m。试验线共有 3 座高架桥（包括桂川桥）及 14 座隧道。之所以隧道很多，是考虑到东京—大阪间的超导磁浮中央新干线计划穿越中部山岭地带及铃鹿山地，而且在东京、大阪、名古屋三大城市圈，预计路线将采用深埋地铁形式，因此，在隧道内最高速度 500 km/h 运行的相关技术开发是重要的研究课题。

The test line has a line spacing of 5.8 m, a limiting gradient of 40‰, and a minimum curve radius of 8,000 m. There are 3 viaducts (including Guichuan Bridge) and 14 tunnels in the test line. The reason why there are many tunnels is that the superconducting maglev Central Shinkansen between Tokyo and Osaka is planned to pass through the central mountains and Suzuka Mountains, and in the three major urban circles of Tokyo, Osaka and Nagoya, it is expected that the route will adopt the form of deep-buried subway. Therefore, the development of related technologies with a maximum speed of 500 km/h in the tunnel is an important research topic.

山梨试验线的实用化以运输大臣批准的山梨试验线计划及技术开发基本计划为指针，属于国家级项目。主要承担者为 JR 东海、JR 综合技术研究所及铁路建设公司。1997年4月，日本开始在此先行区间进行实用化试验，所用的主要建筑物及实验设备有：在都留市的地面区段设立的实验中心、变电站、车辆基地、列车运行道岔装置、试乘时的站台等。

The practical use of the Yamanashi Test Line is guided by the Yamanashi Test Line Plan and the Basic Plan for Technology Development approved by the Minister of Transport, and is a national project. The main undertakers are JR Donghai, JR Comprehensive Technology Research Institute and Railway Construction Company. In April 1997, Japan began to carry out the practical test in this first section. The main buildings and experimental equipment used include the experimental center, substation, vehicle base, turnout device for train operation, and platform for trial ride set up in the ground section of Tsuru City.

三、侧壁悬浮形式

3.2.3 Suspension Form of Side Wall

山梨试验线采用将地上的驱动绕组、悬浮绕组、导向绕组设置在导轨侧壁的侧壁悬浮形式。在宫崎试验线进行基础技术开发时，曾采用将悬浮绕组设置在导轨底部，驱动绕组和导向绕组设置在导轨侧壁的引导反推悬浮形式。当时的技术人员就认为，侧壁悬浮形式更利于超导磁浮列车稳定高效地行驶。因此，山梨试验线采用了侧壁悬浮形式。

The Yamanashi test line adopts a side wall suspension form in which the driving winding, the suspension winding and the guide winding on the ground are arranged on the side wall of the guide rail. During the development of the basic technology of the Miyazaki test line, the suspension winding was set at the bottom of the guide rail, and the driving winding and the guiding winding were set at the side wall of the guide rail. At that time, technicians believed that the sidewall suspension form was more conducive to the stable and efficient operation of the superconducting maglev train. Therefore, the Yamanashi test line uses the sidewall suspension form.

这里简单介绍一下地上绕组的机制。驱动绕组为车辆电机的一部分，当三相交流电在驱动绕组中流动时给车辆产生驱动力，绕组的导体材料是铝线，导体外周由高压绝缘性能良好的环氧树脂覆盖。悬浮绕组和导向绕组的作用与通常的铁路轨道一样，为车辆提供浮力并防止车辆的横向摆动。导体使用铝线，卷成"8"字形，用掺有高强度玻璃纤维的聚酯树脂（Polyester Resin）覆盖。

Here is a brief introduction to the mechanism of the ground winding. The drive winding is a part of the vehicle motor. When three-phase alternating current flows in the drive winding, it generates driving force for the vehicle. The conductor material of the winding is aluminum wire, and the conductor periphery is covered by epoxy resin with good high-voltage insulation performance. The function of the suspension winding and the guide winding is the same as that of the usual railway track, providing buoyancy for the vehicle and preventing the lateral swing of the vehicle. The conductor is made of aluminum wire, rolled into a figure of eight, and covered with Polyester Resin doped with high-strength glass fiber.

第三节　基本原理

Section 3.3　Basic Principles

本节主要介绍日本超导磁浮铁路技术的基本原理，主要包括驱动原理、悬浮原理、导向原理及运行控制原理。

This section mainly introduces the basic principles of superconducting maglev railway technology in Japan, including driving principle, suspension principle, guiding principle and operation control principle.

一、超导原理

3.3.1　Principle of Superconductivity

磁浮铁路的核心驱动装置是直线电机，或称线性电机。根据直线电机绕组所用材料的不同，目前磁浮铁路划分为常导磁浮和超导磁浮两种类型。

The core driving device of maglev railway is linear motor. According to the different materials used in the linear motor windings, the maglev railway is divided into two types: normal magnetic levitation and superconducting magnetic levitation.

德国 TR 系统和日本航空的 HSST 系统均使用常导磁浮技术。常导直线电机中由于绕组电阻的存在会产生大量的能量消耗，也会使绕组温度增加。

The German TR system and the Japan Airlines HSST system both use permanent maglev technology. Due to the existence of winding resistance in the normal conducting linear motor, a large amount of energy will be consumed, and the winding temperature will also increase.

具有超导性质的材料在一定的温度之下出现电阻几乎为零的状态，称为超导状态。在超导状态下，由于超导材料的电阻为零，用它所制成的绕组一旦施加电流之后，其中的电流会永久地流动下去，由此可以得到数十倍永久磁铁的磁场强度。

Materials with superconducting properties have a state of almost zero resistance at a certain temperature, which is called superconducting state. In the superconducting state, because the resistance of the superconducting material is zero, once the current is applied to the winding made of it, the current in it will flow permanently, thus obtaining tens of times the magnetic field strength of the permanent magnet.

根据工作温度的不同，目前超导磁浮铁路技术主要包括高温超导、低温超导两种类型。

According to the different working temperature, the current superconducting maglev railway technology mainly includes two types: high temperature superconducting and low temperature superconducting.

高温超导一般使用液氮作为冷冻液，将绕组线圈保持在 -196 ℃ 之下，使线圈绕组达到超导状态。2001 年 3 月在北京举办的 "863 计划 15 周年成果展"上，我国西南交通大学展示的 "世纪号"磁浮试验车即是采用的高温超导技术。

High temperature superconductors generally use liquid nitrogen as a refrigerant to keep the winding coil at −196 °C, the coil winding is brought into a superconducting state. At the "15th Anniversary Achievements Exhibition of 863 Program" held in Beijing in March 2001, the "Century" maglev test vehicle displayed by Southwest Jiaotong University in China adopted high temperature superconducting technology.

日本磁浮铁路 ML 系统使用低温超导技术。它用液氦作为冷冻液，让线圈绕组达到 -269 ℃ 的温度时车载线圈绕组即进入超导状态。为了提高磁浮车辆上超导材料的稳定性，日本使用铌钛合金作为线圈绕组材料。

Cryogenic superconducting technology is used in the Japanese Maglev railway ML system. It uses liquid helium as a refrigerant to allow the on-board coil windings to enter a superconducting state when the coil windings reach a temperature of −269 °C. In order to improve the stability of superconducting materials on maglev vehicles, real niobium titanium alloy are used as coil winding materials in Japan.

二、超导磁铁

3.3.2 Superconducting Magnet

日本超导磁浮列车上使用的超导绕组使用铌（Nb）钛（Ti）合金制造，在 -269 ℃ 的温度下呈现超导状态。超导线圈放置在低温容器内，上部为液氦冷冻机，每个容器需要 100 L 液氦，每年液氦消耗量为百分之几。

The superconducting windings used on the superconducting maglev trains in Japan are made of niobium (Nb) -titanium (Ti) alloy and assume a superconducting state at a temperature of −269 °C. The superconducting coil is placed in a cryogenic vessel, and the upper part is a liquid helium refrigerator. Each vessel needs 100 L of liquid helium, and the annual consumption of liquid helium is a few percent.

一个超导磁铁共产生 4 个 N、S 极交叉排列的磁场极性（见图 3-1）。为了提高超导磁铁的热效率，还在绕组外面设置了防热辐射板，以防止外面的能量进入超导磁铁内。

A superconducting magnet generates four magnetic field polarities with N and S poles arranged crosswise (see Figure 3-1). In order to improve the thermal efficiency of the superconducting magnet, a heat-proof radiation plate is arranged outside the winding to prevent external energy from entering the superconducting magnet.

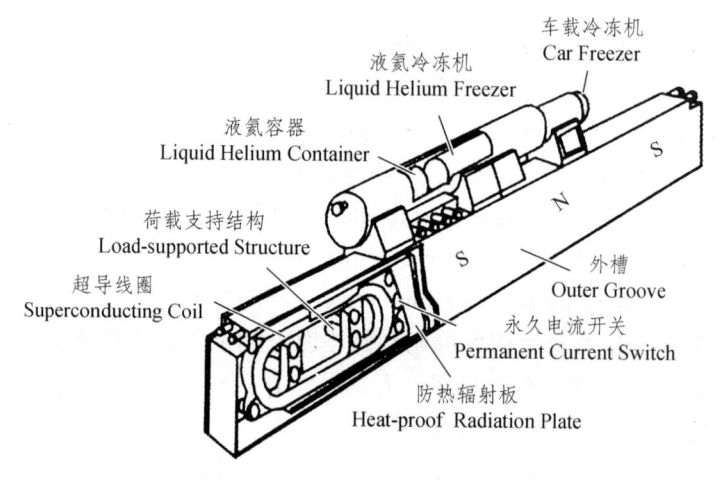

图 3-1　超导磁铁原理及结构

Figure 3-1　Principle and Structure of Superconducting Magnet

三、驱动原理

3.3.3　Driving Principle

常规的电力机车，受电弓从接触网接受电力，之后传送给设在转向架上的传统旋转电机，在电机动力的作用下车轮与轨道之间产生摩擦力进而驱动列车行驶，这也称为黏着牵引。

For conventional electric locomotives, the pantograph receives power from the catenary and then transmits it to the traditional rotating motor on the bogie. Under the action of the motor power, friction is generated between the wheels and the track to drive the train, which is also called adhesive traction.

日本 ML 超导磁浮列车是通过安设在导轨及车辆两侧上的长定子直线电机驱动的。德国 TR 磁浮系统和日本航空的 HSST 磁浮系统的驱动力均设在车辆的底部。

The Japanese ML superconducting maglev train is driven by long stator linear motors installed on the guideway and on both sides of the vehicle. The driving force of the German

TR maglev system and the HSST maglev system of Japan Airlines is located at the bottom of the vehicle.

为了节约能源，超高速磁浮铁路一般将地面上的若干推进绕组相互串联为一个个的分区（Section），各分区的地面绕组中一般情况下无电流通过，只在车辆通过该分区时绕组才接通电流。电流通过地面推进绕组（日本 ML 的推进绕组位于"U"形导轨的侧壁上）后，绕组逐级变成电磁铁（N 极和 S 极），即产生前述的地面直线移动磁场。

In order to save energy, the ultra-high-speed maglev railway generally connects several propulsion windings on the ground in series to form a Section. Generally, no current passes through the ground winding of each Section, and the winding is connected only when the vehicle passes through the Section. After the current passes through the ground propulsion winding (the propulsion winding of the Japanese ML is located on the side wall of the "U" shaped guide rail), the winding becomes an electromagnet (N pole and S pole) step by step, that is, the aforementioned ground linear moving magnetic field is generated.

日本在每节车辆两端都安装有超导磁铁，超导磁铁产生超导磁场 N 极和 S 极。通过控制使得前方地面磁场与车辆超导磁场的极性相反而产生吸力，后面相邻地面磁场与车辆超导磁场产生的极性相同而产生排斥力，使得车辆向前运动。这与常规的旋转电机中转子与旋转磁场协同动作使转子旋转的原理是相同的，见图 3-2。

In Japan, superconducting magnets are installed at both ends of each vehicle, and the superconducting magnets generate the N pole and S pole of the superconducting magnetic field. The polarities of the front ground magnetic field and the vehicle superconducting magnetic field are controlled to be opposite so as to generate an attractive force, and the polarities of the rear adjacent ground magnetic field and the vehicle superconducting magnetic field are the same so as to generate a repulsive force, so that the vehicle moves forward. This is the same as the principle that the rotor rotates in cooperation with the rotating magnetic field in a conventional rotating electrical machine, as shown in Figure 3-2.

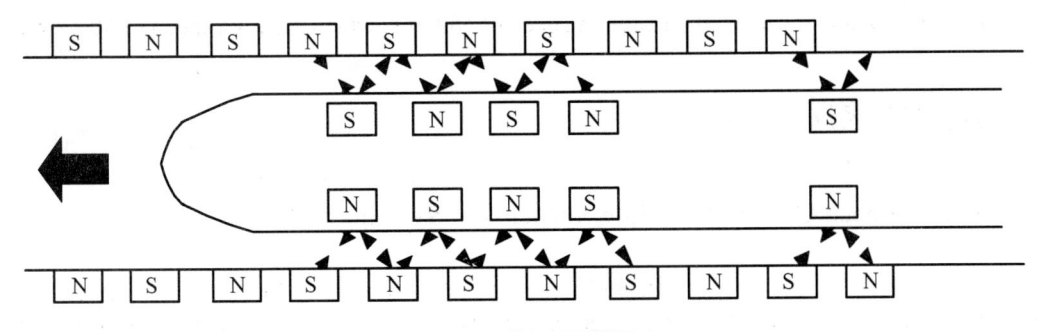

图 3-2 驱动原理图

Figure 3-2　Drive Schematic Diagram

四、速度控制原理

3.3.4 Speed Control Principle

一般轮轨接触的高速列车和中低速磁浮列车均由司机驾驶，列车运行工况和速度均由司机控制。超高速磁浮列车由于速度太快，为保证列车安全地行驶，对车辆的加速、减速、停车等运行工况和速度不能依靠司机控制，必须依靠地面控制中心控制。地面控制中心通过调节变电站送到导轨处驱动绕组的电流的周期（相位）和大小（振幅），改变磁场的强弱，来实现对驱动力的控制。从这个意义上讲，超高速磁浮铁路又称为导轨驱动（或称路轨驱动、地面驱动）的磁浮铁路。

Generally, the high-speed train and medium-low-speed maglev train with wheel-rail contact are driven by the driver, and the running conditions and speed of the train are controlled by the driver. Because the speed of the ultra-high-speed maglev train is too fast, in order to ensure the safe running of the train, the acceleration, deceleration, parking and other operating conditions and speed of the vehicle can not be controlled by the driver, but must be controlled by the ground control center. The ground control center controls the driving force by adjusting the period (phase) and magnitude (amplitude) of the current sent by the substation to the driving winding at the guide rail and changing the strength of the magnetic field. In this sense, the ultra-high-speed maglev railway is also known as the guideway-driven (or rail-driven, ground-driven) maglev railway.

在宫崎试验线的试验中，变电站将电力公司的 60 Hz 电力转换为所需要的频率。1 Hz 的电力即可使列车每秒行驶 4.2 m；将频率上升到 33 Hz 就可达到 139 m/s 的速度，也就是说速度可以达到 500 km/h。

In the test on the Miyazaki test line, the substation converted the 60 Hz power from the power company to the required frequency. 1 Hz of power enables the train to travel 4.2 m/s; increasing the frequency to 33 Hz enables a speed of 139 m/s, which means a speed of 500 km/h.

五、悬浮系统

3.3.5 Speed Control Principle Suspension System

磁浮铁路的最大优点是利用电磁悬浮、电动悬浮的原理将列车悬浮在导轨上方，从而消除了轮轨接触所引起的摩擦、振动等不利因素。这里主要介绍日本超高速磁浮列车的侧壁悬浮原理。

The biggest advantage of maglev railway is that the train is suspended above the guideway by using the principle of electromagnetic suspension and Electrodynamic suspension, thus eliminating the adverse factors such as friction and vibration caused by wheel-rail contact. The sidewall suspension principle of Japan's ultra-high speed maglev train will be mainly introduced.

德国 TR 磁浮系统和日本航空的 HSST 系统的悬浮力均产生于车辆底部，日本超导磁浮系统的悬浮力来自车辆两侧。在导轨两侧的侧壁上，排列着一组组悬浮及导向绕组，当车辆高速通过时，车辆上的超导磁场会在导轨侧壁的悬浮绕组中产生感应电流和感应磁场。控制每组悬浮组上侧的磁场极性与车辆超导磁场的极性相反从而产生引力，下侧极性与超导磁场极性相同而产生斥力，使得车辆悬浮起来，见图 3-3。

The levitation force of the German TR maglev system and the HSST system of Japan Airlines is generated at the bottom of the vehicle, while the levitation force of the Japanese superconducting maglev system comes from both sides of the vehicle. Groups of suspension and guide windings are arranged on the side walls on both sides of the guide rail. When the vehicle passes at high speed, the superconducting magnetic field on the vehicle will generate induced current and induced magnetic field in the suspension windings on the side walls of the guide rail. The polarity of the magnetic field on the upper side of each suspension group is controlled to be opposite to that of the superconducting magnetic field of the vehicle so as to generate an attractive force, and the polarity on the lower side is the same as that of the superconducting magnetic field so as to generate a repulsive force, so that the vehicle is suspended, as shown in Figure 3-3.

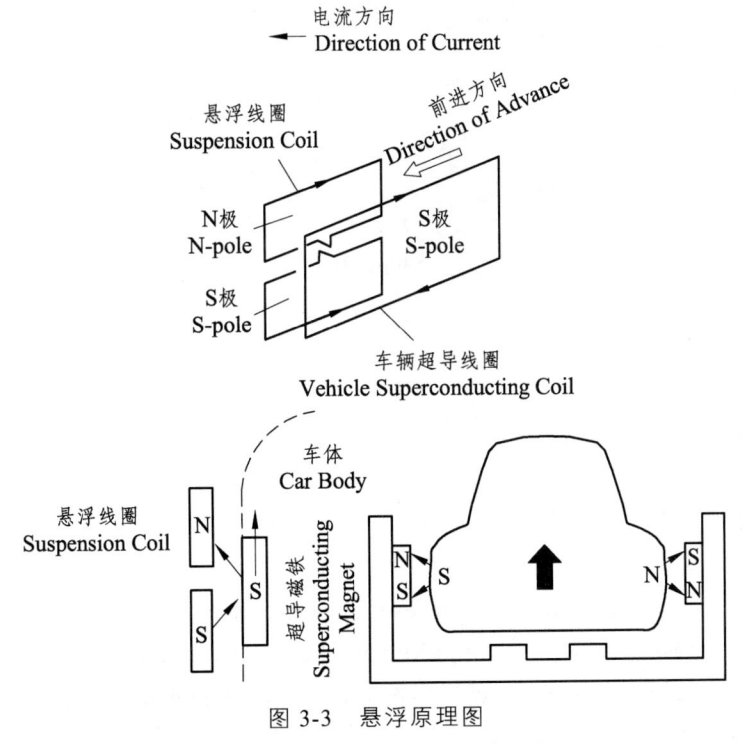

图 3-3　悬浮原理图

Figure 3-3　Suspension Schematic Diagram

由于导轨产生的悬浮磁场为感应磁场,列车运行速度越高,则悬浮力越大。当列车运行速度低于 120 km/h 之后,所产生的悬浮力较小,不足以支承车辆悬浮。故当运行速度低于 120 km/h 时,日本的超导磁浮车辆依靠安装在转向架底部的车轮支承行驶,见图 3-4 中的支承车轮。当速度高于 120 km/h 时,车辆就自动悬浮起来。车辆以 500 km/h 的速度行驶时,其悬浮高度约为 10 cm。

Because the levitation magnetic field generated by the guideway is an induction magnetic field, the higher the train speed is, the greater the levitation force is. When the running speed of the train is lower than 120 km/h, the generated suspension force is too small to support the vehicle suspension. Therefore, when the running speed is lower than 120 km/h, the superconducting maglev vehicle in Japan runs on the wheel support installed at the bottom of the bogie, as shown in Figure 3-4. At speeds above 120 km/h, the vehicle automatically levitates. At a speed of 500 km/h, the vehicle's levitation height is approximately 10 cm.

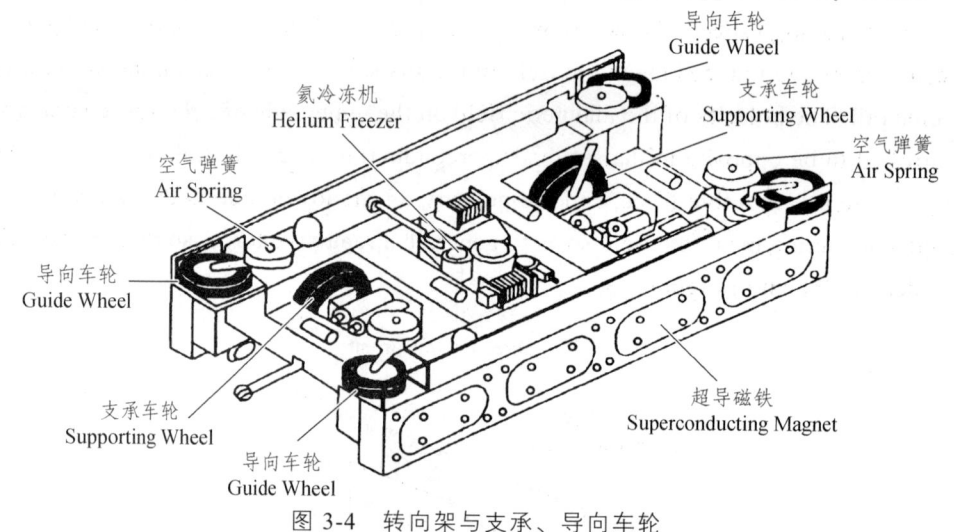

图 3-4 转向架与支承、导向车轮

Figure 3-4 Bogie、Supporting and Guiding Wheels

六、导向原理

3.3.6 Guiding Principle

导向是指在横断面上保证车辆的中心不偏离轨道中心。传统的轮轨接触型铁路,列车的导向是通过轮缘与钢轨的相互作用实现的。

Guidance is to ensure that the center of the vehicle does not deviate from the center of the track on the cross section. In the traditional wheel-rail contact railway, the guidance of the train is realized by the interaction between the wheel flange and the rail.

磁浮车辆在高速运行过程中必须保证与导轨不能有任何形式的接触,不仅在车辆地面不能接触，而且当遇到曲线等情况时也不能与侧壁接触。因此需要建立完善的导向机制。

When the maglev vehicle is running at high speed, it must be ensured that there is no contact with the guide rail in any form, not only on the ground, but also on the side wall when encountering curves. Therefore, it is necessary to establish a sound guiding mechanism.

日本的磁浮铁路在导轨侧壁安装有悬浮及导向绕组。如果车辆在平面上远离了导轨的中心位置，则系统会自动在导轨每侧的悬浮绕组中产生磁场，并且使得偏离侧的地面磁场与车体的超导磁场产生吸引力，靠近侧的地面磁场与车体磁场产生排斥力，从而保持车体不偏离导轨的中心位置，见图3-5。

The maglev railway in Japan is equipped with suspension and guide windings on the side wall of the guide rail. If the vehicle is far away from the center of the guideway on the plane, the system will automatically generate a magnetic field in the suspension winding on each side of the guideway, and make the ground magnetic field on the deviated side and the superconducting magnetic field of the vehicle body generate an attractive force, and the ground magnetic field on the adjacent side and the vehicle body magnetic field generate a repulsive force, so as to keep the vehicle body from deviating from the center of the guideways, see Figure 3-5.

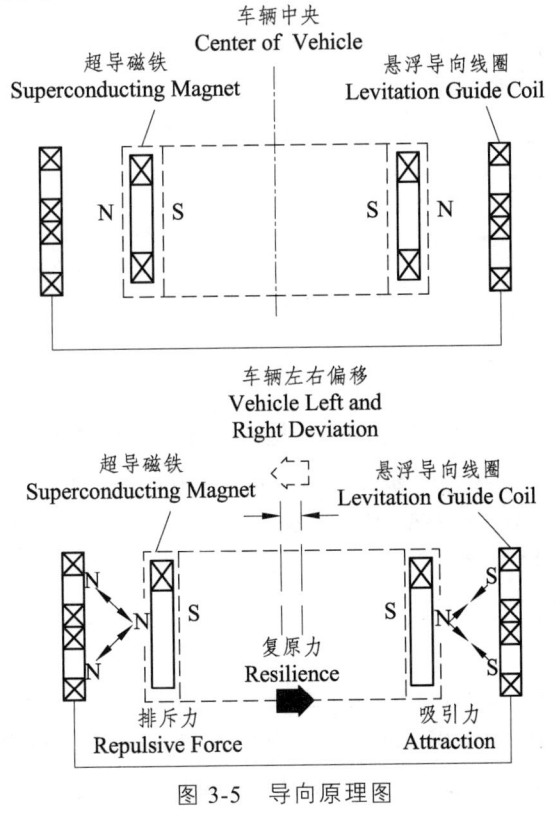

图 3-5 导向原理图

Figure 3-5 Schematic Diagram of Guidance

由于导轨产生的导向磁场也为感应磁场,所以列车运行速度越高,产生的导向力越大。日本的超导磁浮车辆当列车低速运行时,所产生的导向力较小,不足以使车辆自动导向,与前述的悬浮情况类似,此时依靠安装在转向架两侧的导向车轮(参考图3-4)完成导向功能。

Because the guiding magnetic field generated by the guideway is also an induction magnetic field, the higher the train speed is, the greater the guiding force is. When the superconducting maglev vehicle in Japan is running at a low speed, the generated guiding force is too small to guide the vehicle automatically, which is similar to the aforementioned suspension situation. At this time, the guiding function is completed by the guiding wheels installed on both sides of the bogie (refer to Figure 3-4).

第四节　车辆及列车编组

Section 3.4　Vehicle and Train Formation

本节主要介绍在山梨试验线上所使用的列车及车辆,包括列车编组、车辆构造、车辆性能、车辆基地等方面内容。

This section mainly introduces the trains and vehicles used on the Yamanashi Test Line, including train formation, vehicle structure, vehicle performance, vehicle base, etc.

一、车辆基地

3.4.1　Vehicle Base

车辆基地负责进行车辆的日常保养与检查、超导磁铁检修等工作。

The vehicle base is responsible for the daily maintenance and inspection of vehicles and the maintenance of superconducting magnets.

由于液体氦的冷却作用,超导磁铁中的超导绕组平时在－269 ℃工作。但是液氦也会汽化在车辆基地,要将蒸发产生的气体氦进行回收,重新液化,发挥超低温基地的作用。

Due to the cooling effect of liquid helium, the superconducting winding in the superconducting magnet usually runs at －269 ℃. However, liquid helium will also be vaporized in the vehicle base, and the gas helium produced by evaporation should be recovered and re-liquefied to play the role of ultra-low temperature base.

二、营业用的两组列车编组

3.4.2　Two Sets of Train Formation for Business Use

日本超导磁浮铁路有两种形式：中央新干线的长大干线形式与新千岁机场—札幌间及计划中的大宫—成田机场间的短程往返形式。长大干线形式适用于大城市间的大容量高速运输，短程往返形式适用于运行距离 50～70 km 的范围，可用于大城市圈的外环铁路及市中心与机场的连接。

There are two forms of superconducting maglev railway in Japan: the long trunk line form of Chuo Shinkansen and the short round trip form between New Chitose Airport and Sapporo and the planned Omiya-Narita Airport. The form of long trunk line is suitable for high-capacity high-speed transportation between big cities, and the form of short-distance round-trip is suitable for the running distance of 50-70 km, which can be used for the connection between the outer ring railway of big city circle and the city center and the airport.

根据运输省超导磁浮铁路委员会在 1988 年 10 月的第一次聚会中提出的列车编组方案，在中央新干线上长距离运行的列车使用 14 辆编组、定员 950 人、运行间隔控制在 5～6 min、设计客运能力为单程每小时 10 000 人。由于在新干线上轮轨方式的"回声号"及"光号"高速列车也要运行，考虑到各站停车的"回声号"的客运量与东京—名古屋—大阪间的直达列车"光号"相比乘客会减少，因此实际上客运量将为每小时 8 000 人左右。

According to the train marshalling scheme proposed by the Superconducting Maglev Railway Committee of the Ministry of Transport at the first meeting in October 1988, the trains running on the Central Shinkansen for a long distance are composed of 14 cars, with a capacity of 950 people, a running interval of 5 to 6 minutes, and a designed passenger capacity of 10,000 people per hour for a single journey. Due to the operation of the "Echo" and "Hikari" high-speed trains on the Shinkansen, the actual passenger volume will be about 8,000 people per hour, considering that the passenger volume of the "Echo" stopping at each station will be reduced compared with the direct train "Hikari" between Tokyo, Nagoya and Osaka.

与此相比，连接市中心与机场间的短程往返形式为六辆编组，定员 400 人左右，预计客运能力为每小时 1 200 人左右。50～70 km 区间需要时间为 10～15 min，计划每小时 3 个往复运行。

In contrast, the short-distance shuttle between the city center and the airport is a six-car formation with a capacity of about 400 people, and the passenger capacity is expected to be about 1,200 people per hour. The interval of 50-70 km needs 10-15 min, and it is planned to run back and forth 3 times per hour.

中央新干线连接三大城市圈，旅客需求量大，因此为增加运输能力，全线采用复线。考虑到建设费用与经济效益，短程往返形式采用单线。

The Central Shinkansen connects the three metropolitan areas, and there is a large demand for passengers. Therefore, in order to increase the transport capacity, the whole line is double-tracked. In consideration of construction cost and economic benefit, single track is adopted for short distance round trip.

三、山梨试验线的列车编组

3.4.3　Train Formation of Yamanashi Test Line

山梨试验线使用的试验列车分为第一编组（三辆编组）、第二编组（四辆编组）、第三编组（五辆编组）和新旧车辆混合编组。

The test trains used on the Yamanashi Test Line are divided into the first formation (three-car formation), the second formation (four-car formation), the third formation (five-car formation) and the mixed formation of new and old cars.

（一）车辆编号

3.4.3.1　Vehicle Number

1995年7月以后使用的磁浮车辆使用新的名称"MLX01"，编号用名称后的第一位数或两位数表示。位于车头的车辆用一位或三位数表示，位于中间的车辆用两位数表示。

Maglev vehicles used after July 1995 use the new designation "MLX01", and the number is represented by the first digit or two digits after the designation. Vehicles at the front are represented by one or three digits, and vehicles in the middle are represented by two digits.

（二）第一编组

3.4.3.2　The First Formation

第一编组列车由三节车组成。两个车头形状不同，甲府方向车头为双重尖点型（MLX01-01），东京方向车头为流线型（MLX01-02），中间车辆为标准车辆（MLX01-11），见图3-6。

The first train consists of three cars. The two heads are different in shape. The head in Kofu direction is a double cusp type (MLX01-01), the head in Tokyo direction is a streamlined type (MLX01-02), and the middle vehicle is a standard vehicle (MLX01-11). See Figure 3-6.

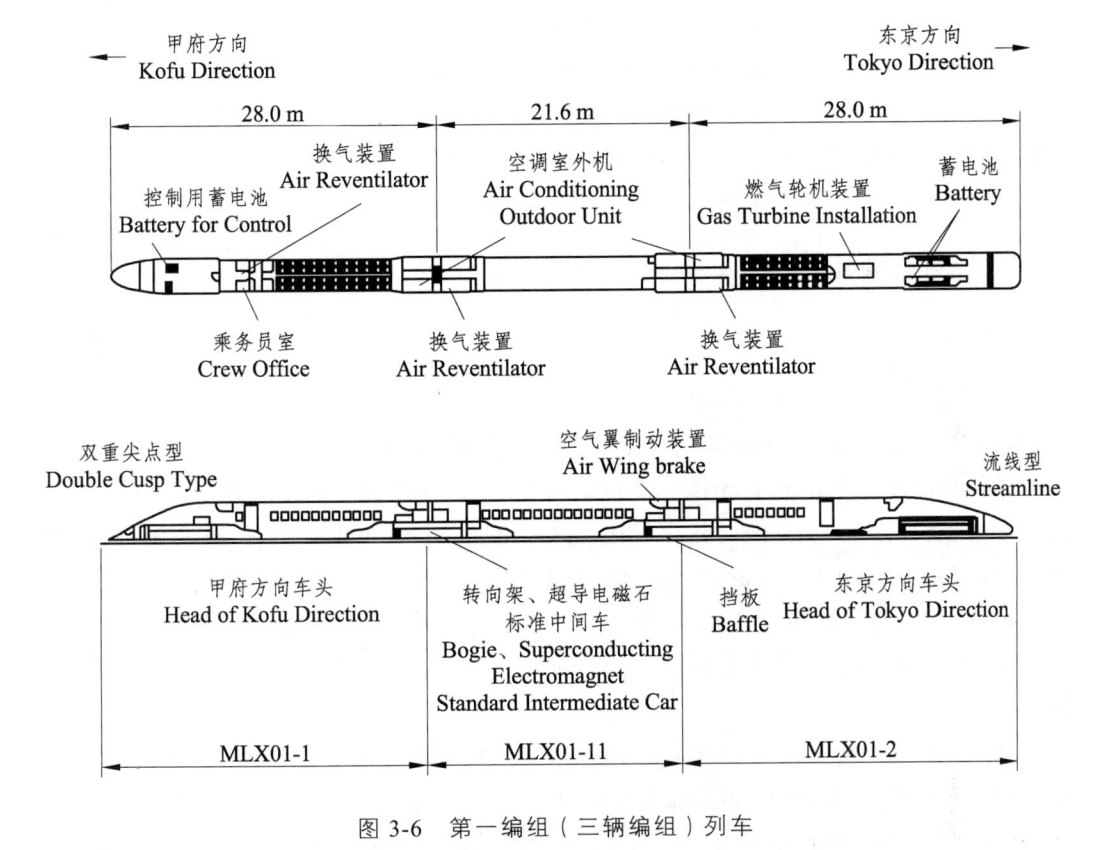

图 3-6　第一编组（三辆编组）列车

Figure 3-6　Train of the First Formation (Three-Car Formation)

1996 年 12 月由维修车辆牵引开始运行试验，此试验为综合调试试验的一部分。综合试验项目包括试验线设备、安装状况的确定；地面设备及车辆性能的确定；导轨等地面构造物与车辆之间的间隙、车辆位置、速度检测功能的确认与调整，以及两种车头的动力性能试验。

In December 1996, the operation test started with the traction of the maintenance vehicle as part of the comprehensive commissioning test. The comprehensive test items include the determination of test line equipment and installation conditions, the determination of ground equipment and vehicle performance, the clearance between ground structures such as guide rail and vehicle, the confirmation and adjustment of vehicle position and speed detection function, and the dynamic performance test of two heads.

"MLX01"型的转向架配置在车辆连接处，为减小空气阻力与空气噪声，依据风洞试验结果将甲府方向的车头设计成双重尖点（Double Cusp）形状，整体为三辆编组四转向架形式。试验时与流线型的特性进行了比较研究，认为双重尖点形状车辆的空气阻力系数与宫崎试验线的车辆 MLU002N 相比减少 45%。

The bogie of "MLX01" type is arranged at the junction of vehicles. In order to reduce the air resistance and air noise, the head of Kofu direction is designed into a Double Cusp shape according to the wind tunnel test results, and the whole is a three-car four-bogie form. The aerodynamic drag coefficient of the double-cusp-shaped vehicle is considered to be 45% less than that of the vehicle MLU002N on the Miyazaki test line by comparing with the streamline characteristics during the test.

（三）第二编组

3.4.3.3　The Second Formation

第二编组由四辆组成，两端车头分别为 MLX01-03 和 MLX01-04，中间车辆为标准中间车辆（MLX01-12）和新生产的加长中间车辆（MLX01-21）混合编组。

The second formation consists of four cars, with MLX01-03 and MLX01-04 at both ends, and the middle cars are mixed formations of standard middle cars (MLX01-12) and newly produced extended middle cars (MLX01-21).

新车 1995 年开始制造，1998 年春以后在山梨试验线导轨上进行与第一编组车辆同样的车轮走行试验与悬浮走行试验。同时，还在第二编组列车上开展了感应发电的试验。

The new car was manufactured in 1995, and after the spring of 1998, the same wheel running test and suspension running test as the first group of cars were carried out on the guideway of Yamanashi test line. At the same time, the induction power generation test was carried out on the second marshalling train.

（四）新编组

3.4.3.4　New Formation

2002 年 6 月新的试验车辆驶入车辆基地后，使用新的列车编组并开始试验。甲府方向的车头为流线型更好的新车（MLX01-901），东京方向车头为选线的 MLX01-04，中间车辆为加长车辆（MLX0l-22）。

In June 2002, after the new test vehicles were driven into the depot, the new train formation was used and the test began. The Kofu direction vehicle is a new vehicle with better streamline (MLX01-901), the Tokyo direction vehicle is a MLX01-04 with route selection, and the middle vehicle is an extended vehicle (MLX01-22).

（五）有关试验

3.4.3.5　Related Tests

1999 年 4 月，5 辆编组（第三编组）的试验列车的载人试验速度达到 552 km/h，创造了当时列车运行试验的最高纪录。

In April 1999, the manned test speed of the five-car (the third formation) test train reached 552 km/h, creating the highest record of train operation test at that time.

导轨地面绕组的加压试验也同时进行。此时无须进行实车行驶，利用模拟器模拟车辆的行驶状态进行加压、调整变电器及运行控制系统等。此次综合试验一直持续到 1997 年 3 月，从 4 月开始进入实用化试验。历时三年的实用化试验，最初实施低速车轮行驶，试验人员也要乘车工作。第二年，进入最高速度达 500 km/h 的高速悬浮行驶阶段，同时也进行了会车试验。JR 东海认为，18 km 长的试验线比较短，虽然速度 550 km/h 时的可行驶时间仅有 1 min 左右，但对于实用化的技术试验没有问题。

The pressurization test of the ground winding of the guide rail is also carried out at the same time. At this time, there is no need to drive the real vehicle, and the simulator is used to simulate the driving state of the vehicle to pressurize, adjust the transformer and run the control system. The comprehensive test lasted until March 1997, and the practical test began in April. During the three-year practical test, low-speed wheel driving was initially implemented, and the test personnel also had to work by car. In the second year, it entered the high-speed suspension driving stage with a maximum speed of 500 km/h, and also carried out the meeting test. JR Donghai believes that the 18 km long test line is relatively short, although the driving time at 550 km/h is only about 1 min, but there is no problem for practical technical test.

四、转向架

3.4.4　Bogie

新的磁浮列车在车辆的连接部设置"连接转向架形式"。日本新干线的试验车辆曾采用过此连接形式，并用于小田急电铁的豪华型车辆。与普通转向架相比，这种"连接转向架形式"有两个好处：首先是常超导磁铁设置在远离座位的连接部，遮断可能会对人体产生有害影响的磁场；其次，与通常的新干线相比，这种形式可以降低座席的高度，这种"低置构造"可减少空气阻力。因此，山梨试验线采用了这种新型车型。转向架的位置见图 3-7。

The new maglev train has a "connecting bogie form" at the connecting part of the vehicle. This type of connection has been used in the test cars of Shinkansen in Japan and in the luxury cars of Odakyu Electric Railway. Compared with the ordinary bogie, this "connected bogie form" has two advantages: first, the superconducting magnet is arranged at the connecting part far away from the seat to block the magnetic field that may have harmful effects on the human body; second, compared with the ordinary Shinkansen, this form can reduce the height of the seat, and this "low-set structure" can reduce air resistance. Therefore, the Yamanashi test line adopts this new model. See Figure 3-7 for the location of the bogie.

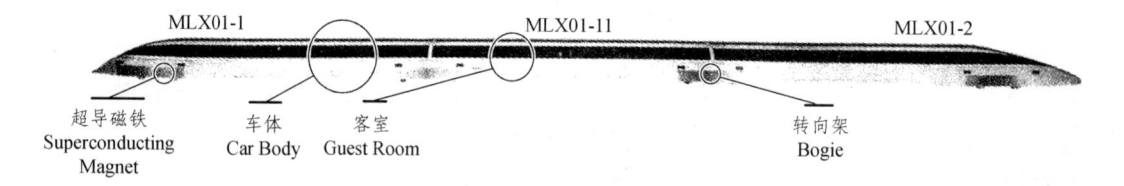

图 3-7 转向架位置图

Figure 3-7 Bogie Location Diagram

安装在车辆连接处的转向架,具有将超导磁铁产生的驱动力与悬浮力传递到车体、保障旅客安全、减少振动（即缓冲）的功能。其构造图见图 3-8。

The bogie installed on the vehicle connection has the functions of transmitting the driving force and suspension force generated by the superconducting magnet to the vehicle body, ensuring the safety of passengers and reducing vibration (buffering). See Fig. 3-8 for its structural diagram.

转向架上还安装有供低速行驶用的支承轮和导向轮。在进入高速悬浮行驶之前的低速行驶阶段，使用飞机采用的高性能轮胎（支承轮和导向轮）在导轨内滑行，当速度超过 120 km/h 后，超导磁铁与地面绕组之间通过电磁感应产生悬浮力和导向力，列车开始进入悬浮无接触行驶状态。

The bogie is also provided with a supporting wheel and a guide wheel for low-speed running. In the low-speed running stage before entering the high-speed suspension running, the high-performance tires (support wheels and guide wheels) used by the aircraft are used to slide in the guide rail. When the speed exceeds 120 km/h, the suspension force and guide force are generated between the superconducting magnet and the ground winding through electromagnetic induction, and the train begins to enter the suspension non-contact running state.

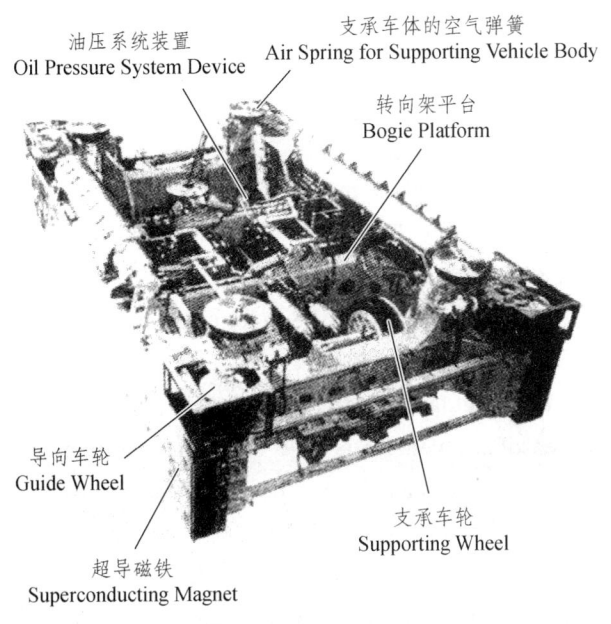

图 3-8 转向架结构

Figure 3-8 Structure of the Bogie

五、车轮及轮胎

3.4.5 Wheels and Tyres

车辆低速行驶时使用车轮行驶和导向，轮上的高性能轮胎由高强度、高耐热的橡胶制成，以层层叠加的方式增加各部分的强度。列车出现异常时，从速度 550 km/h 的悬浮行驶状态紧急着地，进入停车或地上行驶状态，轮胎的性能能够满足需求。重达 300 t 的大型飞机使用橡胶离地起飞或着地滑行，安全上并没有问题。磁浮列车的轮胎承受的荷载比飞机起落架低得多，因此长大的磁浮列车在进入悬浮行驶之前或降落到导轨之后也可以像飞机一样利用轮胎安全行驶。

When the vehicle runs at low speed, it uses wheels to drive and guide. The high-performance tires on the wheels are made of high-strength and heat-resistant rubber, which increases the strength of each part in a layer-by-layer way. When the train is abnormal, it can land on the ground from the suspension running state with a speed of 550 km/h to the parking or ground running state, and the tire performance can meet the requirements. Large aircraft weighing up to 300 t use rubber to take off or taxi on the ground, and there is no problem in safety. The load borne by the tire of the maglev train is much lower than that of the landing gear of the aircraft, so the long maglev train can also use the tire to run safely like the aircraft before entering the suspension running or after landing on the guideway.

六、车　辆

3.4.6 Vehicles

甲府方向车头（MLX01-01）长 28 m，车体最大宽度 2.9 m，转向架部分的最大宽度为 3.22 m，悬浮行驶时的高度为 3.28 m，车轮着地行驶时的高度为 3.32 m，载人时重 29 t，车辆断面面积 8.91 m²。其他车辆及车头与上述长度与质量略有不同。

The Kofu direction head (MLX01-01) is 28 m long, the maximum width of the car body is 2.9 m, the maximum width of the bogie part is 3.22 m, the height of suspension driving is 3.28 m, and the height of wheel landing driving is 3.32 m, the weight is 29 t when carrying people. The sectional area of the vehicle is 8.91 m², Other vehicles and their locomotives are slightly different in length and mass from those mentioned above.

磁浮车辆与以往的新干线车辆相比，在宽度、高度、质量等方面变得更加小而轻。例如，"希望号"的车头长 26 m，宽 3.38 m，高 3.65 m，重 45 t，车体断面面积为 11.2 m²。而第一、第二编组的磁浮车辆高度只有 3.28 m，比"希望号"缩小了 0.37 m。

Maglev vehicles have become smaller and lighter in width, height and mass compared with previous Shinkansen vehicles. For example, the "Hope" has a headstock length of 26 m, a width of 3.38 m, a height of 3.65 m, and a weight of 45 t. The cross-sectional area of the vehicle body is 11.2 m², while the height of the maglev vehicles in the first and second formations is only 3.28 m, which is 0.37 m, smaller than that of the "Hope".

车体的设计融合了飞机与铁路车辆的技术，为铝合金半硬壳结构（semi-monocoque），实现了轻量化，提高了耐久性。考虑到车内的舒适性，车体外板的内侧贴隔热隔音材料，一部分使用了磁场遮断材料。客车天棚的高度为 2.1 m，甲府方向车头的定员为 46 人。座席均为双人座，通过采用 CFRP（碳素纤维补强塑料）壳体构造，大幅度减轻了质量，扩大了座位面积率。为了减少超导磁铁的强磁场对人体的影响，乘客座位尽量远离超导磁铁。另外，监视运行状况的乘务员室很简朴。为保证乘客的空间，车门采用上下推拉及内旋两种形式，均达到不逊飞机的气密性。

The design of the car body combines the technology of aircraft and railway vehicles, and is an aluminum alloy semi-monocoque structure, which achieves lightweight and improves durability. Considering the comfortability inside the car, the inside of the outer panel of the car body is covered with heat insulation and sound insulation materials, and some of them are made of magnetic field blocking materials. The height of the vehicle ceiling is 2.1 m, and the capacity of the vehicle head in the direction of Kofu is 46 people. The seats are all double seats. By adopting the CFRP (carbon fiber reinforced plastic) shell structure, the mass is greatly reduced and the seat area ratio is expanded. In order to reduce the influence of the strong magnetic field of the superconducting magnet on the human body, the passenger seat should be as far away from the superconducting magnet as possible. In addition, the crew office for monitoring the running status is simple. In order to ensure the space of passengers, the door adopts two forms of pushing and pulling up and down and internal rotation, which are not inferior to the air tightness of the aircraft.

七、新型试验车辆

3.4.7 New Test Vehicle

2002 年 6 月 18 日，山梨试验线的新型试验车运入车辆基地。这些车辆是为了将过去使用的试验车辆发展为营业用车辆而制作的试验车，未必就是营业用车辆的原型。

On June 18, 2002, the new test vehicle of Yamanashi Test Line was transported into the vehicle base. These vehicles are test vehicles built to develop previously used test vehicles into commercial vehicles and are not necessarily prototypes of commercial vehicles.

（一）车辆形状

3.4.7.1　Vehicle Shape

新型车辆的最大特点是使得车头流线型的特点更为突出。头车（甲府方向）头部的长度由原来的 9.1 m 增加到 23 m。头车和中间车辆的车体下部的形状也由过去的圆形改为棱角形，减少与转向架连接处的形状变化，改善了整体的空气动力特性。

The biggest feature of the new vehicle is to make the streamline of the front more prominent. The length of the head of the first vehicle (Kofu direction) is increased from 9.1 m to 23 m. The shape of the lower part of the body of the head car and the middle car is also changed from round to angular, which reduces the shape change of the connection with the bogie and improves the overall aerodynamic characteristics.

（二）车体构造

3.4.7.2　Vehicle Body Structure

中间车辆的车体尽量使用"挤出成型材"，实现外板与支撑骨架的一体化，减少了车辆制造工时，降低了制造费用。此外，通过增强车体刚度，提高了乘车的舒适度。采用双层窗确保空气层厚度，使用阻隔振动的内装修材料及加厚外板厚度降低了车内噪声，一次提高了车辆整体水准。

The car body of the intermediate vehicle uses "extruded material" as far as possible to realize the integration of the outer plate and the supporting framework, which reduces the manufacturing time of the vehicle and reduces the manufacturing cost. In addition, by enhancing the rigidity of the car body, the comfort of riding is improved. The use of double-layer windows to ensure the thickness of the air layer, the use of vibration-blocking interior decoration materials and the thickening of the outer plate thickness reduce the noise inside the vehicle and improve the overall level of the vehicle at one time.

（三）车载设备

3.4.7.3 On-board Equipment

空气翼制动装置为紧急制动装置，原先使用油压驱动设在车顶的开闭板片。新型车辆则采用气缸驱动装置，上下滑动板片，简化了构造，减轻了质量。侧门也由原来的电力驱动上下滑动形式改为气缸驱动内旋形式，简化了构造。

The air wing braking device is an emergency braking device, which originally uses oil pressure to drive the opening and closing plate on the roof. The new vehicle uses a cylinder drive device to slide the plate up and down, which simplifies the structure and reduces the mass. The side door is also changed from the original electric drive up and down sliding form to the cylinder drive internal rotation form, which simplifies the structure.

（四）试验计划

3.4.7.4 Test Plan

先使用 3 辆编组确认基本特性，之后使用 4 辆编组实施走行试验。

The basic characteristics shall be confirmed by 3-car formation, and then the running test shall be carried out by 4-car formation.

八、未来感觉与传统协调车厢

3.4.8 The Future Feeling and The Traditional Coordination Carriage

JR 东海、JR 铁道综合研究所就试验车辆做了说明：为减少空气阻力、确保行驶安全等，以提高空气动力特性为重点开发了理想的列车两端车辆与中间车辆。新试验车不仅要确保实用化后大量运输所需要的座位数，而且要意识到磁浮列车安全舒适旅行的特性，因此对其人体工程学意义上的乘坐特性也要考虑。在一部分车辆内，采用日本传统的和纸花色，将未来感觉和传统融于一体。

JR Tokai and JR Railway Comprehensive Research Institute have explained the test vehicles: In order to reduce air resistance and ensure form safety, the ideal vehicles at both ends and in the middle of the train have been developed with emphasis on improving aerodynamic characteristics. The new test vehicle should not only ensure the number of seats needed for mass transportation after practical use, but also realize the safe and comfortable travel characteristics of maglev train, so its ergonomic ride characteristics should also be considered. In some vehicles, traditional Japanese washi colors are used to integrate the feeling of the future with tradition.

室内换气系统巧妙地利用高速行驶时的空气流（Ram Air），开发出节能轻量的换气装置，将新鲜的空气送入车内，使车内既安静又舒适。在隧道内，这种换气装置既能防止气压变动引起的耳鸣，又能连续向车内提供新鲜空气，可以说是一举两得。

The indoor ventilation system ingeniously uses the air flow at high speed to develop an energy-saving and lightweight ventilation device to send fresh air into the car, making the car quiet and comfortable. In the tunnel, this kind of ventilation device can not only prevent tinnitus caused by air pressure changes, but also continuously provide fresh air to the car, which can be said to be two.

车辆的形象设计（外部涂装等）以浅白色为基调，以浅蓝色线条作陪衬，与大城市圈及中部山岳的沿线风景相协调，充满未来世界的感觉。

The image design of the vehicle (exterior painting, etc.) takes light white as the keynote and light blue lines as the foil, which is in harmony with the scenery along the metropolitan area and the central mountains, and is full of the feeling of the future world.

九、改进后的超导磁铁

3.4.9 Improved Superconducting Magnet

作为新试验车辆心脏部分的超导磁铁的性能，与宫崎试验线相比有了大幅度提高。设置在列车连接部转向架的磁铁，在产生磁场后从"U"形导轨的驱动绕组接受推力，从悬浮绕组接受浮力，从导向绕组接受防止车辆左右移动的导向力，具有使车辆在超高速状态下悬浮行驶的重要功能。

The performance of the superconducting magnet, which is the heart of the new test vehicle, has been greatly improved compared with the Miyazaki test line. A magnet arrange on a bogie at that connecting part of a train receive thrust from a drive winding of a U-shaped guide rail after generating a magnetic field, receive buoyancy from a suspension winding, receives guiding force for preventing the vehicle from moving left and right from a guiding winding, and has the important function of suspending and running the vehicle in an ultrahigh speed state.

超导磁铁装置可以说是磁浮铁路系统中最关键的技术。新开发的超导绕组由内槽、外槽以及装有冷却用液体氦的车载制冷机组成，见图3-9。

Superconducting magnet device is the most critical technology in maglev railway system. The newly developed superconducting winding consists of an inner slot, an outer slot, and a vehicle-mounted refrigerator filled with cooling liquid helium, as shown in Figure 3-9.

图 3-9 超导磁铁结构

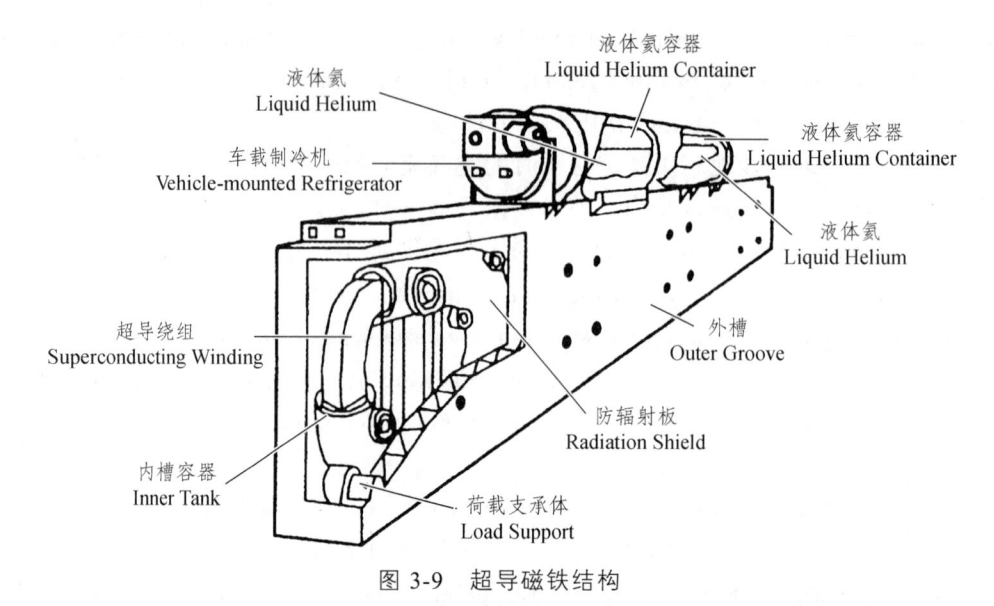

Figure 3-9　Structure Diagram of Superconducting Magnet

宫崎线"MLU002"型车辆的同类装置长 1.7 m，宽 0.5 m，表征磁铁强度的起磁力只有 450~700 kN。山梨试验线的超导磁铁（包括制冷机在内）的体积有所减少，起磁力提高到 -269 ℃ 时即进入零电阻的超导状态。处于超导状态的绕组只要通电一次，电流将流动不息，产生比普通永久磁铁强度高几十倍的强磁场。为了提高超导状态的稳定性，使用了将超导物质铌钛合金的极细多芯线埋设于铜制母材的方法制成绕组。

The similar device of "MLU002" vehicle on Miyazaki Line is 1.7 m long and 0.5 m wide, and the magnetic force representing the magnet strength is only 450-700 kN. The volume of the superconducting magnet (including the refrigerator) of the Yamanashi test line has been reduced, and the superconducting state of zero resistance has been reached when the magnetic force has been increased to -269 ℃. As long as the winding in the superconducting state is electrified once, the current will flow continuously, producing a strong magnetic field tens of times stronger than that of ordinary permanent magnets. In order to improve the stability of the superconducting state, the winding is formed by burying an extremely thin multi-core wire of a niobium-titanium alloy, which is a superconducting substance, in a copper base material.

车载制冷机中的液体氦，受外界热及运行时产生的余热的影响会逐渐蒸发为气体。通过改良制冷机，可以将蒸发的氦气变到液体氦状态从而实现再利用。制冷能力与宫崎试验线的车辆相比提高了 60%。

The liquid helium in the vehicle refrigerator will gradually evaporate into gas under the influence of the external heat and the waste heat generated during operation. By improving the refrigerator, the evaporated helium can be changed into a liquid state for reuse. The cooling capacity is increased by 60% compared with the vehicles on the Miyazaki test line.

在超导磁铁的生产方面,需要进行形状更小、效率更高的常温超导材料的开发及商品化。在 1986 年,IBM 的研究所公布了陶瓷类超导物质的存在,之后又发现了在更高温度下产生超导现象的新材料。在液体氮的温度达到－196 ℃的情况下开发磁浮列车使用的高温超导磁铁已非梦想,在 20 世纪末,我国西南交通大学已研制成功了高温超导磁浮车辆模型"世纪号"。

In the production of superconducting magnets, it is necessary to develop and commercialize room-temperature superconducting materials with smaller shapes and higher efficiency. In 1986, IBM's research Institute announced the existence of ceramic superconductors, and later discovered new materials that produce superconductivity at higher temperatures. When the temperature of liquid nitrogen reaches －196 ℃, it is no longer a dream to develop high-temperature superconducting magnets for maglev trains. At the end of the 20th century, Southwest Jiaotong University in China has successfully developed a high-temperature superconducting maglev vehicle model "Century".

十、失超问题也有所改善

3.4.10　The Problem of Quench Gas Also Been Improved

由于日本超导磁浮没有冗余,为了保证磁浮列车的使用效率,就要求超导磁体具有很高的可靠性。超导磁体的失超问题是影响列车能否正常运行的关键问题。

Because there is no redundancy in the superconducting maglev in Japan, in order to ensure the efficiency of the maglev train, the superconducting magnet is required to have high reliability. The quench of the superconducting magnet is a key problem that affects the normal operation of the train.

所谓失超(Quench)现象,是指安装车辆上的磁铁在运行中由于振动及摩擦而发热,进而丧失磁力的现象,也称为失磁现象。

The so-called Quench phenomenon refers to the phenomenon that the magnet installed on the vehicle is heated due to vibration and friction during operation, and then loses magnetic force, also known as demagnetization phenomenon.

在以往的试验运行中一直存在的失超问题有了大幅度改善。技术人员与绕组制造商协力进行了巨型计算机模拟、电磁加振等试验,经过近十年的研究发现了失超现象的发生机制,从根本上消除了失超的可能性。超导磁体平均无故障工作时间已达到 10 万小时。

The problem of quench, which has always existed in previous test runs, has been greatly improved. Technicians and winding manufacturers have worked together to carry out supercomputer simulation, electromagnetic vibration and other tests. After nearly a decade of research, the mechanism of quench phenomenon has been found, which fundamentally eliminates the possibility of quench. The average fault-free working time of superconducting magnets has reached 100,000 hours.

通过进一步选优绕组材料、改善结构、采用新的绕组固定措施，使绕组的耐振性能提高了 8 倍以上，发热量减少到原来的 1/10。山梨试验线的试验车安装了三家公司提供的依赖性更高的超导磁铁，到目前为止均未出现失超现象。失超现象的解决，使超导磁浮铁路向实用化的目标迈进了一大步。

Through further optimization of winding material, improvement of structure and adoption of new winding fixing measures, the vibration resistance of the winding is improved by more than 8 times, and the calorific value is reduced to 1/10 of the original. The test vehicle on the Yamanashi test line is equipped with more dependent superconducting magnets provided by three companies, and so far there has been no quench phenomenon. The solution of the quench phenomenon makes the superconducting maglev railway a big step towards the goal of practical application.

十一、制动装置

3.4.11 Braking Device

对所有运输工具而言，制动功能特别重要。试验车辆的制动装置为常用的电力再生制动装置。为保障从超高速到停车的各级速度范围都具有稳定的制动力，车上还装有两类制动装置。

The braking function is particularly important for all means of transport. The braking device of the test vehicle is the commonly used electric regenerative braking device. In order to ensure stable braking force at all speeds from ultra-high-speed to parking, the vehicle is also equipped with two types of braking devices.

车轮盘型制动（disk brake）使用轻量 C/C 复合材料（碳素纤维/碳素树脂复合材料），制动盘的能量吸收能力很高。这种制动装置可以进行全自动制动（控制减速度不变）以及防抱死（anti-skid）制动（检测到车轮滑动时减弱制动力，当滑动停止后恢复原来的控制）。

The disk brake uses a lightweight C/C composite material (carbon fiber/carbon resin composite material), and the brake disk has a high energy absorption capacity. This braking device can perform fully automatic braking (control the deceleration unchanged) and anti-skid braking (reduce the braking force when the wheel slip is detected, and restore the original control when the slip stops).

另外一类为空气翼制动。在车体上部向上竖立空气制动翼（或称空气制动板），平常它不向外伸出，当需要空气制动时它伸向上部，产生空气阻力。这与飞机主翼上的制动系统类似，在高速行驶时制动力很大。

The other is air wing braking. An air brake wing (or air brake plate) is erected upwards on the upper part of the vehicle body, and normally, the air brake wing does not extend outwards, and when air braking is needed, the air brake wing extends upwards to generate air resistance. This is similar to the braking system on the main wing of an aircraft, which has a large braking force at high speed.

此外还有紧急制动系统，如绕组短路制动、发电制动等。

In addition, there are emergency braking systems, such as winding short circuit braking, power generation braking, etc.

十二、障碍物排除装置

3.4.12　Obstacle Removal Device

障碍物排除装置指列车与障碍物相撞时防止车体损坏的缓冲器（bumper）。它不但吸收碰撞时的能量，还能借助缓冲材料的变形将障碍物带走。

The obstacle removal device refers to a bumper that prevents the vehicle body from being damaged when the train collides with an obstacle. It not only absorbs the energy of collision, but also takes away the obstacles with the help of the deformation of the buffer material.

第五节　供电及控制

Section 3.5　Power Supply and Control

本节主要介绍日本超导磁浮铁路的供电系统，包括变电站、变流器、运行控制系统及控制中心。

This section mainly introduces the power supply system of superconducting maglev railway in Japan, including substation, converter, operation control system and control center.

一、变电站

3.5.1 Substation

试验线专用变电站占地面积 35 000 m², 内有接收电力设备及变电设备, 于 1995 年 10 月在都留市小形山建成, 由东京电力公司供电。接收电力设备为双路(常用、备用), 电压为 154 kV, 主变压器的容量为 60 MV·A (东海道新干线为 100 MV·A), 故主变压器完全满足列车行驶要求, 将送来的 154 kV 电压降为 66 kV。因为是双路供电, 所以可以确保用电需要。

The special substation for the test line covers an area of 35,000 m², with receiving power equipment and substation equipment. It was built in October 1995 in Ogata Mountain, Tsuru City, and supplied power from Tokyo Electric Power Company. The receiving power equipment is two-way (common and standby), the voltage is 154 kV, the capacity of the main transformer is 60 MV·A (100 MV·A for Tokaido Shinkansen), so the main transformer fully meets the requirements of train running, and the voltage of 154 kV is reduced to 66 kV. Because of two-way power supply. So that the need for electricity can be ensured.

超导磁浮铁路的变电站与普通铁路的变电站不同, 需按列车运行控制要求及时改变输入电流及频率, 使磁浮列车严格按照设定程序自动行驶, 实现列车无人驾驶运行, 同时使列车能准确地停在指定的位置。这样的电力转换由新开发的世界最大级别的变流器控制单元完成。该变流器单元主要由整流器、中间直流环节和逆变器组成, 构成"交-直-交"形式的变流结构。即先通过整流器将交流电转换为直流电, 然后再经逆变器将该直流电变换为频率、幅值和相位可控的三相交流电, 经输出变压器提供给行驶中的列车。

The substation of superconducting maglev railway is different from the substation of ordinary railway. It needs to change the input current and frequency in time according to the requirements of train operation control, so that the maglev train can run automatically in strict accordance with the set program, realize the driverless operation of the train, and at the same time make the train stop accurately at the designated location. Such power conversion is completed by the newly developed world's largest converter control unit. The converter unit is mainly composed of a rectifier, an intermediate DC link and an inverter, forming an AC-DC-AC type converter structure. That is to say, the AC is converted into DC by the rectifier, and then the DC is converted into three-phase AC with controllable frequency, amplitude and phase by the inverter, which is provided to the running train through the output transformer.

超导磁浮铁路的轨道没有控制信号(轨道电路)。因此, 为保证列车安全准确地运行, 将驱动绕组按一定间隔分段(试验线的间隔为 453 m, 将来商用运营线路的间隔为 40～50 m），按列车的位置切换供电开关，确保前后列车的运行安全。此供电系统（三重供电回路）在山梨试验线得到应用。

The track of the superconducting maglev railway has no control signal (track circuit). Therefore, in order to ensure the safe and accurate operation of the train, the drive winding is divided into sections according to a certain interval (the interval of the test line is 453 m, and the interval of the future commercial operation line is 40-50 m), and the power supply switch is switched according to the position of the train to ensure the safe operation of the front and rear trains. This power supply system (triple power supply circuit) has been applied in the Yamanashi test line.

二、变流器

3.5.2 Converter

山梨试验线南、北线分别装有 3 组变流器，提供 20 MV·A、38 MV·A 的电力。该变流器将电力公司提供的商用频率的电力转换为控制列车速度所需要的频率。为了调节列车的运行速度，北线变流器提供的电力频率范围为 0～56 Hz，对应的列车速度为 0～550 km/h，南线的频率范围为 0～46 Hz，对应的列车速度为 0～450 km/h。

The south and north lines of the Yamanashi Test Line are respectively equipped with 3 sets of converter, providing 20 MV·A and 38 MV·A power. The converter converts the commercial frequency power provided by the power company to the frequency required to control the speed of the train. In order to regulate the running speed of the train, the frequency range of the power supplied by the converter of the north line is 0-56 Hz, corresponding to the train speed of 0-550 km/h; the frequency range of the south line is 0-46 Hz, corresponding to the train speed of 0-450 km/h.

变流器的控制过程：根据控制中心的运行管理系统先生成运行曲线，根据这个运行曲线的指示，再通过变电站的驱动控制系统控制变流器的动作。

The control process of the converter is as follows: the operation curve is generated according to the operation management system of the control center, and then the action of the converter is controlled by the drive control system of the substation according to the indication of the operation curve.

三、非接触式供电形式

3.5.3 Form of Non-contact Power Supply

处于超导状态的超导磁铁一旦通电后将半永久性地流动不息，行驶时没有必要像普通电力机车那样从外部供电。但列车运行时，车内的照明、空调等电气设备也需要大量电力。对于超高速磁浮铁路，这种电力不可能像城市轨道交通那样靠供电轨或架空线提供，只能采用无接触供电方式。众所周知，旋转电机可以改造成发电机，与此原理相同，磁浮铁路使用导轨磁铁也可以在车辆绕组产生感应电流，用这种感应电流可以为车内电气设备供电。这种供电方式称为非接触车内供电形式，也称为感应发电装置。其原理及结构见图 3-10 和图 3-11。

Once the superconducting magnet in the superconducting state is electrified, it will flow semi-permanently, and there is no need to supply power from the outside like ordinary electric locomotives. However, when the train is running, the lighting, air conditioning and other electrical equipment in the train also need a lot of electricity. For ultra-high-speed maglev railway, this kind of power can not be provided by power rail or overhead line like urban rail transit, but can only be supplied by contactless power supply. As we all know, the rotary motor can be transformed into a generator. In the same principle, the maglev railway can also generate induced current in the vehicle winding by using guide rail magnets, which can be used to supply power to the electrical equipment in the vehicle. This kind of power supply mode is called non-contact in-car power supply mode, also known as induction power generation device. See Figure 3-10 and Figure 3-11 for its principle and structure.

车辆静止时，可以使用车载蓄电池保证电能供应。车载蓄电池可载列车运行过程中从超导磁铁接收的电力充电，无须与其他物体接触，电力使用效率特别高。

When the vehicle is stationary, the on-board battery can be used to ensure the power supply. The on-board storage battery can be charged by the electric power received from the superconducting magnet during the operation of the train without contacting with other objects, and the electric power utilization efficiency is particularly high.

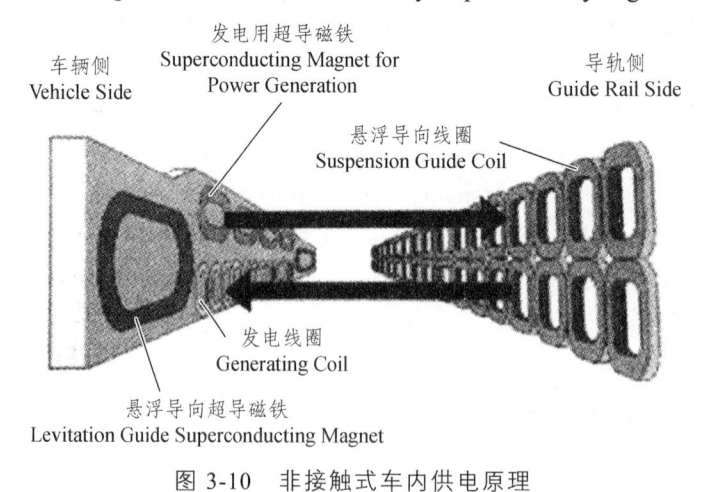

图 3-10　非接触式车内供电原理

Figure 3-10　Schematic diagram of non-contact power supply in the vehicle

悬浮导向用超导磁铁
Superconducting Magnet for Suspension Guidance

感应发电超导磁铁
Induction Power Superconducting Magnet

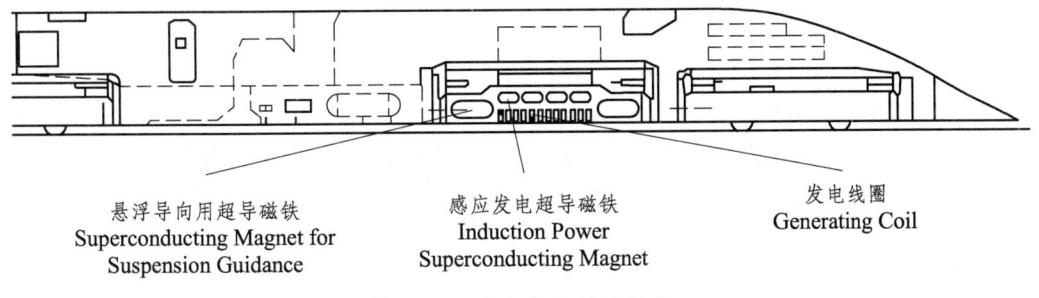

发电线圈
Generating Coil

图 3-11　感应发电装置结构

Figure 3-11　Structure of induction power generation device

四、运行控制系统

3.5.4　Operation Control System

超导磁浮铁路控制系统的总体结构可以分为三个子系统：集中控制子系统、沿线分散的控制子系统和移动的车上控制子系统。

The overall structure of the control system of superconducting maglev railway can be divided into three subsystems: centralized control subsystem, distributed control subsystem along the line and mobile control subsystem on the train.

集中控制子系统即控制中心，控制和监视整个线路和运行设备。

The centralized control subsystem, namely the control center, controls and monitors the entire line and operating equipment.

沿线路分散的控制子系统的分段与变电站的供电区段一致，控制和监测相应的供电区段的线路和磁浮列车的运行情况。分散控制子系统受控制中心控制，并实现与移动子系统的通信。磁浮列车的运行是由地面自动控制的。此外，在变电站还设有地震监测预报装置。

The sections of the control subsystem distributed along the line are consistent with the power supply sections of the substation to control and monitor the operation of the line and the maglev train in the corresponding power supply sections. The decentralized control subsystem is controlled by the control center and communicates with the mobile subsystem. The operation of the maglev train is automatically controlled from the ground. In addition, the substation is also equipped with an earthquake monitoring and prediction device.

磁浮列车上移动的控制子系统对车上的重要设备和系统进行监控。在紧急情况下，车上的控制系统应具有不依赖线路牵引系统和线路侧控制系统独立实现安全保护功能。

The mobile control subsystem on the maglev train monitors and controls the important equipment and systems on the train. In case of emergency, the control system on the train shall have the function of realizing safety protection independently of the line traction system and the line side control system.

移动子系统与沿线路的子系统之间，通过漏泄同轴电缆或无线电毫米波通信。漏泄同轴电缆敷设在线路"U"形槽侧壁顶部。目前这两种通信方式均在试验。车辆的定位和测速采用交叉感应回线。车上设有发射天线，发射一定频率的脉冲信号，沿线路凹槽底部中心有6股每隔45 cm交叉一次的感应回线，能感应车上天线发出的脉冲信号，由此可确定磁浮列车的行驶方向、位移和速度。列车与线路间的安全信号也通过交叉感应回线来传输。此外，在线路上每隔400 m还设有标明线路绝对位置的编码标志，磁浮列车经过时，可得到磁浮列车相对线路的绝对位置，并由此校正交叉感应回线定位系统通过相对技术可能产生的累计定位误差。

Mobile subsystems communicate with subsystems along the line via leaky coaxial cables or radio millimeter waves. The leaky coaxial cable is laid on the top of the side wall of the "U" shaped groove of the line. At present, both communication modes are being tested. Cross induction loop is used for vehicle positioning and speed measurement. The train is equipped with a transmitting antenna to transmit a pulse signal of a certain frequency. Along the center of the bottom of the line groove, there are six induction loops crossing every 45 cm, which can sense the pulse signal sent by the antenna on the train, thus determining the direction, displacement and speed of the maglev train. The safety signal between the train and the line is also transmitted through the cross induction loop. In addition, there are coding marks indicating the absolute position of the line every 400 m on the line. When the maglev train passes by, the absolute position of the maglev train relative to the line can be obtained, and the cumulative positioning error that may be generated by the cross induction loop positioning system through the relative technology can be corrected.

五、试验中心

3.5.5　Test Center

超导磁悬浮列车无人驾驶，它的起动、加速、高速行驶、减速、停止、开关车门、上下车装置的操作均由设在地面的运行控制中心自动控制。

The superconducting maglev train is driverless, and its starting, acceleration, high-speed running, deceleration, stopping, door opening and closing, and operation of getting on and off the train are automatically controlled by the operation control center on the ground.

复习思考题

Questions for Revision

1. 日本磁浮铁路技术发展经过哪几个发展阶段？

1. What are the development stages of maglev railway technology in Japan?

2. 简要介绍日本山梨试验线及侧壁悬浮形式的意义。

2. Briefly introduce the significance of the Yamanashi test line and the suspension form of the side wall.

3. 总结日本超导磁浮铁路的基本工作原理。

3. Summarize the basic working principle of superconducting maglev railway in Japan.

4. 简要介绍山梨试验线所使用车辆的结构及制动装置。

4. Briefly introduce the structure and braking device of the cars used on the Yamanashi Test Line.

5. 简要介绍山梨线路所使用超导磁浮铁路的供电形式。

5. Briefly introduce the power supply form of superconducting maglev railway used in Yamanashi Line.

第四章　德国常导超高速磁浮铁路技术

Chapter 4　Technology of Normal Conducting Ultra-high-speed Maglev Railway in Germany

与超导磁浮相对应，世界著名的磁浮铁路技术还有常导技术。本章简要介绍采用常导技术的德国超高速磁浮铁路运捷 TR（Trans Rapid）技术。德国常导磁浮系统 TR 与日本超导磁浮系统 ML 一样，同是超高速铁路，但在具体实现方面，两者却有很大的不同。

Corresponding to the superconducting maglev, the world famous maglev railway technology also has the normal conductor technology. This chapter briefly introduces the TR (Trans Rapid) technology of German ultra-high speed maglev railway, which adopts the normal conductor technology. The German normal magnetic levitation system (TR) and the Japanese superconducting magnetic levitation system (ML) are both ultra-high-speed railway, but they are quite different in terms of specific implementation.

第一节　概　述

Section 4.1　Overview

在传统轮轨系统铁路中，支承和导向、加速和制动是靠轮轨接触实现的。采用传统轮轨接触的铁路技术在过去的一百多年中已经有了很大的发展，现在日本的新干线、法国的 TGV、德国的 ICE 和我国的高速铁路都在高速铁路领域内取得了辉煌的成就。而轮轨接触原理始终没有改变。由于技术上和经济上的限制，轮轨高速铁路的速度发展已接近极限。为了达到更高的速度范围（350～550 km/h），为了获得比传统技术更好的经济效益及社会效益，为了更有利于环境保护，需要一种更新、更好的技术。这就是：以采用无接触的电磁悬浮、导向和驱动系统的磁浮铁路技术取代传统的轮轨接触的铁路技术。

In traditional railway with wheel/rail system, support and guidance, acceleration and braking are realized by wheel/rail contact. Railway technology with traditional wheel-rail contact has been greatly developed in the past 100 years. Now Japan's Shinkansen, France's TGV, Germany's ICE and China's high-speed railway have made brilliant achievements in the field of high-speed railway. The principle of wheel-rail contact remains unchanged. Due to technical and economic constraints, the speed development of wheel/rail high speed railway is close to the limit. In order to achieve a higher speed range (350-550 km/h), in order to achieve better economic and social benefits than traditional technologies, and in order to be more environmentally friendly, a newer and better technology is needed. This is to replace the traditional railway technology of wheel-rail contact with the maglev railway technology of non-contact electromagnetic suspension, guidance and drive system.

德国的长大干线型磁浮铁路运捷 TR 技术，是由德国政府和民营企业共同开发的。本节主要介绍该技术在德国的发展情况。

The TR technology of the long trunk maglev railway in Germany is jointly developed by the German government and private enterprises. This section mainly introduces the development of this technology in Germany.

一、德国与日本之间的实用化竞争

4.1.1　Practical Competition between Germany and Japan

1922 年，德国的赫尔曼·肯佩尔博士提出了电磁悬浮理论，拟采用真空隧道技术实现 1 000 km/h 的速度。1934 年，他申请了"无轮车辆悬浮铁路"专利。一年之后，他还提出了原型车辆，提出了以电磁引力控制方式为基础的磁浮铁路的概念，展示该系统的承载能力（承载能力为 210 kg）。

In 1922, Dr. Hermann Kemper of Germany proposed the theory of electromagnetic levitation to achieve a speed of 1,000 km/h by using vacuum tunnel technology. In 1934, he applied for a patent for "suspension railway without wheels". A year later, he also proposed a prototype vehicle and the concept of a maglev railway based on electromagnetic gravity control, demonstrating the carrying capacity of the system (210 kg).

1962 年，日本开始直线电机驱动、悬浮铁路的研究；1966 年，美国 Brook Heaven 研究所的鲍威尔、达比两位博士宣布进行超导磁浮列车的技术开发；随后，美国、日本、德国、法国、英国等国家的研究机构及研究人员相继开始了研究开发工作。但在后来的相当长的一段时间内，除日本和德国之外的其他国家基本停止了有关基础研究及系统开发，这样日本和德国在磁浮铁路的实用化技术方面赢得了领先地位。

In 1962, Japan started the research on linear motor drive and suspension railway; in

1966, Drs. Powell and Darby of Brook Heaven Research Institute in the United States announced the technical development of superconducting maglev train; subsequently, research institutions and researchers in the United States, Japan, Germany, France, Britain and other countries started the research and development work one after another. However, for quite a long period of time, other countries except Japan and Germany basically stopped the basic research and system development, so Japan and Germany won the leading position in the practical technology of maglev railway.

日本航空从德国（当时的联邦德国）的克劳斯玛菲公司引进基础技术，开发出短程磁浮列车 HSST，在横滨博览会等地进行载客运行，运输省认为可以作为客运营业线使用，并且发行了营业许可证。现在，HSST 已经进入实用化阶段，在 JR 东海道线的大船站—横滨梦之地之间着手建设营业线路。但是，HSST 属于中低速磁浮的范畴，适合于中短距离的城市轨道交通。

Japan Airlines introduced basic technology from KraussMaffei Company of Germany (Federal Republic of Germany at that time) and developed a short-distance maglev train HSST, which carried passengers in Yokohama Expo and other places. The Ministry of Transport considered that it could be used as a passenger business line and issued a business license. Now, HSST has entered the practical stage, starting to build a business line between Ofuna Station and Yokohama Dream Land on the JR Tokaido Line. However, HSST belongs to the category of medium and low speed maglev, which is suitable for medium and short distance urban rail transit.

在中长距离超高速磁浮铁路方面，之前主要介绍了 ML 系统，目前该技术已经基本成熟，已经达到实用化的程度。德国的 TR 系统也已经完成实用化试验，技术基本成熟。目前，两国在磁悬浮方面的竞争仍然在激烈地进行着。

In the aspect of medium and long distance ultra-high speed maglev railway, the ML system was mainly introduced before. At present, the technology has been basically mature and has reached the practical level. The German TR system has also completed the practical test, and the technology is basically mature. At present, the competition between the two countries in maglev is still going on fiercely.

二、TR 系统的发展过程

4.1.2　The Development Process of TR System

德国磁浮高速铁路的主要研究发展工作是从 1966 年开始的。最初有 3 个发展方向：导轨驱动长定子直线电机斥力电动悬浮系统（EDS）、列车驱动短定子直线电机吸力电磁悬浮系统（EMS）和导轨驱动长定子直线电机吸力电磁悬浮系统（TR），如图 4-1 所示。

The main research and development work of German maglev high-speed railway began in 1966. Initially, there are three development directions: guideway-driven long-stator linear motor repulsion electrodynamic suspension system (EDS), train-driven short-stator linear motor attraction electromagnetic suspension system (EMS), and guideway-driven long-stator linear motor attraction electromagnetic suspension system (TR), as shown in Figure 4-1.

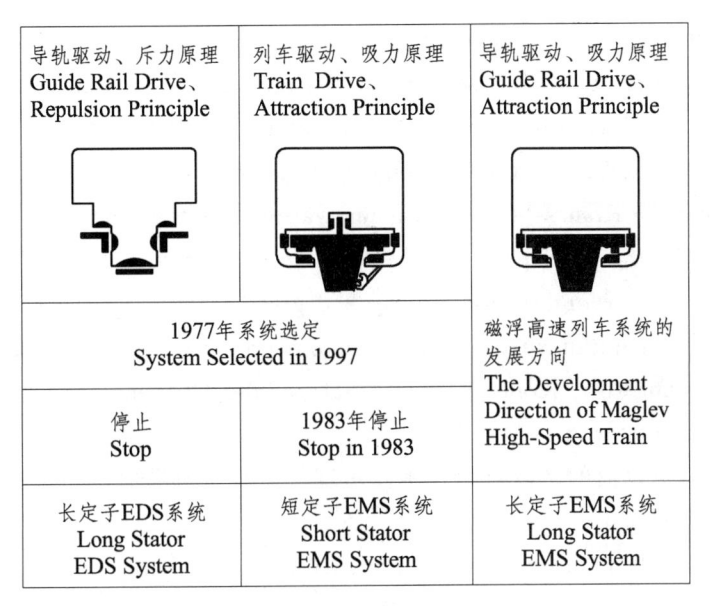

图 4-1 德国 TR 系统的发展过程

Figure 4-1 The Development of TR System in Germany

（一）短定子直线电机列车驱动技术

4.1.2.1 Train Driving Technology of Short Stator Linear Motor

1969 年，原联邦德国运输部长 Georg Leber 授权进行高速铁路研究（High-Speed Railway Study，HSB），目的之一是确认何种形式的交通工具能最好地适应运量的增长。同年，克劳斯玛菲公司（KraussMaffei）采用短定子列车驱动技术，制造出了运捷 01（Transrapid 01，简称 TR01）号磁浮试验车。该项研究于 1972 年结束。

In 1969, Georg Leber, the former Federal Minister of Transport of Germany, authorized the High-Speed Railway Study (HSB), one of the purposes of which was to determine what form of transport could best accommodate the growth of traffic volume. In the same year, Krauss-Maffei manufactured the Transrapid 01 (TR01) maglev test car using the short stator train drive technology. The study was completed in 1972.

1971 年 2 月，梅塞施密特-伯尔考-布洛姆公司（Messerschmitt-Bolkow-Blohm，MBB）在典托布化工厂厂区的试验线路上展示了第一台基于电磁悬浮 EMS 技术载人原型车辆 MBB,该车空车质量 4.8 t,有 4 个座位,在 660 m 长的轨道上已达到 90 km/h 的速度。同年,克劳斯-马菲公司研制出的 TR02 号磁浮试验车投入试验,试验速度达到 164 km/h。1972 年,高速铁路研究计划结束,研究结果表明,高速铁路对国家经济发展具有巨大利益,这种形式的磁浮铁路的运行速度可以达到 400 km/h。在进一步的开发工作中,克劳斯-马菲公司于 1974 年研制出短定子直线电机驱动的 TR04 磁浮车。

In February 1971, Messerschmitt-Bolkow-Blohm (MBB) demonstrated the first manned prototype vehicle MBB based on electromagnetic levitation EMS technology on the test line of Diantobu Chemical Plant, with an empty mass of 4.8 t and four seats. A speed of 90 km/h has been reached on a 660 m long track. In the same year, the TR02 maglev test vehicle developed by Krauss-Maffei Company was put into test, and the test speed reached 164 km/h. In 1972, the high-speed railway research program was terminated. The research results showed that the high-speed railway had great benefits for the national economic development. The operation speed of this form of maglev railway could reach 400 km/h. In further development work, Krauss-Maffei developed the TR04 maglev vehicle driven by a short-stator linear motor in 1974.

德国 TR04 及以前的磁浮铁路技术以短定子直线电机牵引、司机控制列车运行为主,以中低速运行为主。

The maglev railway technology of German TR04 and previous ones is mainly based on short-stator linear motor traction and driver-controlled train operation, mainly at medium and low speed.

(二) 长定子直线电机导轨驱动技术

4.1.2.2 Long Stator Linear Motor Guideway Drive Technology

1975 年,蒂森-亨舍尔公司(Thyssen-Henschel)在卡塞尔(Kassel)的工厂的 HMB 试验线上率先研制成功了在线路上安设长定子线圈的直线同步电机驱动的磁浮车辆 HMB1,车重 2.5 t,有 4 个座位,最高速度 36 km/h。这一试验系统,将直线驱动和悬浮支承结合起来,奠定了今天的 TR 磁浮高速铁路发展的基础。

In 1975, Thyssen-Henschel took the lead in developing a maglev vehicle HMB1 driven by a linear synchronous motor with a long stator coil on the HMB test line in Kassel. The vehicle weighs 2.5 t, has four seats, and has a maximum speed of 36 km/h. This test system, which combines linear drive and suspension support, has laid the foundation for the development of today's TR maglev high-speed railway.

1976 年,蒂森-亨舍尔公司研制了第一辆长定子载人磁浮车辆"彗星号"HMB2。首次证明磁浮车辆的运行速度可以超过 400 km/h。

In 1976, Thyssen-Heischer developed the first long-stator manned maglev vehicle, the "Comet" HMB2. For the first time, it has been demonstrated that maglev vehicles can operate at speeds in excess of 400 km/h.

1977年，德国联邦科研部经过系统比较，选定第三种方案（长定子 EMS）作为磁浮超高速铁路系统的研究发展方向。之后，原联邦德国政府将主要精力用在长定子直线电机导轨驱动磁浮铁路的研究方面。德国 TR05 及以后的研究均以长定子直线电机牵引、控制中心控制列车运行为主，并以高速、超高速运行为主。

In 1977, the German Federal Ministry of Scientific Research selected the third scheme (long stator EMS) as the research and development direction of maglev ultra-high speed railway system after systematic comparison. After that, the former Federal Republic of Germany government focused on the research of long stator linear motor guideway driving maglev railway. German TR05 and its later researches are mainly based on long stator linear motor traction and control center control train operation, and mainly on high-speed and ultra-high-speed operation.

（三）汉堡国际交通博览会磁浮示范线

4.1.2.3　Hamburg International Transport Expo Maglev Demonstration Line

1979年在汉堡国际交通博览会上，TR05 载人试验车首次面世。该车长 26 m，重 30.8 t，有 68 个座位，在 908 m 长的线路上表演运行，并在 3 周的时间内按时刻表运送了 5 万名参观者，平均速度 75 km/h，极大地推动了德国磁浮超高速运输系统的发展。

In 1979, the TR05 manned test vehicle was first introduced at the Hamburg International Transport Fair. With a length of 26 m, a weight of 30.8 t, and a seating capacity of 68, the vehicle performed on a route of 908 m and transported 50,000 visitors on schedule over a period of three weeks at an average speed of 75 km/h, which greatly promoted the development of the German maglev ultra-high-speed transportation system.

（四）艾姆斯兰试验线（TVE）

4.1.2.4　Amsland Test Line (TVE)

汉堡国际交通博览会取得成功后，德国联邦研究部当年宣布，为了在实际运行的条件下测试电磁悬浮技术，将在埃姆斯兰（Emsland）地区的拉滕建设大型试验设施。1980年开发了 TR06 试验车，同时开始建设埃姆斯兰运捷试验设施（TVE）。

After the success of the Hamburg International Transport Expo, the German Federal Ministry of Research announced that in order to test electromagnetic levitation technology under actual operating conditions, a large-scale test facility would be built in Ratten,

Emsland. In 1980, the TR06 test vehicle was developed and the construction of the Emsland Express Test Facility (TVE) began.

1981年在原联邦研究与科技部的基础上，由德国铁路、汉莎航空公司、原联邦德国政府的研究机构共同组建了磁浮试验与规划公司（MVP，总部设在慕尼黑）。MVP由汉莎航空公司和德国铁路集团共同平等经营。第三方的伙伴IABG被委托进行系统试验。

In 1981, on the basis of the former Federal Ministry of Research and Technology, the Maglev Test and Planning Company (MVP, headquartered in Munich) was jointly established by Deutsche Bahn, Lufthansa Airlines and the research institutes of the former Federal German Government. MVP is jointly and equally operated by Lufthansa and Deutsche Bahn AG. The third party's partner, the IABG, was commissioned to conduct the system trial.

第一期工程包括21.5 km的试验线路、试验中心和试验车TR06。1983年6月30日，德国的长定子直线电机驱动的第一个原型车运捷TR06在刚完工的埃姆斯兰试验线TVE第一期工程上开始试验。TR06原型车由两节车辆组成，总长54 m，空车重103 t，有192个座位。

The first phase of the project includes 21.5 km of test line, test center and test vehicle TR06. On June 30, 1983, the first prototype vehicle driven by a long stator linear motor in Germany, TR06, began testing on the first phase of the TVE project of the newly completed Emsland test line. The TR06 prototype consists of two vehicles with a total length of 54 m, an empty weight of 103 t and 192 seats.

为了提高试验速度，1984年决定扩建南环线。1987年，埃姆斯兰试验线第二期工程（南环线）投入使用，这标志着可以循环运行的全长31.5 km的"8"字形的试验线可以开始进行长久的运行试验。1988年，TR06的试验速度达到412.6 km/h。

In order to increase the speed of the test, it was decided to expand the South Link in 1984. In 1987, the second phase of the Emsland Test Line (South Link Line) was put into operation, which marked that the 31.5 km "8" -shaped test line, which can be operated cyclically, could begin to carry out long-term operation tests. In 1988, the TR06 reached a test speed of 412.6 km/h.

1986年开始，Thyssen Henschel公司牵头研制面向应用的TR07列车。1988年，TR07在埃姆斯兰试验线开始运行，该车由两节车辆组成，长51 m，空车重92 t，最高速度500 km/h。

Since 1986, Thyssen Henschel has led the development of TR07 trains for applications. In 1988, the TR07 began operating on the Emsland test line, consisting of two cars, 51 m long, with an empty weight of 92 t and a maximum speed of 500 km/h.

（五）TR 技术走向应用

4.1.2.5 The Application of TR Technology

德国联邦铁路中心局经过近两年的评价和鉴定，于 1991 年年底在慕尼黑证实，运捷的整体系统已经达到了技术成熟的程度。

After nearly two years of evaluation and appraisal, the German Federal Railway Central Bureau confirmed in Munich at the end of 1991 that the overall system of TR has reached the level of technical maturity.

1993 年 3 月，在普通环境下，TR07 的载人试验速度达到 450 km/h，刷新了当时的世界纪录。1997 年，德国决定建造柏林至汉堡之间长 292 km 的磁浮铁路，原定 1998 年下半年开工，2005 年投入商业运行。为此开发拟用于该线的 TR08 型磁浮列车。

In March, 1993, under ordinary environment, the manned test speed of TR07 reached 450 km/h, setting a new world record at that time. In 1997, Germany decided to build a 292 km maglev railway between Berlin and Hamburg, which was originally scheduled to start in the second half of 1998 and put into commercial operation in 2005. Therefore, the TR08 maglev train to be used in this line is developed.

1999 年 9 月，TR08 车头试制完成并在埃姆斯兰试验线投入运行，该车总长 18.8 m，宽 3.7 m，高 4.2 m，客车空重 53 t/节，货车空重 48 t/节，货车有效荷载 15 t/节，座位数两端车最多 92 个，中间车最多 127 个，最高运行速度 500 km/h。采用 3 辆编组列车的最高速度达到 406 km/h。

In September, 1999, the trial production of TR08 headstock was completed and put into operation on Emslan test line. The total length, width and height of TR08 are 18.8 m, 3.7 m and 4.2 m, the empty weight of passenger cars is 53 t/vehicle, the empty weight of freight cars is 48 t/vehicle, the effective load of freight cars is 15 t/vehicle, the maximum number of seats is 92 at both ends, the maximum number of middle cars is 127, the maximum running speed is 500 km/h, and the maximum speed of three marshalling trains is 406 km/h.

2000 年 2 月，由于柏林至汉堡之间磁浮铁路原来预测的客流量偏大，新的预测表明建设新线将面临亏损的危险，德国政府宣布取消该线建设计划。

In February 2000, the German government announced the cancellation of the construction plan of the maglev railway between Berlin and Hamburg because the original forecast of passenger flow was too large, and the new forecast indicated that the construction of the new line would face the danger of losing money.

2000 年 6 月，中国上海市与德国磁浮国际公司合作进行中国高速磁浮列车示范运营线可行性研究。同年 12 月，中国决定建设上海浦东龙阳路地铁站至浦东国际机场的高速磁浮交通示范线。

In June, 2000, Shanghai of China cooperated with German Maglev International Company to carry out the feasibility study of China's high-speed maglev train demonstration operation line. In December of the same year, China decided to build a demonstration line of high-speed maglev transportation from Longyang Road subway station in Pudong, Shanghai, to Pudong International Airport.

2001年3月上海磁浮线正式开工建设,2002年12月31日,该线建成并顺利实现了单线试运行,列车运行速度达到430 km/h。

The construction of Shanghai Maglev Line was officially started in March 2001. In December 31, 2002, the line was completed and the single-line trial operation was successfully realized. The train speed reached 430 km/h.

三、德国政府与民间共同开发

4.1.3 The German Government and Private Jointly Develop

德国的试验车由多个公司在政府的支持下设立 TR 企业共同体制造,当时的磁浮铁路构想属于政府与民间一体的大型项目。

The test car in Germany was manufactured by TR Enterprise Community established by several companies with the support of the government. At that time, the idea of maglev railway was a large-scale project integrating the government and the private.

悬浮空中 1 cm 行驶的德国 TR 与日本的 HSST 一样采用常导电磁铁吸附形式,但驱动装置采用不需要车辆受电的直线同步电动机(LSM)。在使用 LSM 驱动的情况下,当电流被送入设置在导轨的磁铁时,车载发电机被驱动运转,达到将电力送到车辆的目的。因为采用吸附式磁场悬浮,即使停车时或低速行驶时,车辆也可保持悬浮状态,因此不用安装车轮。TR 的车辆与导轨断面见图 4-2,TR 的主要数据见表 4-1。

Like the HSST in Japan, the German TR travelling 1 cm in the air adopts the adsorption form of normally conductive magnets, but the driving device adopts linear synchronous motor (LSM) which does not need the vehicle to receive electricity. In the case of using LSM drive, when the current is sent to the magnet arranged on the guide rail, the vehicle-mounted generator is driven to operate, so as to achieve the purpose of sending electric power to the vehicle. Because the adsorption magnetic field suspension is adopted, the vehicle can maintain the suspension state even when stopping or running at low speed, so there is no need to install wheels. See Figure 4-2 for vehicle and guide rail section of TR, and Table 4-1 for main data of TR.

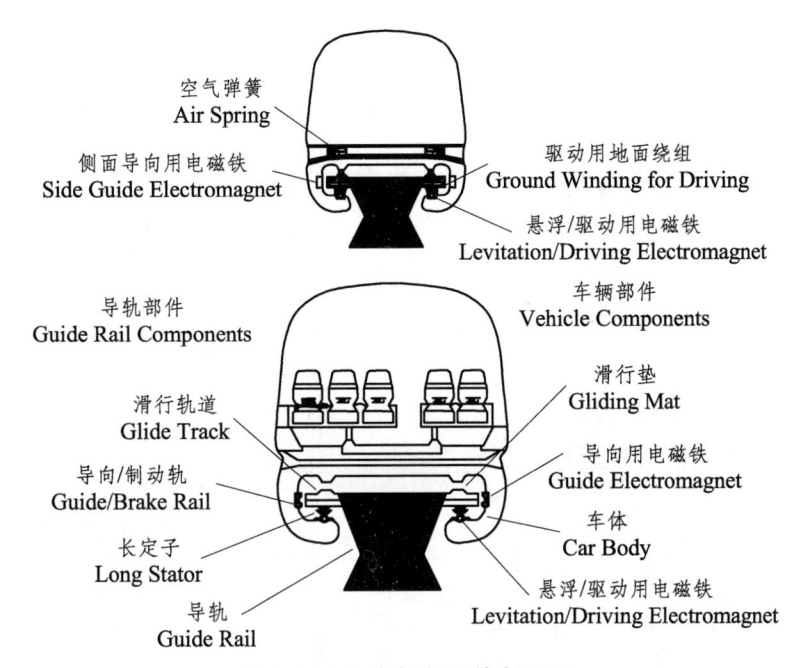

图 4-2 TR 车辆与导轨断面图

Figure 4-2　Section of TR Vehicle and Guideway

表 4-1　TR 的主要数据

Table 4-1　Main Data of TR

项目 Items			试验线（Emsland） Testline (Emsland)			营业线 Business Line
				TR06	TR07	TR08	
系统 System		支承形式 Support Form			吸附式磁力悬浮 EMS（驱动用电磁铁兼用） Adsorption Magnetic Levitation EMS (Drive Electromagnet)		
^		导向形式 Guide Form			吸附式磁力导向 Adsorptive Magnetic Guidance		
^		驱动形式 Driving Form			地面驱动直线同步电机（LSM） Ground Drive Linear Synchronous Motor (LSM)		
^		上下气隙/mm Upper and Lower Air Gap/mm			10		10
^		左右气隙/mm Left and Right Air Gap/mm			10		10
导轨 Guide rail		线路长度/km Length of the Route/km			31.5（两端为回环线） 31.5(The two Ends are Loop Lines)		40～50 km 以上 Above 40-50 km
^		曲线半径/m Radius of Curve/m			1 000（200 km/h）		400～500（最小值） 400-500(Minumum Value)
^		^			1 690（250 km/h）		4 000（400 km/h）

续表

项 目 Items		试验线（Emsland） Testline (Emsland)			营业线 Business Line
		TR06	TR07	TR08	
导轨 Guide rail	限制坡度/‰ Limiting Slope/‰	35			最大 100 Maximum 100
	轨道宽/m Track Width/m	2.8			2.8
列车 Train	最高速度/（km/h） Maximum Speed/(km/h)	400	450	406（1999 年） 406（in1999）	300-500
	车辆尺寸（长×宽×高）/m Vehicle Dimension (Length × Height × Width)/m	27.1×3.7×4.2			
	座席数/（人/列） Number of Seats/(Person/Line)	120	96	190	（72~100）×辆 （72-100）×Cars
	质量/（t/列） Mass/(t/Line)	125	113	200	39.4×辆 39.4×Car
	编组数/辆 Number of Marshalling/Car	2		3	2-8

德国政府及汉莎航空公司等有关企业对开发新型高速铁路表现积极，努力解决至今为止在基础试验、实用化试验中发现的问题，对磁浮铁路技术实现实用化更加充满信心。

The German government, Lufthansa Airlines and other relevant enterprises are active in the development of new high-speed railway, striving to solve the problems found in the basic and practical tests so far, and are more confident in the practical application of maglev railway technology.

第二节 基本原理

Section 4.2 Basic Principle

德国常导超高速磁浮铁路的基本原理与日本的 ML 大体相似，故本节只作简要介绍，主要包括悬浮原理、导向原理和驱动原理。

The basic principle of the conventional ultra-high-speed maglev railway in Germany is similar to that of the conventional ultra-high-speed maglev railway in Japan, so this section only gives a brief introduction, mainly including the suspension principle, the guiding principle and the driving principle.

一、悬浮原理

4.2.1 Suspension Principle

德国磁浮铁路的悬浮和导向系统是按照电磁悬浮 EMS 原理，即利用在车体底部的可控悬浮电磁铁和安装在导轨底面的反应轨（定子部件）之间的吸引力工作，悬浮磁铁从导轨下面利用吸引力使列车浮起，导向磁铁从侧面使车辆与轨道保持一定的侧向距离，保持运行轨迹。列车从头到尾都安装着支承磁铁和导向磁铁。每一节车辆拥有 15 个独立的悬浮磁铁和 13 个独立的导向磁铁。悬浮磁铁和导向磁铁安装在列车的两侧，沿列车全长分布，见图 4-3。

The levitation and guidance system of German maglev railway is based on the principle of electromagnetic levitation EMS, that is, it works by using the attraction between the controllable levitation electromagnet at the bottom of the car body and the reaction rail (stator component) installed at the bottom of the guide rail, and the levitation magnet uses the attraction to make the train float from below the guide rail. The guide magnet keeps a certain lateral distance between the vehicle and the track from the side to keep the running track. The train is equipped with support magnets and guide magnets from beginning to end. Each vehicle has 15 independent levitation magnets and 13 independent guide magnets. Levitation magnets and guide magnets are installed on both sides of the train and distributed along the full length of the train, as shown in Figure 4-3.

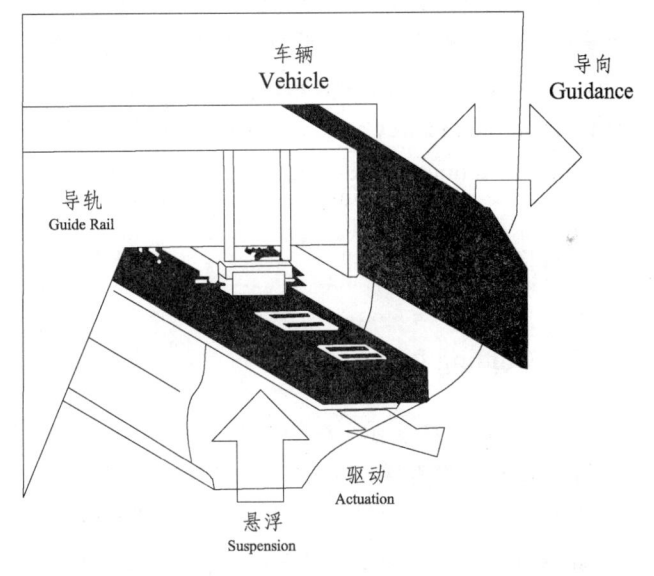

图 4-3 TR 工作原理

Figure 4 3 Operating principle of TR

高度可靠的电磁控制系统保证列车与轨道之间的平均悬浮间隙保持在 10 mm。轨道平面和列车底部之间的浮动距离是 15 cm，这样一来，列车在悬浮时可以翻越轨面上低于 15 cm 高的障碍物或积雪。悬浮高度控制原理见图 4-4。

The highly reliable electromagnetic control system ensures that the average suspension clearance between the train and the track is maintained at 10 mm, and the floating distance between the track level and the bottom of the train is 15 cm, so that the train can climb over obstacles or snow less than 15 cm high on the track level while suspending. The levitation height control principle is shown in Figure 4-4.

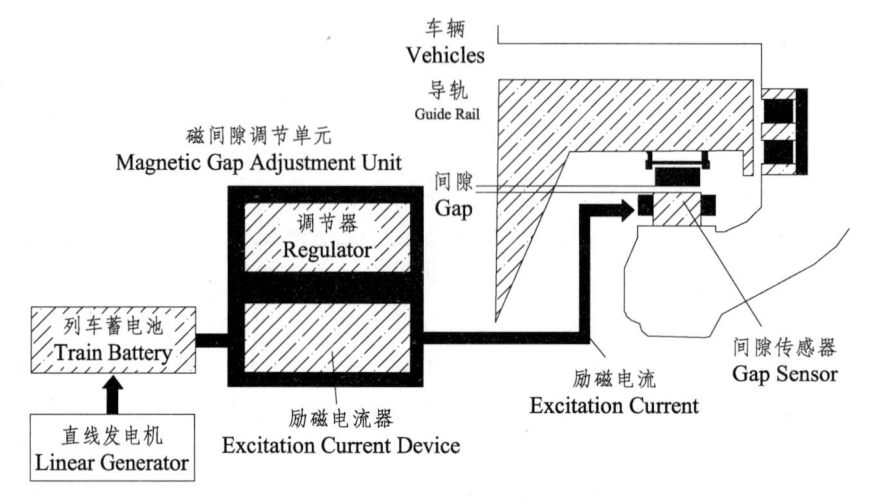

图 4-4　TR 悬浮高度控制原理

Figure 4-4　Schematic Diagram of TR Levitation Control

TR 磁浮列车的支承、导向和驱动系统是模块式的，有容许失效的冗余结构并配备自动诊断系统。这就保证个别部件的失效不会导致运行故障。

The support, guidance and drive systems of the TR maglev train are modular, with failure-tolerant redundancy and an automatic diagnostic system. This ensures that the failure of individual components does not result in operational failure.

二、导向原理

4.2.2　Guiding Principle

如图 4-2 和图 4-3 所示，在线路两侧垂直地布置有钢板（图中导向和制动钢轨），车辆两侧相应地布置有导向电磁铁，它与线路的钢板形成闭合磁路，电磁铁线圈通电后产生横向导向力，两边横向气隙均为 8～10 mm。

As shown in Figure 4-2 and Figure 4-3, steel plates (guide rails and brake rails) are arranged vertically on both sides of the line, and guiding electromagnets are correspondingly arranged on both sides of the vehicle, forming a closed magnetic circuit with the steel plates of the line. The electromagnet coil generates a transverse guiding force when energized, and the transverse air gap on both sides is 8-10 mm.

车辆正好在中心线位置时，两边气隙和横向电磁力相等，而方向相反，互相平衡；通过曲线时，车辆一旦产生横向位移偏差，位移传感器会检测其变化，通过控制系统改变左右两侧电磁铁线圈电流的大小，使气隙小的一侧电流减少，电磁吸力减少，而气隙大的一侧电流增加，电磁吸力增大，合成产生的导向恢复力与列车离心力相平衡，使得偏离中心线的车辆自动恢复到中心线位置。

When the vehicle is in the center line position, the air gap and transverse electromagnetic force on both sides are equal, but opposite, and balance each other. When passing the curve, once the vehicle produces lateral displacement deviation, the displacement sensor will detect its change, and change the size of the electromagnet coil current on both sides through the control system, so that the side with a small air gap reduces the current and electromagnetic suction, while the side with a large air gap increases the current and electromagnetic suction. The resultant steering restoring force is balanced with the centrifugal force of the train, so that the deviated vehicles automatically return to the center line position.

三、驱动原理

4.2.3　Driving Principle

超高速磁浮铁路的驱动和制动均靠长定子直线同步电机 LSM 实现。这个无接触的驱动和制动系统的工作原理类似于旋转电动机，它的定子被切开并在轨道下面沿两侧向前展直延伸（见图 4-5）。列车上的悬浮磁铁相当于电动机的转子（励磁元件）。直线电机的驱动部件，即具有三相行波场绕组的铁磁定子部件，不是安装在车上而是安装在导轨上，故称为导轨驱动的长定子同步直线电动机。

The driving and braking of ultra-high-speed maglev railway are realized by long stator linear synchronous motor LSM. The contactless drive and braking system works like a rotary motor, with its stator cut and stretched straight forward on both sides under the track (see Figure 4-5). The suspension magnet on the o train acts as the rotor (excitation element) of the motor. The driving parts of linear motor, namely the ferromagnetic stator parts with three-phase traveling wave field windings, are not installed on the car but on the guide rail, so it is called the long stator synchronous linear motor driven by the guide rail.

在三相 LSM 电动机地面绕组里，通过三相电流产生移动的电磁场，它作用于列车上的驱动磁铁，它产生的不再是旋转磁场，而是一个移动的行波磁场，从而带动列车前进。

In the ground winding of three-phase LSM motor, a moving electromagnetic field is generated by three-phase current, which acts on the driving magnet on the train. Instead of rotating magnetic field, it generates a moving traveling wave magnetic field, thus driving the train forward.

用逆变器改变交变电流的强度和频率可以在静止和运行之间无级调节驱动力，对列车从停车状态到最高运行速度进行无级调整。如果改变行波场的方向，将使电动机变成发电机，致使列车无接触制动。制动的能量可反馈回电网重新利用，进而实现再生制动。

By changing the intensity and frequency of the alternating current with the inverter, the driving force can be stepless adjusted between rest and running, and the train can be stepless adjusted from the stop state to the maximum running speed. If the direction of the traveling wave field is changed, the motor will become a generator, resulting in non-contact braking of the train. The braking energy can be fed back to the power grid for reuse, thus realizing regenerative braking.

图 4-5 TR 定子

Figure 4-5 TR stator

德国 TR 系统的悬浮、导向和驱动系统普遍装有冗余部件，同时装有自动化检测装置。当某个单独部件发生故障时，冗余部件立即接替工作。这样就保证了整个系统的运行不会因为出现单个故障而中断。在最不利的情况下，也只是功率受到限制而已。

The suspension, guidance and drive systems of German TR systems are generally equipped with redundant components and automatic detection devices.When a single component fails, the redundant component immediately takes over. This ensures that the operation of the entire system will not be interrupted by a single failure. In the most unfavorable case, only the power is limited.

导轨上的长定子直线电机由许多区段组成，每个区段的供电只是当列车经过时才被接通，两个相互独立的变电站分别将电网的电流从工作区段导轨电机两端输入，见图 4-6，这样可避免能量损失。变电站的距离和装机功率根据需求而定。在需要巨大牵引力的路段（如陡上坡、加速或者制动阶段），电机功率就设计得高于平缓的匀速行驶地段。而在传统交通系统中，列车电机必须全程按其最高功率供电，这在不需要最高功率的区段是不必要而且不经济的。从这个意义上讲，磁浮铁路比传统的轮轨接触铁路的能量利用率更高一些，限制坡度可以更陡一些。

—126—

The long stator linear motor on the guideway is composed of many sections. The power supply of each section is connected only when the train passes. Two independent substations input the current of the power grid from both ends of the guideway motor in the working section, as shown in Figure 4-6, so as to avoid energy loss. The distance and installed power of the substations are based on demand. The motor power is designed to be higher than the gentle uniform driving section in the road section requiring great traction force (such as steep uphill, acceleration or braking phase). In the traditional traffic system, the train motor must be powered at its highest power all the way, which is unnecessary and uneconomical in the section where the highest power is not needed. In this sense, the energy utilization rate of maglev railway is higher than that of traditional wheel-rail contact railway, and the limiting gradient can be steeper.

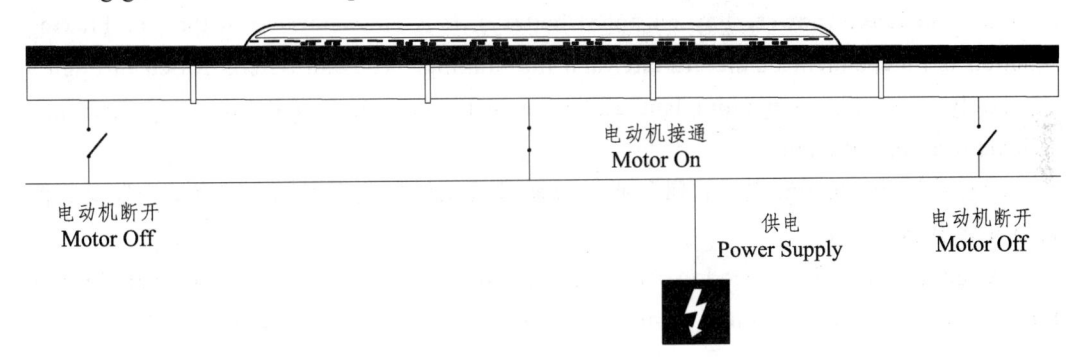

图 4-6　TR 列车分段供电

Figure 4-6　Power Supply by Section for TR Train

悬浮和导向系统以及车上的装置由悬浮磁铁中的直线发电机无接触发电供电。因此这种磁浮铁路在区间内既不需要上部架空线，也不需要第三轨集电器供电，实现了完全无接触运行的目标，这是与用于城市轨道交通的中低速磁浮铁路的不同之处。只是列车在车站范围内停车时，车上电气设备的用电通过接触轨供给。当供电中断时，列车由车上的蓄电池供电。这些蓄电池在列车运行的同时被充电。

The levitation and guidance system as well as the devices on the vehicle are powered by the contactless power generation of the linear generator in the levitation magnet. Therefore, this kind of maglev railway does not need the upper overhead line or the third rail collector to supply power in the section, and achieves the goal of completely non-contact operation, which is different from the medium and low speed maglev railway used in urban rail transit.Only when the train stops within the station, the electricity for the electrical equipment on the train is supplied through the conductor rail.When the power supply is interrupted, the train is powered by the battery on the train.These batteries are charged while the train is running.

四、制动原理

4.2.4 Braking Principle

采用独立于牵引系统和外部电源的安全制动系统，受自动列车控制与保护系统控制。

The safety braking system shall be independent of the traction system and external power supply, and shall be controlled by the automatic train control and protection system.

在运行速度由 500 km/h 降至 10 km/h 的过程中，列车采用涡流制动器制动（通过车载蓄电池供电）。其特点是：制动功能与气候无关，制动力可控制，通过单独控制和冗余的电磁制动回路，保证安全可靠的制动功能。

When the running speed is reduced from 500 km/h to 10 km/h, the train is braked by eddy current brake (powered by on-board battery). It is characterized in that the braking function is independent of the climate, and the braking force can be controlled through a separately controlled and redundant electromagnetic braking circuit to ensure safe and reliable braking function.

当速度降至 10km/h 之后，列车通过滑橇降落在滑行轨上滑行，靠摩擦力制动，保证列车停在预定位置。

When the speed is reduced to 10 km/h, the train will slide on the sliding track through the skid and brake by friction to ensure that the train stops at the predetermined position.

第三节　列车与车辆

Section 4.3　Train and Vehicle

德国第一辆应用型的磁浮高速列车称为运捷 07 "欧罗巴号"，它于 1989 年初在埃姆斯兰磁浮试验中心开始试验运行。

Germany's first practical maglev high-speed train, named TR07 "Europa", was put into trial operation at the Amsland Maglev Test Center in early 1989.

一、列车编组

4.3.1 Train Marshalling

磁浮运捷快车可以根据不同的要求特征任意组合。列车车厢用轻型结构制造，可以根据使用情况和交通量情况，由至少两节（164 个座位）到最多十节（820 个座位）组成列车。

Maglev express trains can be combined at will according to different requirements and characteristics.The train cars are manufactured by the light construction and can be composed of at least two (164 seats) to a maximum of ten (820 seats) depending on the use and traffic.

两节车是 TR 列车的最短组合形式，适用于机场客运；在城市间客运方面，一般可使用 6 节编组的列车；根据客流需求，一组列车最多可由十节车厢组成，适用于长距离运输。

Two-car train is the shortest combination form of TR train, which is suitable for airport passenger transport; in terms of inter-city passenger transport, 6-car trains can generally be used; according to passenger flow demand, a group of trains can be composed of up to ten cars, which is suitable for long-distance transport.

二、车　辆

4.3.2　Vehicles

车辆是高速磁浮客运系统中最重要的部分，包括悬浮架及其上安装的电磁铁、二次悬挂系统和车厢。此外还有车载蓄电池、应急制动系统和悬浮控制系统等电气设备。

The vehicle is the most important part of the high-speed maglev passenger transport system, including the suspension frame, the electromagnet installed on it, the secondary suspension system and the carriage.In addition, there are electrical equipment such as on-board batteries, emergency braking systems and suspension control systems.

车厢由铝型材料和三明治蜂窝铝板通过焊接和铆接的方式构成。各部分具有优化设计的外形和平滑的表面。侧面窗户由两层玻璃组成，分别从内侧和外侧固定在车体上，前方玻璃则由三层经化学硬化的活动玻璃板组成。为了增加车体的刚度，车门设在车辆的端部。车内装修按航空防火标准进行设计。TR08 的导轨和车辆见图 4-7。

The carriage is made of aluminum type material and sandwich honeycomb aluminum plate by welding and riveting. Each part has an optimally designed profile and a smooth surface.The side windows consist of two layers of glass fixed to the car body from the inside and outside, while the front glass consists of three layers of chemically hardened movable glass plates.In order to increase the rigidity of the vehicle body, doors are provided at the ends of the vehicle.The interior decoration of the vehicle is designed according to the aviation fire protection standard. Figure 4-7 shows the guide rails and vehicles of the TR08.

图 4-7 德国 TR 的导轨和车辆

Figure 4-7 Guide Rail and Vehicle of the TR in Germany

TR07 每节车辆平均安装 90 个座位。列车的功率不受其长度以及随之增加的客运量的影响。列车的内部设施组件使用标准化的固定方法固定，这种方法能够高度灵活地满足客户的要求。

TR07 has an average of 90 seats per vehicle. The power of a train is not affected by its length and the consequent increase in passenger capacity. The internal facility components of the train are fixed using a standardised fixing method that is highly flexible to customer requirements.

车辆几乎完全用空气动力学的观点来设计，所以运捷列车驶过时几乎不产生空气涡流。采用在航空和航天已证实有效的方法进行研究并通过现场测试得到证实，沿着列车的压力分布及其对迎面驶来的列车产生的影响符合设计要求。由于车厢结构密封好，两车会车时不会使旅客感到不舒适。

The vehicle is designed almost entirely from an aerodynamic point of view, so there is almost no air turbulence when the express train passes by. The pressure distribution along the train and its effect on the oncoming train are in accordance with the design requirements, as confirmed by field tests using methods proven in aeronautics and astronautics. Because the carriage structure is well sealed, passengers will not feel uncomfortable when two cars meet.

因为 TR 磁浮铁路驱动装置的初级绕组安装在地面导轨里，TR 车辆只安装比较简单的次级绕组，不必像其他交通工具那样装备最大荷载所需的功率；再加上车上没有车轮、车轴、传动箱、制动器和集电器，因此采用导轨驱动的磁浮车辆比普通铁路车辆技术简单、转向架尺寸减小、质量减轻。

Because the primary winding of the driving device of the TR maglev railway is installed in the ground guide rail, the TR vehicle is only installed with a relatively simple secondary winding, and does not need to be equipped with the power required by the maximum load like other vehicles; In addition, there are no wheels, axles, transmission boxes, brakes and collectors on the vehicle, so the guideway driven maglev vehicle has simpler technology, smaller bogie size and lighter mass than ordinary railway vehicles.

磁浮铁路基本上没有磨损，而且不需要维护的电子部件取代了易磨损的经常需要维护的机械部件，因此磁浮铁路的养护维修工作量比传统铁路要低得多。

Maglev railway basically has no wear and tear, and the electronic components that do not need maintenance replace the mechanical components that are easy to wear and often need maintenance, so the maintenance workload of maglev railway is much lower than that of traditional railway.

三、悬浮架

4.3.3 Suspension Frame

悬浮架又称转向架，见图 4-8，其作用是装载电磁铁，并保证列车具有顺利通过曲线和坡道的能力。每节车厢设 4 个悬浮架，用于传递驱动、悬浮、导向和制动能量，悬浮架与车厢用水平调节的空气弹簧和摆式悬挂连接起来。车厢和磁铁之间所有的活动机械部件都由减振的橡胶/金属材料支承。悬浮导向磁铁和悬浮制动磁铁都安装在悬浮架的架梁上，成为一个磁铁模块。

Suspension frame is also called bogie, as shown in Figure 4-8. Its function is to load the electromagnet and ensure that the train has the ability to pass through the curve and ramp smoothly. Each carriage is provided with 4 suspension frames for transmission of driving, suspension, guiding and braking energy, and the suspension frames are connected with the carriage by horizontally adjustable air springs and pendulum suspension. All moving mechanical parts between the carriage and the magnet are supported by a damping rubber/metal material. The suspension guiding magnet and the suspension braking magnet are both arranged on the frame beam of the suspension frame to form a magnet module.

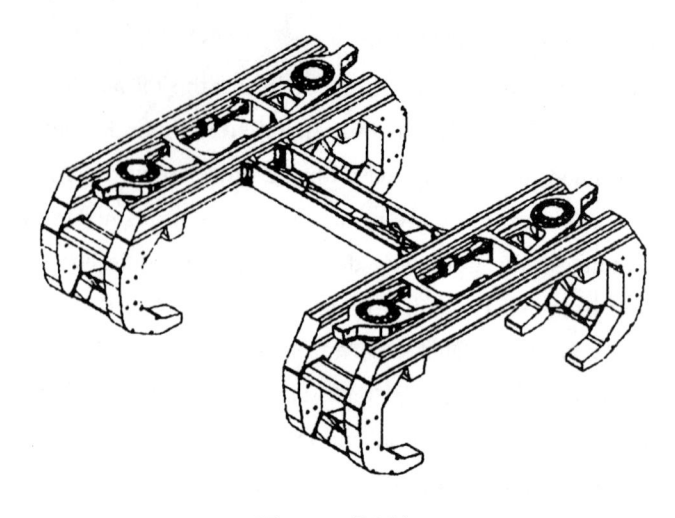

图 4-8 悬浮架

Figure 4-8 Suspension Frame

每个悬浮架在车体两侧底部各安装一个悬浮电磁铁,相邻两个悬浮架之间也在每侧有一个悬浮电磁铁连接在两个悬浮架上,即车辆两侧是由悬浮电磁铁首尾相接布满全列车。每个悬浮电磁铁的两端分为两个独立的控制单元,如果电磁铁的某个控制单元发生故障,另一控制单元仍能控制该电磁铁继续工作,这就是通常说的电气冗余设计,能够提高系统的可靠性。另外,因为悬浮电磁铁是满铺于车辆两侧的,所以即使一辆车甚至一列车上有几个电磁铁同时失效,剩余的电磁铁仍能提供足够的悬浮力保证列车安全运行。

A suspension electromagnet is respectively arranged at the bottom of the two sides of the vehicle body of each suspension frame, and a suspension electromagnet is connected to the two suspension frames on each side between two adjacent suspension frames, namely, the suspension electromagnets are connected end to end on the two sides of the vehicle and are distributed on the whole vehicle. The two ends of each suspension electromagnet are divided into two independent control units. If one control unit of the electromagnet fails, the other control unit can still control the electromagnet to continue working, which is commonly known as the electrical redundancy design, which can improve the reliability of the system. In addition, because the suspension electromagnets are fully laid on both sides of the vehicle, even if several electromagnets on a vehicle or even a train fail at the same time, the remaining electromagnets can still provide enough suspension force to ensure the safe operation of the train.

与悬浮电磁铁的安装对应,车辆悬浮架的侧面用于安装导向电磁铁,其中部分位置(每隔两个磁浮架的中间)用于安装涡流制动器。由于采用冗余设计,个别导向电磁铁的故障不会导致列车运行中断。

Corresponding to the installation of the suspension electromagnet, the side of the vehicle suspension frame is used to install the guide electromagnet, and some of them (in the middle of every two magnetic suspension frames) are used to install the eddy current brake. Due to the redundant design, the failure of individual guiding electromagnets will not cause the train operation to be interrupted.

四、二次悬挂系统

4.3.4　Secondary Suspension System

二次悬挂系统的作用是将车厢荷载传递给悬浮架，同时通过减振装置使车辆/线路界面间的振动在传递到车厢之前得到衰减，其部件包括空气弹簧、摆动机构和防侧滚稳定器。二次悬挂系统使悬浮架与车厢之间的相对横向和垂向位移成为可能，从而使列车能够在曲线和坡道上运行。

The function of the secondary suspension system is to transfer the carriage load to the suspension frame, while the vibration between the vehicle/line interface is damped by the damping device before it is transferred to the carriage. Its components include air spring, swing mechanism and anti-roll stabilizer. The secondary suspension system enables the relative lateral and vertical displacement between the levitation frame and the carriage, thus enabling the train to run on curves and ramps.

车厢的减振装置共有两层，第一层减振装置是电磁铁与悬浮架之间的弹簧，而空气弹簧则提供车体与轨道间的第二层减振作用。在每节车的车厢和悬浮架之间安装了16个空气弹簧，每个弹簧载质量为2 t。

The damping device of the carriage has two layers, the first layer of damping device is the spring between the electromagnet and the suspension frame, and the air spring provides the second layer of damping between the car body and the track. Sixteen air springs are installed between the carriage and the suspension frame of each car, and each spring has a load mass of 2 t.

车辆的车厢是刚性的，列车在曲线上运行时，悬浮电磁铁相对于车厢要发生相对位移。为了允许悬浮架相对于车厢有侧向运动自由度，且不阻碍垂直方向空气弹簧的功能，故设置了摆杆结构。每节车厢有16个导向摆杆与悬浮架相连，可以同时产生侧向和纵向运动。

The carriage of the vehicle is rigid. When the train runs on the curve, the suspension electromagnet will have relative displacement with respect to the carriage. In order to allow the suspension frame to have the freedom of lateral movement relative to the carriage and not hinder the function of the air spring in the vertical direction, a swing rod structure is provided. Each carriage has 16 guide swing rods connected with the suspension frame, which can produce lateral and longitudinal movement at the same time.

当列车运行中遇侧向风力，或者存在未被平衡离心加速度时，车厢将产生侧滚运动。为了衰减车辆的侧滚运动，车厢与悬浮架之间的摇臂上还设计了防侧滚稳定器，这种液压装置可有效地减轻车厢的侧滚效应。

When the train encounters lateral wind force or unbalanced centrifugal acceleration, the carriage will roll. In order to attenuate the roll motion of the vehicle, an anti-roll stabilizer is also designed on the rocker arm between the carriage and the suspension frame, which is a hydraulic device that can effectively reduce the roll effect of the carriage.

五、电气设备

4.3.5　Electrical Equipment

车载电气设备包括悬浮、导向、紧急制动、车载控制系统、照明、空调和车载电源设备。车载电源通过车上的直线发电机获得电能，并由车载蓄电池储存。列车运行时，发电机定子线圈中产生感应电动势，当列车达到一定速度（100 km/h 左右）后，该感应电动势可提供足够的电能，供车体用电，同时对车载蓄电池充电。当列车需要紧急停车时，使用车载的涡流制动器。

On-board electrical equipment includes suspension, guidance, emergency braking, on-board control system, lighting, air conditioning and on-board power supply equipment. The vehicle power supply obtains electric energy through the linear generator on the vehicle and is stored by the vehicle battery. When the train is running, the induced electromotive force is generated in the stator coil of the generator. When the train reaches a certain speed (about 100 km/h), the induced electromotive force can provide enough electric energy for the car body and charge the on-board battery. When the train needs to be stopped in an emergency, the on-board eddy current brake shall be used.

悬浮和导向控制系统的作用是保证电磁铁与轨道之间维持正常的间隙。

The function of the levitation and guidance control system is to maintain the normal clearance between the electromagnet and the rail.

磁浮列车的大部分部件为电气和电子部件，设计中采用多重冗余设计，大大提高了车辆运行的可靠性。此外，磁浮列车的大部分构件还采用了模块化设计，更换方便。对于故障诊断系统监测到的故障部件，可以迅速更换，维修时间短，整车的利用率高。

Most of the components of the maglev train are electrical and electronic components, and the multiple redundancy design is adopted in the design, which greatly improves the reliability of vehicle operation. In addition, most of the components of the maglev train adopt modular design, which is convenient for replacement. The fault parts detected by the fault diagnosis system can be quickly replaced, the maintenance time is short, and the utilization rate of the whole vehicle is high.

六、货车车辆

4.3.6　Freight Vehicles

TR 磁浮列车不仅运送旅客，而且也运送货物。在快速货运时将使用专门的货运车厢。需要时可以将客车和货车组成混合列车。TR 列车配备的高速货车车辆，每节可最多承载 18.3 t 货物。

TR maglev trains transport not only passengers, but also goods.Special freight cars will be used for express freight.When necessary, passenger cars and freight cars can be combined into a mixed train.The TR train is equipped with high-speed freight cars, each of which can carry up to 18.3 t of goods.

第四节　线　路

Section 4.4　Line

本节主要介绍德国常导超高速磁浮铁路的线路，包括线路导轨、桥梁、道岔、设计参数等技术。

This section mainly introduces the line of the German ultra-high-speed maglev railway, including the line guide rail, bridge, turnout, design parameters and other technologies.

一、导　轨

4.4.1　Guideway

导轨引导列车的前进方向，同时承受列车荷载并将之传至地基。线路上部结构为用于连接长定子的精密焊接的钢结构或钢筋混凝土结构的支承梁，下部结构为钢筋混凝土支墩和基础。支承梁本身在力学性质上与传统土木工程简支梁桥或连续梁桥的梁部相同，由于其上需安装磁浮系统的定子线圈和铁心，因此制造和施工精度要求较高。

The guideway guides the forward direction of the train, bears the load of the train and transfers it to the foundation. The superstructure of the line is the support beam of the precision welded steel structure or reinforced concrete structure for connecting the long stator, and the substructure is the reinforced concrete buttress and foundation. The mechanical properties of the supporting beam itself are the same as those of the simply supported beam bridge or continuous beam bridge in traditional civil engineering. Because the stator coil and iron core of the maglev system need to be installed on the supporting beam, the manufacturing and construction accuracy requirements are higher.

磁悬浮铁路可以分为单线铁路和双线铁路，TR 双线铁路的线间距是 4.4 m（300 km/h）、4.8 m（400 km/h）和 5.1 m（500 km/h），建筑接近限界宽度为 10.1~11.4 m，轨距为 2.8 m。

Maglev railway can be divided into single-track railway and double-track railway.The distance between tracks of TR double-track railway is 4.4m (300 km/h), 4.8 m (400 km/h) and 5.1 m (500 km/h), the width of construction approach clearance is 10.1-11.4 m, and the gauge is 2.8 m, which is also a super high-speed railway.

同样是超高速铁路，德国 TR 系统的悬浮高度为 10 mm，而日本 ML 系统的悬浮高度为 100 mm，德国 TR 系统的悬浮高度只有日本 ML 系统的 1/10。因此德国 TR 系统对导轨梁加工和装配的质量和精度提出了很高的要求。为了达到这些要求，德国专门开发了全自动机器人焊接技术进行钢梁的焊接，以保证焊接的高精度。

The German TR system has a levitation height of 10 mm, while the Japanese ML system has a levitation height of 100 mm. The German TR system has only 1/10 of the Japanese ML system.Therefore, the German TR system has put forward high requirements for the quality and accuracy of the processing and assembly of the guideway beam.In order to meet these requirements, Germany has developed a fully automatic robot welding technology for steel beam welding to ensure high precision of welding.

使用计算机控制的装配方法把批量生产的长定子直线电动机电磁部件装配在支承梁上。与此同时，该电磁部件在线路上的位置也被设定了。这样避免了错误，提高了安装精度，而且非常经济。在制梁厂里进行支承梁预加工，可以缩短现场建路的时间。

A computer-controlled assembly method is used to assemble the electromagnetic components of a mass-produced long-stator linear motor on a support beam. At the same time, the position of the electromagnetic component on the line is also set.This avoids errors, improves installation accuracy, and is very economical.The pre-processing of supporting beams in the beam fabrication plant can shorten the time of road construction on site.

二、高架轨道

4.4.2 Elevated Track

由于磁浮列车与线路的耦合关系，磁浮铁路的线路必须具有一定的高度，并采用梁式结构。线路可以高架,也可以根据地形直接将梁固定在基础上(称为低置线路);可以敷设在桥梁上,也可以敷设在隧道里。无论是在地面上,还是在空中,无论是用钢梁,还是用混凝土梁,磁浮运捷系统的轨道均能满足运行平稳与安全的要求。

Due to the coupling relationship between the maglev train and the line, the line of the maglev railway must have a certain height and adopt a beam structure. The line can be elevated or directly fixed on the foundation according to the terrain (called low line), which can be laid on the bridge or in the tunnel. Whether on the ground or in the air, whether with steel beams or concrete beams, the track of the maglev system can meet the requirements of smooth and safe operation.

单个的导轨梁长度为 6~62 m,标准跨度为 31 m,可以将两个标准跨度(31 m)的简支梁连接成 62 m 的连续梁。支承梁预加工在工厂里进行,这样可以缩短现场施工的时间。

The length of a single guideway beam is 6-62 m, and the standard span is 31 m. Two simply supported beams with standard span (31 m) can be connected to form a continuous beam of 62 m. The prefabrication of the supporting beam is carried out in the factory, which can shorten the construction time on site.

三、低置轨道

4.4.3　Low Track

在磁浮线路与现有的交通线(公路、铁路)平行的情况下,轨道首先在平地上铺设,在路堑、隧道和原结构如桥梁或者车站建筑物等处,轨道一般也铺设在平地上。如果条件允许或者鉴于防噪的要求,可以选择地面轨道。低置轨道一般采用 6~12 m 的标准跨度和 1.25~3.5 m 的高度,这个高度可以保证排水及小动物通过的要求。

When the maglev line is parallel to the existing traffic line (highway, railway), the track is first laid on the flat ground, and the track is generally laid on the flat ground at the cutting, tunnel and original structure such as bridge or station building. Ground track can be selected if conditions permit or in view of noise prevention requirements. The standard span of 6-12 m and the height of 1.25-3.5 m are generally adopted for the low track, which can meet the requirements of drainage and the passage of small animals.

无论是使用地面轨道,还是高架轨道,磁浮铁路导轨占地面积都比其他交通系统少。

Whether using ground track or elevated track, maglev rail tracks cover less area than other transportation systems.

四、桥梁基础

4.4.4 Bridge Foundation

根据地基基础的不同，在一般情况下，桥梁基础采用浅基础就足够了。桩基只是在很复杂的地质情况下才有必要。

According to the difference of foundation, in general, shallow foundation is sufficient for bridge foundation. Pile foundations are only necessary in very complex geological situations.

五、道　岔

4.4.5 Turnout

线路的另一个重要组成部分是道岔。由于磁浮铁路的"轨道"——支承梁刚度较大，因此道岔的设计和施工较为复杂。磁浮铁路的道岔是一个多跨连续钢梁，长度与道岔侧向允许通过速度有关，侧向过岔速度不大于 200 km/h 者称为高速道岔，侧向过岔速度不大于 100 km/h 者称低速道岔，长度分别为 148.6 m 和 78.4 m。最近蒂森克虏伯公司又开发了一种侧向过岔速度可达 400 km/h 的超高速道岔，可用于干线分岔的特殊地段。

Another important part of the line is the turnout. The design and construction of turnouts are complicated due to the large rigidity of the supporting beam, which is the "track" of the maglev railway. The turnout of maglev railway is a multi-span continuous steel beam, and its length is related to the allowable lateral speed of turnouts. The turnout with a lateral speed not more than 200 km/h is called a high-speed turnout, and the turnout with a lateral speed not more than 100 km/h is called a low-speed turnout, with lengths of 148.6 m and 78.4 m respectively. Recently, ThyssenKrupp has developed an ultra-high-speed turnout with a lateral turnout speed of up to 400 km/h, which can be used in special sections of the main line bifurcation.

列车借助钢弯曲道岔换道，见图 4-9，借助电动扳道装置使钢梁弹性弯曲左右分段移动即可达到换道目的，换道完成后用道岔闩将活动部件锁定在终端位置上。换道过程由微处理机控制，微处理机受中心计算机的监控，见图 4-10。

The train changes track with the help of steel bending turnout, as shown in Figure 4-9. The purpose of track change can be achieved by using the electric switch device to make the steel beam move left and right by elastic bending. After the track change is completed, the movable parts are locked at the terminal position with the turnout latch. The lane change process is controlled by the microprocessor, which is monitored by the central computer, as shown in Figure 4-10.

图 4-9 道岔

Figure 4-9　TR Turnout

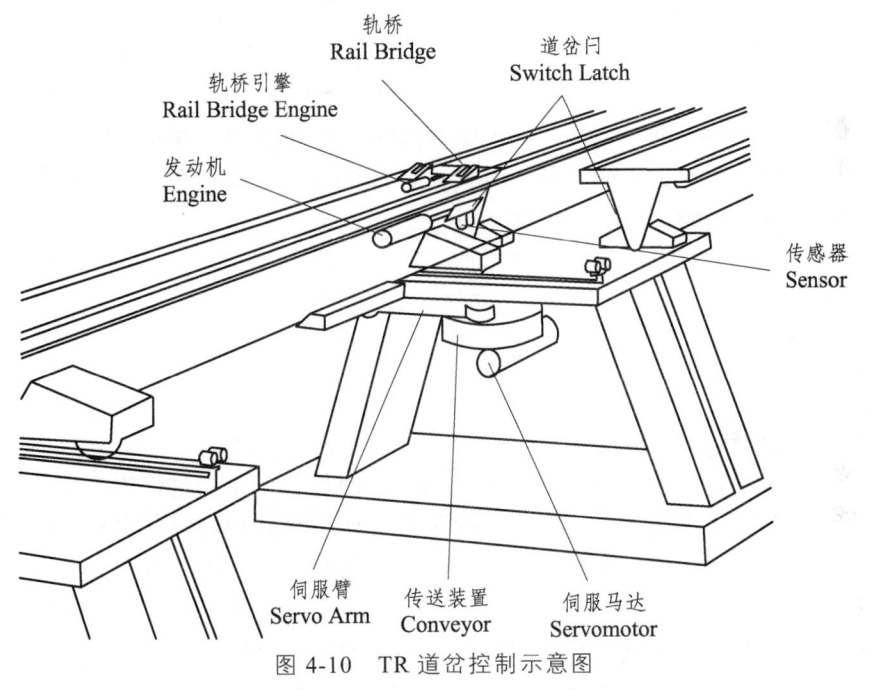

轨桥 Rail Bridge
轨桥引擎 Rail Bridge Engine
道岔闩 Switch Latch
发动机 Engine
传感器 Sensor
伺服臂 Servo Arm
传送装置 Conveyor
伺服马达 Servomotor

图 4-10　TR 道岔控制示意图

Figure 4-10　Diagram of TR Turnout Control

道岔可以是单开道岔（快速道岔）或双开道岔（慢速道岔）。当道岔处于正线通过位置时，允许列车以其正常速度（300～500 km/h）驶过，列车运行速度不受限制；处于侧线通过时，允许的行驶速度是 200 km/h 和 100 km/h。道岔可以铺在地面，也可以架设在空中。在停车场和维修保养区换道也可以通过一个轨道组件在移动平台上平行推移来进行。

Turnouts may be single (fast) or double (slow). When the turnout is in the main line passing position, the train is allowed to pass at its normal speed (300-500 km/h), and the running speed of the train is not limited; when the turnout is in the siding passing position, the allowed running speed is 200 km/h and 100 km/h. The turnout can be laid on the ground or erected in the air. Lane changing in the parking lot and maintenance area can also be carried out by parallel movement of a track assembly on a mobile platform.

六、隧　道

4.4.6　Tunnels

由于磁浮铁路选线灵活，其线路能很好地适应地形，所以，即使在丘陵地带和山区地带，也不需要修筑隧道。磁浮铁路的隧道横断面取决于空气动力学的要求。二至八节编组列车通过大于150 m 长的隧道时，所需要的隧道断面面积取决于列车的运行速度。

Because of the flexible route selection of maglev railway, its route can well adapt to the terrain, so even in hilly and mountainous areas, there is no need to build tunnels. The tunnel cross section of the maglev railway depends on the aerodynamic requirements.The required tunnel section area for trains of two to eight cars passing through tunnels longer than 150 m depends on the speed of the train.

七、功能件

4.4.7　Functional Parts

功能件是磁浮线路轨道设备之一，磁浮列车的支承、导向和驱动都与功能件有关。功能件的主要功能部件包括顶部滑行板、侧面导向板及定子固定件等。顶部滑行板在列车停止状态起支承作用，在列车运行时悬浮架两个悬浮控制电路出现故障或列车安全制动时，磁浮列车通过滑橇降落在滑行板上，滑行板承受机械支承力和摩擦力。顶部滑行板使用 S355N 钢板，厚度 15 mm，宽度 360 mm。侧面导向板与列车导向系统完成列车的导向功能，在列车运行时，当悬浮架两个导向控制电路失效或列车完全制动时，导向磁铁极靴或制动磁铁极靴接触导向板，起机械导向作用功能或摩擦制动作用。侧面导向板使用软磁结构钢，厚度为 30 mm，高度为 305 mm。

The support, guidance and drive of the maglev train are all related to the functional parts, which are one of the maglev line track equipment.The main functional parts of the functional parts include the top sliding plate, the side guide plate and the stator fixing part. The top sliding plate plays a supporting role when the train is stopped. When the two suspension control circuits of the suspension frame fail or the train is safely braked during the operation of the train, the maglev train lands on the sliding plate through the skid, and the sliding plate bears mechanical supporting force and friction force. The top sliding plate is made of S355N steel plate with thickness of 15 mm and width of 360 mm. The side guide plate and the train guide system complete the guide function of the train. When the train is running, once the two guide control circuits of the suspension frame fail or the train is completely braked, the guide magnet pole shoe or the brake magnet pole shoe contacts the guide plate to achieve the mechanical guide function or friction braking function. The side guide plates are made of soft magnetic structural steel with a thickness of 30 mm and a height of 305 mm.

定子固定件用于安装直线电机定子铁心。根据定子类型，在型钢下缘加工横槽及螺栓孔，用于固定定子铁心。

The stator fastener is used to install the stator core of a linear motor. According to the type of stator, the transverse groove and bolt hole are processed at the lower edge of the section steel to fix the stator core.

腹板、竖向及水平肋板也是功能件结构的重要组成部分，用于连接及加强顶部滑行板、侧面导向板和定子固定件。

Webs, vertical and horizontal ribs are also important parts of the structure of functional parts, which are used to connect and strengthen the top sliding plate, side guide plate and stator fixing.

八、供电轨

4.4.8　Power Rail

在车站、维修基地以及中途停车站等处，磁浮列车的集（受）电靴要通过供电轨给列车的悬浮机构、空调、照明等提供电能，并能给车载蓄电池充电。

At the station, maintenance base and midway stop station, the collecting (receiving) electric shoes of the maglev train provide electric energy for the suspension mechanism, air conditioning and lighting of the train through the power supply rail, and can charge the on-board battery.

供电轨也称动力轨，采用支架固定在轨道梁上。支架固定在轨道梁腹板上，位置可作调整。供电轨的标准长度是 8 242 mm，自重 91 kg。供电轨由铝合金和不锈钢材料复合加工而成。它分为正、负和 PE 三极，见图 4-11。

Power rail, also known as power rail, is fixed on the track beam by bracket. The support is fixed on the web plate of the track beam, and the position can be adjusted. The standard length of the power rail is 8,242 mm, and the weight of the power rail is 91 kg, which is made of aluminum alloy and stainless steel. It is divided into positive, negative and PE poles, as shown in　figure 4-11.

供电轨与支架间采用绝缘子（器）连接，绝缘子是供电轨与供电轨支架间用于连接的具有良好绝缘性能的自锁式内螺纹连接件。

The power rail and the support are connected by insulator (insulator). The insulator is a self-locking internal thread connector with good insulation performance for connection between the power rail and the power rail support.

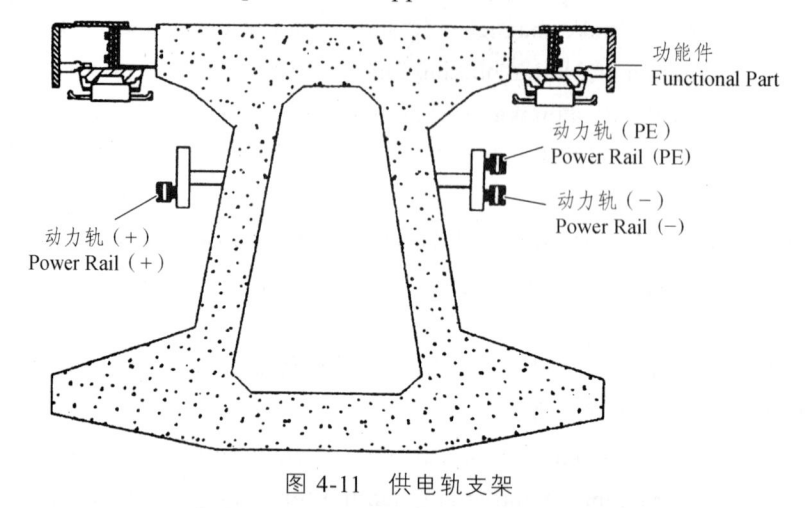

图 4-11 供电轨支架
Figure 4-11　Layout of the Power Supply Rail Support

九、有关线路参数

4.4.9　Relevant Line Parameters

由于在导轨上采用了有效的磁导向和与各路段特点相适应的电机功率分配技术，所以使得磁浮铁路具有很好的选线特性。

Due to the effective magnetic guidance and the motor power distribution technology adapted to the characteristics of each section, the maglev railway has good route selection characteristics.

（一）限制坡度

4.4.9.1　Limiting Gradient

由于磁浮铁路地面驱动绕组的数量、驱动绕组的功率可以根据地形的需要灵活布置，所以它的爬坡能力很强，限制坡度高达100‰，比普通高速铁路（12‰~40‰）高得多。因此，磁浮铁路线路可以灵活地适应地形环境，不必像修筑普通铁路那样，不得不修建长大桥梁和隧道。

Because the number and power of the ground drive windings of the maglev railway can be flexibly arranged according to the needs of the terrain, its climbing ability is very strong, and the limiting gradient is as high as 100‰ , which is higher than that of the ordinary high-speed railway(12‰-40‰). Therefore, the maglev railway line can flexibly adapt to the terrain environment, and does not have to build long bridges and tunnels like the construction of ordinary railway.

(二) 最小曲线半径

4.4.9.2　Minimum Curve Radius

磁浮铁路的最小曲线半径比普通铁路小得多。德国 TR 系统在速度 300 km/h 时仅为 1 590 m，而普通轮轨铁路在同样的速度条件下却需要 5 000 m。

The minimum curve radius of maglev railway is much smaller than that of ordinary railway. The German TR system is only 1,590 m at a speed of 300 km/h, while the ordinary wheel-rail railway requires 5,000 m at the same speed.

(三) 缓和曲线

4.4.9.3　Transition Curve

缓和曲线采用正弦曲线。根据列车运行速度、线路允许最大侧向冲击、扭转角和法向冲击，可以确定最小缓和曲线长度。

The transition curve is a sine curve. The minimum transition curve length can be determined according to the train running speed, the maximum lateral impact allowed by the line, the torsion angle and the normal impact.

(四) 竖曲线

4.4.9.4　Vertical Curve

竖曲线半径是根据列车运行速度和舒适度要求确定的。

The radius of vertical curve is determined according to the requirements of train speed and comfortability.

(五) 竖曲线缓和曲线长度

4.4.9.5　Length of Transition Curve for Vertical Curve

由于磁浮列车运行速度快，对舒适度要求高，因此，它对竖曲线也要求设置缓和曲线，这是与轮轨高速铁路的不同之处。竖曲线缓和曲线采用回旋曲线。

Because the maglev train runs fast and requires high comfortability, it also requires transition curve for vertical curve, which is different from wheel-rail high-speed railway. Clothoid curve is used for transition curve of vertical curve.

(六) 横坡设计参数

4.4.9.6　Cross Slope Design Parameters

在线路曲线区段，为了平衡列车运行时的部分侧向加速度，轨道梁须设置超高。

在直线区段，为了便于排水，轨道梁也需设置排水横坡。

In the curve section of the line, in order to balance part of the lateral acceleration when the train is running, the track beam must be set with superelevation. In the straight section, in order to facilitate drainage, the track beam also needs to be provided with a drainage cross slope.

在线路区间，轨道梁的最大横坡为12°；在车站，横坡角不大于3°；在道岔范围，横坡角为0°。

In the section of the line, the maximum transverse slope of the track beam is 12°; At the station, the cross slope angle shall not be greater than 3°. In the turnout range, the cross slope angle is 0°.

十、与其他交通工具和交通路线的连接

4.4.10 Connection with Other Means of Transport and Transport Routes

磁浮铁路的车站也经常需要与其他既有交通系统（铁路、高速铁路、城市轨道交通、公路）连接。旅客在这些连接点应尽可能容易、舒适地转乘别的交通工具，尤其是高速铁路，以便能够方便地到达更远的目的地。因此，普通铁路和磁浮高速铁路这两种轨道导向的交通系统应该实现同车站甚至同站台换乘。

Maglev railway stations also often need to connect with other existing transportation systems (railway, high-speed railway, urban rail transit, highway). Passengers should transfer to other means of transport, especially high-speed rail, as easily and comfortably as possible at these connections, so that they can easily reach more distant destinations. Therefore, the two kinds of rail oriented transportation systems, the ordinary railway and the maglev high-speed railway, should realize the transfer at the same station or even at the same platform.

第五节　供电与运行控制

Section 4.5　Power Supply and Operation Control

一、供电系统

4.5.1 Power Supply System

供电系统包括变电站、沿线供电电缆、开关站和其他供电设备。

The power supply system includes substations, power supply cables along the line, switching stations and other power supply equipment.

磁浮列车供电系统通过给地面长定子线圈供电来提供列车运行所需的电能。首先，从 110 kV 的公用电网引入交流高压电，通过降压变压器降至 20 kV 和 1.5 kV，然后整流成为直流电，再由逆变器变成 0~300 Hz 的交流电，升压后通过线路电缆和开关站供给线路上的长定子线圈，在定子和车载电磁铁之间形成牵引力。供电系统逻辑示意图如图 4-12 所示。

The power supply system of the maglev train provides the electric energy needed by the train operation by supplying power to the long stator coil on the ground. First, AC high voltage is introduced from the 110 kV utility grid, reduced to 20 kV and 1.5 kV by a step-down transformer, then rectified to DC, and then converted to AC of 0 to 300 Hz by an inverter. After boosting, it is supplied to the long stator coil on the line through the line cable and the switching station, forming a traction force between the stator and the on-board electromagnet. The logic diagram of the power supply system is shown in Figure 4-12.

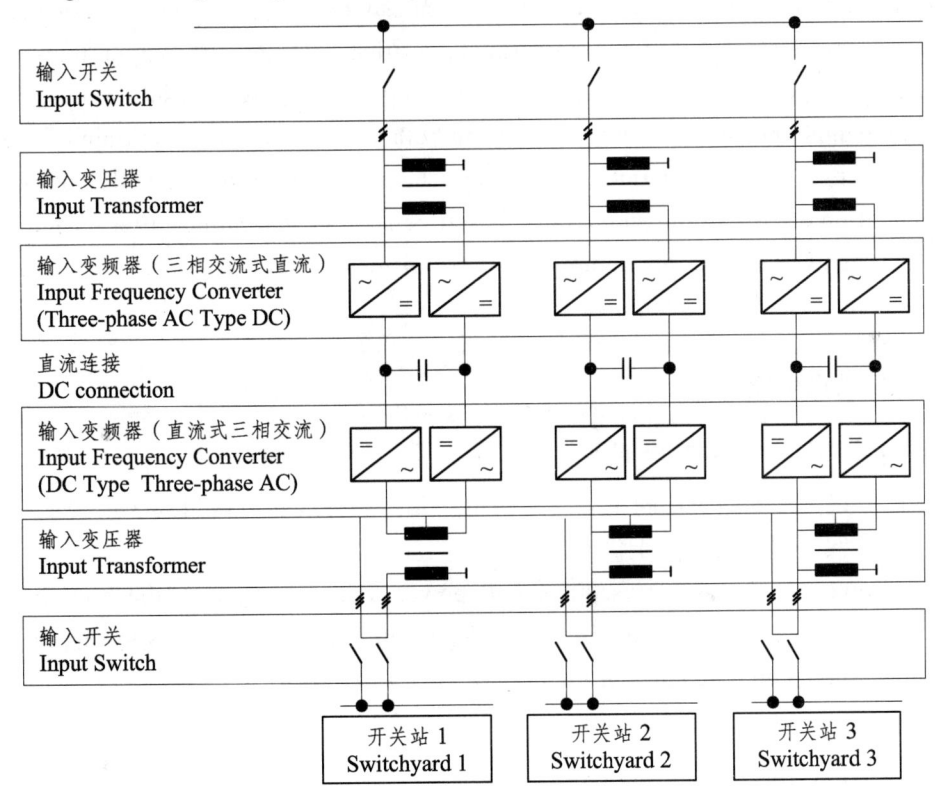

图 4-12　供电系统逻辑示意图

Figure 4-12　Logic Diagram of Power Supply System

磁浮列车系统的整流、变流及电机定子等设备均在地面，对设备的体积和质量以及抗振性能没有严格要求。

The rectifier, converter and motor stator of the maglev train system are all on the ground, so there is no strict requirement for the volume, mass and anti-vibration performance of the equipment.

（一）变电站

4.5.1.1　Substation

变电站内实现高压交流电的降压、整流并再逆变成 0～300 Hz 的交流电，因此站内设备有降压变压器、整流变压器、整流器、逆变器和输出变压器。变电站一般设在线路旁边，一条线路设若干变电站，每个变电站可向两旁的线路区段供电。由于两个变电站之间每条线路只能运行一列列车，因此变电站的间距实际上控制了全线的列车运行密度，其设置应根据运输需求、列车编组和技术约束综合考虑，经技术经济分析后确定。

The substation realizes the step-down, rectification and inversion of high-voltage alternating current into 0-300 Hz alternating current, so the equipment in the station includes step-down transformer, rectifier transformer, rectifier, inverter and output transformer. Substations are generally located next to the line, and a line has several substations, each of which can supply power to the line sections on both sides. Since only one train can run on each line between two substations, the distance between substations actually controls the train operation density of the whole line. Its setting shall be determined after technical and economic analysis based on comprehensive consideration of transport demand, train formation and technical constraints.

（二）供电电缆

4.5.1.2　Power Supply Cable

供电电缆用于对牵引电机的长定子供电。每条磁浮线路有两组或 3 组相互独立的三相电缆对线路两侧的长定子供电。

The power supply cable is used to supply power to the long stator of the traction motor. Each maglev line has two or three sets of independent three-phase cables to supply power to the long stators on both sides of the line.

（三）开关站

4.5.1.3　Switchyard

开关站沿线路分布，将同一供电区间的电机长定子分为若干小段（数百米），在列车通过时交替接通。设置开关站的目的是减少供电电流在定子段上的功率损失，其设置间距根据技术和经济分析确定。

The switchyard is distributed along the line, and the long stator of the motor in the same power supply section is divided into several small sections (hundreds of meters), which are alternately connected when the train passes.The purpose of setting the switchyard is to reduce the power loss of the power supply current on the stator section, and its spacing is determined according to the technical and economic analysis.

(四) 其他供电设备

4.5.1.4　Other Power Supply Equipment

除了对长定子供电以外，还需要相关电气线路为道岔、车/线数据传输天线、车站或停车点的静止列车等供电。

In addition to the power supply to the long stators, the associated electrical wiring is required to supply power to turnouts, train/line data transmission antennas, stationary trains at stations or depots, etc.

二、运行控制系统

4.5.2　Operation Control System

磁浮铁路的运行控制系统（简称 OCS）是一个安全控制与防护系统，其基本任务是控制列车的运行，确保列车运行的安全，提高运输组织的效率，实现列车运行的自动化。所以，磁浮铁路的运行控制系统不仅仅是实现列车运行的安全控制和防护，它还兼有列车运行的管理和调度等功能。

The Operation Control System (OCS) of Maglev Railway is a safety control and protection system. Its basic task is to control the operation of trains, ensure the safety of train operation, improve the efficiency of transport organization, and realize the automation of train operation. Therefore, the operation control system of maglev railway is not only to realize the safety control and protection of train operation, but also to manage and dispatch train operation.

要保证磁浮列车高速、安全地运行，并能根据运行中车辆、线路的状况随时调整运行计划，迅速处理运行中的各种突发事件，列车的运行控制就必须自动化进行。磁浮铁路运行控制系统按照已存储的行车时刻表对列车运行进行中央自动化控制，包括准确按照时间和地点操纵列车的驱动和制动过程。常规的列车控制任务不是由司机操作，而是完全由运行控制系统来执行。因此该系统具有很高的自动控制和防护特性，一般无须人工干预列车的运行，只是在需要清除故障时才需控制人员按操作顺序进行人工干预。

In order to ensure the high-speed and safe operation of maglev train, adjust the operation plan at any time according to the conditions of running vehicles and lines, and quickly deal with various emergencies in operation, the operation control of maglev train must be automated. The maglev train operation control system automatically controls the train operation according to the stored timetable, including controlling the driving and braking process of the train accurately according to the time and place. Routine train control tasks are not performed by the driver, but are performed entirely by the operation control system. Therefore, the system has high automatic control and protection characteristics. Generally, there is no need for manual intervention in the operation of the train. Only when the fault needs to be cleared, the controller needs to intervene manually according to the operation sequence.

运行控制系统是整个磁浮交通系统正常运转的根本保障。它包括所有用于安全保护、控制、执行和计划的设备，还包括用于设备之间相互通信的设备。运行控制系统由运行控制中心、通信系统、分散控制系统和车载控制系统组成。运行控制系统的任务还包括调度、处理与记录列车运行和各方面的故障诊断数据，为操作人员与乘客介绍最新信息。

The operation control system is the fundamental guarantee for the normal operation of the whole maglev transportation system. It includes all the equipment used for security, control, execution, and planning, and also includes the equipment used to communicate with each other. The operation control system consists of operation control center, communication system, distributed control system and on-board control system. The task of the operation control system also includes dispatching, processing and recording train operation and all aspects of fault diagnosis data, and introducing the latest information to operators and passengers.

（一）运行控制中心

4.5.2.1 Operation Control Center

运行控制中心负责安排行车计划，编制运行图。它根据线路条件按计划发出列车；当出现故障或冲突时，根据情况的变化改变或撤销计划；通过比较预定计划和实际运行情况，实现整个系统的优化运行。为了保证计划的正常执行，控制中心通过数据传输设备从下属分散控制系统取得各种信息，进行计算分析并提出运行调整计划。同时，运行控制中心还负责保存各种技术数据，用于进一步的统计分析和故障诊断。此外，运行控制中心还负责向乘客发布列车运行信息。

The operation control center is responsible for arranging the train operation plan and preparing the train diagram. It sends out the trains according to the line conditions. When there is a fault or conflict, it changes or cancels the plan according to the change of the situation. By comparing the scheduled plan with the actual operation, it realizes the optimal operation of the whole system. In order to ensure the normal implementation of the plan, the control center obtains all kinds of information from the subordinate distributed control system through data transmission equipment, calculates and analyzes, and puts forward the operation adjustment plan.At the same time, the operation control center is also responsible for saving various technical data for further statistical analysis and fault diagnosis.In addition, the operation control center is also responsible for issuing train operation information to passengers.

（二）分散控制系统

4.5.2.2 Distributed Control System

分散控制系统直接参与列车的控制和运行。它的功能是保证本区段内列车的运行安全，对本段各种设备状况进行监控和维护，将各种信息传给运行控制中心，并在非计划情况下执行运行控制中心的指示，对设备状态和列车运行进行人工干预。

The distributed control system is directly involved in the control and operation of trains. Its function is to ensure the safe operation of trains in this section, monitor and maintain the status of various equipment in this section, transmit various information to the operation control center, execute the instructions of the operation control center under unplanned conditions, and conduct manual intervention on the status of equipment and train operation.

控制系统借助轨道上的数字密码化的位置标记准确地测定列车的位置，不断监控列车是否超过了容许速度的限制。如果超过，则系统会自动切断相应供电区间的电源。如果需要，还可以开启列车制动装置，保证运行安全。此外，系统还可以确保路段上列车之间的距离、保护岔道及车站里的人员安全以及保证运营设施其他功能和过程的安全。

The control system accurately determines the position of the train by means of digitally coded position markers on the track and continuously monitors whether the train exceeds the allowable speed limit. If it exceeds, the system will automatically cut off the power supply of the corresponding power supply area. If necessary, it can also open the train brake device to ensure the safety of operation. In addition, the system can ensure the distance between trains on the road section, protect the safety of personnel in turnouts and stations, and ensure the safety of other functions and processes of operation facilities.

（三）车载控制系统

4.5.2.3 On-board Control System

车载控制系统的主要任务是对各种车载设备进行检测和控制，保证它们正常工作。

通过移动无线传输，车上的列车保护系统始终和分散控制系统保持联系。同时，它也与运行控制中心保持无线通信联系，随时将列车运行状况数据传给运行控制中心并接受后者对行车计划的调整命令。车载控制系统的监控设备会随时比较当前运行数据与计划运行数据，一旦两者的差别超出允许范围，就启动列车保护系统，使列车迅速减速或停车。虽然磁浮铁路的运行控制系统的费用只占总投资的 4%左右，但它却是各种高技术（包括检测技术、有线和无线通信技术、数据处理技术和自动控制技术等）的集成，在磁浮交通系统中占有非常重要的地位。

The main task of the on-board control system is to detect and control various on-board equipment to ensure their normal operation. Through mobile wireless transmission, the train protection system on the train keeps in touch with the distributed control system all the time. At the same time, it also keeps wireless communication with the operation control center, transmits the train operation status data to the operation control center at any time and receives the adjustment command of the latter to the train operation plan. The monitoring equipment of the on-board control system will compare the current operation data with the planned operation data at any time. Once the difference between the two exceeds the allowable range, the train protection system will be started to slow down or stop the train quickly. Although the cost of the operation control system of maglev railway only accounts for about 4% of the total investment, it is the integration of various high technologies (including detection technology, wired and wireless communication technology, data processing technology and automatic control technology, etc.) And plays a very important role in the maglev transportation system.

（四）通信系统

4.5.2.4　Communication System

列车与控制台之间的联络使用配备冗余部件的定向无线电数据传输设备。无线电台天线杆安装在导轨旁边，间距数千米。通过无线电天线杆沿着轨道的特殊排列，能够保证列车上的两个天线总是同时处于两个无线电台天线杆的接收和发射范围之内，见图 4-13。

Communication between the train and the control console uses directional radio data transmission equipment with redundant components. Radio station masts are installed next to the guide rail at a distance of thousands of meters. The special arrangement of radio masts along the track can ensure that the two antennas on the train are always within the receiving and transmitting range of the two radio masts at the same time, as shown in Figure 4-13.

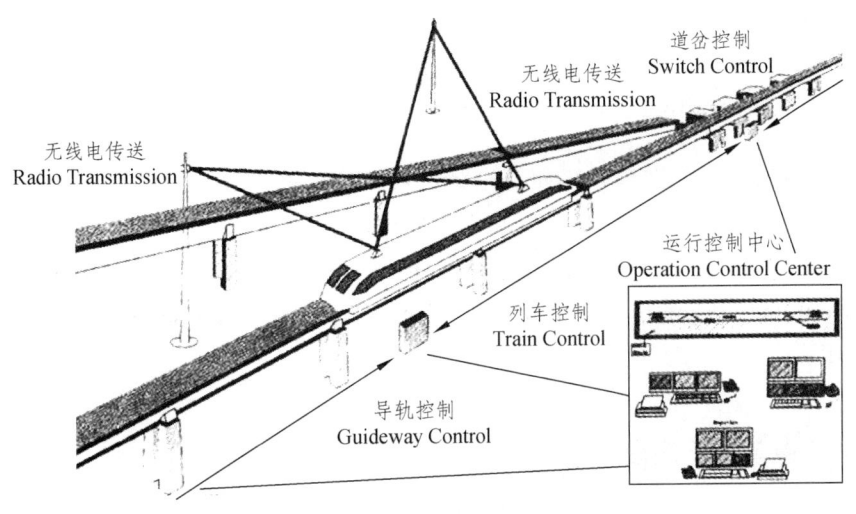

图 4-13 德国 TR 运行控制系统原理

Figure 4-13 Schematic Diagram of German TR Operation Control System

第六节 安全性能

Section 4.6 Safety Performance

德国 TR 磁浮交通系统在开发、制造过程中经历了系统性的安全分析和验证以及严格的第三方安全评估，许多方面已在德国埃姆斯兰试验线（TVE）的试验运行中得到检验。该系统在正常运行（按照列车运行时刻表的运行）及故障运行（偏离列车运行时刻表的运行）时，在技术上安全都是完全有保障的。超高速磁浮铁路技术结构本身可以预防传统交通系统的事故。因此尽管速度最高可达 500 km/h，乘坐 TR 磁浮列车还是比任何别的交通方式都更安全。

The German TR maglev transportation system has undergone systematic safety analysis and verification as well as strict third-party safety assessment during its development and manufacturing process, and many aspects have been tested and verified in the test operation of the German Emsland Test Line (TVE). The technical safety of the system is fully guaranteed during normal operation (operation according to the train operation timetable) and fault operation (operation deviating from the train operation timetable). The technical structure of the ultra-high speed maglev railway itself can prevent accidents in the traditional transportation system. So even at speeds of up to 500 km/h, the TR Maglev is safer than any other mode of transport.

一、不脱轨

4.6.1　No Derailment

普通铁路列车只是靠车轮踏面及轮缘使其保持在钢轨上，这有可能造成列车脱轨。TR 磁浮列车紧紧地抱住轨道，所以它不会脱轨。

An ordinary railway train is only kept on the rail by the wheel tread and the wheel flange, which may cause the train to derail. The TR maglev train clings to the track so it can't derail.

二、不撞车、不追尾

4.6.2　No Collision, No Rear-end Collision

由于使用导轨驱动的同步直线电机 LSM，并且 LSM 的地面部分以分段方式接通，使得列车和驱动电动机移动场的运行是同步的，也就是说，它们以同样的速度并且往同一个方向运行。此外，只有列车所在的那一段长定子直线电动机是接通的。因此在同一路段上行驶的两辆或多辆列车不可能以不同的速度或朝不同的方向行驶，故绝对不会发生两辆列车追尾及迎头相撞的现象。

Due to the use of synchronous linear motor LSM driven by rail, and the ground part of LSM is connected in a segmented way, the movement of the train and the moving field of the drive motor is synchronous, that is, they run at the same speed and in the same direction. In addition, only the section of the long-stator linear motor where the train is located is connected. Therefore, it is impossible for two or more trains running on the same section of road to travel at different speeds or in different directions, so there is absolutely no rear-end collision or head-on collision between two trains.

三、安全悬浮

4.6.3　Safe Suspension

安全悬浮指的是磁浮列车在假设最严重故障情况或紧急情况下仍能保持悬浮功能，以确保列车能强行制动并到达就近停车区。

Safe suspension means that the maglev train can still maintain the suspension function in the most serious fault or emergency situation, so as to ensure that the train can brake forcibly and reach the nearest parking area.

保证安全悬浮功能的技术措施有：所有与安全相关的重要子系统和部件都采用冗余设计、检测和诊断装置的故障报警、强制制动、定子在线路上的冗余固定、轨道自动检测装置等。

The technical measures to ensure the safety suspension function include: redundancy design for all safety-related important subsystems and components, fault alarm of detection and diagnosis device, forced braking, redundant fixation of stator on the line, automatic detection device of track, etc.

四、安全制动

4.6.4　Safe Braking

在列车运行时，如果发生供电中断的情况，系统只是驱动功能失效。支承和导向系统以及车上设施的电源供应完全靠车上电池供给继续工作。这样一来，列车依靠安全制动系统仍然可以保持原有的"活力"继续悬浮行驶。

When the train is running, if the power supply is interrupted, the system only fails to drive. The support and guidance system and the power supply of the on-board facilities continue to work entirely on the on-board battery supply. In this way, the train can still maintain its original "vitality" and continue to suspend by relying on the safety braking system.

安全制动功能的特征是：采用独立于牵引系统和外部电源的安全制动系统，受自动列车控制与保护系统控制。在运行速度由 500 km/h 降至 10 km/h 的过程中，列车采用涡流制动器制动（通过车载蓄电池供电）。其特点是：制动功能与气候无关，制动力可控制，通过单独控制和冗余的电磁制动回路，保证安全可靠的制动功能。当速度降至 10 km/h 后，列车通过滑橇降落在滑行轨上滑行，靠摩擦力制动，保证列车停在预定位置。

The safety braking function is characterized by a safety braking system independent of the traction system and external power supply and controlled by the automatic train control and protection system. When the running speed is reduced from 500 km/h to 10 km/h, the train adopts eddy current brake for braking (powered by on-board battery). It is characterized in that the braking function is independent of the climate, the braking force can be controlled, and the safe and reliable braking function is ensured through a separately controlled and redundant electromagnetic braking circuit. When the speed is reduced to 10 km/h, the train will slide on the sliding track through the skid and brake by friction to ensure that the train stops at the predetermined position.

五、列车自动控制与保护

4.6.5　Automatic Train Control and Protection

列车自动控制与保护系统保证列车自动、安全运行，具有产生运行指令、道岔动作指令、牵引系统控制参数等控制功能，监视列车运行速度范围及其他与安全有关的列车功能和状态、开通安全区间及停车区、触发安全制动系统、产生列车运行状态信息等安全功能。

The automatic train control and protection system ensures the automatic and safe operation of the train, and has the control functions of generating operation instructions, switch action instructions, traction system control parameters, monitoring the train operation speed range and other safety-related train functions and status, opening safety sections and parking areas, triggering safety braking system, generating train operation status information and other safety functions.

正常运行为自动模式，并依靠安全保护系统的保护。列车运行按照存储在运行控制系统中的程序自动地进行。因此正常的运行安全完全依靠设备保障，而车站工作及值班人员、车上工作人员的主要工作是为旅客服务。

Normal operation is in automatic mode and is protected by the safety protection system.Train operation is performed automatically in accordance with a program stored in the operation control system.Therefore, the normal operation safety depends entirely on the equipment guarantee, and the main work of the station staff, on-duty staff and on-board staff is to serve the passengers.

六、自动监测

4.6.6　Automatic Monitoring

牵引驱动系统、运行控制、安全防护系统设备依靠其自身的自动监测及故障诊断子系统保障其可靠性、可用性及故障安全性。

Traction drive system, operation control and safety protection system equipment rely on their own automatic monitoring and fault diagnosis subsystems to ensure their reliability, availability and safety.

运行的车载设备自动检测线路轨道，以确定轨道结构几何尺寸的变化或者附属设备的偏移。车上的设备可有规律地监测各功能区域，将所测的数据与参考值相比较，显示各类偏差并确定其位置，以便检修、调整。

The running on-board equipment automatically detects the track of the line to determine changes in the geometric dimensions of the track structure or deviations of auxiliary equipment. The equipment on the vehicle can regularly monitor each functional area, compare the measured data with the reference value, display all kinds of deviations and determine their locations for maintenance and adjustment.

七、辅助停车区

4.6.7　Auxiliary Parking Area

辅助停车区是线路上某些用于列车计划外停车的特定路段，配置动力轨，是保护乘客的重要措施。列车即使在严重故障情况下也能到达下一个停车区（车站停车区或辅助停车区），在这里可以实施计划救援方案。

The auxiliary parking area is a specific section of the line for unplanned parking of trains, and the power rail is an important measure to protect passengers.The train can reach the next parking area (station parking area or auxiliary parking area) even in the case of serious failure, where the planned rescue plan can be implemented.

即使在罕见的系统技术失灵的情况下，如果下一站距离太远，列车将在下一个沿着轨道按一定距离设立的技术停车站（辅助停车区）停靠。制动借助于涡流制动装置来实现，这个装置同样也由车上的蓄电池供电。它使列车的速度减到 10 km/h，然后将列车放到滑板上停住。

Even in the extremely rare case of a technical failure of the system, if the next station is too far away, the train will stop at the next technical stop (auxiliary parking area) set up at a certain distance along the track.Braking is achieved by means of an eddy-current brake, which is also powered by the on-board battery. It reduces the speed of the train to 10 km/h and then stops the train on the skateboard.

八、车上防火保护

4.6.8　On-board Fire Protection

车上火灾的预防措施包括：①采用电子式电源断路器、电流监测器监测电气设备，当发生故障时，自动将车辆内的电源系统切断。②采用超负荷电流和短路电流保护装置切断车内设备电源。③采用具有绝缘监控功能的车载电源系统，并由分布式冗余绝缘监测器监测其接地故障，各套车载冗余电源系统之间设置电气隔离。④车载蓄电池具有双重绝缘，并有可靠的通风设备。蓄电池连接电缆皆具有可靠的防短路和接地保护性能。电池冷却及其废气排放依靠冗余通风装置及监测装置，故不会聚集爆炸性气体。⑤当车辆停止或者车速低于直线发电机使用的速度时，为车上供电的电流接触器将单独连接，并且在电流为零时从动力轨上断开，避免产生火花。⑥车上设施皆不具备可燃性。车上没有燃料或者易燃冷却材料。列车使用的全部是无聚氯乙烯材料，这种材料很难点燃，不易导热，耐烧透和耐温度变化。⑦采用防止车上火灾蔓延的措施，如车辆的内部配件及电气装备均按照飞机防火标准设计，设置车载火灾报警系统，车内设置手持式化学灭火器，车厢过道门均按防火、防烟模式设计等。

Fire prevention measures on the vehicle include: ① Use electronic power circuit breaker and current monitor to monitor electrical equipment, and automatically cut off the power system in the vehicle in case of failure. ② Overload current and short-circuit current protection devices are used to cut off the power supply of the equipment in the vehicle. ③ On-board power supply system with insulation monitoring function shall be adopted, and its grounding fault shall be monitored by distributed redundant insulation monitor. Electrical isolation shall be set between each set of on-board redundant power supply system. ④ The on-board battery shall be provided with double insulation and reliable ventilation equipment.The connecting cables of the battery have reliable anti-short circuit and grounding protection performance. Battery cooling and its exhaust emissions rely on redundant ventilation and monitoring devices, so there is no accumulation of explosive gases. ⑤ When the vehicle is stopped or the vehicle speed is lower than the speed used by the linear generator, the current contactor supplying power to the vehicle will be connected separately and disconnected from the power rail when the current is zero to avoid sparks. ⑥ The facilities on the vehicle are not flammable.There is no fuel or flammable coolant on board. All the materials used in the train are non-polyvinyl chloride materials, which are difficult to ignite, not easy to conduct heat, and resistant to burning through and temperature changes. ⑦ Measures shall be taken to prevent the spread of fire on the vehicle, for example, the internal accessories and electrical equipment of the vehicle shall be designed in accordance with the aircraft fire protection standards, the on-board fire alarm system shall be set, the hand-held chemical fire extinguisher shall be set in the vehicle, and the compartment doors shall be designed in accordance with the fire and smoke protection modes.

列车上防火设施的安全性超过了飞机的安全标准。另外，每一节车厢都可以关闭所有的门窗进行有效防火。在发生火灾的时候，同样有预防措施。通常列车将驶入下一个技术停车站，在紧急情况下还可以在原地下车。

The safety of fire protection facilities on trains exceeds the safety standards of aircraft. In addition, all doors and windows of each carriage can be closed for effective fire prevention. In the event of a fire, there are also precautions. Normally the train will enter the next technical stop and can alight in place in an emergency.

九、车站旅客保护

4.6.9　Station Passenger Protection

为了保证乘客在车站上下车以及在站台候车时的安全，最佳方案是在站台边缘设置屏蔽门系统。根据建设标准需求，也可考虑先预留屏蔽门系统（运行控制系统等预留完备的接口、车站设计考虑屏蔽门安装条件），或者设置隔离栏杆等设施。

In order to ensure the safety of passengers getting on and off at the station and waiting at the platform, the best solution is to set up a platform screen door system at the edge of the platform. According to the requirements of construction standards, it can also be considered to reserve the platform screen door system first (complete interfaces are reserved for the operation control system, and the installation conditions of the platform screen door are considered in the station design), or to set up isolation railings and other facilities.

车站设置消防报警系统和灭火设施，如消火栓、化学灭火设施等，配置情况应按列车发生火灾进入车站进行扑救的具体要求考虑。

The station is equipped with fire alarm system and fire extinguishing facilities, such as fire hydrant, chemical fire extinguishing facilities, etc. The configuration shall be considered according to the specific requirements for the train to enter the station for fire fighting in case of fire.

进一步的安全措施包括自动列车安全设备、为了避免轨道结构和车站建筑受到损坏而装备的被动保护设施、自动化的轨道检查系统等。

Further safety measures include automatic train safety equipment, passive protection against damage to track structures and station buildings, automated track inspection systems, etc.

第七节　环保性能

Section 4.7　Environmental Protection Performance

磁浮超高速铁路从生态环境、生活环境方面来看也有诸多优点。例如，因无接触技术而没有车轮和驱动产生的噪声，不受原始能源的制约，沿途没有废气和其他有害物质的排放，高架轨道和低置轨道占地面积都很少，高架轨道下面仍然可以继续利用（如用于农业），高架轨道不破坏风景线、动物和植物的生活环境，高架轨道对野生动物的出没无不良影响，低置轨道也给两栖动物和小动物留有通道，广泛地避免使用路堤和路堑,对自然景色的影响很小。通过不同的轨道建筑形式和灵活的选线参数而具有对地形情况的适应能力。

Maglev super-high-speed railway also has many advantages in terms of ecological environment and living environment. For example, because of non-contact technology, there is no noise generated by wheels and driving, no restriction from original energy, no emission of exhaust gas and other harmful substances along the way, the area occupied by elevated track and low track is very small, the elevated track can still be used under it (such as for agriculture), and the elevated track does not destroy the landscape, the living environment of animals and plants. The elevated track has no adverse effect on the presence of wild animals, and the low track also provides access for amphibians and small animals. The use of embankments and cuttings is widely avoided, and the impact on natural scenery is very small. It has the ability to adapt to the terrain conditions through different track construction forms and flexible route selection parameters.

一、噪 声

4.7.1 Noise

传统交通系统的噪声来源于电机噪声、滚动噪声和空气动力(风)噪声。

The noise of traditional traffic system comes from motor noise, rolling noise and aerodynamic (wind) noise.

磁浮系统采用直线电机,电机噪声较低;通过无接触方式实现支承、导向、驱动、制动和供电,避免了车/线界面的接触,不产生机械噪声;在速度高达 250 km/h 时,TR 磁浮列车几乎无声地悬浮驶过城市和人口密集的地区;只是在速度超过 200 km/h 之后,会产生随速度增加的空气动力学噪声;磁浮列车以 400~500 km/h 的速度运行时,其噪声主要来源于空气动力噪声。故在常用的速度范围内,在相同的速度条件下,磁浮铁路的噪声比普通轮轨接触系统铁路所产生的噪声要低得多。

The maglev system adopts the linear motor with low motor noise; the non-contact support, guidance, driving, braking and power supply are realized to avoid the contact of the vehicle/line interface and generate no mechanical noise; when the speed is as high as 250 km/h, the TR maglev train is suspended almost silently through cities and densely populated areas; Only when the speed exceeds 200 km/h, the aerodynamic noise increases with the speed; when the maglev train runs at a speed of 400-500 km/h, the noise mainly comes from the aerodynamic noise. Therefore, in the common speed range, under the same speed conditions, the noise of the maglev railway is much lower than that of the ordinary wheel-rail contact system railway.

磁浮列车车体在转向架以下的部分最大限度地实施了外壳封闭,尤其是没有传统铁路的轮轨走行部，其空气阻力大为减少，同等速度下相应的空气动力噪声将比轮轨铁路低。同时，磁浮铁路的无接触供电，也消除了传统轮轨铁路的受电弓空气噪声。

The part of the maglev train body under the bogie is enclosed by the shell to the maximum extent, especially without the wheel-rail running part of the traditional railway, its air resistance is greatly reduced, and the corresponding aerodynamic noise is lower than that of the wheel-rail railway at the same speed. At the same time, the contactless power supply of maglev railway also eliminates the pantograph air noise of traditional wheel-rail railway.

（一）噪　声

4.7.1.1　Noise

噪声可能令人感到不舒服，甚至可能令人感到痛苦。可以测量的是声压级，也就是声源在空气中产生的压力波动。声压级用分贝（dB）来表示，用这种国际统一的测量单位能够模仿出人的听力感觉。声压级刻度分为 0 dB（听阈）到 130 dB（痛苦极限）。分贝刻度用对数的方式表示。提高 10 dB 时感觉到的音量增加一倍。通常接触到的噪声见表 4-2。

Noise can be uncomfortable and can even be painful. What can be measured is the sound pressure level, which is the pressure fluctuation in the air produced by the sound source. Sound pressure levels are expressed in decibels (dB), an internationally unified unit of measurement that mimics the human sense of hearing. Sound pressure levels are scaled from 0 dB (hearing threshold) to 130 dB (pain threshold). The decibel scale is expressed logarithmically. Double the perceived volume when increased by 10 dB. See Table 4-2 for common noise exposure.

表 4-2　通常接触到的噪声
Table 4-2　Common Noise Exposure

噪声源 Noise Source	距离/m Distance/m	噪声/dB Noise/dB
喷气式飞机 A Jet Plane	200	130
风动锤 Pneumatic Hammer	5	120
圆盘锯 Disc Saw	5	110
汽车喇叭 Car Horn	5	100
卡车 Truck	5	90
正常的公路交通 Normal Road Traffic	5	70

续表

噪声源 Noise Source	距离/m Distance/m	噪声/dB Noise/dB
正常的谈话 A Normal Conversation	5	60
很轻的收音机音乐 Very Light Radio Music	5	50
小声说话 Speak in a Low Voice	5	30
钟表的滴答声 The Ticking of a Clock	5	20
计算机 Computer	5	10

（二）TR与其他铁路的噪声比较

4.7.1.2 Noise Comparison Between TR and Other Railways

根据德国有关机构进行的测试，德国高速磁浮列车与德国高速轮轨列车的具体噪声值比较见表4-3。测量位置为距线路25 m处，测量结果为列车驶过时的瞬时值。可见，在相同速度的条件下，各种铁路形式中，磁浮铁路的噪声水平是最低的。

According to the test conducted by relevant German institutions, the specific noise values of German high-speed maglev train and German high-speed wheel-rail train are compared in Table 4-3. The measurement location is 25 m away from the line, and the measurement result is the instantaneous value when the train passes. It can be seen that under the condition of the same speed, the noise level of maglev railway is the lowest among all kinds of railway forms.

表4-3 磁浮列车与轮轨列车驶过的噪声对比

Table 4-3 Comparison of Passing Noise of Maglev Train and Wheel-Rail Train

运行速度/ (km/h) Operating Speed/ (km/h)	轮轨铁路噪声/dB Wheel-Rail Railway Noise/dB	磁浮铁路噪声/dB Maglev Railway Noise/dB
100	72	
160	79	70
200	83	73
250	88	78
280	89	81
300	91	83
400		91

由德国技术监督协会做出的比较测试表明，磁浮列车通过稠密居民区，以通常速

度行驶时产生的噪声，比任何其他交通系统都低。即使在 400 km/h 的速度情况下，它比轮轨铁路系统产生的噪声水平也要低得多。

Comparative tests conducted by the German Association of Technical Supervisors show that maglev trains generate less noise at normal speeds than any other transport system when traveling through dense residential areas. Even at speeds of 400 km/h, it produces much lower noise levels than wheel-rail systems.

（三）TR 与其他铁路及高速公路的噪声平比较

4.7.1.3　Noise Level Comparison Between TR and Other Railways and Expressways

对交通噪声的评价除了使用上述瞬时噪声之外，更常用的指标是在一段时间内的持续声平（噪声平）。根据测试可知，即使 TR 磁浮铁路速度达到 400 km/h，其所产生的噪声平仍然比速度为 250 km/h 时的 ICE 高速铁路、速度为 100 km/h 时的德国城郊铁路及高速公路的噪声平要低。

In addition to the transient noise mentioned above, The more commonly used indicator is the sustained sound level (noise level) over a period of time. According to the test, even if the TR maglev railway reaches 400 km/h, the noise level generated by it is still lower than the noise level of the ICE high-speed railway at 250 km/h, the German suburban railway and highway at a speed of 100 km/h.

二、振　动

4.7.2　Vibration

在运捷列车通过时，振动通过路基传入地下。列车引起的振动受德国联邦环境保护法约束。测量值根据 DIN4150 称之为振动强度 KB，并像判断噪声声级那样考虑其影响时间和影响强度。

When the express train passes, the vibration is transmitted into the ground through the roadbed. Train-induced vibrations are subject to the German Federal Environmental Protection Act. The measured value is called the vibration intensity KB according to DIN4150, and its influence time and influence intensity are taken into account in the same way as the noise level.

德国埃姆斯兰区磁悬浮高速铁路试验场（TVE）的测量表明，在列车以 250 km/h 的规定速度运行时，距离列车 25 m 处的振荡在人的"感觉阈"之下。在全部速度范围内，距离 50 m 没有任何振动的感觉。

Measurements at the Maglev High Speed Railway Test Site (TVE) in the Emsland region of Germany show that when the train is running at a specified speed of 250 km/h, the oscillation at 25 m from the train is below the human "sensory threshold". There is no feeling of vibration at a distance of 50 m over the entire speed range.

三、电磁污染强度

4.7.3　Electromagnetic Pollution Intensity

磁浮系统依靠巨大的磁吸引力实现列车的悬浮、导向和驱动，因此其磁场对人体的影响成为人们关注的重要问题。

The maglev system relies on the huge magnetic attraction to realize the suspension, guidance and drive of the train, so the influence of its magnetic field on the human body has become an important problem.

磁浮的强磁场存在于车辆、线路界面的间隙处。对人体的影响来自从间隙处泄漏的磁通量。德国磁浮铁路 TR 系统采用磁吸式悬浮原理，由于车、路界面的间隙很小（约 10 mm），且磁力线通过间隙闭合，故磁通的泄漏量很少，电磁污染强度非常低。它与地球磁场相当，远低于家用电器。吹风机或电视机周围的磁场强度远远高于在 TR 车厢里的磁场强度。车厢外面线路沿线的磁场强度就更低了。

The strong magnetic field of maglev exists in the gap between vehicle and line interface. The effect on the human body comes from the magnetic flux leaking from the gap. The German maglev railway TR system adopts the principle of magnetic levitation. Because the gap between the vehicle and the road is very small (about 10 mm), and the magnetic line of force is closed through the gap, the leakage of magnetic flux is very small, and the intensity of electromagnetic pollution is very low. It is comparable to the Earth's magnetic field and much lower than household appliances. The magnetic field strength around the hair dryer or television is much higher than that in the TR compartment. The magnetic field intensity along the line outside the carriage is even lower.

四、能　耗

4.7.4　Energy Consumption

高速运行条件下，空气阻力在列车所受的阻力中将占主导地位，由于空气阻力与速度的平方成正比，随着行车速度的提高，空气阻力迅速增大，列车能耗也明显增加，因此有必要分析行车速度对高速磁浮铁路运输能耗的影响，为磁浮铁路建设项目的技术经济分析提供依据。

Under the condition of high speed, the air resistance will be dominant in the resistance of the train, because the air resistance is proportional to the square of the speed, with the increase of the running speed, the air resistance increases rapidly, and the energy consumption of the train also increases significantly, so it is necessary to analyze the impact of running speed on the energy consumption of high-speed maglev railway transportation. It provides the basis for the technical and economic analysis of the maglev railway construction project.

经测试得知，在速度相同的情况下，德国磁浮 TR 系统比德国高速铁路 ICE 系统减少能耗 30%。换言之，在相同的能耗下，磁浮系统能多做 1/3 左右的功。

According to the test, the energy consumption of the German maglev TR system is 30% less than that of the German high-speed railway ICE system at the same speed. In other words, under the same energy consumption, the maglev system can do about 1/3 more work.

与公路和空中交通相比，超高速磁浮铁路系统的低能耗就更明显了。在可相比的距离情况下，小汽车的单位能量需要是 TR 磁浮铁路的 3 倍，飞机是 TR 磁浮铁路的 5 倍。

Compared with road and air traffic, the low energy consumption of ultra-high-speed maglev railway system is even more obvious. At comparable distances, the specific energy requirement of a car is three times that of a TR maglev railway, and that of an airplane is five times that of a TR maglev railway.

五、有害物质排放

4.7.5　Discharge of Harmful Substances

磁浮系统采用的能源为电能，运行中不排放有害物质。

The maglev system uses electric energy and does not emit harmful substances during operation.

六、土地占用

4.7.6　Land Occupation

土地是最重要的环境资源。磁浮系统作为大容量公共交通工具，与轮轨铁路一样，对土地的占用量少于高速公路。同时，由于磁浮系统在同等速度下容许的曲线半径比轮轨铁路小（最高速度 v_{max} = 300 km/h 时，轮轨铁路最小曲线半径 R_{min} = 4 000 ~ 5 000 m，磁浮系统最小曲线半径 R_{min} = 1 590 m）、坡度比轮轨铁路大（轮轨铁路最大坡度 i_{max} = 4%；磁浮系统最大坡度 i_{max} = 10%），线路能够更好地适应地形，减少填挖工程数量，从而使土地被占用和地表被破坏的数量更少。

Land is the most important environmental resource. As a high-capacity public transport, maglev system, like wheel-rail railway, occupies less land than highway. At the same time, because the allowable curve radius of maglev system is smaller than that of wheel-rail railway at the same speed (when the maximum speed v_{max} = 300 km/h, The minimum curve radius of the wheel-rail railway is R_{min} = 4,000-5,000 m, and the minimum curve radius of the maglev system is R_{min} = 1,590 m), and the slope is larger than that of the wheel-rail railway (the maximum gradient of the wheel-rail railway is i_{max} = 4%; the maximum gradient of the maglev system is i_{max} = 10%), the line can better adapt to the terrain, reduce the number of filling and excavation works, so that the number of land occupied and surface damage is less.

在平原地区，地形地质障碍少，土地开挖量少，磁浮系统的选线灵活优势在用地方面不明显，磁浮系统与轮轨铁路的土石方工程数量比较接近。

In the plain area, there are few topographic and geological obstacles, and the amount of land excavation is small. The advantage of flexible route selection of maglev system is not obvious in terms of land use. The amount of earthwork of maglev system is close to that of wheel-rail railway.

在山区，磁浮系统在选线参数上的灵活性得到充分体现，填挖高度将显著低于轮轨铁路，从而使路基开挖宽度和开挖断面面积大为减少。

In mountainous areas, the flexibility of maglev system in route selection parameters is fully reflected, and the filling and excavation height will be significantly lower than that of wheel-rail railway, thus greatly reducing the excavation width and excavation section area of subgrade.

磁浮高速铁路 TR 系统与其他交通系统相比，轨道和其他必要的设施占地最少。

Compared with other transportation systems, the maglev high-speed railway TR system occupies the least land for track and other necessary facilities.

七、气 流

4.7.7　Air Flow

德图埃姆斯兰试验线（TVE）对列车周围的气流进行了全面测量，结果如下：在高架轨道下面，在全部速度范围内均感觉不到气流；在低置轨道线路旁边，当磁浮列车驶过时感觉到的气流和典型的自然风一样。列车下面地上的小砾石在列车通过时原地不动；在速度为 350 km/h 时，在轨道旁边距离列车 1 m 处的气流速度小于 10 km/h。

The Detou-Emsland Test Line (TVE) carried out a comprehensive measurement of the airflow around the train, and the results were as follows: under the elevated track, the airflow was not felt at all speeds; beside the low track line, the airflow felt when the maglev train passed was the same as the typical natural wind. Small gravels on the ground under the train remain in place as the train passes; at 350 km/h, the airflow velocity at 1 m from the train beside the track is less than 10 km/h.

八、受天气情况的影响

4.7.8　Affected by Weather Conditions

比较而言，全部采用轨道导向的交通工具较少受天气情况的影响，磁浮铁路也一样。TR 铁路采用无接触技术，使其在极其特殊的天气形势下也照常运营。

Comparatively speaking, all rail-guided vehicles are less affected by weather conditions, as is the maglev railway. The TR railway uses contactless technology to enable it to operate as usual in very special weather conditions.

TR 磁浮列车的驱动部分被安装在轨道下面保护起来，那里既不会积雪，也不会结冰。只要轨道上出现超过规定数值的雪或冰，系统就将借助专用车辆予以清理。

The drive section of the TR Maglev is protected under the track, where there is neither snow nor ice. Whenever there is snow or ice on the track that exceeds the specified value, the system will clear it with the help of special vehicles.

第八节　德国、日本超高速磁浮铁路技术经济比较

Section 4.8　Technical and Economic Comparison of Ultra-high-speed Maglev Railway in Germany and Japan

目前在超高速磁浮铁路领域，德国常导磁浮铁路 TR 技术和日本超导磁浮铁路 MLX 技术是两个具有代表性的技术。本节首先将两种形式的系统技术特点进行总结，之后再讨论两者之间的不同之处。

At present, in the field of ultra-high-speed maglev railway, the TR technology of Germany and the MLX technology of Japan are two representative technologies. In this section, we first summarize the technical characteristics of the two forms of systems, and then discuss the differences between them.

一、德国 TR 系统的特点

4.8.1 Characteristics of German TR system

德国的 TR 超高速磁浮铁路系统采用电磁悬浮（EMS）原理。

The TR ultra-high-speed maglev railway system in Germany adopts the principle of electromagnetic levitation (EMS).

（一）主要技术特点

4.8.1.1 Main Technical Features

（1）借助气隙传感器和加速度传感器，通过对电磁铁的主动控制，实现车辆的悬浮和导向，悬浮气隙保持在 8～10 mm，悬浮高度与车速无关。

（1）With the help of air gap sensor and acceleration sensor, the suspension and guidance of the vehicle are realized through the active control of the electromagnet. The suspension air gap is kept at 8-10 mm, and the suspension height is independent of the vehicle speed.

（2）悬浮和导向功能采用可靠性高的冗余设计。

（2）Suspension and guidance functions adopt redundant design with high reliability.

（3）通过长定子直线电机，实现无接触的牵引和再生制动，制动时可向电网反馈电能。

（3）Non-contact traction and regenerative braking are realized through the long stator linear motor, and electric energy can be fed back to the power grid during braking.

（4）牵引功率的控制和转换通过地面固定设备实现。

（4）Control and conversion of traction power shall be realized through fixed equipment on the ground.

（5）车载 440 V 辅助电网由直线发电机供电。

（5）The on-board 440 V auxiliary power grid is powered by the linear generator.

（6）地面控制中心对列车位置的控制信号通过频率为 38 GHz 的无线电传送。

（6）The control signal of the ground control center to the train position is transmitted by the radio with the frequency of 38 GHz.

（7）当牵引系统失效时，采用车载的涡流制动器实现列车的目标定点制动。

（7）When the traction system fails, the on-board eddy current brake shall be used to realize the target fixed point braking of the train.

（8）线路高架或地面低置。

（8）The line is elevated or the ground is low.

（9）支承梁采用钢结构或混凝土结构。

（9）The supporting beam is of steel structure or concrete structure.

（10）道岔采用连续的钢结构梁，在电力、液压传动系统的推动下，产生弹性弯曲，实现列车换线。

（10）Continuous steel structure beam is adopted for the turnout, which is driven by the electric and hydraulic transmission system to produce elastic bending, so as to realize the train line change.

（11）系统运行由计算机全自动控制。

（11）The system operation is fully controlled by the computer.

（12）TR 磁浮列车由功能相对独立的多节车辆组成，其中包括两节头车和 0~8 节中间车，每节车可用作客运或运送贵重货物。

（12）The TR maglev train is composed of several cars with relatively independent functions, including two head cars and 0-8 intermediate cars, each of which can be used for passenger transport or transportation of valuable goods.

（二）系统特征

4.8.1.2　System Characteristics

（1）比较宽的应用范围，如速度范围为 200~500 km/h。

（1）Wide application range, such as the speed range of 200-500 km/h.

（2）客运能力（单向）为每年 700 万~4 000 万人。

（2）The passenger transport capacity (one-way) is 7 million to 40 million people per year.

（3）悬浮和导向的电子控制较复杂。

（3）The electronic control of suspension and guidance is complicated.

（4）在静止状态仍保持悬浮，不需要车轮。

（4）Remain suspended in a stationary state without wheel.

（5）由于牵引功率设备不在车上，所以车上有较大的使用空间。

（5）Since the traction power equipment is not on the vehicle, the vehicle has a large space for use.

（6）车上悬浮线圈沿车辆均匀分布，线路荷载小，且随着车速的升高，线路荷载增加不大。

（6）The suspension coils on the vehicle are evenly distributed along the vehicle, the line load is small, and with the increase of the vehicle speed, the line load increases slightly.

（7）优越的选线参数（转弯半径小，爬坡能力强）。

（7）Superior route selection parameters (small turning radius and strong climbing ability).

（8）能耗低。

（8）Low energy consumption.

（9）噪声低。

（9）Low noise.

（10）电磁场辐射可忽略不计。

（10）Electromagnetic field radiation is negligible.

（11）由于悬浮和导向的不稳定性，在功率电子和控制电子方面的耗费较大。

（11）The cost of power electronics and control electronics is large due to the instability of levitation and guidance.

（12）列车环抱着线路，安全性能好。

（12）The train encircles the line and has good safety performance.

二、日本 MLX 系统的特点

4.8.2　Characteristics of Japanese MLX System

日本超高速磁浮铁路 MLX 系统采用电动悬浮（EDS）技术。

Electric suspension (EDS) technology is adopted for MLX system of ultra-high-speed maglev railway in Japan.

（一）技术特点

4.8.2.1　Technical Features

（1）磁浮列车速度超过大约 120 km/h 时，实现无接触的悬浮和导向。

（1）Achieving non-contact levitation and guidance when the speed of the maglev train exceeds about 120 km/h.

（2）在 120 km/h 速度以下，依靠车轮支承和导向。

（2）Under the speed of 120 km/h, it depends on wheel support and guidance.

（3）通过无铁心的长定子同步直线电机实现牵引和正常的运行制动，采用空气芯铝线圈。

（3）The traction and normal operation braking are realized by the long stator synchronous linear motor without iron core, and the air core aluminum coil is adopted.

（4）混凝土结构的线路断面呈"U"字形，在侧壁的内侧安装用于悬浮、导向的"8"字形线圈和用于牵引的直线电机定子线圈。

（4）The line section of the concrete structure is U-shaped, and the inner side of the side wall is provided with an 8-shaped coil for suspension and guidance and a linear motor stator coil for traction.

（5）车辆的两端装有超导线圈，形成超导强磁体，当车速达到 120 km/h 以后，超导磁体产生的运动磁场在线路内侧的"8"字形线圈中感应出电流，感应电流与超导磁体的磁场相互作用，产生悬浮力和导向力，悬浮力和导向力不需要主动控制，列车的稳定悬浮气隙约 100 mm。

（5）Superconducting coils are installed at both ends of the vehicle to form a strong superconducting magnet. When the vehicle speed reaches 120 km/h, the moving magnetic field generated by the superconducting magnet induces current in the "8" shaped coil inside the line. The interaction between the induced current and the magnetic field of the superconducting magnet produces levitation force and guidance force, which do not need active control. The stable suspension air gap of the train is about 100 mm.

（6）在紧急情况下安全制动时，使用空气翼动力制动（较高速度时）、再生制动和车轮盘型制动。

（6）When braking safely in emergency, use air wing dynamic braking (at higher speed), regenerative braking and wheel disc braking.

（7）第一列磁浮列车上的 300 V 电网由车载的燃气轮发电机经蓄电池组缓冲后供电，之后的磁浮列车采用直线感应发电机对车载电网供电。

（7）The 300 V power grid on the first maglev train is powered by the on-board gas turbine generator after buffering by the battery pack, and the subsequent maglev train uses the linear induction generator to supply power to the on-board power grid.

（8）列车运行由计算机全自动控制。

（8）Train operation is fully controlled by computer.

（二）系统特点

4.8.2.2　System Characteristics

（1）应用速度为 500~550 km/h。

（1）The application speed is 500-550 km/h.

（2）适合于超高速场合，因为在中低速下，悬浮力与涡流阻力损耗的比例不佳。

（2）It is suitable for ultra-high speed applications, because the ratio of levitation force to vortex resistance loss is not good at medium and low speeds.

（3）车体质量较轻。

（3）The weight of the car body is light.

（4）由于线路呈"U"形，列车运行时，辐射噪声较低。

（4）Due to the "U" shape of the line, the radiation noise is low when the train is running.

（5）悬浮和导向系统中，不需要对超导磁体进行反馈控制，但采用液氦对超导线圈制冷，低温超导体和制冷设备的能量耗费较大。

（5）In the suspension and guidance system, the feedback control of the superconducting magnet is not needed, but the cryogenic superconductor and the refrigeration equipment consume a lot of energy when liquid helium is used to refrigerate the superconducting coil.

（6）由于涡流损耗，在中低速运行时，能耗相对较高。

（6）Due to the eddy current loss, the energy consumption is relatively high at medium and low speeds.

（7）悬浮气隙较大，对导轨的加工精度要求较低。

（7）The suspension air gap is large, and the requirement for the machining accuracy of the guide rail is low.

（8）起动和制动时都需要带有车轮的运行装置。

（8）Running devices with wheels are required for starting and braking.

（9）由于采用超导强磁铁及电动悬浮技术，系统原理决定了较高的电磁辐射。

（9）Due to the use of superconducting strong magnet and electric suspension technology, the system principle determines the higher electromagnetic radiation.

（10）电动悬浮系统悬浮的一级抗振动阻尼较低，需要额外的措施来保证乘坐的舒适性。

（10）The primary anti-vibration damping of the electric suspension system is low, and additional measures are needed to ensure the ride comfortability.

三、悬浮系统及适用速度比较

4.8.3　Comparison of Suspension System and Applicable Speed

悬浮原理不同，导致技术特征亦不同。

Different suspension principles lead to different technical characteristics.

（一）EDS斥力型磁浮特征

4.8.3.1　Characteristics of EDS Repulsion Maglev

EDS斥力型磁浮铁路的特点是：列车运行速度等于零时不能静止悬浮，它依靠车辆上的磁体（超导磁体、永磁铁或常导线圈）在运动时切割线路上的导体（短路环、"8"字形线圈或导体板）产生感应电流，该电流产生的磁力线必然与产生它的磁力线相反，形成斥力。这类磁浮列车的垂直悬浮力和通过曲线时的横向导向力都是利用这个原理实现的，所以在静止时没有悬浮力和导向力。

The characteristics of the EDS repulsion type maglev railway are as follows: the train cannot be suspended when the running speed is equal to zero. It relies on the magnet (superconducting magnet, permanent magnet or normal conducting coil) on the vehicle to cut the conductor (short-circuit ring, "8" coil or conductor plate) on the line to generate induced current when it moves. The magnetic line of force generated by the current must be opposite to the magnetic line of force generated by it, forming a repulsive force. The vertical levitation force and the lateral guidance force of this kind of maglev train are realized by this principle, so there is no levitation force and guidance force at rest.

磁浮铁路的车辆与线路有磁场耦合，在运动时必然会产生磁阻力。轮轨列车运行时有机械摩擦阻力，不存在磁阻力，机械摩擦阻力随着速度线性增加；而斥力型磁浮列车的磁阻力在低速时大，而在高速时随着速度增高而下降，这也就是斥力型磁浮列车适用于高速运行的一个原因。在磁浮铁路中，悬浮力（或导向力）与运行磁阻力的比值是一个重要指标。这个比值对于斥力型磁浮列车是随着速度提高而增大的。

There is a magnetic field coupling between the vehicle and the line of the maglev railway, which will inevitably produce magnetic resistance when moving. Wheel-rail train has mechanical friction resistance, but no magnetic resistance, and the mechanical friction resistance increases linearly with the speed; the magnetic resistance of the repulsion type maglev train is large at low speed, and decreases with the increase of speed at high speed, which is one of the reasons why the repulsion type maglev train is suitable for high-speed operation. The ratio of levitation force (or guidance force) to running detent force is an important index in maglev railway. This ratio increases with the increase of the speed of the repulsion maglev train.

从以上分析可以看出，斥力型磁浮列车适用于超高速，速度越高，悬浮力越大，磁阻力下降，效率提高。而在低速（如速度低于 120 km/h）时，不能产生足够的悬浮力使列车离开地面线路。因此这类斥力型磁浮铁路只适用于大城市间长距离高速运输，日本开发研制低温超导磁浮列车的目的是准备在东京到大阪 517 km 线路上应用。现在速度为 250 km/h 的轮轨高速约需 3 h，而采用速度 500 km/h 的磁浮列车 1 小时多就能跑完全程。另外，日本专家认为，日本是个多地震国家，不宜采用德国 TR 吸力型高速磁浮列车，因为常导吸力型磁浮列车的悬浮气隙仅 8~10 mm，精度要求太高。

From the above analysis, it can be seen that the repulsion type maglev train is suitable for ultra-high speed, the higher the speed, the greater the levitation force, the lower the magnetic resistance and the higher the efficiency. At low speeds (e.g., less than 120 km/h), it is not possible to generate enough levitation force to keep the train off the ground line. Therefore, this kind of repulsion maglev railway is only suitable for long-distance and high-speed transportation between big cities. The purpose of developing the cryogenic superconducting maglev train in Japan is to prepare for the application on the 517 km line from Tokyo to Osaka. At present, the wheel-rail high-speed train with a speed of 250 km/h takes about 3 hours, while the maglev train with a speed of 500 km/h can complete the whole journey in more than one hour. In addition, Japanese experts believe that Japan is an earthquake-prone country, and it is not appropriate to adopt the German TR suction high-speed maglev train, because the suspension air gap of the normal conduction suction maglev train is only 8-10 mm, and the accuracy requirement is too high.

（二）EMS 吸力型磁浮特征

4.8.3.2　Characteristics of EMS Suction Type Maglev

德国 TR 型磁浮列车的垂向悬浮力是由线路的同步电机铁心与车辆上同步电机的磁极之间形成气隙磁通产生的，驱动力（纵向牵引力）与垂向悬浮力两个系统合二为一，这也是德国 TR 磁浮铁路的优势所在。

The vertical levitation force of German TR maglev train is generated by the air gap flux formed between the synchronous motor core of the line and the magnetic pole of the synchronous motor on the vehicle. The two systems of driving force (longitudinal traction force) and vertical levitation force are combined into one, which is also the advantage of German TR maglev railway.

与斥力型磁浮列车相同，吸力型磁浮列车在钢轨上运动时，也会产生运动磁阻力。因为车上磁体产生的磁力线，运动时在钢轨内会引起感应电流（涡流）而产生能耗，形成磁阻力。德国 TR 磁浮列车运行的磁阻力主要在导向钢板中产生涡流，而在垂向悬浮系统中，因为地面电机定子铁心是用矽钢片叠成的，涡流很小，磁阻力可忽略不计。

Like the repulsion type maglev train, the attraction type maglev train will also produce moving magnetic resistance when it moves on the rail. Because the magnetic line of force generated by the magnet on the vehicle will cause induced current (eddy current) in the rail when moving, resulting in energy consumption and magnetic resistance. The magnetic resistance of German TR maglev train mainly produces eddy current in the guide steel plate, while in the vertical suspension system, because the stator core of the ground motor is made of silicon steel sheets, the eddy current is very small and the magnetic resistance can be ignored.

（三）小　结

4.8.3.3　Summary

由上述分析可知，从磁浮铁路的悬浮特征、磁阻力特征来看，德国 EMS 型 TR 磁浮铁路的适用速度范围要宽一些，日本 EDS 型 MLX 磁浮铁路的适用速度要高一些。

It can be seen from the above analysis that the applicable speed range of German EMS type TR maglev railway is wider and the applicable speed of Japanese EDS type MLX maglev railway is higher in terms of the levitation characteristics and magnetic resistance characteristics of maglev railway.

四、主要技术特点比较

4.8.4　Comparison of Main Technical Features

下面介绍德国常导超高速磁浮铁路 TR 与日本超导超高速磁浮铁路 MLX 系统的

主要技术性能方面的比较，见表4-4。

See Table 4-4 for the comparison of the main technical performance of the German normal conducting ultra-high-speed maglev railway TR and the Japanese superconducting ultra-high-speed maglev railway MLX system.

表 4-4 主要技术特点比较
Table 4-4 Comparison of Main Technical Features

项 目 Items	德国 TR 系统 German TR System	日本 MLX 系统 Japanese MLX System
悬浮方式 Suspension Mode	电磁吸引式 Electromagnetic Attraction Type	侧壁电动式 Side Wall Electric Type
悬浮气隙 Levitation Air Gap	8-10 mm	100 mm 以上 More than 100 mm
运行速度 Operating Speed	高低均可 Both High and Low	超高速 Ultra High Speed
低速时悬浮状态 Levitation at Low Speed	悬浮 Suspension	车轮支承和导向 Wheel Support and Guidance
悬浮、导向控制 Levitation and Guidance Control	需闭环控制 Closed-Loop Control Required	不需控制，具有自稳定性 No Need of Control, With Self-Stability
线路荷载分布 Line Load Distribution	连续分散 Continuous Dispersion	相对集中 Relatively Concentrated
电磁铁的安全冗余 Safety Redundancy of Electromagnet	常导电磁铁有安全冗余 Normally Conducting Electromagnet With Safety Redundancy	超导电磁铁无安全冗余 Superconducting Electromagnet Without Safety Redundancy
最高试验速度 Maximum Test Speed	450 km/h	552 km/h
最高应用速度 Maximum Application Speed	430 km/h	约 500 km/h About 500 km/h
车内磁力线泄漏 Leakage of Magnetic Line of Force in the Vehicle	几乎没有，对人体无碍 Almost None. No Harm to the Human Body.	相对较强，但经测试对生物无害，使用心脏起搏器者不宜乘车 Relatively Strong, Be Harmless to Organisms After Testing, Unsuitable for Cardiac Pacemakers Users Riding
技术难点 Technical Difficulties	精确控制技术 Precise Control Technology	低温超导制冷技术 Cryogenic Superconducting Refrigeration Technology
线路造价 Line Cost	较低 Lower	较高 Higher

（一）运行速度

4.8.4.1 Running Speed

TR 系统的最高试验速度和最高运营速度分别是 450 km/h 和 430 km/h，而 MLX 系统分别为 552 km/h 和 500 km/h。因此，从最高速度方面比较，MLX 系统优于 TR 系统。

The maximum test speed and maximum operating speed of the TR system are 450 km/h and 430 km/h, respectively, while the MLX system is 552 km/h and 500 km/h, respectively. Therefore, the MLX system is superior to the TR system in terms of top speed.

（二）荷载分布

4.8.4.2 Load Distribution

TR 车辆以均匀荷载的形式作用在线路结构上，MLX 车辆以相对集中的荷载形式作用在线路结构上。因此，TR 的荷载在车辆结构、线路结构中产生的内应力和相应的冲击系数小于 MLX 车辆。

TR vehicles act on the line structure in the form of uniform load, while MLX vehicles act on the line structure in the form of relatively concentrated load. Therefore, the internal stress and corresponding impact coefficient generated by TR load in vehicle structure and line structure are less than those of MLX vehicle.

（三）电磁铁

4.8.4.3 Electromagnet

MLX 车辆需要复杂的车载低温冷却系统且要防止失超现象发生，而 TR 车辆采用常导技术，容易实现。不过 TR 系统需要多闭环控制悬浮系统，该系统是多因素的、随机的，难度大；MLX 则不需要，它本身具有稳定特性。

MLX vehicle requires a complex on-board cryogenic cooling system and needs to prevent the occurrence of quench phenomenon, while TR vehicle uses conventional technology, which is easy to achieve. However, the TR system requires a multi-closed-loop control levitation system, which is multi-factor, random and difficult, while the MLX does not, because it has its own stability characteristics.

（四）长定子电机、制动系统比较

4.8.4.4 Comparison of Long Stator Motor and Braking System

下面介绍两者在与控制有关的性能（包括直线电机、变压器、制动等内容）方面的不同，见表 4-5。

The following describes the differences between the two in terms of control-related performance (including linear motor, transformer, braking, etc.), as shown in Table 4-5.

表 4-5 直线电机、制动系统比较

Table 4-5 Comparison of Linear Motor and Braking System

项 目 Items	德国 TR 系统 German TR System	日本 MLX 系统 Japanese MLX System
定子 Stator	长定子有铁心 The Long Stator With an Iron Core	长定子无铁心，空气芯铝线圈 Long Stator Without Iron Core, Air Core Aluminum Coil
驱动绕组 Drive Winding	波形绕组 Wave Winding	环形绕组 Toroidal Winding
长定子开关站分段长度 Section Length of Long Stator Switchyard	300-2,000 m	456 m
长定子开关 Long Stator Switch	机械式开关，无电流时开合 Mechanical Switch, Open and Close Without Current	机械式开关，无电流时开合 Mechanical Switch, Open and Close Without Current
悬浮线圈 Suspension Coil	长电子铁心用于悬浮 Long Stator Core for Levitation	另设悬浮、导向共用的"8"字形感应线圈 A Common "8" Shaped Induction Coil for Suspension and Guidance is Arranged
供电方式 Power Supply Mode	交-直-交供电（GTO） AC-DC-AC Power Supply (GTO)	交-直-交供电（GTO） AC-DC-AC Power Supply (GTO)
逆变器容量 VVVF Inverter Capacity	15 MV・A	南线 38 MV・A，北线 20 MV・A South 38 MV・A, North 20 MV・A
变电站间距 Substation Spacing	20-50 km	50 km
正常制动方式 Normal Braking Mode	直线电机再生制动 Linear Motor Regenerative Braking	再生制动、低速时车轮盘型制动 Regenerative Braking, Wheel Disc Braking at Low Speed
紧急制动 Emergency Braking	涡流制动 Eddy Current Braking	空气动力制动（高速时） 车轮盘型制动（低速时） Aerodynamic Brake (at High Speed) Wheel Disc Brake (at Low Speed)
紧急制动停车点 Emergency Braking Stop	预定的有救援、疏散设施的停车点 Reserved Parking Spots With Rescue and Evacuation Facilities	任意位置，旅客从双线之间的通道疏散 Passengers Can Evacuate from Any Position Through the Passage Between the Two Lines

（五）导轨结构

4.8.4.5　Guide Rail Structure

TR 车辆环抱 T 形导轨，MLX 车辆在 U 形导轨槽中运行，列车在这两种结构形式上运行都很安全，不会产生脱轨、翻车等事故。其中，MLX 的槽形结构有利于降低车辆的高度，进而在隧道地段有利于降低工程造价。另外，MLX 系统的道岔采用分段移动 U 形导轨槽技术，而 TR 系统的道岔采用连续弯曲连续钢梁技术。

The TR vehicle encircles the T-shaped guide rail, and the MLX vehicle runs in the U-shaped guide rail groove. The train runs safely on these two structures, and there will be no derailment, rollover and other accidents. Among them, the trough structure of MLX is conducive to reducing the height of vehicles, and then to reducing the project cost in the tunnel section. In addition, the turnout of MLX system adopts the technology of sectional moving U-shaped guide rail groove, while the turnout of TR system adopts the technology of continuous bending continuous steel beam.

（六）悬浮性能

4.8.4.6　Suspension Performance

运捷 TR 的悬浮高度约为 MLX 的 1/10，对轨面的平顺性要求高，控制悬浮气隙较难，抗振性能较差，且必须保证线路及轨道结构具有足够的高度，避免承载结构因车辆引起的弹性挠度过大而干扰气隙量的控制。MLX 系统由于采用感应电流使车辆悬浮，故车辆在低速运行时悬浮力很小，车辆需要车轮支承，而在 100～150 km/h 以上才有足够的悬浮力使得车辆悬浮起来。TR 车辆在静止或低速行驶时都能悬浮，所以不需要辅助支承，但这部分的耗电量会增加。

The suspension height of TR is about 1/10 of that of MLX, which requires high smoothness of rail surface. It is difficult to control the suspension air gap, and the anti-vibration performance is poor. In addition, it is necessary to ensure that the line and track structure have sufficient height to avoid interference with the control of air gap due to excessive elastic deflection of the bearing structure caused by vehicles. MLX system uses induced current to suspend the vehicle, so the suspension force is very small when the vehicle is running at low speed, and the vehicle needs wheel support, but there is enough suspension force to suspend the vehicle above 100-150 km/h. The TR vehicle can levitate at rest or at low speed, so it does not need auxiliary support, but the power consumption of this part will increase.

（七）电磁污染

4.8.4.7　Electromagnetic Pollution

为了降低超导强磁场辐射问题，MLX 车辆的超导磁铁设置在车厢两头底部的连接转向架上，远离乘客，在连接车厢的通道处采取了磁屏蔽措施。TR 系统的外泄磁场强度很低，不必采用特殊的屏蔽措施。两种车辆的磁场强度分别为 0.2 mT 和 0.1 mT，都不会对健康乘客造成危害。

In order to reduce the problem of superconducting strong magnetic field radiation, the superconducting magnet of MLX vehicle is set on the connecting bogie at the bottom of both ends of the carriage, far away from passengers, and magnetic shielding measures are taken at the passage connecting the carriage. The leakage magnetic field intensity of TR system is very low, so it is not necessary to adopt special shielding measures. Magnetic field strengths of 0.2 mT and 0.1 mT for both vehicles are not hazardous to healthy passengers.

（八）噪　声

4.8.4.8　Noise

1996 年开始试验的 MLX01-01、MLX01-02 车辆分别采用双重尖点（双尖交角）和流线型（航空模型）形状，产生的噪声比 TR07 系统车辆略低一些。当车速为 300 km/h 时，在距离线路 25 m、高度 1.2 m 处测量，MLX01 的噪声比 TR07 低 6 dB。自 2002 年开始，日本采用新型的 MLX01-901 车头，其流线特性更加突出，它所产生的噪声水平比 TR07 更低一些。

The MLX01-01 and MLX01-02 vehicles tested in 1996 adopt double cusp (double cusp intersection angle) and streamline (aviation model) shapes respectively, and the noise generated is slightly lower than that of TR07 system vehicles. At 300 km/h, the noise of MLX01 is 6 dB lower than that of TR07, measured at a distance of 25 m from the line and a height of 1.2 m. Since 2002, Japan has adopted the new MLX01-901 locomotive, which has more prominent streamline characteristics and produces lower noise levels than TR07.

五、主要经济性能比较

4.8.5　Comparison of Main Economic Performance

（一）总投资及分项投资比较

4.8.5.1　Comparison of Total Investment and Itemized Investment

德国柏林—汉堡磁浮铁路计划总投资 98 亿马克（1 马克约 10.791 元人民币），投资指标约为 3 360 万马克/km。其中，土建部分造价 61 亿马克，占总投资的 62.2%；

机电、运行部分 28 亿马克，占总投资的 28.6%；车辆购置费为 9 亿马克，造价指标 7.25 万马克/辆，车辆部分造价仅占总投资的 9.2%。

The Berlin-Hamburg Maglev Railway in Germany is planned to have a total investment of 9.8 billion marks (1 mark is about 10.791 yuan), with an investment index of about 33.6 million marks/km. Among them, the cost of civil construction is 6.1 billion marks, accounting for 62.2% of the total investment; the cost of electromechanical and operation is 2.8 billion marks, accounting for 28.6% of the total investment; the purchase cost of vehicles is 900 million marks, the cost index is 72,500 marks per vehicle, and the cost of vehicles only accounts for 9.2% of total investment.

东京至大阪间中央新干线总投资指标约 58 亿日元/km（1 日元约 0.06 元人民币），土建部分以线路及车站为主体。其中，线路造价总计 7 650 亿日元；车站 5 处共计 250 亿日元；土地购置费 8 600 亿日元。绕组、电路等电力电气设备费用按 18 亿日元/km 计算，全线共计 9 000 亿日元，占总投资的 30%；40 列 14 辆编组列车的费用：车辆造价约 8 亿日元/辆，车辆购置费总计 4 500 亿日元，占总投资的 15%。

The total investment index of the Central Shinkansen between Tokyo and Osaka is about 5.8 billion yen/km (1 yen is about 0.06 yuan), and the civil part is mainly composed of lines and stations. Among them, the total cost of the line is 765 billion yen; the total cost of the five stations is 25 billion yen; and the land acquisition cost is 860 billion yen. The cost of winding, circuit and other electrical equipment is calculated as 1.8 billion yen/km, and the total cost of the whole line is 900 billion yen, accounting for 30% of the total investment; the cost of 40 14-car trains: The vehicle cost is about 800 million yen/vehicle, and the vehicle purchase cost is 450 billion yen, accounting for 15% of the total investment.

由此看来，日本中央磁浮新干线投资指标约是德国柏林—汉堡磁浮铁路投资的 3 倍。

From this point of view, the investment index of Japan's Central Maglev Shinkansen is about three times that of Germany's Berlin-Hamburg Maglev Railway.

（二）磁浮铁路与轮轨高速铁路的投资比较

4.8.5.2 Investment Comparison Between Maglev Railway and Wheel-Rail High-Speed Railway

根据德国对实际交通项目的测算，当在平原地区修建高速铁路时，选用 TR 磁浮铁路的综合投资比选用 ICE 轮轨高速铁路高 20%～30%；如线路主要通过中等山区，由于磁浮铁路选线更灵活、限制坡度更陡的原因，TR 系统综合造价与 ICE 相当或更低；考虑到 TR 运营费用低于轮轨铁路，所以从系统整个生命周期耗费来看，TR 应当优于 ICE。

According to the calculation of actual traffic projects in Germany, when high-speed railway is built in plain areas, the comprehensive investment of TR maglev railway is 20%-30% higher than that of ICE wheel-rail high-speed railway. If the line mainly passes through medium mountainous areas, the comprehensive cost of TR system is equivalent to or lower than that of ICE because the route selection of maglev railway is more flexible and the limiting slope is steeper; Considering that the operating cost of TR is lower than that of wheel-rail railway, TR should be superior to ICE in terms of the whole life cycle cost of the system.

东京至大阪间磁浮中央新干线的投资指标约 58 亿日元/km，与上越新干线不相上下，这与铁路工程专家及其他调研机构的估算结果大体相同。日本专家还根据山梨试验线总造价和新建的轮轨高速新干线建设投资对比，认为将来投入应用的超导磁浮铁路的造价可能比轮轨高 10%～20%。由于日本 MLX 磁浮铁路采用 U 形导轨断面，降低了车厢地板高度，减少了车辆断面，从而有利于减少隧道断面和隧道工程数量，因此在山区采用 MLX 系统，其造价应该低于传统轮轨高速铁路造价。

The investment target for the Maglev Central Shinkansen between Tokyo and Osaka is approximately 5.8 billion yen/km, which is comparable to the Joetsu Shinkansen. This is roughly consistent with the estimation results of railway engineering experts and other research institutions. According to the comparison between the total cost of the Yamanashi test line and the investment in the construction of the new wheel-rail high-speed Shinkansen, Japanese experts believe that the cost of the superconducting maglev railway to be put into use in the future may be 10% -20% higher than that of wheel-rail. Because the MLX maglev railway in Japan adopts U-shaped guide rail section, which reduces the floor height of the carriage and the vehicle section, thus helping to reduce the number of tunnel sections and tunnel projects, the cost of using MLX system in mountainous areas should be lower than that of traditional wheel-rail high-speed railway.

因此可以认为，在平原地区，磁浮铁路造价比轮轨高速铁路高 10%～30%；而在山区，磁浮铁路造价应该与轮轨高速铁路相当或低于轮轨高速铁路。综合来看，磁浮铁路造价并不比轮轨高速铁路造价有明显增加。

Therefore, it can be considered that in the plain area, the cost of maglev railway is 10% -30% higher than that of wheel-rail high-speed railway, while in the mountainous area, the cost of maglev railway should be equivalent to or lower than that of wheel-rail high-speed railway. Generally speaking, the cost of maglev railway is not significantly higher than that of wheel-rail high-speed railway.

（三）占　地

4.8.5.3　Land Occupation

在土地使用量方面，德国运捷 TR 线路由于均设置为高架或低置梁，并且由于使用 T 形梁，使得占地减少。TR 线路比日本 MLX 线路占地减少 10%～15%。

In terms of land use, the German Express TR line is set as elevated or low beams, and because of the use of T-shaped beams, the land occupation is reduced. The occupied area of TR line is reduced by 10%-15% compared with MLX line in Japan.

(四) 车体质量

4.8.5.4　Vehicle Body Quality

在减轻自重降低能耗方面，MLX 车辆的起浮和落地系统以及超导装置和冷却系统质量要占车辆质量的相当比例。但超导线圈无铁心，车体较轻。MLX 磁浮列车第二编组（4 辆编组）空车总质量只有 75 t，座位 208 个，列车总长 101.9 m，平均每座 360 kg，平均每延米质量 740 kg。而 TR 车辆下每侧装有 8 条，两侧共有 16 条相当大的电磁铁，车体较重。TR07 四辆编组列车总重 192.8 t，座位数 336 个，列车总长 103.5 m，平均每座 570 kg，平均每延米质量 1.86 t。可见，MLX 车体质量比 TR 轻很多。MLX 每座位平均质量只为 TR 的 63%，每延米质量只为 TR 的 40%。

In terms of reducing weight and energy consumption, the mass of the MLX vehicle's lifting and landing system, as well as the superconducting device and cooling system, accounts for a considerable proportion of the vehicle mass. However, the superconducting coil has no iron core, and the vehicle body is light. The second marshalling (4-car marshalling) of MLX maglev train has a total empty mass of only 75 t, 208 seats, a total length of 101.9 m, an average of 360 kg per seat, and an average mass of 740 kg per linear meter. The TR vehicle is equipped with 8 electromagnets on each side, and there are 16 quite large electromagnets on both sides, so the body is heavy. The total weight of TR07 four-car train is 192.8 t, the number of seats is 336, the total length of the train is 103.5 m, the average weight of each seat is 570 kg, and the average mass per linear meter is 1.86 t. It can be seen that the body mass of MLX is much lighter than that of TR. MLX has an average mass of only 63% of TR per seat and 40% of TR per linear meter.

(五) 能　耗

4.8.5.5　Energy Consumption

MLX 车辆通过超导线圈同时实现悬浮、驱动和导向 3 种功能，且车载超导线圈无铁心，只需很小的供电电流，所以耗电量很小。其耗电量主要用于地面定子绕组和维持液氢的超低温制冷用电，且在列车停站和低速行驶时依靠车轮实现支承和导向，此时在悬浮和导向方面不消耗电力。TR 车辆除了在驱动方面消耗电能之外，由于车辆在停站和低速行驶过程中始终处于悬浮状态，故与 MLX 系统相比，TR 系统增加了在悬浮和导向方面的能耗。

The MLX vehicle realizes three functions of suspension, driving and guiding at the same time through the superconducting coil, and the on-board superconducting coil has no iron core and only needs a small power supply current, so the power consumption is very small. Its power consumption is mainly used for the ground stator winding and maintaining the ultra-low temperature refrigeration of liquid helium, and when the train stops and runs at low speed, it relies on the wheels to achieve support and guidance, at this time, it does not consume power in suspension and guidance. In addition to the electric energy consumption in driving, the TR system increases the energy consumption in suspension and guidance compared with the MLX system because the vehicle is always in suspension during stop and low-speed driving.

（六）养护维护

4.8.5.6　Maintenance and Repair

与轮轨系统铁路相比，磁浮铁路的养护维修工作量很小。MLX 的养护维修工作主要集中在支承、导向橡胶车轮的拆换方面；而 TR 系统则没有车轮磨耗，养护维修工作量就更少了。

Compared with the wheel-rail system railway, the maintenance and repair workload of maglev railway is very small. The maintenance and repair work of MLX mainly focuses on the removal and replacement of supporting and guiding rubber wheels, while the TR system has no wheel wear, so the maintenance and repair workload is even less.

六、结　论

4.8.6　Conclusion

综合对比分析日本电动悬浮 MLX 与德国电磁悬浮 TR 系统在技术、经济、环境三方面的性能，可以得出如下结论：

The following conclusions can be drawn from the comprehensive comparison and analysis of the technical, economic and environmental performance of the Japanese electric levitation MLX and the German electromagnetic levitation TR system:

（1）MLX 系统造价高、超导技术难度大；TR 系统造价相对较低，虽然控制系统复杂、精确，但技术相对成熟，大部分零部件具有通用性，市场供应方便。

（1）The cost of MLX system is high and the superconducting technology is difficult; the cost of TR system is relatively low. Although the control system is complex and accurate, the technology is relatively mature, most of the parts are universal and the market supply is convenient.

（2）MLX系统车辆悬浮气隙较大，对轨面平整度要求较低，抗振性能好，速度快并且还有进一步提高速度的可能性，它还具有低速时不能悬浮的特点，因此更适合于大运量长距离、更高速度的客运。

（2）The MLX system vehicle has a large suspension air gap, low requirements for rail surface flatness, good anti-vibration performance, high speed and the possibility of further increasing the speed. It also has the characteristics that it can not be suspended at low speed, so it is more suitable for passenger transport with large capacity, long distance and higher speed.

（3）MLX系统集当代超导技术、磁浮铁路技术等高新技术于一体，其发展将与相关高新技术产业的发展相辅相成，发展潜力巨大。

（3）MLX system integrates modern superconducting technology, maglev railway technology and other high and new technologies, and its development will complement the development of related high-tech industries, with great potential for development.

（4）MLX与TR的噪声与能耗相近，MLX车辆屏蔽后的电磁辐射与TR车辆相差不大。

（4）The noise and energy consumption of MLX and TR are similar, and the electromagnetic radiation of MLX vehicle after shielding is not much different from that of TR vehicle.

（5）TR线路占地和养护维修费用较少，但MLX隧道限界较小，隧道工程造价更低，在隧道较多的山区更具有优越性。

（5）The land occupation and maintenance cost of TR line is less, but the tunnel clearance of MLX tunnel is smaller, the cost of tunnel engineering is lower, and it has more advantages in mountainous areas with more tunnels.

（6）关于适用速度范围，日本曾负责宫崎试验线超导磁浮车辆设计方案的西条教授认为，从经济和效率来看，在500 km/h以上速度运行时，日本电动悬浮（EDS）的磁浮铁路MLX优于德国电磁悬浮（EMS）的磁浮铁路TR；在300~500 km/h的速度范围内运行时，电磁悬浮铁路比较优越；在300 km/h以下时，采用轮轨高速可能更好。

（6）With regard to the applicable speed range, Professor Saijo, who was in charge of the design scheme of the superconducting maglev vehicle for the Miyazaki test line in Japan, believes that, in terms of economy and efficiency, the maglev railway MLX of Japan's electric suspension (EDS) is superior to the maglev railway TR of Germany's electromagnetic suspension (EMS) when running at a speed above 500 km/h; The electromagnetic levitation railway is superior when it runs at a speed of 300-500 km/h; when it runs below 300 km/h, the wheel-rail high speed may be better.

具体选用何种形式的轨道交通方式，主要取决于对运行速度和经济性的要求。

The specific choice of rail transit mode depends mainly on the requirements of running speed and economy.

复习思考题

Questions for Revision

1. 什么是导轨驱动长定子直线电机斥力电动悬浮系统？

1. What is the guideway driven long stator linear motor repulsion electric suspension system?

2. 什么是列车驱动短定子直线电机吸力电磁悬浮系统？

2. What is a train-driven short-stator linear motor suction electromagnetic levitation system?

3. 什么是导轨驱动长定子直线电机吸力电磁悬浮系统？

3. What is the guideway driven long stator linear motor suction electromagnetic suspension system?

4. 简要叙述德国常导超高速磁浮铁路的基本原理（悬浮原理、导向原理、驱动原理）。

4. Briefly describe the basic principles (suspension principle, guidance principle, driving principle) of the German ultra-high-speed maglev railway.

5. 简要叙述运捷07"欧罗巴号"的列车编组、车辆、悬浮架、二次悬挂系统、电气设备。

5. Briefly describe the train formation, vehicle, suspension frame, secondary suspension system and electrical equipment of TR07 "Europa".

6. 简要叙述德国常导超高速磁浮铁路供电系统与运行控制系统。

6. Briefly describe the power supply system and operation control system of the conventional ultra-high speed maglev railway in Germany.

7. 简要叙述德国TR磁浮交通系统的安全性能。

7. Briefly describe the safety performance of German TR maglev transportation system.

8. 简要对德国和日本的超高速磁浮铁路进行技术经济比较。

8. Briefly make a simple technical and economic comparison between the ultra-high speed maglev railway in Germany and Japan.

第五章　中国上海磁浮示范线

Chapter 5　China Shanghai Maglev Demonstration Line

上海磁浮列车示范运营线又称上海磁浮铁路、上海磁浮列车示范线、上海磁浮商业运营线、上海磁浮高速列车工程等，简称上海磁浮示范线，是"十五"期间上海市交通发展的重大项目，建成后已成为世界上第一条投入商业化运营的线路，具有交通、展示、旅游观光等多重功能，为上海又营造了一条亮丽的风景线。

Shanghai Maglev Train Demonstration Line, also known as Shanghai Maglev Railway, Shanghai Maglev Train Demonstration Line, Shanghai maglev commercial operation line, Shanghai maglev high-speed train project, etc., is a major project of Shanghai's transportation development during the "Tenth Five-Year Plan" period, and has become the first commercialized operation line in the world since its completion. It has multiple functions such as transportation, exhibition, tourism and sightseeing, and has created a beautiful scenery for Shanghai.

该工程项目大体分为车辆、控制、驱动（牵引供电）、线路（含轨道梁及土建工程）四大部分。该工程整个运行系统的设备，包括车辆、控制系统、驱动系统以及附属在轨道梁上的定子铁心和线圈电缆，全部由德方按成套设备方式供货。系统调试由德方负责；轨道梁在德方技术转让的基础上，由中方负责设计、制造；土建工程及设备安装由中方负责。

The project is generally divided into four parts: vehicle, control, drive (traction power supply) and line (including track beam and civil works). The equipment of the whole operation system of the project, including the vehicle, control system, drive system and the stator core and coil cable attached to the track beam, are all supplied by German Party in the form of complete equipment. The German Party shall be responsible for the system commissioning; the Chinese Party shall be responsible for the design and manufacture of the track beam based on the German Party's technology transfer; the Chinese Party shall also be responsible for civil engineering and equipment installation.

上海磁浮列车是常导磁吸型磁浮列车，是利用"异性相吸"原理设计的一种吸力悬浮系统，利用安装在列车两侧转向架上的悬浮电磁铁和铺设在轨道上的磁铁（实际上是线圈通电产生的磁场），在磁场作用下产生的吸力使车辆浮起来。车辆、控制部分均采用德国 TR 技术（详见第四章）。本章主要介绍磁浮线路及沿线铁路建筑物方面的有关内容。

Shanghai maglev train is a normal magnetic levitation train, which is a kind of suction levitation system designed by using the principle of "opposites attract". It uses the suspension electromagnets installed on the bogies on both sides of the train and the magnets laid on the track (in fact, the magnetic field generated by the coil electrification) to make the vehicle float under the action of the magnetic field. German TR technology is adopted for vehicle and control parts (see Chapter 4 for details). This chapter mainly introduces the relevant contents of the maglev line and the railway buildings along the line.

第一节　概　述

Section 5.1　Overview

20 世纪 80 年代，因初步掌握了高速磁浮铁路技术而成竹在胸的德国人，对欧洲以外最有可能修建磁浮铁路的国家和地区进行了排序：①美国和加拿大；②东南亚；③日本；④澳大利亚；⑤苏联；⑥沙特阿拉伯；⑦中国；⑧南美国家。

In the 1980s, the Germans, who had initially mastered the technology of high-speed maglev railway, ranked the countries and regions outside Europe that were most likely to build maglev railway: ① the United States and Canada; ② Southeast Asia; ③ Japan; ④ Australia; ⑤ the Soviet Union; ⑥ Saudi Arabia; ⑦ China; ⑧ South American countries.

然而，20 多年后，在这份排序表中差一位垫底的中国却拔得头筹，甚至走到了磁浮铁路的"鼻祖"德国人的前面。2002 年 12 月 31 日，世界上首条高速磁浮商业运营线——上海磁浮线正式开通并投入试运营，中德两国总理参加了开通仪式并乘坐了首趟列车。

However, more than 20 years later, China, which is one place short of the bottom in this ranking table, has won the first place, even ahead of the Germans, the "originator" of the maglev railway. On December 31, 2002, Shanghai Maglev Line, the world's first high-speed maglev commercial line, was officially opened and put into trial operation. Chinese and German prime ministers attended the opening ceremony and took the first train.

一、立项背景

5.1.1　Background of Project Establishment

1999年，国家在进行京沪高速铁路可行性研究论证的过程中，部分专家提出：鉴于高速磁浮交通系统具有无接触运行、速度高、起动快、能耗低、环境影响小等诸多优点，同时考虑到德国的高速常导磁浮试验线已经经历了十余年的运行，累计安全运行里程超过6 000万千米，而且德国政府也已宣布高速磁浮交通系统技术已经成熟等情况，认为要充分运用发展中国家的技术后发效应实现轨道交通跨越式发展，建议国家在京沪干线上采用高速磁浮技术。

In 1999, during the feasibility study of Beijing-Shanghai high-speed railway, some experts pointed out: Considering that the high-speed maglev transport system has many advantages such as non-contact operation, high speed, fast starting, low energy consumption and small environmental impact, and taking into account that the high-speed permanent maglev test line in Germany has been in operation for more than ten years, with a cumulative safe operating mileage of more than 60 million kilometers, and the German government has also announced that the high-speed maglev transport system technology has matured, etc. It is believed that the high-speed maglev technology should be adopted on the Beijing-Shanghai trunk line in order to make full use of the late effect of technology in developing countries to realize the leap-forward development of rail transit.

与此同时，大部分铁路专家则提出了相反的意见，认为高速轮轨系统技术经过几十年的实践已经完全成熟，我国国内对高速轮轨系统技术的开发也已经取得了重大进展；尽管高速磁浮技术拥有诸多优点，世界上不少国家也都在开展研究，但均停留在试验阶段，缺乏商业化运行实践，它的技术性、安全性和经济性尚未得到进一步验证，相对高速轮轨系统技术，磁浮技术在技术上、经济上都存在着很大风险。

At the same time, most railway experts put forward the opposite opinion that the high-speed wheel-rail system technology has been fully mature after decades of practice, and the development of high-speed wheel-rail system technology in China has also made significant progress; Although high-speed maglev technology has many advantages, many countries in the world are also carrying out research, but they are still in the experimental stage, lack of commercial operation practice, its technical, safety and economy have not been further verified, compared with high-speed wheel-rail system technology, maglev technology has great risks in technology and economy.

在论证过程中，两种意见一度相持不下，经过激烈的争论，专家们最终形成共识，建议先建设一段商业化运行示范线，以验证高速磁浮交通系统的成熟性、可用性、经济性和安全性。此建议得到了国务院领导的关注与支持，随即在对北京、上海、深圳三个地区进行比选后于2000年6月确定在上海建设。

In the process of demonstration, the two opinions were once at loggerheads. After a heated debate, experts finally reached a consensus, suggesting that a commercial operation demonstration line should be built first to verify the maturity, availability, economy and safety of the high-speed maglev transportation system. This proposal received the attention and support of the leaders of the State Council, and then decided to build in Shanghai in June 2000 after comparing the three regions of Beijing, Shanghai and Shenzhen.

二、工程简介

5.1.2　Project Introduction

上海磁浮列车示范运营线项目，结合上海经济和社会发展的需要，确定线路西起浦东新区规划的地铁枢纽龙阳路车站，东至浦东国际机场，主要解决连接浦东国际机场和市区的大运量高速交通需要。正线全长 30 km，并附有 3.5 km 的辅助路线，双线上下行折返运行，设两个车站、两个牵引变电站、1 个运行控制中心（设在龙阳路车站内部）和 1 个维修中心。初期配置 3 套车底，共 15 节车，设计最高运行速度为 430 km/h，单向运行时间约 8 min，发车间隔为 10 min。

Shanghai Maglev Train Demonstration Line Project, in combination with the needs of Shanghai's economic and social development, determines that the line starts from Longyang Road Station, the planned subway hub in Pudong New Area, in the west and ends at Pudong International Airport in the east, mainly to meet the needs of large-scale high-speed traffic connecting Pudong International Airport and the urban area. The total length of the main line is 30 km, with an auxiliary line of 3.5 km, double-track up and down turn-back operation, two stations, two traction substations, one operation control center (inside the Longyang Road Station) and one maintenance center. In the initial stage, it is equipped with 3 sets of car bottoms, totaling 15 cars, with the designed maximum running speed of 430 km/h, one-way running time of about 8 min, and departure interval of 10 min.

线路与上海地铁 2 号线平行向东，跨越新建的罗山路后，在罗山路东侧绿化带外侧边缘往南，分别跨越高科路、张衡路，一直到川杨河，过了川杨河以大半径曲线由北向东转，连接到迎宾大道。在迎宾大道北侧道路红线以外的规划绿地之中与迎宾大道并行向东，先后上跨申江路、外环线、华东路等主要道路，然后下穿迎宾立交，沿浦东国际机场主进场路的中间分隔带直抵机场的候机楼。沿线经过浦东新区的花木、张江、孙桥、黄楼、川沙、机场等镇及南汇区的康桥开发区。线路基本走向见图 5-1。

The line is parallel to Shanghai Metro Line 2 to the east. After crossing the newly built Luoshan Road, it crosses Gaoke Road and Zhangheng Road to the south at the outer edge of the green belt on the east side of Luoshan Road, and reaches Chuanyang River. After crossing Chuanyang River, it turns from north to east with a large radius curve and connects to Yingbin Avenue. Parallel to Yingbin Avenue in the planned green space outside the red line on the north side of Yingbin Avenue, it crosses the main roads such as Shenjiang Road, Outer Ring Road and Huadong Road successively, then crosses the Yingbin Interchange, and reaches the airport terminal along the median of the main entrance road of Pudong International Airport. It passes through Huamu, Zhangjiang, Sunqiao, Huanglou, Chuansha, Airport and other towns in Pudong New Area and Kangqiao Development Zone in Nanhui District. See Fig. 5-1 for the basic route of the line.

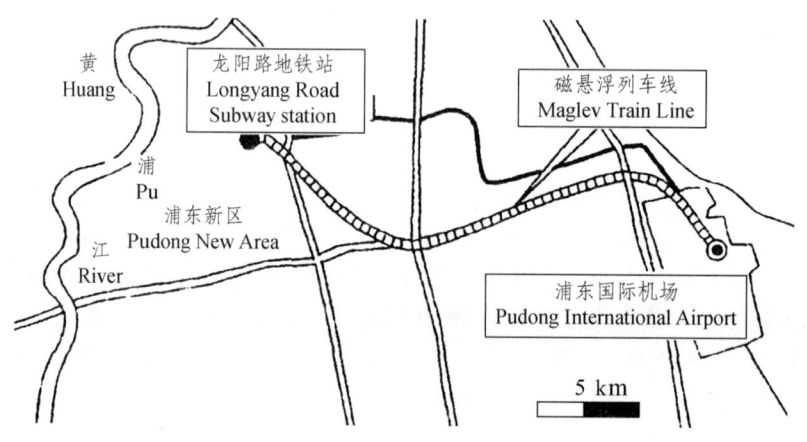

图 5-1 上海磁浮示范线走向图

Figure 5-1 Direction of Shanghai Maglev Demonstration Line

由于磁浮线路及轨道梁的设计、制造技术（线路设计理论与计算软件、混凝土钢复合梁设计理论与计算软件）是德方多年研究的专有技术，德国政府为帮助中方掌握磁浮线路的选线和轨道梁建造技术，先后两次提供赠款，用于技术转让费的支付。

As the design and manufacturing technology of maglev line and track beam (line design theory and calculation software, concrete steel composite beam design theory and calculation software) is the proprietary technology developed by the German side for many years, the German government has provided grants twice for the payment of technology transfer fees in order to help the Chinese side master the technology of maglev line selection and track beam construction.

磁浮轨道梁既是承载列车的承重结构，又是列车运行的导向结构，其制造的精度要求极高，梁体的加工和组装都必须在恒温车间进行。为了生产、加工磁浮轨道梁，特在浦东新区建立了磁浮轨道梁生产基地。

The maglev track beam is not only the load-bearing structure of the train, but also the guiding structure of the train operation. Its manufacturing accuracy requirements are extremely high, and the processing and assembly of the beam body must be carried out in the constant temperature workshop. In order to produce and process maglev track beams, a maglev track beam production base has been established in Pudong New Area.

三、速度目标值

5.1.3 Target Value of Speed

一条线路的速度目标值的选择，应考虑技术上可行，经济上合理；应与世界先进水平相适应，也与经济发展水平相适应；应考虑在综合交通运输体系中的竞争能力等诸多因素。磁浮列车的最大特点就是消除了传统的轮轨摩擦，因而能体现高速度、起动快、爬坡能力大等诸多优点。磁浮列车行车速度取决于列车的牵引能力（牵引加速度）、所受到的空气阻力（与车体形状有关）以及线路设计的各项参数。上海磁浮示范线的历史使命是为中国高速客运交通的模式选择提供可借鉴的经验，因此，它的速度应取较高的目标值，即列车商业运行最高速度为 430 km/h；列车示范运行最高速度为 505 km/h。

The selection of the speed target value of a line should consider many factors, such as technical feasibility, economic rationality, adaptation to the world's advanced level and the level of economic development, and the competitiveness in the comprehensive transportation system. The biggest characteristic of maglev train is that it eliminates the traditional wheel-rail friction, so it can reflect many advantages such as high speed, fast starting, good climbing ability and so on. The speed of maglev train depends on the traction capacity (traction acceleration), the air resistance (related to the shape of the train body) and the parameters of the line design. The historical mission of Shanghai Maglev Demonstration Line is to provide referential experience for the mode selection of high-speed passenger transport in China. Therefore, its speed should take a higher target value, that is, the maximum speed of trains in commercial operation is 430 km/h, and the maximum speed of trains in demonstration operation is 505 km/h.

四、运输能力

5.1.4 Transport Capacity

磁浮列车的运输能力与每辆车的定员、列车编组、发车间隔以及每天可以发送列车的时间有关。轨道交通系统的运输能力一般受车站分布或闭塞分区控制，即由运行图周期或列车追踪时间决定。同样，磁浮系统的变电站间距、运营速度、列车在车站区的运行方式和停站时间等对磁浮系统的列车最小追踪时间具有决定性的影响。这里所提的车站区运行方式，是指列车进出站时的速度限制，它对列车之间的允许时间间隔和旅行时间具有重要影响。

The transport capacity of maglev train is related to the capacity of each vehicle, train formation, departure interval and the time when trains can be sent every day.The transport capacity of rail transit system is generally controlled by station distribution or block section, that is, determined by the cycle of train diagram or train tracking time. Similarly, the distance between substations of maglev system, operating speed, operation mode and dwell time of trains in the station area have a decisive impact on the minimum train tracking time of maglev system. The operation mode in the station area mentioned here refers to the speed limit when trains enter and leave the station, which has an important impact on the allowable time interval and travel time between trains.

（一）列车的追踪时间间隔

5.1.4.1 Tracking Time Interval of Train

根据安全行车的要求，磁浮列车的追踪时间间隔包括下列情形：①区间列车最小追踪时间间隔；②前方列车正线停站时的追踪时间间隔；③前方侧线停车时的列车追踪时间间隔；④列车出站追踪时间间隔。

According to the requirements of safe operation, the tracking time interval of maglev train includes the following situations: ① the minimum tracking time interval of interstation train; ② the tracking time interval when the front train stops at the station on the main line; ③ the tracking interval when the front train stops at the side line; ④ the tracking interval for train leaving the station.

实际运行中的列车追踪时间间隔，应同时满足上述各项追踪时间间隔要求。追踪时间间隔取决于下列技术参数：①列车加速和减速特性，即加速度和制动减速度限制值；②列车正常运行的最高速度；③道岔允许通过的速度；④车站供电区段和区间供电区段的长度；⑤站内停车位置处车头距进站道岔末端的距离。

The tracking time interval of the train in actual operation shall meet the requirements of the above tracking time intervals. The tracking time interval depends on the following technical parameters: ① the acceleration and deceleration characteristics of the train, i.e., the limit values of acceleration and braking deceleration; ② the maximum speed of the train for normal operation; ③ the speed at which the turnout is allowed to pass; ④ the length of the station power supply section and the section power supply section; ⑤ the distance between the headway at the parking position in the station and the end of the turnout entering the station.

（二）磁浮铁路的通过能力

5.1.4.2 Carrying Capacity of Maglev Railway

铁路通过能力为每天通过特定断面的列车对数或列数。对于高速客运专线，为保证旅行速度，一般都采用双线，通过能力为每天每方向能够通过的列车数，按下式计算：

$$N = T_{实运}/\tau$$

The railway carrying capacity is the number of pairs or trains passing through a specific section every day. For high-speed passenger dedicated lines, in order to ensure the travel speed, double lines are generally used, and the carrying capacity is the number of trains that can pass in each direction every day, which is calculated according to the following formula:

$$N = T_{\text{Actural Running}} / \tau$$

式中，N 为通过能力；$T_{实运}$ 为每天实际用于行车的时间；τ 为列车运行的追踪时间间隔。

Where, N is the carrying capacity; $T_{\text{Actural Running}}$ is the time actually used for running every day; τ is the tracking time interval of train operation.

1. $T_{实运}$

1. $T_{\text{Actural Running}}$

对于高速客运专线，$T_{实运}$ 受两个因素的影响。一是具有商业运营价值的时间，即适应市场需求，满足旅客交通需要的时间。在高速客运系统中，一般旅程均能在数小时内完成，乘客无须在车上过夜，因此人们都愿意在白天旅行。通常情况下，一天之内具有商业运营价值的时段是 7：00～22：00。为了使整个旅行过程处于这个时期，断面通过能力计算中采用的 $T_{实运}$ 实际范围将小于 7：00～22：00。二是系统技术条件所约束的允许运行时间。由于系统需要进行线路、供电系统及其他运营设备的维护和检修，故一天之内需扣除若干时间用于各种固定设备和移动设备的检修。根据目前国外已运行的轮轨高速列车的经验，技术维护完全可以在不具商业运营价值的夜间进行。磁浮交通系统各组成部分的状态主要采用电子技术进行监测，发现出现问题的部件则迅速更换其所在的模块，因此维护所需时间更短，不会占用具有商业运营价值的时间。

For the high-speed passenger dedicated line, $T_{\text{Actural Running}}$ is affected by two factors. One is the time with commercial operation value, that is, the time to adapt to market demand and meet passenger traffic needs. In the high-speed passenger transport system, the average journey can be completed in a few hours, and passengers do not have to spend the night in the car, so people are willing to travel in the daytime. Usually, the time period with commercial operation value in a day is from 7:00 to 22:00. In order to make the whole travel process in this period, the actual range of $T_{\text{Actural Running}}$ used in the calculation of section carrying capacity will be less than 7:00-22:00. The second is the allowable running time restricted by the technical conditions of the system. As the system requires maintenance and repair of lines, power supply system and other operating equipment, a certain amount of time shall be deducted for the maintenance of various fixed and mobile equipment in a day. According to the experience of wheel-rail high-speed trains in operation abroad, technical maintenance can be carried out at night without commercial operation value. The status of each component of the maglev transportation system is mainly monitored by electronic technology, and the module where the component is found to be in trouble is quickly replaced, so the maintenance time is shorter and the time with commercial operation value will not be occupied.

2. τ 值

2. τ Value

从磁浮铁路的技术条件来看，列车追踪间隔主要受供电站间距和列车制动安全保障的影响。具体实际线路的 τ 值将根据运输需求情况，经技术经济分析后确定。德国 TR 磁浮系统资料给出的理论最小追踪时间为 2.5 min，推荐的最小追踪时间为 5 min。

According to the technical conditions of maglev railway, the train tracking interval is mainly affected by the distance between power supply stations and the safety guarantee of train braking. The τ value of the actual line will be determined after technical and economic analysis according to the transportation demand. The theoretical minimum tracking time given in the data of German TR maglev system is 2.5 min, and the recommended minimum tracking time is 5 min.

3. 输送能力

3. Conveying Capacity

输送能力是交通系统设计中最重要的指标。在通过能力一定的条件下，输送能力取决于列车编组辆数和每辆车的载客能力。

Transportation capacity is the most important index in the design of transportation system. Under the condition of certain carrying capacity, the transport capacity depends on the number of trains and the passenger carrying capacity of each train.

在高速客运系统设计中，需要从市场需求出发，尽可能缩短旅客"门到门"的旅行时间，故一般遵循小编组、高密度的原则。目前已成熟的常导高速磁浮系统是在德国开发的，较多地考虑了德国乃至欧洲的人文社会环境，认为 10 辆编组已经足以满足市场的需要，所以 TR 磁浮系统目前是以 10 辆作为最大编组。

In the design of high-speed passenger transport system, it is necessary to start from the market demand and shorten the "door-to-door" travel time of passengers as far as possible, so the principle of small marshalling and high density is generally followed. At present, the mature normal high-speed maglev system is developed in Germany, considering the human and social environment of Germany and even Europe. It is considered that the 10-car marshalling is enough to meet the needs of the market, so the TR maglev system currently takes 10 cars as the largest marshalling.

反映磁浮铁路输送能力的另一个重要因素是每辆车的定员，磁浮列车车体较宽，可以设置比轮轨高速车辆更多的座位。德国 TR08 磁浮车辆内宽 3.43 m，座位编排为一等舱 4 座/排，经济舱 6 座/排。

Another important factor reflecting the transport capacity of maglev railway is the capacity of each vehicle. Maglev trains are wider and can be equipped with more seats than high-speed wheel-rail vehicles. The German TR08 maglev vehicle has an interior width of 3.43 m, and the seating arrangement is 4 seats/row in first class and 6 seats/row in economy class.

还有一种观点认为，在交通系统设计中，旅行时间较短时可适当降低对乘坐空间大小的要求，如在速度较高的飞机上，人均占有的座席空间就小于轮轨高速铁路的相应值。按此推理，磁浮列车因速度较高而可以显著缩短旅行的时间，故相应可以适当加密座位。这在不增加列车长度的情况下，将增加约 10%的定员。

There is also a view that in the design of transportation system, when the travel time is short, the requirement for the size of the seat space can be reduced appropriately. For example, on a high-speed aircraft, the seat space per capita is less than the corresponding value of the wheel-rail high-speed railway. According to this reasoning, the maglev train can significantly shorten the travel time because of its higher speed, so the seats can be properly encrypted accordingly. This will increase the capacity by about 10% without increasing the length of the train.

实际运行中，由于列车可能采用不同的停站方案，将导致列车的越行，从而产生通过能力扣除问题，实际运输能力将小于平行图运输能力。由于高速磁浮列车运行速度比较一致，扣除系数较小。

In the actual operation, the train may adopt different stop schemes, which will lead to the overtaking of the train, resulting in the deduction of the carrying capacity, and the actual transport capacity will be less than that of the parallel diagram. Because the speed of high-speed maglev train is relatively consistent, the deduction coefficient is relatively small.

4. 上海磁浮线设计能力

4. Design Capacity of Shanghai Maglev Line

按设计水平，9 节车厢可坐乘客 959 人，每小时发车 12 列，按每天运行 18 h 计，每天客流量为 4 万人左右，年客运量可达 1.5 亿人次。初期引进德国常导长定子超高速型的最新磁悬浮列车 3 列，其中两列运营。

According to the design level, 9 carriages can seat 959 passengers, 12 trains per hour, running 18 hours per day, the daily passenger flow is about 40,000 people, and the annual passenger volume can reach 150 million people. In the initial stage, three of the latest German maglev trains with long stator and ultra-high speed were introduced, two of which were in operation.

五、环境保护措施

5.1.5 Environmental Protection Measures

针对磁浮系统所产生的环境影响，可以从设计上采取措施，尽量予以减轻。

In view of the environmental impact of the maglev system, measures can be taken from the design to reduce it as far as possible.

（一）噪声影响防治

5.1.5.1 Noise Impact Prevention

根据噪声水平叠加原理：同时存在两种以上的噪声源时，噪声水平的叠加值与各噪声源声平值之和的对数成正比，因此，在选线阶段，可根据沿线的声环境情况，使磁浮系统线路尽量与其他噪声源接近，从而显著地降低磁浮系统所产生的噪声负荷。

According to the superposition principle of noise level: when there are more than two noise sources at the same time, the superposition value of noise level is proportional to the logarithm of the sum of the sound level values of each noise source. Therefore, in the line selection stage, the maglev system line can be as close as possible to other noise sources according to the acoustic environment along the line, so as to significantly reduce the noise load generated by the maglev system.

在线路设计中，合理控制线路与噪声敏感目标的距离，以免列车速度受限。

In the line design, the distance between the line and the noise-sensitive target should be reasonably controlled to avoid the limitation of train speed.

在技术设计中，可根据环境影响评价大纲设定沿线主要环境影响敏感目标，在线路两侧设置声屏障，以确保环境敏感目标的声环境质量达标。

In the technical design, the main environmental impact sensitive targets along the line can be set according to the environmental impact assessment outline, and sound barriers can be set on both sides of the line to ensure that the acoustic environmental quality of the environmental sensitive targets meets the standards.

（二）电磁辐射影响控制措施

5.1.5.2 Electromagnetic Radiation Impact Control Measures

沿线设备设置良好的接地，并在穿越敏感目标区域的路段加大密度设置接地设施。建设项目的变电站、开关站，采用钢筋混凝土结构，窗户玻璃夹衬金属丝网、主变压器外壳采取良好的接地措施。同时，确保规划红线控制距离，以此减缓磁浮列车在运营中对轨道两侧目标的电磁辐射影响。

The equipment along the line shall be well grounded, and the grounding facilities shall be set up in the sections crossing the sensitive target areas with increased density. The substation and switch station of the construction project adopt reinforced concrete structure, and the window glass is lined with wire mesh, and the main transformer shell adopts good grounding measures. At the same time, the control distance of the planned red line is ensured, so as to mitigate the electromagnetic radiation impact of the maglev train on the targets on both sides of the track during operation.

（三）其他防治措施

5.1.5.3 Other Control Measures

对于水污染、固体废弃物等环境污染的问题，磁浮列车并不产生有别于现有各种交通工具（尤其是轮轨铁路）的污染物排放，故可采用常规交通环境保护措施。

For the environmental pollution problems such as water pollution and solid waste, the maglev train does not produce pollutant emissions different from the existing vehicles (especially the wheel-rail railway), so conventional traffic environmental protection measures can be adopted.

（四）对视觉环境及景观的保护

5.1.5.4 Protection of Visual Environment and Landscape

磁浮铁路与其他现代工业产品一样，在对视觉环境和景观的影响方面具有两重性：一方面，它作为现代高科技的产物，能够展示人类技术进步的成果，创造出人文景观；另一方面，随着现代工业文明对自然环境的一再破坏，人们更加崇尚自然界的原始美，故应尽量避免对地表的改变，减少水土流失。

Like other modern industrial products, the maglev railway has a dual nature in its impact on the visual environment and landscape: on the one hand, as a product of modern high-tech, it can display the achievements of human technological progress and create a human landscape; on the other hand, with the repeated destruction of the natural environment by modern industrial civilization, People advocate the primitive beauty of nature, so they should try their best to avoid changes to the surface and reduce soil erosion.

六、上海磁浮列车建设工程进展大事记

5.1.6 Memorabilia of Shanghai Maglev Train Construction Project

2000年6月30日，中德两国政府正式签订双方合作开展上海磁浮列车示范运营线项目可行性研究的协议。

In June 30, 2000, the Chinese and German governments formally signed an agreement on the feasibility study of the Shanghai Maglev Train Demonstration Line Project.

2000年8月，上海申通集团有限公司等6家公司联合出资注册成立上海磁浮交通发展有限公司；国家计委经国务院同意，批准了工程项目建议书。

In August 2000, six companies including Shanghai Shentong Group Co., Ltd. jointly invested and registered to establish Shanghai Maglev Transportation Development Co., Ltd.; the State Planning Commission approved the project proposal with the consent of the State Council.

2000年10月，上海市委、市政府批准成立上海磁浮列车工程指挥部。

In October 2000, the Shanghai Municipal Committee and the Municipal Government approved the establishment of the Shanghai Maglev Train Engineering Command.

2000年11月20日，中德双方如期合作编制完成工程可行性研究报告，同月由市计委上报国家计委审批。

In November 20, 2000, China and Germany completed the feasibility study report of the project as scheduled, which was submitted to the State Planning Commission for approval by the Municipal Planning Commission in the same month.

与此同时，中方开始与德方联合体（由西门子公司、蒂森克虏伯、磁浮国际公司组成）进行设备供贷和服务合同谈判。

At the same time, the Chinese side began to negotiate equipment supply and service contracts with the German consortium (composed of Siemens, ThyssenKrupp and Maglev International).

2001年1月，上海磁浮快速列车工程项目启动，上海磁浮快速工程设备供贷及服务合同在沪正式签署。

In January 2001, the Shanghai Maglev Express Train Project was launched, and the Shanghai Maglev Express Engineering Equipment Supply and Service Contract was formally signed in Shanghai.

2001年3月，上海磁浮列车示范运营线工程在浦东新区正式开工。

In March 2001, the Shanghai Maglev Train Demonstration Line Project was officially started in Pudong New Area.

2001年7月，重达70多吨的上海磁浮列车工程首根轨道梁"出炉"，这也是我国自行设计和生产的首根中心受压预应力混凝土梁。

In July 2001, the first track beam of Shanghai Maglev Train Project weighing more than 70 tons came out, which is also the first central compression prestressed concrete beam designed and produced by our country.

2001年8月，首批上海磁浮列车设备自德国汉堡启程，安全抵达上海港，其中包括约1 000 km长的定子线圈电缆。同月，磁浮列车工程的第一根大梁在浦东造梁基地顺利装车，运往浦东国际机场的磁浮列车维修基地。

In August 2001, the first batch of Shanghai maglev train equipment arrived safely at Shanghai Port from Hamburg, Germany, including about 1,000 km of stator coil cables. In the same month, the first girder of the maglev train project was successfully loaded at the Pudong girder building base and transported to the maintenance base of the maglev train at Pudong International Airport.

2001年9月，上海磁浮工程进入技术攻坚关键性阶段。

In September 2001, Shanghai Maglev Project entered the key stage of technical fortification.

2001年11月，上海磁浮列车工程龙阳路站架梁成功，标志着磁浮工程取得重大进展。

In November 2001, the successful erection of beams at Longyang Road Station of Shanghai Maglev Train Project marked a significant progress in the Maglev Project.

2002年3月，世界首条磁浮列车商运线在沪全线贯通，从上海市区到浦东国际机场只需7 min，将在第二年初变成现实。

In March 2002, the world's first commercial maglev train line was completed in Shanghai. It takes only 7 minutes to travel from downtown Shanghai to Pudong International Airport, which will become a reality at the beginning of the second year.

2002年7月，上海磁浮快速列车轨道梁制作提前完成，工程建设又获重要进展，关键部件轨道梁的生产全部到位。

In July 2002, the production of track beams for Shanghai Maglev Express Train was completed ahead of schedule, and important progress was made in the construction of the project, with the production of all key components of track beams in place.

2002年8月，磁浮列车首批三节车厢运抵上海，并运往磁浮工程维修基地组装、调试。同月，磁浮列车开始安装磁铁模块。

In August 2002, the first three carriages of the maglev train arrived in Shanghai and were transported to the maglev engineering maintenance base for assembly and commissioning. In the same month, Maglev trains began to install magnet modules.

2002年9月5日，上海磁浮工程实现了轨道梁全线贯通。

In September 5, 2002, the Shanghai Maglev Project completed the completion of the track girder.

2002年12月31日，上海磁浮列车开始试运行。

On December 31, 2002, Shanghai Maglev Train began trial operation.

2003年1—2月，上海磁浮列车示范性运行。

From January to February 2003, Shanghai Maglev Train was put into demonstration operation.

2003年5月，上海磁浮列车A线轨道运行速度达到430 km/h。

In May 2003, the speed of Shanghai Maglev Line A reached 430 km/h.

2003年8月，上海磁浮列车完成系统调试。

In August 2003, Shanghai Maglev Train completed system commissioning.

2003 年 10—11 月，上海磁浮列车进行安全论证，并达到世界纪录的运行速度 501 km/h。

From October to November 2003, the Shanghai Maglev train was demonstrated for safety and reached the world record running speed of 501 km/h.

七、上海磁浮示范线磁浮列车的工作原理

5.1.7　Working Principle of Maglev Train of Shanghai Maglev Demonstration Line

中国第一条磁浮列车示范运营线——上海磁浮列车是"常导磁吸型"（简称"常导型"）磁浮列车，是利用"异性相吸"原理设计的一种吸力悬浮系统，利用安装在列车两侧转向架上的悬浮电磁铁和铺设在轨道上的磁铁，在磁场作用下产生的吸力使车辆浮起来。

Shanghai Maglev Train, the first Maglev Train Demonstration Line in China, is a "normal conducting magnetic attraction type" ("normal conducting type" for short) maglev train, which is a kind of attraction suspension system designed by using the principle of "opposites attract". It uses the suspension electromagnets installed on the bogies on both sides of the train and the magnets laid on the track to generate attraction under the action of magnetic field to make the vehicle float.

列车底部及两侧转向架的顶部安装电磁铁，在"工"字轨的上方和上臂部分的下方分别设反作用板和感应钢板，控制电磁铁的电流，使电磁铁和轨道间保持 10 mm 的间隙，使转向架和列车间的吸引力与列车重力相互平衡，利用磁铁吸引力将列车浮起 10 mm 左右，使列车悬浮在轨道上运行。这必须精确控制电磁铁的电流。

Electromagnets are installed at the bottom of the train and the top of bogies on both sides, and reaction plates and induction steel plates are respectively installed above the I-shaped rail and below the upper arm to control the current of the electromagnets, so that a gap of 10 mm is maintained between the electromagnets and the rail, and the attraction between the bogie and the train is balanced with the gravity of the train. The attraction of the magnet is used to float the train about 10 mm, so that the train is suspended on the track. This requires precise control of the current to the electromagnet.

悬浮列车的驱动和同步直线电动机原理一模一样。通俗说，在位于轨道两侧的线圈里流动的交流电，能将线圈变成电磁体，由于它与列车上的电磁体的相互作用，使列车开动。

The driving principle of the levitation train is the same as that of the synchronous linear motor. Generally speaking, the alternating current flowing in the coils on both sides of the track can turn the coils into electromagnets, which interact with the electromagnets on the train to move the train.

列车头部的电磁体 N 极被安装在靠前一点的轨道上的电磁体 S 极所吸引, 同时又被安装在轨道上稍后一点的电磁体 N 极所排斥。列车前进时, 线圈里流动的电流方向就反过来, 即原来的 S 极变成 N 极, N 极变成 S 极, 循环交替, 列车就向前运行。

The N pole of the electromagnet at the head of the train is attracted by the S pole of the electromagnet installed on the rail at a point in front, and is repelled by the N pole of an electromagnet installed at a point later on the rail. When the train moves forward, the direction of the current flowing in the coil is reversed, that is, the original S pole becomes N pole, N pole becomes S pole, cycle alternates, and the train moves forward.

稳定性由导向系统来控制。"常导型磁吸式"导向系统, 是在列车侧面安装一组专门用于导向的电磁铁。列车发生左右偏移时, 列车上的导向电磁铁与导向轨的侧面相互作用, 产生排斥力, 使车辆恢复正常位置。列车如运行在曲线或坡道上时, 控制系统通过对导向磁铁中的电流进行控制, 达到控制运行的目的。

Stability is controlled by the guidance system. The "normal conducting magnetic attraction" guiding system is to install a group of electromagnets specially used for guiding on the side of the train. When the train deviates left and right, the guide electromagnet on the train interacts with the side of the guide rail to generate a repulsive force to restore the vehicle to its normal position. When the train runs on a curve or a ramp, the control system controls the current in the guide magnet to achieve the purpose of controlling the operation.

中国上海磁浮示范线列车制动原理:

Train braking principle of Shanghai Maglev Demonstration Line in China:

上海磁浮示范线属于高速磁浮, 全程都是电制动 (再生制动、电阻制动); 在电制动故障或需要紧急制动时, 依靠电涡流制动; 速度小于 10 km/h 时采用滑撬制动。

The Shanghai Maglev Demonstration Line is a high-speed maglev line, and electric braking (regenerative braking and resistance braking) is used in the whole process; in case of electric braking failure or emergency braking, eddy current braking is used; when the speed is less than 10 km/h, skid braking is used.

高速运行时采用再生制动,将列车动能转化为电能回馈给电网;列车速度较低时, 再生制动改为电阻制动; 列车速度很低时, 直线电机改为反接制动, 即电机的牵引方向与列车的运行方向相反, 直到列车停止。当直线电机制动失灵或需要紧急制动时, 采用电涡流制动, 即车上的涡流制动电磁铁励磁, 使侧向导轨上产生涡流, 形成制动力。磁悬浮列车速度小于 10 km/h 时, 采用滑撬制动。

When the train runs at high speed, regenerative braking is used to convert the kinetic energy of the train into electric energy and feed it back to the power grid. When the train runs at a low speed, the regenerative braking is changed to resistance braking. When the train runs at a very low speed, the linear motor is changed to reverse braking, that is, the traction direction of the motor is opposite to the running direction of the train until the train stops. When the linear motor fails to brake or needs emergency braking, eddy current braking is used, that is, the eddy current braking electromagnet on the vehicle is excited to generate eddy current on the lateral guide rail to form braking force. When the speed of maglev train is less than 10km/h, skid braking is adopted.

第二节 线路设计

Section 5.2 Line Design

本节主要介绍上海磁浮示范线设计的内容，包括限界、线间距及线路平、纵、横断面的设计。

This section mainly introduces the design of Shanghai Maglev Demonstration Line, including the design of clearance, distance between tracks and horizontal, vertical and cross sections of the line.

一、线路主要特点

5.2.1 Main Characteristics of the Line

由于磁浮列车系统车辆与轨道之间的无接触、无磨损的支承和导向，无接触的牵引和制动特性，对线路的曲线半径和爬坡能力有了极大改善，为线路的选线提供了较大的灵活性。

Due to the non-contact and wear-free supporting and guiding, non-contact traction and braking characteristics between the vehicle and the track of the maglev train system, the curve radius and climbing ability of the line have been greatly improved, which provides greater flexibility for the route selection of the line.

首先，转弯半径小。在曲线地段，为平衡侧向自由加速度，不论是公路还是铁路，均设置横坡（超高）。速度越快，半径越小，横坡值要求越大。由于不存在轮轨接触，不会脱轨，磁浮列车在高速时也不会对轨道造成磨损，因此，有可能采用较大的横坡；缓和曲线和横坡的线形采用正弦曲线，其线形变化是圆顺的，动力学特性较佳，不产生突变点，而且其横坡角度变化完全以舒适度作为控制，不再受脱轨控制。

First of all, the turning radius is small. In the curve section, in order to balance the lateral free acceleration, cross slope (superelevation) is set for both highway and railway.

The faster the speed, the smaller the radius, and the larger the required crossfall value. Since there is no wheel-rail contact, there will be no derailment, and the maglev train will not wear the track at high speed, so it is possible to use a larger cross slope; The line shape of the transition curve and the cross slope adopts the sine curve, the line shape change is smooth, the dynamic characteristics are good, no mutation point is generated, and the change of the cross slope angle is completely controlled by the comfort level and is no longer controlled by the derailment.

其次，爬坡能力强。列车在坡道上运行时，除其他阻力外，会增加一个沿坡道向下的重力分力。坡度越陡，载客越多，重力分力越大，机车牵引能力要求越高。法国TGV的最大坡度是35‰。磁浮列车的牵引能力和轨道上供电能力较强，再加上没有轮轨黏着限制，列车的爬坡能力可达100‰。

Secondly, the climbing ability is strong. When the train runs on the ramp, it will add a component of gravity downward along the ramp in addition to other resistances. The steeper the slope, the more passengers, the greater the gravity component, and the higher the locomotive traction capacity requirements. The maximum gradient of the French TGV is 35‰. Maglev trains have strong traction capacity and power supply capacity on the track, and there is no wheel-rail adhesion restriction, so the climbing capacity of the train can reach 100‰.

二、限界和线间距

5.2.2 Clearance and Line Spacing

为了确保列车在线路上运行的安全，防止列车撞击邻近的建筑物或设备，每条线路都必须保持一定的空间，这个空间的轮廓线便是限界。

In order to ensure the safety of trains running on the line and prevent trains from hitting adjacent buildings or equipment, each line must maintain a certain space, and the outline of this space is the clearance.

磁浮线路的限界划分为三个层次：列车运行动态边界、固定设施边界和净空包络限界。

The clearance of maglev line is divided into three levels: dynamic boundary of train operation, boundary of fixed facilities and clearance envelope gauge.

（一）限界图

5.2.2.1 Clearance Diagram

直线区间地段的限界图、有横坡角地段限界、无横坡角地段限界值要遵循有关要求。当线路有横坡角 α 时,其限界要进行加宽。

The gauge diagram of the straight section, the gauge of the section with cross slope angle and the gauge of the section without cross slope angle shall comply with relevant requirements.When the line has a transverse slope angle α, its gauge shall be widened.

(二)线间距

5.2.2.2 Line Spacing

磁浮线路的线间距如表 5-1 所示。

The line spacing of maglev line is shown in Table 5-1.

表 5-1 线间距表

Table 5-1 Line Spacing

速度/(km/h)	≤500	≤400	≤300
线间距/m	5.1	4.8	4.4

三、线路平面

5.2.3 Line plane

该运营线除了浦东国际机场景观水池到机场站一段为地面线外,其余均为高架线路。全线有高架桥墩(台)1 554 座。一般地段轨道离地面的高度为 12~13 m。

Except for the ground line from the landscape pool of Pudong International Airport to the airport station, the rest of the line is elevated. There are 1,554 viaduct piers (platforms) along the whole line. In general, the height of the track above the ground is 12-13 m.

(一)曲线半径

5.2.3.1 Radius of Curves

根据市政规划要求,该磁浮线路的走向必须避开张江高科技园区,这就意味着一辆如此快速的列车不可能实现直线行驶,线路有 2/3 为弯道。经过精密测算,设计人员为它"定制"了一条呈正弦曲线走向的路线,即使列车在拐弯处,也不用降低车速。

According to the requirements of municipal planning, the direction of the maglev line must avoid Zhangjiang High-tech Park, which means that such a fast train can not run in a straight line, and 2/3 of the line is curved. After precise calculation, the designer "customized" a sinusoidal route for it, even if the train is turning, it does not need to reduce the speed.

两条直线之间需要圆曲线连接,而圆曲线的半径对列车的通过速度起了很大的制约作用,圆曲线半径当然越大越好,而实际上线路受地物地形等因素影响,总是在保证线路速度目标值的前提下,选择一个比较经济合理的曲线半径,根据线路所处地段的地形地物、允许侧向加速度标准及行车速度,确定的极限最小圆曲线半径见表 5-2。

Two straight lines need to be connected by a circular curve, and the radius of the circular curve plays a very important role in restricting the passing speed of the train, of course, the larger the radius of the circular curve, the better, but in fact, the line is affected by factors such as ground features and topography, always on the premise of ensuring the target speed of the line, choose a more economical and reasonable curve radius. See Table 5-2 for the determined limit minimum circular curve radius according to the landform and surface features of the section where the line is located, allowable lateral acceleration standard and driving speed.

表 5-2 极限最小圆曲线半径
Table 5-2 Limit Minimum Radius of Circular Curve   m

行车速度/(km/h) Driving Speed/(km/h)	自由侧向加速度 Free Lateral Acceleration	
	一般地段 1.0 m/s^2 General Location 1.0 m/s^2	困难地段 1.25 m/s^2 Difficult Location 1.25 m/s^2
100	509	437
200	994	918
300	2,235	2,065
400	3,973	3,671
430	4,591	4,242
505	6,333	5,736

(二) 缓和曲线

5.2.3.2 Transition Curves

为保证列车运行的平顺,在直线与圆曲线之间要设置缓和曲线连接。公路的缓和曲线线形一般采用回旋曲线,铁路的缓和曲线线形一般采用三次抛物线,它们的特点是线形简单、维护容易。磁浮线路的平面缓和曲线采用一正弦曲线,它的线形平顺,动力学特性好,因而磁浮线路一经建成,维护工作量极少。由于正弦曲线的曲率过渡非常平顺,因此,相邻两曲线的两个缓和曲线可以直接相连。

In order to ensure the smooth operation of the train, the transition curve should be set between the straight line and the circular curve. Generally, the transition curve of highway is clothoid, and the transition curve of railway is cubic parabola, which are characterized by simple alignment and easy maintenance. The plane transition curve of the maglev line is a sine curve, which has smooth alignment and good dynamic characteristics, so once the maglev line is built, the maintenance workload is very small. Because the curvature transition of the sine curve is very smooth, the two transition curves of two adjacent curves can be directly connected.

同圆曲线半径一样，缓和曲线也需要在保证速度目标值的前提下，选择比较经济合理的长度；根据线路允许最大侧向冲击、扭转率和法向冲击等指标，对应各种速度和曲线半径确定。

Like the radius of circular curve, the transition curve also needs to select a more economical and reasonable length on the premise of ensuring the target speed; it is determined according to the allowable maximum lateral impact, torsion rate, normal impact and other indicators of the line, corresponding to various speeds and curve radius.

（三）线路构成与特征

5.2.3.3 Line composition and characteristics

上海磁浮示范线由三部分构成：一是正线，即 A 线、B 线；二是车辆维修基地维修线和进出线，即 C 线、D 线、E 线；三是渡线，即 F 线、H 线和 G 线。F 线和 H 线各有两跨 24 m 的标准梁，G 线为道岔直接相连，见图 5-2。

The Shanghai Maglev Demonstration Line consists of three parts: the first is the main line, i.e. Line A and Line B; the second is the maintenance line and incoming and outgoing lines of the vehicle maintenance base, i.e. Line C, Line D and Line E; and the third is the crossover line, namely Line F, Line H and Line G. Line F and Line H each have two standard beams with a span of 24 m, and Line G is directly connected to the turnout, as shown in Figure 5-2.

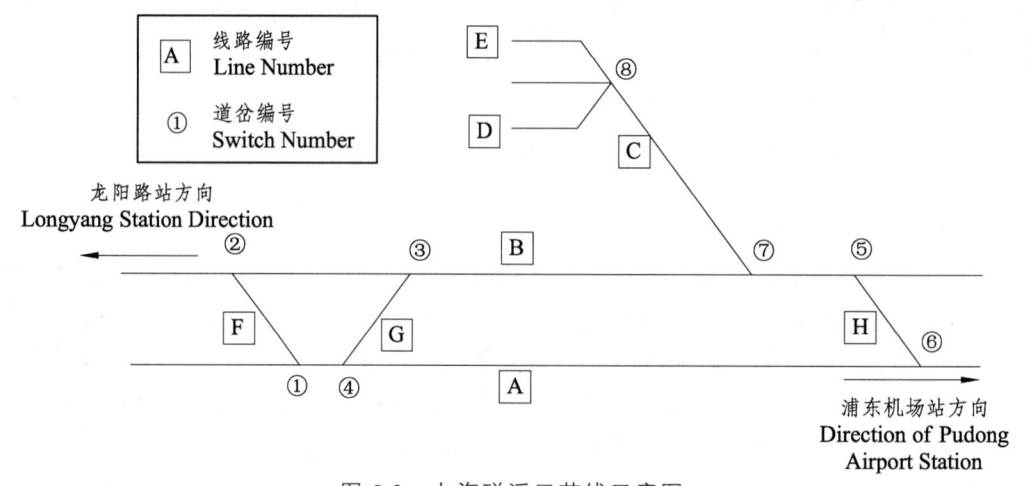

图 5-2　上海磁浮示范线示意图

Figure 5-2　Schematic Diagram of Shanghai Maglev Demonstration Line

四、线路纵断面

5.2.4　Vertical Section of The Line

线路纵断面也是由直线、圆曲线和缓和曲线组成的。

The line profile is also composed of straight line, circular curve and transition curve.

（一）限制坡度

5.2.4.1　Limiting Gradient

磁浮列车特点之一是它的爬坡能力强，在线路区间范围内（非辅助停车区），它的纵坡可达到100%。在车站、停车场及辅助停车区，坡度一般不大于5%。在困难条件下，经过批准也可采用不大于5%的纵坡度。

One of the characteristics of the maglev train is its strong climbing ability, and its longitudinal slope can reach 100% within the line section (non-auxiliary parking area). In stations, parking lots and auxiliary parking areas, the gradient is generally not more than 5%. In difficult conditions, the longitudinal gradient of not more than 5% can also be adopted after approval.

（二）竖曲线

5.2.4.2　Vertical Curve

竖曲线的半径是根据列车的速度和舒适度要求来决定的。

The radius of the vertical curve is determined according to the speed and comfort requirements of the train.

五、线路横坡及横断面

5.2.5　Cross Slope and Cross Section of the Line

在线路曲线区段，为了平衡列车运行时的部分侧向加速度，轨道梁须设置超高。在直线区段，为了便于排水，轨道梁设置排水横坡。

In order to balance part of the lateral acceleration of the train running in the curve section of the line, the track beam must be set with superelevation. In the straight section, in order to facilitate drainage, the track beam is provided with a drainage cross slope.

在缓和曲线区段以及其他线路横坡角有变化的区段，其横坡角的变化按照正弦曲线规律变化，该区段轨道梁的表面在空间呈现为一个扭曲的空间曲面。超高缓和段的长度要保证横坡角扭转率不超限。

In the transition curve section and other sections where the cross slope angle of the line changes, the change of the cross slope angle changes according to the law of sine curve, and the surface of the track beam in this section presents a distorted space surface in space. The length of the superelevation transition section shall ensure that the torsion rate of the cross slope angle does not exceed the limit.

（一）横坡设计参数

5.2.5.1　Cross Slope Design Parameters

在线路区间，轨道梁的最大横坡为 12°；在车站，横坡角不大于 3°；在道岔范围，横坡角为 0°。

In the section of the line, the maximum transverse slope of the track beam is 12°; in the station, the transverse slope angle is not more than 3°; In the turnout range, the cross slope angle is 0°.

线路超高横坡角缓和曲线采用正弦曲线，旋转轴为线路中心线。超高横坡缓和曲线范围一般与线路平面缓和曲线相对应，特殊情况也可以延伸至平面曲率为常数的路段上。

The transition curve of superelevation cross slope angle of the line is a sine curve, and the rotation axis is the center line of the line. The range of superelevation transverse slope transition curve generally corresponds to the horizontal transition curve of the line, and in special cases, it can also be extended to the road section where the plane curvature is constant.

因舒适度要求，线路超高的变化是渐变的过程。线路轨道每米的扭转角度称为扭转率。

Due to comfort requirements, the change of line superelevation is a gradual process.The angle of twist per meter of line track is called the twist rate.

（二）横坡设计

5.2.5.2　Cross Slope Design

线路横坡设计除了在直线区段按规定设置排水坡之外，主要是根据列车运行舒适度的要求确定曲线区段线路的横坡角（轨面超高）。

In addition to setting the drainage slope in the straight section according to the regulations, the design of line cross slope is mainly to determine the cross slope angle (rail surface superelevation) of the curve section according to the requirements of train operation comfort.

在进行线路横坡角设计时，重点要解决好线路排水坡与线路曲线区段超高横坡的连接问题。当线路排水坡与线路曲线区段超高横坡是同向时，线路排水坡就是线路曲线区段超高横坡的起点坡；当线路排水坡与线路曲线区段超高横坡是反向时，那么应在线路曲线起点前 20 m 处作为线路排水坡的终点，而线路曲线起点的横坡角为零。

When designing the transverse slope angle of the line, it is important to solve the connection problem between the drainage slope of the line and the superelevation transverse slope in the curve section of the line.When the drainage slope of the line and the superelevation cross slope of the curve section of the line are in the same direction, the drainage slope is the starting point slope of superelevation cross slope in the curve section of the line; when the drainage slope is in reverse direction to that in the curve section, 20 m before the starting point of the curve shall be taken as the end point of drainage slope, and the cross slope angle at the starting point of the line curve is zero.

第三节 轨道结构

Section 5.3 Track Structure

轨道结构是磁浮工程的关键部分。上海磁浮示范线共生产了 2 551 根轨道梁。轨道梁主要为箱形梁，呈"工"字形，顶宽 1.78 m，底宽 3 m，高 2.2 m。

Track structure is the key part of maglev engineering. A total of 2,551 rail girders were produced for the Shanghai Maglev Demonstration Line. The track beam is mainly a box beam in the shape of "I", with a top width of 1.78 m, a bottom width of 3 m and a height of 2.2 m.

全线轨道梁共有 5 种不同长度、1 000 多种规格。在预应力达到 1 800 t 的台座上，采用严格的制作工艺要求，一根长达 25 m 的轨道梁构件几何尺寸平面误差不许超过 2 mm。该轨道梁对收缩、徐变性能要求也极高，是当今混凝土行业的顶级产品。

There are five different lengths and more than 1,000 specifications of track beams along the whole line. On the pedestal with prestress of 1,800 t, the plane error of the geometric dimension of a 25 m long track beam member should not exceed 2 mm by adopting strict manufacturing process requirements. The track beam also has high requirements for shrinkage and creep performance, and is the top product in the concrete industry today.

施工中对轨道梁加工要求严格。轨道梁在承重后，梁与梁之间的变形误差不能超过 5 mm，这个设计误差不到铁路的 1/6；轨道梁上的长定子在钻孔后装上去，整个线路需打 28 万个钉孔，定子铁心的组装误差不能超过 ±0.2 mm，精确度相当高。

During the construction, the processing of the track beam is strictly required. After the track beam is loaded, the deformation error between the beams should not exceed 5 mm, which is less than 1/6 of the design error of the railway. The long stator on the track beam is installed after drilling, and the whole line needs to drill 280,000 nail holes. The assembly error of the stator core should not exceed ±0.2 mm, which is quite accurate.

铺设完成后的轨道梁及在其上运行的列车见图 5-3。

See Figure 5-3 for the laid track beam and the train running on it.

图 5-3 轨道梁及车辆

Figure 5-3　Track beam and vehicle

一、轨道结构的基本形式

5.3.1　Basic Form of Track Structure

20 世纪 80 年代，德国在埃姆斯兰建造了一条磁浮列车试验线，该试验线上对多种形式的轨道结构进行了开发与研究。之后，德国又进行了柏林至汉堡磁浮列车商业运营线的可行性研究，对线路在不同地形、地貌及地物条件下可能采用的轨道结构进行了研究，提出了多种新型轨道结构，可分为以下几种基本形式：

In the 1980s, a maglev train test line was built in Emsland, Germany, on which various forms of track structures were developed and studied. After that, Germany carried out the feasibility study of the Berlin-Hamburg maglev train commercial operation line, studied the possible track structures under different terrain, geomorphology and surface features, and proposed a variety of new track structures, which can be divided into the following basic forms:

（一）一般路段轨道结构

5.3.1.1　Track Structure of General Section

一般路段轨道结构可分为两种，即低置轨道结构及高架轨道结构。

Generally, the track structure of the road section can be divided into two types, namely, the low track structure and the elevated track structure.

（1）低置轨道结构就是建造在平地上或基本上贴着地面建造的轨道结构，轨道顶面距地面高度为 1.35～3.5 m。

（1）Low-set track structure is a track structure built on the flat ground or basically close to the ground, and the height of the top surface of the track from the ground is 1.35 to 3.5 m.

（2）高架轨道结构就是架设在空中的轨道结构，轨道顶面至地面的高度为 2.2～20 m。

（2）The elevated track structure is a track structure erected in the air, and the height from the top of the track to the ground is 2.2-20 m.

（二）特殊节点轨道结构

5.3.1.2 Track Structure of Special Nodes

特殊节点指线路沿线所遇常规高架轨道结构无法跨越的河流、公路、铁路及立交等构筑物节点。特殊节点轨道结构有两种：桥上轨道梁和隧道结构。

Special nodes refer to the nodes of structures such as rivers, highways, railways and interchanges that cannot be crossed by conventional elevated track structures along the line. There are two kinds of track structures with special nodes: track beam on bridge and tunnel structure.

桥上轨道梁就是将一般路段上采用的轨道梁架设在桥梁结构上。德国有关磁浮系统技术标准将轨道梁下的桥梁结构称作基本承载结构，轨道梁采用 6.192 m 长的Ⅲ形梁，建议该种形式使用在轨面高度大于 20 m 的线路中。

The track beam on the bridge is to erect the track beam used on the general road section on the bridge structure. The bridge structure under the track beam is called the basic load-bearing structure in the relevant German maglev system technical standards, and the track beam is a 6.192 m long Ⅲ shape beam, which is recommended to be used in the line with a rail surface height of more than 20 m.

隧道结构就是线路在穿越大江大河或山岭等特殊地段时建造的隧道结构，隧道内架设轨道梁，德国的磁浮系统技术标准建议采用 6.192 m 长的Ⅲ形梁。

The tunnel structure is the tunnel structure built when the line crosses special sections such as rivers or mountains, and the track beam is erected in the tunnel. The German maglev system technical standard recommends that the Ⅲ-type beam with a length of 6.192 m should be used.

二、轨道梁

5.3.2 Track Beam

由于磁浮列车与轨道梁之间耦合工作的特点，线路系统对轨道梁提出了非常严格的要求，用传统的结构设计方法已无法实现。

Because of the characteristics of the coupling work between the maglev train and the track beam, the line system is very strict with the track beam. The traditional structural design method has been unable to achieve the requirements.

在德国 TVE 试验线上，德方试用过许多结构形式的轨道梁。但是，真正有可能符合技术要求的却只有极少的 2～3 种。其中，跨度 25～31 m 的双跨钢梁技术上能完全满足系统要求，但加工制造却必须使用六坐标铣镗床，该机床价格昂贵且难以购买；全线使用钢结构，也不符合我国国情，只得放弃。另一种 6 m 的轨道梁，虽加工较易，亦可使用钢筋混凝土结构，却又必须有良好的地基，使用场合极为有限。唯一有参考价值的预应力钢筋混凝土复合梁，德国仅有一根双跨直线梁的试验结果，加工工艺和计算理论均需进一步完善。

On the German TVE test line, the German side has tried many structural forms of track beams. However, there are only a few 2 to 3 kinds that are really likely to meet the technical requirements. Among them, the double-span steel beam with a span of 25-31 m can fully meet the requirements of the system technically, but the six-axis milling and boring machine must be used for processing and manufacturing, which is expensive and difficult to purchase; the steel structure used in the whole line is not in line with China's national conditions, so it has to be abandoned. Another 6 m track beam, although easy to process, can also use reinforced concrete structure, but must have a good foundation, the use of occasions is very limited. There is only one test result of double-span straight beam in Germany, which is the only prestressed reinforced concrete composite beam with reference value, and the processing technology and calculation theory need to be further improved.

下面就上海示范线研究开发的各种轨道梁做简要介绍。

The following is a brief introduction to the various track girders developed by Shanghai Demonstration Line.

（一）预应力钢筋混凝土复合梁

5.3.2.1 Prestressed Reinforced Concrete Composite Beam

预应力钢筋混凝土复合梁是由功能区钢结构（简称功能件）与预应力混凝土通过连接件复合成的轨道梁。预应力混凝土梁设计、制造时均按零挠度控制，以确保梁体混凝土发生收缩、徐变后仍能保持直线状态。然后用特殊的五坐标双铣镗床系统对连接件的连接面及螺栓孔、定位销孔进行整梁机加工。最后用特制的功能件拟合成所需曲面。

Prestressed reinforced concrete composite beam is a kind of track beam which is composed of functional steel structure and prestressed concrete through connectors.

Prestressed concrete beams are designed and manufactured according to zero deflection control to ensure that the beam concrete can still maintain a straight line after shrinkage and creep. Then a special five-coordinate double milling and boring machine system is used to machine the whole beam of the connecting surface, bolt hole and positioning pin hole of the connecting piece. Finally, a special functional part is used to fit the required surface.

为减少轨道梁长度种类及简化功能件、定子铁心布置，线路内外侧轨道梁采用等跨布置，标准跨径为 12.384 m、24.768 m（空间线路轴线长度）。在线路曲线段，由于外侧线路长度大于内侧线路长度，按功能件长度模数（3.096 m）确定非跨径，如 18.576 m、21.672 m。在线路遇到横向道路、立交、河流等位置，也采用上述非标跨径与标准跨径组合调整孔跨位置，以满足横向构筑物界限及河流通航要求。

In order to reduce the length and types of track beams and simplify the layout of functional parts and stator cores, the track beams inside and outside the line are arranged in equal spans, with standard spans of 12.384 m and 24.768 m (length of spatial line axis). In the curve section of the line, since the length of the outer line is greater than that of the inner line, the non-span is determined according to the length modulus of functional parts (3.096 m), such as 18.576 m and 21.672 m. When the line meets the transverse road, interchange, river and other positions, the combination of the above non-standard span and standard span is also used to adjust the position of the span, so as to meet the requirements of transverse structure boundaries and river navigation.

预应力钢筋混凝土复合梁是在德国技术转让的基础上优化和创新产生的，主要构造特点为：①主体结构预应力混凝土梁采用直线布置，断面根据横坡角整体倾斜，支座处设水平垫块，支座水平设置；②功能件系统长度为 3.096 m，采用直线布置，连接件按空间位置预埋，不设预拱；③预应力混凝土梁的预应力，在先张法的基础上，再做两次后张预应力，并预留了设置体外预应力钢筋的可能，使轨道梁线形在线路运营后仍可根据需要调整；④复合梁在制造安装阶段均为简支梁，精确定位后利用简支梁连续构造转变为双跨连续梁。

The prestressed reinforced concrete composite beam is optimized and innovated on the basis of German technology transfer. The main structural characteristics are as follows: ① The prestressed concrete beam of the main structure is arranged in a straight line, the section is inclined as a whole according to the transverse slope angle, the horizontal cushion block is set at the support, and the support is set horizontally; ② The length of the functional part system is 3.096 m, which is arranged in a straight line, and the connectors are embedded according to the spatial position without pre-arch; ③ For the prestress of the prestressed concrete beam, on the basis of the pretensioning method, two post-tensioning prestresses are made, and the possibility of setting external prestressed reinforcement is reserved, so that the alignment of the track beam can still be adjusted as required after the line is put into operation; ④ The composite beams are simply supported beams in the manufacturing and installation stage, and after accurate positioning, they are transformed into double-span continuous beams by using the continuous structure of simply supported beams.

(二) 钢复合梁

5.3.2.2 Steel Composite Beam

钢复合梁是由功能件与钢梁通过连接件连接复合成的轨道梁。其构造与预应力钢筋混凝土复合梁类似。

The steel composite beam is a track beam composed of functional parts and steel beams connected by connectors. Its structure is similar to that of prestressed reinforced concrete composite beam.

为了试验研究,选择在上海磁浮线路中部列车运行速度 430 km/h 的位置设计了一根 2×24.78 m 的双跨连续钢复合梁。钢复合梁为直线梁,采用单箱单室断面,顶板设双向排水坡。

For the purpose of experimental study, a 2 × 24.78 m double-span continuous steel composite girder was designed in the middle of Shanghai Maglev Line, where the train speed is 430 km/h. The steel composite beam is a straight beam with a single-box and single-chamber section, and the top plate is provided with a two-way drainage slope.

功能件采用与预应力钢筋混凝土复合梁相同的形式。连接件采用钢结构,使用材料与钢梁相同（S355N）,并设计为一整体。

The form of functional parts is the same as that of prestressed reinforced concrete composite beam. The steel structure is adopted for the connecting piece, the material used is the same as that of the steel beam (S355N), and the connecting piece is designed as a whole.

(三) 桥上轨道梁

5.3.2.3 Track Beam On the Bridge

桥上轨道梁为双层组合式结构,由上层轨道梁、下层桥梁结构及上下层连接结构组成。上层轨道梁一般采用 6.192 m 的板梁;下层桥梁结构根据所需跨径、地形地质及施工条件确定结构形式,可采用梁式、拱式或斜拉桥等桥型;连接结构是上下层结构间的传力构件,采用钢结构。

The track beam on the bridge is a double-layer combined structure, which is composed of the upper track beam, the lower bridge structure and the upper and lower connecting structures. The upper track beam generally adopts 6.192 m plate girder; the lower bridge structure can adopt beam type, arch type or cable-stayed bridge according to the required span, topography, geology and construction conditions; the connecting structure is the force transmission component between the upper and lower structures and adopts steel structure.

（四）维修基地钢梁

5.3.2.4　Steel Beam of Maintenance Base

维修基地钢梁为磁浮列车提供检修平台，由功能件及支承横梁等组成。维修基地钢梁除构造上应满足列车检修时所需传感器定位的要求外，同时还必须满足与主线轨道梁相同的各项技术要求，如动力性能、变形要求及操作限界等。上海磁浮线维修钢梁采用整体框架式结构，共有3种基本类型：3.096 m可移动钢梁、3.096 m和6.192 m固定式钢梁。

The steel beam of the maintenance base provides a maintenance platform for the maglev train, which is composed of functional parts and supporting beams. The steel beam of the maintenance base shall not only meet the requirements of sensor positioning during train maintenance, but also meet the same technical requirements as the main line track beam, such as dynamic performance, deformation requirements and operation clearance. The maintenance steel girders of Shanghai Maglev Line adopt the integral frame structure, which has three basic types: 3.096 m movable steel girder, 3.096 m and 6.192 m fixed steel girder.

（五）可调支座

5.3.2.5　Adjustable Support

由于轨道结构的自重较大，在软土地基上建造的下部承重结构又不可避免地产生一定沉降。对于高速磁浮交通系统来说，必须限制相邻两支墩之间的不均匀沉降引起的上部轨道结构移位。一种可行的方法是，在相邻支墩之间的沉降差超限后，通过支座位置的调节来达到消除偏差的目的。为此，上海磁浮交通发展有限公司牵头研制了多种三向无级可调支座（见图5-4），较好地解决了这一问题。

Because of the heavy weight of the track structure, the lower bearing structure built on the soft soil foundation will inevitably produce a certain settlement. For the high-speed maglev transportation system, it is necessary to limit the displacement of the upper track structure caused by the differential settlement between two adjacent piers. A feasible method is to eliminate the deviation by adjusting the bearing position after the settlement difference between adjacent piers exceeds the limit. For this reason, Shanghai Maglev Transportation Development Co., Ltd. has taken the lead in developing a variety of three-way stepless adjustable bearings (see Figure 5-4), which has solved this problem well.

图 5-4　可调支座

Figure 5-4　Adjustable Support

三、道　岔

5.3.3　Turnout

与常见的铁路道岔相比，相同侧向过岔速度下的道岔长度相差不大。区别较大的是：铁路道岔只动尖轨和心轨，基本轨保持不动，而磁浮道岔则是整个轨道梁一起移动。磁浮道岔实际上是一根可连续弹性弯曲的钢梁，由液压或电动机械驱动道岔钢梁从直股转换到侧股，低速道岔的钢梁下共设置 6 个墩柱，其中 0 号墩柱上设置道岔基座，1~5 号墩柱上设置了作用在基础底板上的道岔移动横梁，可以使道岔沿横梁向固定滑轨移动。除 0 号墩柱外，其余支座上均设置定位和锁定装置，以保证道岔钢梁可以弯曲到设计的位置。

Compared with the common railway turnouts, the length of turnouts under the same lateral speed is not much different. The big difference is that the railway turnout only moves the switch rail and the point rail, and the stock rail remains motionless, while the maglev turnout moves the whole track beam together. The maglev turnout is actually a steel beam that can be bent continuously and elastically. The steel beam of the turnout is driven by hydraulic or electric machinery to convert from straight strand to side strand. Six piers are set under the steel beam of the low-speed turnout, of which the No.0 pier is equipped with a turnout base, and the No.1 to No.5 piers are equipped with a turnout moving beam acting on the foundation slab, which can make the turnout move along the beam to the fixed slide rail. Locating and locking devices shall be set on the rest of the bearings except for the pier stud No.0 to ensure that the turnout steel beam can be bent to the designed position.

道岔在线形上采用直线-回旋曲线-圆曲线-回旋曲线-直线组成的平面组合来拟合道岔钢梁的弯曲曲线。道岔之所以采用回旋曲线，是为了缩短整个道岔的长度。

In terms of turnout alignment, the plane combination consisting of straight line, clothoid curve, circular curve, clothoid curve and straight line is adopted to fit the bending curve of turnout steel beam. The clothoid curve is adopted for the turnout to shorten the length of the whole turnout.

为避免钢梁的扭转，道岔上不设置横坡。道岔范围内不允许设置竖曲线。为满足舒适度的要求，除渡线外，在侧向过岔后的线路上应设置一段运行时间不小于 2 s 的直线段。道岔允许的最大驱动和制动加速度为 1.5 m/s²，道岔允许的最大自由侧向加速度为 2.0 m/s²。

In order to avoid the torsion of the steel beam, no cross slope is set on the turnout. Vertical curves are not allowed to be set within the turnout range. In order to meet the requirements of comfort, a straight line section with a running time of not less than 2 s shall be set on the line after the lateral turnout except the crossover. The maximum allowable driving and braking acceleration of the turnout is 1.5 m/s², and the maximum allowable free lateral acceleration of the turnout is 2.0 m/s².

上海磁浮示范线共设置 8 组低速道岔，其中 1 组是三开道岔。道岔均为电动机械驱动，道岔移动一次的时间约 28 s，如图 5-5 所示。

There are 8 sets of low-speed turnouts in Shanghai Maglev Demonstration Line, one of which is a three-way turnout. All turnouts are driven by electric machinery, and the time for turnouts to move once is about 28 s, as shown in Figure 5-5.

图 5-5 上海磁悬浮线路道岔

Figure 5-5 Turnout of Shanghai Maglev Line

四、轨道功能区

5.3.4 Track Function Area

轨道结构起将轨道设备安装在轨道梁上的作用。轨道设备的主要部分是轨道功能区，位于轨道结构的顶部两侧。轨道功能区有3个工作面，包括顶板滑行轨面、两侧磁性导向板面及定子铁心底面。

The track structure serves to mount the track equipment on the track beam. The main part of the track equipment is the track functional area, which is located on both sides of the top of the track structure. There are three working faces in the track functional area, including the sliding rail surface of the top plate, the magnetic guide plate surface on both sides and the bottom surface of the stator core.

定子铁心底面，也称为定子面，是长定子直线同步电机的组成部分。电机的定子沿整个线路铺设，电机的转子安装在车上。列车的牵引和制动，由地面固定设备调节频率、电压、电流及相位角，通过长定子直线同步电机来实施控制。磁性导向板面，也称侧面导向轨面，起控制列车方向的作用。滑行轨面，起在车站或辅助停车区等停车区域支承落下列车的作用。

The bottom surface of the stator core, also known as the stator face, is an integral part of the long stator linear synchronous motor. The stator of the motor is laid along the entire line, and the rotor of the motor is mounted on the vehicle. The frequency, voltage, current and phase angle of train traction and braking are adjusted by ground fixed equipment, and controlled by long stator linear synchronous motor. The magnetic guide plate surface, also known as the side guide rail surface, plays a role in controlling the direction of the train. The sliding rail surface is used to support the falling train in the parking area such as the station or the auxiliary parking area.

五、线路轨道的精度要求

5.3.5 Accuracy Requirements of Track

磁浮列车运行时悬浮电磁铁和导向电磁铁与线路功能面之间的平均距离保持在 10 mm 左右，为保证列车在高速运行时的安全性和舒适性，磁浮列车系统对轨道提出了较高的设计及制造要求。

When the maglev train is running, the average distance between the levitation electromagnet and the guiding electromagnet and the functional surface of the track is about 10 mm. In order to ensure the safety and comfort of the train running at high speed, the maglev train system puts forward higher design and manufacturing requirements for the track.

（一）轨道结构力学性能方面的要求

5.3.5.1 Requirements for Mechanical Properties of Track Structure

（1）结构刚度要求。系统要求轨道结构在列车载荷、外界环境影响（如温度变化、风力等）作用时，其变形和挠度控制在很小范围内。如要求单跨简支轨道梁在静车载作用下的跨中挠度小于 $L/4\,800$（L 为简支梁跨径），而公路及铁路的一般要求小于 $L/600 \sim L/800$。

(1) Structural stiffness requirements. The system requires that the deformation and deflection of the track structure should be controlled within a very small range under the action of train load, external environmental effects (such as temperature changes, wind, etc.). For example, the mid-span deflection of a single-span simply supported track beam under static load is required to be less than $L/4,800$ (L is the span of the simply supported beam), while the general requirements of highways and railways are less than $L/600 \sim L/800$.

（2）结构动力性能要求。为减少轨道结构在列车运行时的动力反应（振动），系统对轨道结构的动力性能有严格的限制，轨道梁的一阶自振频率必须大于 1.1 倍的列车运行速度与轨道梁跨之比。

(2) Structural dynamic performance requirements. In order to reduce the dynamic response (vibration) of the track structure during train operation, the system has strict restrictions on the dynamic performance of the track structure, and the first natural frequency of the track beam must be greater than 1.1 times the ratio of train speed to track beam span.

（二）轨道功能区制造精度要求

5.3.5.2 Requirements for Manufacturing Accuracy of Track Functional Area

磁浮列车系统对轨道功能区提出了严格的制造精度要求，对 3 个功能面的制造安装精度都要求在 1 mm 以内。系统对轨道功能区的精度要求直接影响轨道结构的设计制造要求，如轨道梁采用预应力混凝土梁时，混凝土收缩、徐变等引起轨道梁跨中竖向变形须控制在 1 mm 以内。

The maglev train system puts forward strict requirements for the manufacturing accuracy of the track functional areas, and the manufacturing and installation accuracy of the three functional areas is required to be within 1 mm. The accuracy requirements of the system for the track functional area directly affect the design and manufacture requirements of the track structure, for example, when the track beam is a prestressed concrete beam, the vertical deformation of the track beam caused by concrete shrinkage and creep must be controlled within 1 mm.

（1）功能面的几何公差主要包括两个方面：一是可直接测量的公差，如位置偏差、相互之间的错位、相互之间的间隙、轨道宽度、钳距等；二是根据测量的数据，进行一定的加工计算得出的公差，如长波误差、短波误差、坡度变化指标等。

(1) The geometric tolerance of functional surface mainly includes two aspects: one is the tolerance that can be directly measured, such as position deviation, mutual dislocation, mutual gap, track width, clamp distance, etc.; the other is the tolerance calculated by certain processing according to the measured data, such as long wave error, short wave error, slope change index, etc.

（2）间隙。

(2) Gap.

① 定子铁心之间的允许间隙：同一梁跨内相邻功能件之间定子间隙 2.5~5.0 mm；相邻梁跨之间定子间隙 90~100 mm。

① Allowable clearance between stator cores: the stator clearance between adjacent functional parts in the same beam span is 2.5-5.0 mm; the stator clearance between adjacent beam spans is 90-100 mm.

② 功能件之间的允许间隙：同一梁跨内功能件间隙 5.5~12.5 mm；相邻梁跨之间功能件间隙 55~70 mm。

② Allowable clearance between functional parts: 5.5-12.5 mm in the same beam span; 55-70 mm between adjacent beam spans.

（3）坡度变化指标（NGK）。

(3) Gradient Change Index (NGK).

坡度变化指标（NGK）的定义是每 1 m 长的功能面相对于相邻的 1 m 长功能面的倾斜度的偏差值，用以控制各功能面的平顺变化，这是一项非常重要的指标。其中以定子面要求最高，其最大绝对值为 1.5 mm/m；滑行轨面要求最低，其最大允许值为 3.0 mm/m。

The slope change index (NGK) is defined as the deviation of the inclination of each 1 m long functional surface relative to the adjacent 1 m long functional surface, which is used to control the smooth change of each functional surface, and it is a very important index.The stator surface has the highest requirement, with the maximum absolute value of 1.5 mm/m; the sliding rail surface has the lowest requirement, with the maximum allowable value of 3.0 mm/m.

（4）长波误差和短波误差。长波误差是拟合位置与理论位置比较的差值，短波误差是拟合位置与实测位置比较的差值。这两个误差保证实测值、拟合曲线值、理论位置之间的差值在一定的范围内。

(4) Long wave error and short wave error. The long wave error is the difference between the fitting position and the theoretical position, and the short wave error is the

difference between the fitting position and the measured position.These two errors ensure that the difference between the measured value, the fitting curve value and the theoretical position is within a certain range.

（三）线路空间位置误差

5.3.5.3 Line Space Position Error

轨道梁的定位精度除了要满足前面所限定的梁间功能面相对关系精度外，还要满足下列相对于空间曲线和线路桩位理论位置的安装公差要求：①x方向：±1 mm（参考位置为固定支座轴线）；②y方向：±1 mm（参考位置为距固定支座轴线 100 mm 处两侧侧面导向轨中心）；③z方向：±1 mm（参考位置为距固定支座轴线 100 mm 处定子底面中心）。

The positioning accuracy of the track beam shall not only meet the accuracy of the relative relationship between the functional surfaces of the beams defined above, but also meet the following installation tolerance requirements relative to the space curve and the theoretical position of the line pile: ①x direction: ±1 mm (the reference position is the axis of the fixed support); ②y direction: ±1 mm (the reference position is the center of the guide rail on both sides 100 mm away from the axis of the fixed support) ③z direction: ±1 mm (the reference position is the center of the stator bottom surface 100 mm away from the axis of the fixed support) .

六、安全设施

5.3.6 Safety Facilities

磁浮铁路沿线各装有 25 m 宽的隔离网，列车上下均设置了防护措施，既避免各类物体落入轨道影响行驶，也防止车上有物品砸向地面。

25 m wide isolation net is installed along the maglev railway, and protective measures are set up above and below the train to prevent all kinds of objects from falling into the track and affecting the running, and to prevent objects from hitting the ground on the train.

磁浮列车还按飞机的防火标准配置了消防设施。为了防止磁浮列车高速运行时对行驶在高架道路上的机动车产生影响，在高架道路的内侧栏杆处还安装了防眩板。

Maglev trains are also equipped with fire fighting facilities according to the fire protection standards of aircraft. In order to prevent the maglev train from affecting the motor vehicles running on the elevated road at high speed, an anti-glare plate is also installed at the inner railing of the elevated road.

第四节 车站与维修基地

Section 5.4　Station and Maintenance Base

上海磁浮示范线的车站设计独特。车站外形设计新颖，具有现代气息，为上海浦东地区又增添了新的景观。车站内设施先进、功能齐全。上海磁浮示范线只设两个车站，即龙阳路站和浦东机场站。

The station design of Shanghai Maglev Demonstration Line is unique.The appearance design of the station is novel and modern, which adds a new landscape to the Pudong area of Shanghai. The station has advanced facilities and complete functions. There are only two stations on the Shanghai Maglev Demonstration Line, namely Longyang Road Station and Pudong Airport Station.

一、龙阳路站

5.4.1　Longyang Road Station

龙阳路站位于地铁车站的南广场，站中心处线路中线距离地铁站房约为 38 m。线路中线与地铁站房主轴线有一小的偏角。车站处的设计轨面标高为 17.0 m。

Longyang Road Station is located in the south square of the subway station, and the central line of the station center is about 38 m away from the subway station building.There is a small angle between the central line of the line and the main axis of the subway station building. The design rail surface elevation at the station is 17.0 m.

龙阳路站因地形的限制，采用前折返的运行方式。考虑到列车运行间隔与站台的布置形式，采用岛、侧组合式站台。按结构需要，两线间距为 12.080 5 m，这样实际的站台宽度为 8.28 m。同时，两侧各设宽为 7.0 m 的侧式站台。从运行组织上可以通过不同站台的发车来提高其通过能力。

Due to the limitation of terrain, Longyang Road Station adopts the operation mode of front turn-back. Considering the train running interval and the layout of the platform, the island and side combined platform is adopted. According to the structural requirements, the distance between two lines is 12.080 5 m, so the actual platform width is 8.28 m. At the same time, a side platform with a width of 7.0 m is set on both sides. From the operation organization, the carrying capacity can be improved through the departure of different platforms.

二、浦东机场站

5.4.2 Pudong Airport Station

浦东机场站的站位中心正对候机楼的中央廊道。候机楼全长 400 m，在其上方已建有 3 个廊道。而本线路设计的站台长度为 210 m，考虑站房上方开发的需要，车站中心位于中间廊道中心以北 100 m 处，把后折返道岔区设置在候机楼南侧。而线路标高已考虑廊道的标高，使站厅层能与廊道水平连接。浦东机场站的中心在候机楼的中央廊道中线以北 100 m。本站采用站后折返方式。为了设置一条渡线，在站台南将线间距由 5.1 m 扩大到 7.4 m。同时，为了运行组织与停放车辆的方便，站后设两条折返线。折返线的有效长度按 8 辆编组计算并设 30 m 的安全距离，全长为 240 m。

The center of Pudong Airport Station is facing the central corridor of the terminal building. The total length of the terminal building is 400 m, and three corridors have been built above it. The designed platform length of this line is 210 m. Considering the development needs above the station building, the station center is located 100 m north of the center of the middle corridor, and the rear turn-back turnout area is located on the south side of the terminal building. The elevation of the corridor has been considered for the elevation of the line, so that the station hall floor can be horizontally connected with the corridor. The center of Pudong Airport Station is 100 m north of the central corridor centerline of the terminal building. The station adopts the turn-back mode after the station. In order to set a crossover, the distance between tracks is expanded from 5.1 m to 7.4 m in the south of the platform. At the same time, for the convenience of operation organization and parking, two turn-back lines are set behind the station. The effective length of the turn-back line shall be calculated according to the 8-car formation and a safety distance of 30 m shall be set, and the total length shall be 240 m.

三、辅助停车区

5.4.3 Auxiliary Parking Area

列车运行中一旦发生故障而停车时，依靠列车的惯性和车载安全制动器的控制使它停到指定区段，以便能够给列车充电并重新浮起，该区段即为辅助停车区。辅助停车区的位置与列车的行驶速度有关，低速区较密，高速区较稀。辅助停车区内应铺设供电轨，同时具有疏散乘客的条件。

Once the train breaks down and stops during operation, it will be stopped to the designated section by the inertia of the train and the control of the on-board safety brake, so that the train can be charged and floated again. This section is the auxiliary parking area. The location of the auxiliary parking area is related to the running speed of the train, with the low speed area being dense and the high speed area being sparse. Power supply rails shall be laid in the auxiliary parking area, and the conditions for evacuating passengers shall be provided.

四、维修基地

5.4.4 Maintenance Base

磁浮列车的车辆、牵引供电系统、运行控制系统、基础通信系统、轨道结构之间始终保持相互联系、相互影响、相互制约。车辆、轨道的运行及工作状况通过列车配置的监测设备自动检测，并自动传递至维护管理系统（MMS）；牵引供电系统、运行控制系统的运行及工作状况通过自身的诊断子系统进行监测记录，同时自动传递至维护管理系统。因此，磁浮系统设备检测的自动化程度高，其维护工作相对较少。

The vehicle, traction power supply system, operation control system, basic communication system and track structure of maglev train are always connected, influenced and restricted each other. The operation and working conditions of the vehicle and track are automatically detected by the monitoring equipment configured for the train and automatically transmitted to the maintenance management system (MMS); The operation and working conditions of traction power supply system and operation control system are monitored and recorded by its own diagnostic subsystem, and automatically transmitted to the maintenance management system. Therefore, the detection of maglev system equipment has a high degree of automation, and its maintenance work is relatively small.

车辆、牵引供电系统、运行控制系统的维修对象主要是电子器件，依靠更换模块的方式进行，不需要大规模的专用检修设施，线路结构（含道岔、定子铁心、定子线圈、供电轨等）的维护主要包括日常检查、清扫及必要的调整，配置的检修设施宜简易、便捷。

The maintenance objects of vehicle, traction power supply system and operation control system are mainly electronic devices, which are carried out by replacing modules and do not require large-scale special maintenance facilities. The maintenance of line structure (including turnout, stator core, stator coil, power rail, etc.) mainly includes daily inspection, cleaning and necessary adjustment. The maintenance facilities should be simple and convenient.

复习思考题

Questions for Revision

1. 叙述中国上海磁浮示范线建设工程进展历程。

1. Describe the progress of Shanghai Maglev Demonstration Line Construction Project in China.

2. 叙述中国上海磁浮示范线磁悬浮列车的工作原理。

2. Describe the working principle of the maglev train of Shanghai Maglev Demonstration Line in China.

3. 叙述中国上海磁浮示范线的主要特点。

3. Describe the main characteristics of Shanghai Maglev Demonstration Line in China.

4. 叙述中国上海磁浮示范线的道岔结构及特点。

4. Describe the turnout structure and characteristics of Shanghai Maglev Demonstration Line in China.

5. 叙述中国上海磁浮示范线采取的环境保护措施。

5. Describe the environmental protection measures taken by Shanghai Maglev Demonstration Line in China.

6. 为什么说中国上海磁浮示范线的车辆和控制部分采用德国 TR 技术？

6. Why do we say that the vehicle and control part of Shanghai Maglev Demonstration Line in China adopts German TR technology?

第六章　日本中低速磁浮 HSST 系统

Chapter 6　Japan Medium and Low Speed Maglev HSST System

前面第三、四、五章主要介绍了超高速磁浮铁路技术，包括日本的 ML 技术和德国的 TR 技术，它们主要适用于长大干线铁路和城际铁路。本章主要介绍中低速磁浮铁路的典型代表——日本的 HSST 技术。HSST 系统主要应用于速度较低的城市轨道交通和机场铁路。我国的磁浮铁路研究目前大都侧重于中低速范围，并且大都参照 HSST 技术。

In chapter 3, 4 and 5, it mainly introduced the ultra-high-speed maglev railway technology, including the Japan's ML technology and Germany's TR technology, which are mainly applicable to long main-line railway and intercity railway. In this chapter, it mainly introduces the HSST technology of Japan, which is the typical representative of medium and low speed maglev railway. The HSST system is mainly used in urban rail transit and airport railway with low speed. At present, the research of maglev railway in China mostly focuses on the range of medium and low speed, and mostly refers to HSST technology.

第一节　概　述

Section 6.1　Overview

本节主要介绍日本 HSST 系统的基本情况，包括发展过程、主要特色及适用范围等内容。

This section mainly introduces the basic information of the Japan's HSST system, including the development process, main features, scope of application, etc.

一、早期发展过程

6.1.1 Early Development Process

HSST（High Speed Surface Transport）称为"高速地面运输系统"。但从目前开发出的产品的实际最高运行速度划分，它还不能属于高速铁路的范畴，而应该称作中低速地面运输系统。

HSST is also called "High Speed Surface Transport System". However, according to the actual maximum running speed of the products developed at present, it can not belong to the category of high-speed railway, but should be called medium and low speed surface transport system.

HSST 最初由日本航空公司投资，40多年前从德国（当时的联邦德国）的克劳斯玛菲公司引进基础技术，希望用于机场到市区的快速轨道交通，后又与名古屋铁路公司等共同投资建立了"HSST 开发公司"（总部设在东京）。

HSST was originally invested by Japan Airlines. More than 40 years ago, it introduced basic technology from KraussMaffei Company in Germany (the Federal Republic of Germany at that time), hoping to use it for rapid rail transit from airport to urban area. Later, it jointly invested with Nagoya Railway Company to establish "HSST Development Company" (headquartered in Tokyo).

（一）HSST-01

6.1.1.1　HSST-01

20世纪70年代中期，为了开发一种连接机场和市区的速度快、噪声低、乘坐舒适的交通工具，日本航空公司开始组织专家对磁浮技术进行研究。1974年4月，小型磁浮试验装置的浮起试验获得成功。1975年制造出了 HSST 试验车 HSST-01，电磁悬浮和直线电机驱动的磁浮试验车运行试验取得了成功。借助于火箭和直线电机驱动，HSST-01 在11.6 km长的试验线上达到了308 km/h 的试验速度。

In the mid-1970s, in order to develop a fast, low-noise and comfortable means of transportation connecting airports and urban areas, Japan Airlines began to organize experts to study maglev technology. In April 1974, the floating test of the small maglev test device was successful. In 1975, the HSST test vehicle HSST-01 was manufactured, and the operation test of the magnetic levitation test vehicle driven by electromagnetic levitation and linear motor was successful. Driven by a rocket and a linear motor, the HSST-01 reached a test speed of 308 km/h on an 11.6 km long test line.

（二）HSST-02

6.1.1.2　HSST-02

日本航空公司 1978 年向公众展出了 HSST-02 磁浮车，最高速度约为 100 km/h，总共有 9 个座位。为了改善舒适性，在车厢和悬浮框架之间采用了二系弹簧悬挂系统。在 1978—1981 年的试验期间，大约有 3 000 人次试乘了 HSST-02 磁浮车。

Japan Airlines exhibited the HSST-02 maglev vehicle to the public in 1978, with a maximum speed of about 100 km/h, and 9 seats in total. In order to improve comfort level, a secondary spring suspension system is used between the carriage and the suspension frame. During the test period from 1978 to 1981, about 3,000 people took the HSST-02 maglev vehicle.

（三）HSST-03

6.1.1.3　HSST-03

为了向公众展示新的磁浮交通技术，并在接近应用的条件下对新的磁浮交通技术最重要的部分功能进行试验，日本从 1983 年开始建造试验和展览车 HSST-03，并于 1985 年在筑波国际工艺博览会上展出。试验和展览设施由一条 300 m 长的线路、一个进出站、一套供电设备和一个维修站组成。该车有 48 个座位，车速限制在 30 km/h。展览会期间，总共有 60 万人次乘坐了该磁浮车。

In order to demonstrate the new maglev transportation technology to the public and test some of the most important functions of the new maglev transportation technology under conditions close to application, Japan began to build the test and exhibition vehicle HSST-03 in 1983 and exhibited it at the Tsukuba International Craft Fair in 1985. The test and exhibition facilities consist of a 300 m long line, an access station, a power supply unit and a maintenance station. The vehicle has 48 seats and a speed limit of 30 km/h. During the exhibition, a total of 600,000 people rode the maglev vehicle.

1986 年，HSST-03 磁浮车被送到温哥华国际博览会展出。在一段 450 m 长、有弯道的线路上，磁浮车的运行速度达到 40 km/h。

In 1986, the HSST-03 maglev vehicle was sent to the Vancouver International Expo for display. On a 450 m long line with curves, the maglev vehicle ran at a speed of 40 km/h.

（四）HSST-04

6.1.1.4　HSST-04

日本 1987 年研制成 HSST-04 磁浮车，车重 24 t，长 19.4 m，可容纳约 70 名乘客，设计速度为 200 km/h。它与 HSST-03 车一样，也采用了复合支承、导向和驱动模块化技术，不同的是，新车走行模块从外侧包住线路。1988 年 5 月，HSST-04 型车在琦玉国际博览会展示,展示线路长 327 m,混凝土高架梁跨 12 m,轨道包括两个半径为 150 m 的曲线段,超高 2.3°,试验速度为 40 km/h。

The HSST-04 maglev vehicle developed by Japan in 1987 weighs 24 t, is 19.4 meters long, can accommodate about 70 passengers, and has a design speed of 200 km/h. Like the HSST-03, it also uses the modular technology of composite support, guidance and drive, but the difference is that the running module of the new car wraps the line from the outside. In May 1988, the HSST-04 train was displayed at the Saitama International Expo. The track was 327 m long, with a concrete viaduct span of 12 m. The track consisted of two curved sections with a radius of 150 m, a superelevation of 2.3°, and a test speed of 40 km/h.

(五) HSST-05

6.1.1.5　HSST-05

1989 年 5—10 月,HSST-05 型车在横滨国际博览会上展示,展示线长 568 m,线路采用单片箱形梁结构,梁跨有 12 m 和 16 m,净空高 4.5 m,动载荷下梁的挠跨比为 1/3 800,由反应板和钢轨组成的走行轨通过钢枕与梁体连接。

From May to October in 1989, the HSST-05 train was displayed at the Yokohama International Exposition. The length of the line was 568 m. The line was a single box beam structure with a span of 12 m and 16 m and a clearance height of 4.5 m. The ratio of deflection to span of the beam under dynamic load was 1/3,800. The running rail composed of reaction plate and steel rail was connected with the beam body through steel sleepers.

早期的 HSST 发展及车辆特征情况见表 6-1（至 1996 年为止）。

Early HSST development and vehicle characteristics are shown in Table 6-1 (as of 1996).

表6-1　HSST早期车辆特征比较表

Table 6-1　Comparison of HSST Early Vehicle Characteristics

编　号 No.	HSST-01	HSST-02	HSST-03	HSST-04	HSST-05	HSST-100
生产年代 Year	1975	1978	1985	1987	1989	1991—1993
长/m Length/m	4.2	8.84	13.8	19.4	19.4	17
宽/m Width/m	2.6	2.0	2.95	3.0	3.0	2.6
高/m Height/m	1.1	1.75	3	3.6	3.6	3.3
席位 Seats	0	9	48	50（70）	160	160
质量/t Mass/t	1.2	1.8（2.4）	12.3（18.0）	19.8（27.0）	39.5（54.0）	18（30）

续表

编号 No.	HSST-01	HSST-02	HSST-03	HSST-04	HSST-05	HSST-100
悬浮气隙/mm Levitation Air Gap /mm	13	8-10	11	9	9	8
供电/V Supply/V	蓄电池164 BATTERY164	蓄电池120 BATTERY 120	直流280 DC280	直流280 DC280	直流280 DC280	直流280 DC280
斩波频率/kHz Chop Frequency /kHz	2	2	2	2	2	2

二、HSST-100

6.1.2 HSST-100

为了使适合于城市交通的HSST型实现商业运行，1989年8月，以名古屋铁路公司（名铁）、爱知省、HSST公司为中心，成立了"中部HSST开发股份公司"，着手HSST技术的进一步开发与试验。

In order to realize the commercial operation of the HSST type which was suitable for urban traffic, in August 1989, with Nagoya Railway Company (Meitetsu), Aichi Province and HSST Company as the center, the "Central HSST Development Co., Ltd." Was established to further develop and test the HSST technology.

1990年，日本对HSST磁浮铁路系统与德国磁浮铁路系统进行了比较和评估，得出采用电磁悬浮的HSST和TR系统接近实用的结论，并计划研制HSST-100型磁浮列车。

In 1990, Japan compared and evaluated the HSST maglev railway system with the German maglev railway system, and concluded that the HSST and TR systems using electromagnetic levitation were close to practical use, and planned to develop the HSST-100 maglev train.

（一）名古屋试验线

6.1.2.1 Nagoya Test Line

1991年，日本在名古屋附近的大江，建成一条新的面向应用的试验线。试验线总长1 530 m，最小平曲线半径为100 m（主线）和25 m（支线），最小竖曲线半径为1 000 m，最大超高为8°，最大坡度为70‰。

In 1991, Japan completed a new application-oriented test line in Oe, near Nagoya. The total length of the test line is 1,530 m, the minimum horizontal curve radius is 100 m (main line) and 25 m (branch line), the minimum vertical curve radius is 1,000 m, and the maximum superelevation is 8°, Maximum slope is 70‰.

较早的名古屋 HSST 车辆导轨断面见图 6-1。

An earlier Nagoya HSST vehicle guideway section is shown in Figure 6-1.

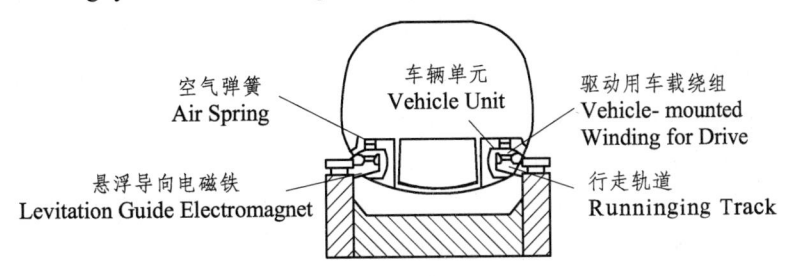

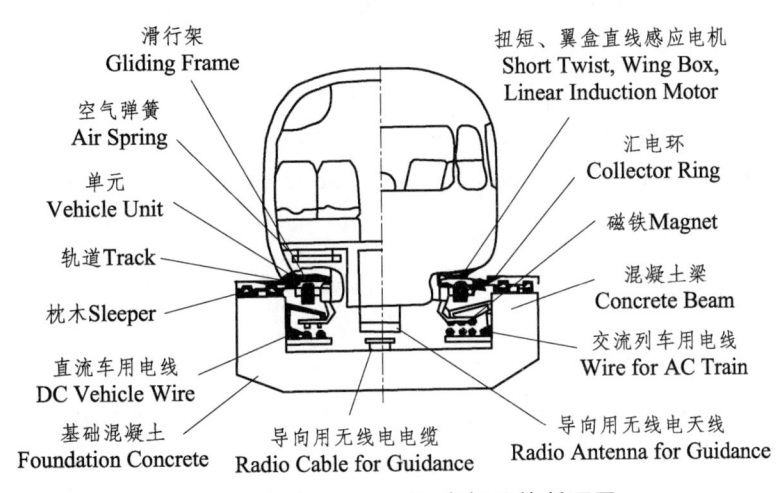

图 6-1 原名古屋 HSST 车辆导轨断面图

Figure 6-1 Cross Section of HSST Vehicle Rail in Nagoya

(二) HSST-100S

6.1.2.2 HSST-100S

HSST-100 适合于市区外围环线和放射形线路，在市内狭窄道路的情况下，其灵活性有利于选线。其设计车速为 110 km/h，限制坡度为 70‰。HSST-100 又分为两种型号：较短的 HSST-100S 和较长的 HSST-100L。

HSST-100 is suitable for urban peripheral loop lines and radial lines, and its flexibility is conducive to route selection in the case of narrow roads in the city. The design speed is 110 km/h and the limiting gradient is 70‰. The HSST-100 is further divided into two variants: the shorter HSST-100S and the longer HSST-100L.

从 1991 年开始，在名古屋试验线上，HSST-100S 已成功地开始运行。HSST-100S 系统由 1 500 V 直流电供电，采用 VVVF（可变电压可变频率）逆变器供给直线电机。

The HSST-100S has been in successful operation on the Nagoya test line since 1991. The HSST-100S system is powered by 1,500 V DC and uses a VVVF (variable voltage variable frequency) inverter to supply the linear motor.

HSST-100S 采用较短的车辆，车辆长度为 8 500 mm，宽度为 2 600 mm，高度为 3 300 mm，高峰载客量约 67 人，最小曲线半径为 25 m。其最高运行速度达到 130 km/h。

The HSST-100S uses shorter vehicles with a vehicle length of 8,500 mm, a width of 2,600 mm, a height of 3,300 mm, peak capacity of approximately 67 passengers, and a minimum curve radius of 25 m. Its maximum operating speed reaches 130 km/h.

依照爱知省的委托，日本成立了城市交通磁浮直线电机列车实用化研究调查委员会，从 1991 年开始到 1995 年对 HSST-100S 型磁浮列车进行了 100 多项面向应用要求的运行试验。测试结果表明，HSST-100S 型磁浮列车是成功的。

According to the commission of Aichi Province, Japan has established the Research Committee on the Practical Application of Maglev Linear Motor Trains for Urban Transportation, which has carried out more than 100 application-oriented operation tests on HSST-100S Maglev Trains from 1991 to 1995. The test results show that the HSST-100S maglev train is successful.

（三）HSST-100L

6.1.2.3　HSST-100L

1995 年，在 HSST-100S 型的基础上，日本又研制了一台加长型样车，称为 HSST-100L，其模块由 6 个增加到 10 个，车辆长度由 8.5 m 增加到 14.4 m，一些器件在 HSST-100S 型试验结果的基础上进行了改进。HSST-100L 型磁浮列车是一列两辆编组的、商业运营车的样车，从 1995 年开始，在大江的试验线路上进行运行试验。

In 1995, on the basis of HSST-100S, Japan developed a lengthened prototype vehicle, called HSST-100L, whose modules were increased from 6 to 10, and the length of the vehicle was increased from 8.5 m to 14.4 m. Some devices were improved on the basis of the test results of HSST-100S. The HSST-100L maglev train is a two-car, commercially operated prototype, which has been tested on the Oe test line since 1995.

HSST-100L 设计速度 130 km/h，车辆长度为 14 000 mm（中间车为 13 500 mm），宽度为 2 600 mm，高度为 3 300 mm，高峰载客量约 118 人（中间车约 129 人），最小曲线半径为 50 m。

The HSST-100L has a design speed of 130 km/h, a vehicle length of 14,000 mm (13,500 mm for intermediate vehicles), a width of 2,600 mm, a height of 3,300 mm, a peak passenger capacity of about 118 (129 for intermediate vehicles), and a minimum curve radius of 50 m.

三、HSST 的发展

6.1.3　The Development of HSST

日本航空公司开发的 HSST-100 已达到成熟应用程度，已经进入实用化阶段。日本目前正在 JR 东海道的大船站—横滨梦之地之间着手建设营业路线，还正在建设名古屋东部丘陵线。

The HSST-100 developed by Japan Airlines has reached a mature application level and has entered the practical stage. Japan is currently building a business route between JR Tokaido's Ofuna Station and Yokohama Dream Land, as well as the Nagoya Eastern Hills Line.

HSST-100 系列目前是 HSST 的主力车型，实际上它属于低速（或称普速）铁路。日本目前正在致力于研究速度更高的 HSST 系统，包括 HSST-200 和 HSST-300 系统。

HSST-100 series is currently the main model of HSST, in fact, it belongs to low-speed (or ordinary speed) railway. Japan is currently working on higher speed HSST systems, including the HSST-200 and HSST-300 systems.

（一）HSST-200

6.1.3.1　HSST-200

HSST-200 适合于城市与近郊的连接交通线，可以大幅度缩短通勤、就学的时间。其设计车速为 200 km/h，限制坡度为 70‰。车辆长度为 18 500 mm（中间车为 17 100 mm），宽度为 3 000 mm，高度为 3 600 mm，高峰载客量约 143 人，最小曲线半径为 100 m。

HSST-200 is suitable for connecting traffic lines between cities and suburbs, which can greatly shorten commuting and school time. The design speed is 200 km/h and the limiting gradient is 70‰. The vehicle has a length of 18,500 mm (17,100 mm for intermediate vehicles), a width of 3,000 mm, a height of 3,600 mm, a peak passenger capacity of approximately 143, and a minimum curve radius of 100 m.

HSST-200 的设计速度实际上已达到高速铁路的速度，但目前 HSST-200 只是处于设计阶段，还未实际车辆投入试验运行。

The design speed of HSST-200 has actually reached the speed of high-speed railway, but at present, HSST-200 is only in the design stage, and has not yet been put into test operation.

（二）HSST-300

6.1.3.2　HSST-300

HSST-300 适合于城市之间或市区与机场之间的连接交通线，其设计车速为

300 km/h。HSST-300 的设计速度也达到了高速铁路的速度，但目前其技术还没有达到实际应用的程度。另外，由于 HSST 采用第三轨供电方式，实际上并未实现列车完全无接触行驶，这使得其最高运行速度无法达到日本 MLX、德国 TR 那样的超高速水平。故日本 HSST-300 将来能否达到 300 km/h 的设计速度，能否达到实用化水平，还有待将来实践的检验。

HSST-300 is suitable for connecting transportation lines between cities or between urban areas and airports, and its design speed is 300 km/h. The design speed of HSST-300 also reaches the speed of high-speed railway, but its technology has not yet reached the level of practical application. In addition, because HSST uses the third rail power supply mode, in fact, it does not realize the complete non-contact running of the train, which makes its maximum running speed unable to reach the super-high speed level of MLX in Japan and TR in Germany. Therefore, whether the Japanese HSST-300 can reach the design speed of 300 km/h in the future and whether it can reach the practical level remains to be tested by future practice.

几种主要形式 HSST 的主要数据对比见表 6-2。

See Table 6-2 for the main data comparison of several main forms of HSST.

表 6-2　HSST 的主要数据
Table 6-2　Main Data of HSST

项目 Project		温哥华博览会试验线 Vancouver Expo Test Line	HSST-100		营业线 Operating Line
		HSST-03	HSST-100S	HSST-100L	HSST-200
系统 System	支承形式 Support Form	吸附式磁力悬浮 Adsorption Type Magnetic Levitation			
	导向形式 Guide Type	吸附式磁力导向（与悬浮电磁铁兼用，交错形式配置） Adsorption Magnetic Guide (Used With Suspension Electromagnet, Interlaced Configuration)			
	驱动形式 Drive Form	车辆驱动异步直线电机（单侧直线感应电机） Vehicle Drive Asynchronous Linear Motor (Single-Sided Linear Induction Mmotor)			
	悬浮气隙/mm Levitation Air Gap /mm	11	8（名古屋试验线） 8 (Nagoya Test Line)		7-9
导轨 Guide Raill	路线长度/km Length/km	0.45（单线） 0.45 (Single Line)	1.5（名古屋试验线） 1.5 (Nagoya test line)		根据需要 As Required
	最小曲线半径/m Minimum Curve Radius/m	250	50（名古屋试验线最小值） 50 (Nagoya Test Line Min)		最小值 100，1 100（200 km/h）Min100, 1,100（200 km/h）

续表

项目 Project		温哥华博览会试验线 Vancouver Expo Test Line	HSST-100		营业线 Operating Line
		HSST-03	HSST-100S	HSST-100L	HSST-200
导轨 Guide Raill	限制坡度/‰ Limiting Slope/‰	5	最大 70 Max70		最大 70 Max70
车辆 Vehicle	设计速度/ （km/h） Design Speed /(km/h)	60 （运营速度 40） 60 (operating speed 40）	110	130	200
	宽度/m Width/m	2.95	2.6	2.6	3.0
	高度/m Height/m	3.0	3.4	3.2	3.6
	头车长度/m Head Car Length/m	13.8	8.5	14.4	19.1
	中车长度/m Middle Car Length /m		8.3	13.5	18.2
	单元/（台/辆） Unit/ (Set/Vehicle)		6	10	
	空车重/（t/辆） Empty Vehicle Weight （t/Vehicle）	18	10	15	24
	满载重/（t/辆） Full Load/ （t/Vehicle）		15	25	32
	座席数/（人/辆） Number of Seats / (Person/Vehicle)	68+11 个辅助座席 68+11 Auxiliary Seats	高峰载客量 67 Peak Capacity 67	高峰载客量 118 （中间车约 129） Peak Capacity 118 (about 129 in the Middle)	50（含 10 个辅助座席），高峰载客量 143 50 (Including 10 Auxiliary Seats), Peak Capacity143
乘客数 （坐/站/总数） Number of Passengers (Seat/Station /Total)	4 辆编组 4-Car Formation		112/82/194	146/156/302	240/214/454
	6 辆编组 6-Car Formation		176/126/302	228/238/466	368/324/692
	8 辆编组 8-Car Formation		240/170/410	310/320/630	496/434/930

四、HSST 的特色

6.1.4　Features of HSST

日本的 HSST 系统具有如下特色：
The Japanese HSST system has the following features:

（一）舒适、无公害

6.1.4.1　Comfortable and Pollution-free

HSST 不需要车轮，利用电磁铁的吸力作用悬浮走行，没有车轮与轨道接触所产生的噪声和振动，因此，HSST 不仅乘坐舒适，同时消除了公害问题。

The HSST does not need wheels and uses the attraction of the electromagnet to suspend and run without noise and vibration caused by the contact between the wheels and the track. Therefore, the HSST is not only comfortable to ride, but also eliminates the problem of public nuisance.

（二）安全、不必担心事故发生

6.1.4.2　Safe, No Need to Worry about Accidents

在构造上车辆环抱着轨道，不会出现脱轨、翻车等事故。此外，HSST 的悬浮系统利用了电磁铁的吸力作用，磁场不向外扩散，故对人体、磁卡完全没有影响。

In the structure, the vehicle encircles the track, so there will be no derailment, rollover and other accidents. In addition, the suspension system of HSST uses the attraction of the electromagnet, and the magnetic field does not diffuse outward, so it has no effect on the human body and the magnetic card.

（三）建设费用、养护维修费用低

6.1.4.3　Low Construction Cost and Maintenance Cost

由于 HSST 的车体质量轻，构造物规模小，轨道的建设费用、养护维修等运行费用可以降低，无须像传统铁道那样，投入巨额设备资金。

Since the weight of the car body of the HSST is light and the scale of the structure is small, the construction cost, maintenance and other operating costs of the track can be reduced, and there is no need to invest a huge amount of equipment funds as in the conventional railway.

（四）技术成熟、可以早日实现实用化

6.1.4.4　Mature Technology, Can Be Put into Practice As Soon As Possible

HSST 从 1974 年开始开发，已经进行了无数次的试验和改良。使用了经过实践检验的 HSST，可以说是最接近实用化的磁浮城市轨道交通系统。

The HSST has been in development since 1974 and has undergone numerous tests and modifications. HSST, which has been tested in practice, can be said to be the closest practical maglev urban rail transit system.

（五）新交通系统、适应各种条件

6.1.4.5　New Transportation System to Adapt to Various Conditions

使用直线电机驱动，可以毫不费力地在陡坡区间行走，小巧的车体即使急弯处也能够顺畅通过。由于使用专用的高架轨道，不会有堵车问题。能够悬浮停车，适合于站间距离较短的城市交通系统。

Driven by linear motor, it can walk effortlessly on steep slopes, and the compact car body can pass smoothly even at sharp bends. Because of the use of dedicated elevated tracks, there will be no traffic jams. It can suspend parking and is suitable for urban traffic systems with short distance between stations.

（六）不受距离因素限制、适用于众多场所

6.1.4.6　Not Limited by Distance, Suitable for Many Places

HSST 不仅适合低速悬浮运行，也适合高速悬浮运行。在不久的将来，在城际交通运输、机场铁路等速度高达 200～300 km/h 的高速运输系统也有可能发挥其作用。

HSST is not only suitable for low speed suspension operation, but also for high speed suspension operation. In the near future, it may also play a role in high-speed transportation systems with speeds of up to 200-300 km/h, such as inter-city transportation and airport railway.

第二节　工作原理

Section 6.2　Operating Principle

本节主要介绍 HSST 系统的工作原理，包括悬浮原理、导向原理和驱动原理。

This section describes the operating principles of the HSST system, including the suspension principle, the guiding principle, and the driving Principle.

一、悬浮原理

6.2.1 Suspension Principle

HSST 的工作原理与德国的 TR 原理类似，均使用磁吸电磁式（EMS）工作原理。HSST 应用了磁铁吸引铁板的原理，轨道梁的两侧为悬空倒"U"形钢质铁磁性轨道，固定在磁浮列车上的悬浮兼导向的电磁铁正好置于轨道下方，且铁心呈正"U"形，与倒"U"形的轨道相对。安装在车体的电磁铁从下方产生吸引轨道的吸力，列车利用此吸力而悬浮。

The operating principle of the HSST is similar to that of the German TR, which uses a magnetically attracted electromagnetic (EMS) operating principle. HSST applies the principle that magnets attract iron plates. The two sides of the track beam are suspended inverted "U"-shaped steel ferromagnetic tracks. The suspension and guidance electromagnet fixed on the maglev train is just under the track, and the iron core is in a positive "U" shape, opposite to the inverted "U"-shaped track. The electromagnet installed on the vehicle body generates a suction force to attract the track from below, and the train is suspended by the suction force.

如果放任吸力作用，磁铁将吸附在轨道上，因此在磁铁和轨道之间设置感应器，实时探测电磁铁与轨道的距离，通过调节电磁铁的励磁电流，调整电磁铁与轨道之间的引力，以保持电磁铁与轨道之间的距离（间隙）稳定在 8 mm 左右，实现列车稳定悬浮。

If the attraction is allowed, the magnet will be adsorbed on the rail. Therefore, an inductor is set between the magnet and the rail to detect the distance between the electromagnet and the rail in real time. By adjusting the excitation current of the electromagnet, the attraction between the electromagnet and the track can be adjusted to keep the distance (gap) between the electromagnetic and the track stable at about 8 mm, so as to realize the stable suspension of the train.

在名古屋试验线上早期应用的 HSST 的悬浮原理见图 6-2。

The levitation principle of the early HSST application on the Nagoya test line is shown in Figure 6-2.

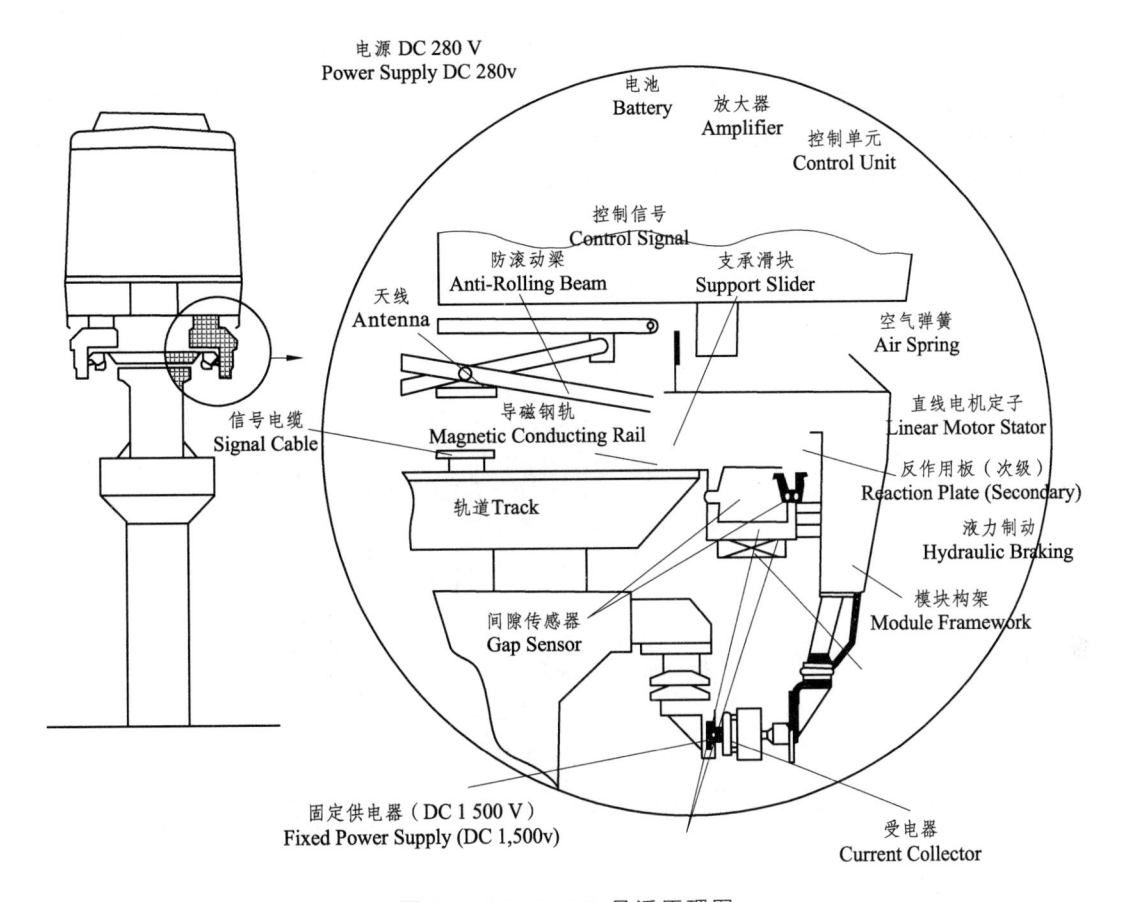

图 6-2　HSST-100 悬浮原理图

Figure 6-2　HSST-100 Suspension Schematic Diagram

二、导向原理

6.2.2　Guiding Principle

列车在运行过程中会产生左右偏离，使得正"U"形电磁铁的铁心与倒"U"形轨道错位，两者之间的引力倾斜，产生一个与偏离方向相反的横向分量，利用其产生的作用力与轨道（倒"U"字形）、磁铁（"U"字形）之间的吸力相互作用进行纠正，使列车返回中心线，见图 6-3。也就是说，HSST 磁浮列车的导向是自动的，不需要导向电磁铁的主动控制。

The train can generate left and right deviation in the running process, so that the iron core of the positive U-shaped electromagnet and the inverted U-shaped track are misplaced, the attractive force between the two is inclined, a transverse component opposite to the deviation direction is generated, and the interaction between the generated acting force and the attractive force between the track (inverted U-shaped) and the magnet (U-shaped) is used for correction, to make the the train return to the centerline, as shown in Figure 6-3. That is to say, the guidance of the HSST maglev train is automatic and does not require the active control of the guidance electromagnet.

导磁钢轨
Magnetic Rail

电磁铁铁心
Electromagnet Core

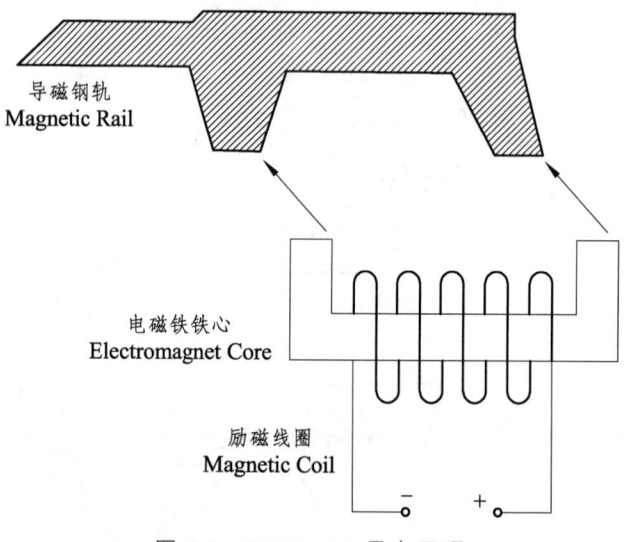

励磁线圈
Magnetic Coil

图 6-3　HSST-100 导向原理

Figure 6-3　HSST-100 Guidance Schematic Diagram

三、驱动原理

6.2.3　Driving Principle

日本 HSST 的车辆及导轨结构与德国 TR 系统有些类似。两者的主要不同之处在于驱动原理方面。TR 采用地面驱动方式，电机为长定子直线同步电机（LSM），而 HSST 采用列车驱动方式，电机为短定子直线感应电机（LIM）。电机的初级线圈（定子，或称一次侧）安装在车辆上，与普通旋转电机相似的转子（或称二次侧、次级线圈）沿列车前进方向展开设置在轨道上，见图 6-4。

The vehicle and guideway structure of the Japanese HSST is somewhat similar to the German TR system. The main difference between the two lies in the driving principle. The TR is a ground drive and the motor is a long-stator linear synchronous motor (LSM), while the HSST is a train drive and the motor is a short-stator linear induction motor (LIM). The primary coil of the motor (stator, or primary side) is mounted on the vehicle. The rotor (or secondary side, secondary coil) similar to the common rotating motor is set on the track along the forward direction of the train, as shown in Figure 6-4.

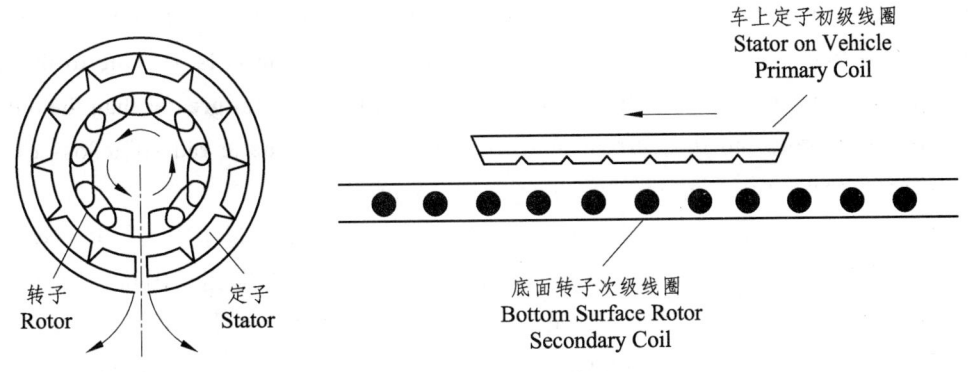

图 6-4 HSST 直线电机原理

Figure 6-4 Schematic Diagram of HSST Linear Motor

在倒"U"形轨道的背面（上方）敷设有铜质或铝质的反应板，正对其上方车体上安装有该直线电机的定子，当定子通入三相电流后，产生一个移动磁场，该磁场在感应板上感应出电流和磁场，由于磁场的作用产生推力，牵引列车前进或后退。

A reaction plate made of copper or aluminum is laid on the back (above) of the inverted U-shaped track, and a stator of the linear motor is mounted on the vehicle body right above the reaction plate. When a three-phase current is applied to the stator, a moving magnetic field is generated, and the magnetic field induces a current and a magnetic field on the reaction plate. Due to the action of the magnetic field, a thrust is generated to pull the train forward or backward.

由于直线电机定子在车上，HSST 牵引功率的控制和转换由车上的设备来完成，而不像 TR 或 MLX 磁浮铁路那样，在地面实现牵引功率的转换和控制。

Because the linear motor stator is on the vehicle, the control and conversion of HSST traction power is completed by the equipment on the vehicle, unlike TR or MLX maglev railway, which realizes the conversion and control of traction power on the ground.

采用短定子直线感应电机牵引的优点是，轨道结构简单（线路上无铁心和线圈）、控制方便（车上控制）、发车频率较高（采用类似轮轨铁路区间闭塞的方式防止列车追尾）、造价较低。缺点是电机功率因数较低（$\cos\phi<0.7$）和效率较低（$\eta<0.7$）。这是因为当列车处于悬浮状态时，定子与反应板的距离（间隙）大约为 10 mm（而旋转电机间隙不到 1 mm），励磁功耗较大。电机功率因数低，导致功率设备容量远大于电机输出功率，设备的电流热损耗和电磁辐射损耗增大，导致能耗较大。

The advantages of short-stator linear induction motor traction are simple track structure (no iron core and coil on the line), convenient control (on-board control), high departure frequency (similar to the way of wheel-rail railway section blocking to prevent train rear-end collision) and low cost. The disadvantage is that the motor power factor is low ($\cos\phi<0.7$) and less efficient ($\eta<0.7$). This is because when the train is levitated, the distance (gap) between the stator and the reaction plate is about 10 mm (while the gap between the rotating motor is less than 1 mm), and the excitation power consumption is large. Due to the low power factor of the motor, the capacity of the power equipment is far greater than the output power of the motor, and the current heat loss and electromagnetic radiation loss of the equipment increase, resulting in large energy consumption.

直线感应电机牵引的磁浮列车在较高速度下（如 300 km/h 以上）运行时，效率和功率因数还会更低，且在高速下，通过机械接触向车上供电也相当困难。因此，像 HSST 磁浮列车这样的系统适合在较低的速度（低于 120 km/h）下应用。

The efficiency and power factor of the maglev train driven by linear induction motor will be even lower when it runs at a higher speed (such as more than 300 km/h), and it is also very difficult to supply power to the train through mechanical contact at high speed. Therefore, systems such as the HSST maglev train are suitable for application at lower speeds (below 120 km/h).

第三节　HSST 试验线

Section 6.3　HSST Test Line

本节主要介绍位于名古屋附近的大江 HSST 试验线及试验结果评估。

This section focuses on the Oe HSST test line located near Nagoya and the evaluation of the test results.

一、试验线概况

6.3.1　Test Line Overview

日本于 1990 年在名古屋附近的大江建造了大约 1.5 km 的 HSST 试验线，并于 1991 年 5 月开始试运行。在这条试验线上，主要利用两辆编组 HSST-100 型列车进行运行试验，最高运行速度为 110 km/h。

About 1.5 km of the HSST test line was constructed in Japan at Oe near Nagoya in 1990 and began trial operation in May 1991. On this test line, two HSST-100 trains are mainly used for operation test, and the maximum running speed is 110 km/h.

为了验证 HSST 列车在陡坡和急弯处的运行性能，该试验线特别设计了 60‰、70‰

的坡度和 100 m（适用于正线）、50 m 的曲线半径，并在原大江车站站场内设置了道岔系统。该试验线上列车的最高运行速度为 110 km/h。

In order to verify the operation performance of HSST trains on steep slopes and sharp bends, the test line is specially designed with a gradient of 60‰ and 70‰ and a curve radius of 100 m (applicable to the main line) and 50 m, and a turnout system is set in the yard of the original Oe Station. The maximum running speed of the train on the test line is 110 km/h.

二、试验结果评估

6.3.2 Evaluation of Test Results

HSST 试验线 1991 年开始运行试验，试验逐渐进行。日本研究的 HSST 磁浮技术中，中低速（100 km/h 左右）技术最为成熟。截止到 1999 年 10 月，在该大江试验线上，HSST-100S 已运行了 6.3 万千米，试乘 1.3 万人；HSST-100L 已运行 5 万千米，试乘 1.7 万人。

The HSST test line began operational testing in 1991 and the testing was conducted gradually. Among the HSST maglev technologies studied in Japan, the medium and low speed (about 100 km/h) technology is the most mature. As of October 1999, HSST-100S has been operated for 63,000 kilometers on the Oe test line, with 13,000 test passengers; HSST-100L has been operated for 50,000 kilometers, with 17,000 test passengers.

试验结果由以东京大学技术系正田英介教授为主席，由运输省、建设省和其他单位的专家学者组成的可行性研究委员会进行评估。专家考察了 HSST 的噪声、振动和磁场影响等，结论是：HSST 磁浮铁路系统是舒适的低污染系统，能够应对紧急情况，长期的运行试验证明它是可靠的，并且由于其悬浮的优点使得它的维修量降低。作为城市交通系统，HSST 磁浮铁路系统已进入实用阶段，将来定会在城市交通系统中显示其特长。现在的任务是利用新技术使其更加完善。

The test results were evaluated by a feasibility study committee chaired by Professor Hidesuke Masada of the Department of Technology of the University of Tokyo and composed of experts and scholars from the Ministry of Transport, the Ministry of Construction and other units. The experts examined the noise, vibration, and magnetic field effects of the HSST, and concluded that the HSST maglev rail system is a comfortable, low-pollution system that can cope with emergencies, is proven reliable by long-term operational tests, and requires less maintenance due to its levitation advantages. As an urban transportation system, the HSST maglev railway system has entered the practical stage and will show its advantages in urban transportation systems in the future. The task now is to make it better with new technology.

对利用磁铁悬浮 1 cm 运行的常规磁浮铁路技术，日本运输省认为，在安全性、可靠性、舒适性等方面，技术上是成熟的，作为铁路运输工具也是可以认可的，进行营业运行没有问题，可以作为客运营业线使用。1993 年 4 月，日本运输省正式确认 HSST-100 系统是一种安全、可靠的交通系统，可以用于城市公共交通。运输省已发放了 HSST 的营业许可证。

The Ministry of Transport of Japan believes that the conventional maglev railway technology, which uses magnets to suspend 1 cm for operation, is technically mature in terms of safety, reliability and comfort, and can be recognized as a railway transport tool. There is no problem in business operation, and it can be used as a passenger transport line. In April 1993, the Ministry of Transport of Japan officially confirmed that the HSST-100 system is a safe and reliable transportation system and can be used for urban public transport. The Ministry of Transport has issued an operating license for HSST.

在 1986 年举行的温哥华交通博览会上有 47 万人试乘了 HSST，1989 年的横滨博览会上试乘人数达到 126 万人。普遍的评价是噪声低、横向晃动小、感觉舒适。从实际客运试验方面也证明 HSST 技术是成熟的、实用的。

At the Vancouver Transport Expo in 1986, 470,000 people rode the HSST, and at the Yokohama Expo in 1989, 1.26 million people rode the HSST. The general evaluation is that the noise is low, the lateral shaking is small and the feeling is comfortable. It is also proved that the HSST technology is mature and practical from the actual passenger test.

到 1998 年为止，在中低速磁浮铁路系统中，只有日本的 HSST 常导低速磁浮铁路系统发展到实用水平，并具有商业应用的可能性。

Up to 1998, among the medium-low-speed maglev railway systems, only the HSST low-speed maglev railway system in Japan has been developed to a practical level and has the possibility of commercial application.

第四节 车 辆

Section 6.4　Vehicles

本节主要介绍 HSST 的车辆，包括车辆结构、单元、电磁铁和直线电机。

This section describes the HSST vehicles, including the vehicle structure, units, electromagnets, and linear motors.

一、车　体

6.4.1　Car Body

试验线使用两种类型的车辆，包括基本上与新交通系统大小相同的 HSST-100S 型以及与铁路车辆基本相同的 HSST-100L 型。HSST-100L 车辆比原先的 HSST-100S 车辆的长度更长一些，从 1995 年开始试验。

Two types of vehicles were used on the test line, including the HSST-100S, which is essentially the same size as the new transit system, and the HSST-100L, which is essentially the same size as the rail vehicle. The HSST-100L vehicle is longer than the original HSST-100S vehicle and has been tested since 1995.

车辆长度按照实际线路的要求进行设计。之后还要进行运行速度为 200 km/h 和 300 km/h 的 HSST-200 和 HSST-300 两种车辆的试验。此外，为了减轻质量，车体使用了铝合金结构。

The length of the vehicle shall be designed according to the requirements of the actual line. This will be followed by testing of the HSST-200 and HSST-300 vehicles at speeds of 200 km/h and 300 km/h. In addition, in order to reduce the mass, the body uses aluminum alloy structure.

HSST-100L 磁浮列车主要技术指标见表 6-3。

See Table 6-3 for main technical indexes of HSST-100L maglev train.

表 6-3　HSST-100L 磁浮列车主要技术指标
Table 6-3　Main Technical Indexes of HSST-100L Maglev Train

最高速度 Maximum Speed	130 km/h
悬浮气隙 Levitation Air Gap	8 mm
车辆组成 Vehicle Composition	5 台转向架，40 台悬浮电磁铁和车体 5 Bogies, 40 Suspension Electromagnets and Car Body
二次悬挂 Secondary Suspension	空气弹簧 Air Spring
车体材料 Body Material	铝合金 Aluminum Alloy
转弯机构 Turning Mechanism	机构转弯控制 Mechanism Turning Control
导向方式 Guidance Mode	悬浮磁铁侧向力导向，最大为悬浮力的 20% Lateral Force Steering of Suspension Magnet, The Maximum is 20% of the Suspension Force
牵引电机 Traction Motor	直线交流异步电动机，10 台/车 Linear AC Asynchronous Motor, 10 sets/vehicle
电机功率 Motor Power	50 kW/台 50 kW/set
主逆变器 Main Inverter	1 台/车，1 200 kV·A，为 10 台电机供电 1set/vehicle, 1,200kV·A, Supplying Power for 10 Motors

续表

辅助逆变器 Auxiliary Inverter	AC 380 V/50 kV·A，为空调供电 AC 380 V/50kV·A, Supplying Power for Air Conditioning
牵引控制 Traction Control	等滑差控制 Equal Slip Control
正常制动 Normal Braking	电阻制动 Resistance Braking
应急制动 Emergency Braking	液压制动和滑块制动 Hydraulic Braking and Slide Braking
加速度 Acceleration	起动不小于 0.9 m/s² Starting Not Less Than 0.9 m/s²
减速度 Deceleration	常规制动不小于 0.8 m/s²，紧急制动不小于 1.5 m/s² No less than 0.8 m/s² for Normal Braking, No less than 1.5 m/s² for Emergency Braking
供电电压 Supply Voltage	DC 1,500 V
受流方式 Current Collection Mode	正负受流轨双受流器受流 Positive and Negative Current Collection Rail Double Current Collection
辅助电源 Auxiliary Power Supply	DC 280 V 和 DC 110 V DC 280 V and DC 110 V
车辆限界 Vehicle Gauge	符合城市地铁标准 Meets the Urban Subway Standard
海拔范围 Altitude Range	不超过 1 200 m No more than 1,200 m
环境温度 Ambient Temperature	－20 ～ ＋45 ℃
车辆种类 Type of Vehicles	有驾驶室的头车 Mc 和无驾驶室的中车 M，全为动车 The First Car Mc with a Cab and the Middle Car M without a Cab are all Motor Cars.
车辆长度 Vehicle Length	Mc 头车 14 400 mm，M 中间车 13500 mm Mc Head Car 14,400 mm, M Middle Car 13,500 mm
车辆宽度 Vehicle Width	2,600 mm
车辆高度 Vehicle Height	3,190 mm
车辆质量 Vehicle Mass	空车 15 t，满载 25 t Empty 15 t, Loaded 25 t
车辆载人 Vehicle Occupancy	Mc 头车 69 人，M 中间车 82 人 Mc Head Car 69 People, M Middle Car 82 People
列车编组 Train Formation	6 辆编组（Mc＋M＋M＋M＋M＋Mc） 6-car Formation (Mc＋M＋M＋M＋M＋Mc)
列车全长 Total Length	2×14.4 m＋4×13.5 m＝82.8 m（6 辆编组） 2×14.4 m＋4×13.5 m＝82.8 m(6-car Formation)
列车载人 Train Occupancy	466 人（6 辆编组） 466 People (6-car Formation)
噪声 Noise	车内不大于 60 dB，车外 10m 不大于 64 dB No more than 60 dB Inside the Vehicle, No more than 64 dB 10 m Outside the Vehicle.

二、单　元

6.4.2 Unit

单元相当于通常铁路车辆的转向架。HSST 的车身一般由 4 个或更多沿纵向首尾相接的磁转向架共同悬浮。每个转向架都具有独立的悬浮、导向和驱动功能，相互之间可以互补，整车悬浮能力具有一定的冗余。转向架与车身通过空气弹簧连接。每个转向架有 4 组 8 个空气弹簧，因此 4 个转向架的车就有 32 个空气弹簧。这些弹簧的压缩气体通过管线和控制系统相互连接构成一个统一的支承系统，使车厢的质量分布在各个转向架上，同时减少车身的振动，为乘客提供舒适的乘车感觉。每个转向架为两侧既相对独立又通过防侧滚梁而连成一体的模块化结构。即每一侧为一个模块组件，由 4 个悬浮兼导向电磁铁和一台直线电机定子组装而成，具有独立的悬浮、导向和驱动功能，其运动在防侧滚梁所限制的一个小范围内不受另一侧模块的约束（即机械解耦）。正是由于这种模块化机械解耦的功能，使得两侧轨道不必严格地保持绝对平行，降低了精度要求和控制的难度，允许列车通过较小半径的弯道。

The unit corresponds to the bogie of a normal railway vehicle. The body of the HSST is generally suspended by four or more magnetic bogies connected end to end in the longitudinal direction. Each bogie has independent suspension, guidance and driving functions, which can complement each other, and the suspension capacity of the whole vehicle has certain redundancy. The bogie is connected with the vehicle body through an air spring. Each bogie has four sets of eight air springs, so a four-bogie car has 32 air springs. The compressed gas of these springs is interconnected through pipelines and control systems to form a unified support system, so that the mass of the carriage is distributed on each bogie, while reducing the vibration of the body and providing passengers with a comfortable ride. Each bogie is of a modular structure with two relatively independent sides which are connected into a whole through an anti-rolling beam. That is to say, each side is a module assembly, which is assembled by four levitation and guidance electromagnets and a linear motor stator. It has independent levitation, guidance and driving functions, and its movement is not constrained by the module on the other side within a small range limited by the anti-rolling beam (mechanical decoupling). It is precisely because of this modular mechanical decoupling function that the tracks on both sides do not have to be strictly kept absolutely parallel, which reduces the accuracy requirements and the difficulty of control, and allows the train to pass through smaller radius curves.

HSST-100S 的每辆车上装有 6 个单元（转向架），HSST-100L 型的每辆车上装有 10 个单元。使用这样的构造，使车辆、轨道结构变得简便，平稳走行变得可能。单元的结构见图 6-5。

Each vehicle of HSST-100S is equipped with 6 units (bogies), and each vehicle of HSST-100L is equipped with 10 units. With such a structure, the vehicle and the track structure become simple, and smooth running becomes possible. See Figure 6-5 for the structure of the unit.

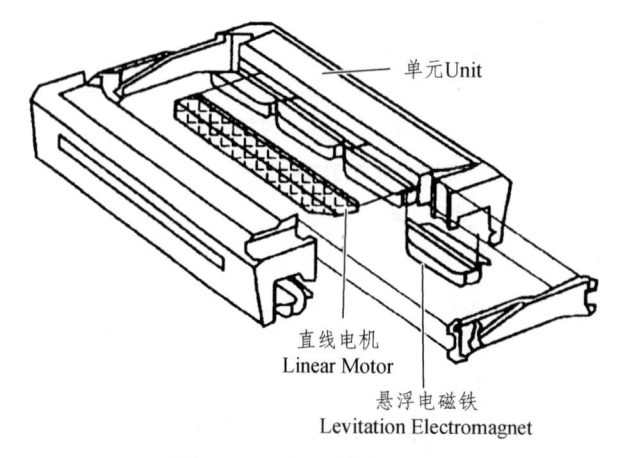

图 6-5　HSST 车辆单元

Figure 6-5　HSST Vehicle Unit

三、悬浮电磁铁

6.4.3　Suspension Electromagnet

每个单元装有 4 个悬浮电磁铁。在 HSST-100S 型车辆上共安装有 24 个电磁铁，而在 HSST-100L 车辆上则有 40 个悬浮电磁铁，电磁铁使用 280 V 直流电，紧急情况断电时，蓄电池维持悬浮走行直到停车。

Each unit is equipped with 4 suspension electromagnets. A total of 24 electromagnets are installed on the HSST-100S vehicle, while 40 levitation electromagnets are installed on the HSST-100L vehicle. The electromagnets use DC 280 V. In case of emergency power failure, the battery maintains levitation until the vehicle stops.

四、直线电机定子

6.4.4　Linear Motor Stator

1 个单元装有 1 个直线感应电机 LIM 定子，保证列车能够以速度 100 km/h 行驶，直线感应电机定子安装在车辆上，使用小型并且质量较轻的 VVVF 逆变控制器控制。

One unit is equipped with a linear induction motor LIM stator to ensure that the train can run at a speed of 100 km/h. The linear induction motor stator is installed on the vehicle and controlled by a small and lightweight VVVF inverter controll.

五、制　动

6.4.5　Braking

HSST-100L 磁浮列车通过牵引直线电机和液压制动器制动。在常规运行中，速度在 10 km/h 以上时，完全靠直线电机制动；速度为 5～10 km/h 时，采用直线电机和液压制动器共同制动；速度低于 5 km/h 时，仅使用液压制动器进行机械制动。液压制动器是通过液压装置使转向架上的机械制动装置钳住倒"U"形轨道槽沿，依靠摩擦阻力制动。在紧急情况下，当上述制动措施均失效时，磁浮列车可以通过支承滑靴降落在支承轨上，依靠摩擦使列车制动。

The HSST-100L maglev train is braked by a traction linear motor and a hydraulic brake. In normal operation, when the speed is above 10 km/h, the linear motor is used for braking; when the speed is between 5 and 10 km/h, the linear motor and the hydraulic brake are used for braking; when speed is lower than 5 km/h, only the hydraulic brake is used for mechanical braking. The hydraulic brake makes the mechanical braking device on the bogie clamp the inverted "U" shaped track groove edge through the hydraulic device, and brakes by friction resistance. In case of emergency, when the above braking measures fail, the maglev train can land on the supporting rail through the supporting slipper and brake the train by friction.

六、列车运行控制及信号传输

6.4.6　Train Operation Control and Signal Transmission

HSST 的定位方式与日本超导磁浮高速铁路类似，也采用交叉感应回线。交叉感应回线敷设在轨道中间的轨枕上，在磁浮列车底架上，正对交叉感应回线上方，安装有用于定位的信号接收探头。车上还设有通过交叉感应回线与地面设备实现数据通信的天线。磁浮列车可以无人驾驶，完全由地面控制中心操作磁浮列车运行。同时，在车上还设有操作台，也可由车上司机操作磁浮列车运行。

The positioning method of HSST is similar to that of the superconducting maglev high-speed railway in Japan, and the cross induction loop is also used. The cross induction loop is laid on the sleeper in the middle of the track, and a signal receiving probe for positioning is installed on the underframe of the maglev train over the cross induction loop. The vehicle is also equipped with an antenna for data communication with the ground equipment through the cross induction loop. The maglev train can be driverless and operated entirely by the ground control center. At the same time, there is also a console on the train, which can also be operated by the driver on the train.

第五节 轨 道

Section 6.5　Track

HSST 的轨道安置在梁跨结构上。与 TR 磁浮列车类似，线路既可以高架，也可以低置于地面，但不可能同别的交通线路在同一水平面交叉。由于悬浮间隙（HSST 还包括直线电机与反应板的间隙）较小，所以该轨道对线路的精度要求较高。

The tracks of the HSST are placed on the girder span structure.Similar to the TR maglev train, the line can be elevated or placed low on the ground, but it is impossible to cross other traffic lines on the same level. Because the suspension gap (HSST also includes the gap between the linear motor and the reaction plate) is small, the track requires high accuracy of the line.

本节主要介绍 HSST 的轨道，包括与传统轮轨铁路类似的"钢轨"、起直线电机转子作用的反作用板及道岔。

This section focuses on the track of the HSST, including the "steel rail" similar to the traditional wheel-rail railway, and the reaction plates which works as the linear motor rotor, and turnouts.

一、感应轨

6.5.1　Induction Rail

在 HSST 轨道的顶面两侧，设置了起驱动、悬浮和导向作用的纵向构造物，由于其形状类似传统轮轨铁路的钢轨，也称为导磁钢轨，见图 6-2 和图 6-6，为车辆提供驱动、悬浮、导向功能，故称为感应轨。

On both sides of the top surface of the HSST track, there are longitudinal structures for driving, suspension and guidance. Because their shapes are similar to the rails of traditional wheel-rail railway, they are also called magnetic rails, as shown in Figure 6-2 and Figure 6-6. They provide driving, suspension and guidance functions for vehicles, so they are called induction rails.

不过 HSST 的钢轨与传统意义上的钢轨不同，车辆的驱动力、支承力和导向力不是靠轮轨接触提供的，而是由电磁力提供。HSST 的钢轨断面为"∩"形，车辆上的电磁铁吸引两侧"∩"形钢轨的底面产生悬浮力。

However, the HSST rail is different from the traditional rail in that the driving force, supporting force and guiding force of the vehicle are not provided by wheel-rail contact, but by electromagnetic force. The rail section of HSST is " ∩ " shaped, and the electromagnet on the vehicle attracts the bottom surface of the "∩" shaped rail on both sides to generate levitation force.

图 6-6　HSST 的轨道

Figure 6-6　Track of the HSST

二、反作用板

6.5.2　Reaction Plate

在导磁钢轨上面设有铝制反作用板（或称感应板、反作用力板），作为直线电机地面侧的"转子"部分为车辆提供驱动力，见图 6-2 和图 6-6。

Aluminum reaction plate (or reaction plate, reaction force plate) is provided on the magnetic steel rail as the "rotor" on the ground side of the linear motor to provide driving force for the vehicle, as shown in Figure 6-2 and Figure 6-6.

三、道　岔

6.5.3　Rail Switch

HSST 的道岔使用钢梁。道岔由三部分组成，转辙时道岔钢梁水平方向整体移动。

其工作原理与日本 ML 的导轨平移式道岔及德国 TR 的高速道岔相同，见图 6-7。

Steel beams are used for the HSST rail switchs. The rail switch consists of three parts, and the rail switch steel beam moves horizontally as a whole during switching. Its working principle is the same as that of the guideway translation rail switch of ML in Japan and the high-speed rail switch of TR in Germany, as shown in Figure 6-7.

图 6-7　HSST 的道岔

Figure 6-7　HSST Rail Switch

第六节　供电系统

Section 6.6　Power Supply System

名古屋试验线上的应用型 HSST 系统，利用车辆上磁铁的磁场与导轨磁铁铝板之间的电磁作用驱动列车行驶，牵引功率的转换和控制是在车上实现的，车辆上装有电源和产生移动磁场的装置，需要向车辆输送初始电流。

The application-oriented HSST system on the Nagoya test line uses the electromagnetic interaction between the magnetic field of the magnet on the vehicle and the aluminum plate of the guideway magnet to drive the train. The conversion and control of traction power are realized on the vehicle. The vehicle is equipped with a power supply and a device for generating a moving magnetic field, which needs to deliver initial current to the vehicle.

早期 HSST 系统中，列车上需要的直流电和交流电均从导轨内侧供应。改进后的

HSST 系统，列车上需要的电力直接从导轨外下侧设置的直流供电器上获得。新的供电系统在导轨底部侧面设置有固定供电轨（Rigid Conductor Trolley），为车辆供应 1 500 V 的直流电。车辆底部设置有受电器（或称电刷），对磁浮列车接触供电。这样处理，就大大简化了导轨结构。

In the early HSST system, both DC and AC power required on the train was supplied from the inside of the guideway. In the modified HSST system, the power required on the train is directly obtained from the DC power supply installed on the lower side of the guideway. The new power supply system is equipped with a fixed power supply rail (Rigid Conductor Trolley) on the side of the bottom of the guideway to supply the vehicle with DC 1,500V. A current collector (or electric brush) is arrange at that bottom of the vehicle to supply power to the contact of the maglev train. In this way, that structure of the guide rail is greatly simplify.

在导向轨下方轨道梁侧面，敷设有两根供电轨，上面通有 1 500 V 或 750 V 直流电。当出现事故停电时，车载蓄电池将提供列车在紧急状态下所需的电能，控制列车安全停车和降落。

On the side of the track beam below the guide rail, two power supply rails are laid with DC 1,500V or 750 V. In case of power failure, the on-board storage battery will provide the electric energy required by the train in emergency to control the train to stop and land safely.

设在导轨下的固定送电轨由铝和不锈钢制成，这就使得车辆上的受电器即使在列车高速运行情况下也能从固定供电器稳定地获得电力供应。

The fixed power transmission rail provided under the guide rail is made of aluminum and stainless steel, which enables the power collector on the vehicle to receive a stable power supply from the fixed power supplier even when the train is running at a high speed.

第七节　安全与救援措施

Section 6.7　Safety and Rescue Measures

磁浮线路基本为高架线，以避免与地面交通发生相互干扰。导轨梁上运行的车辆通常距离地面 7 m 以上。磁浮列车与普通列车有所不同，梁的两侧没有供乘客在应急情况下使用的路肩通道。因此，安全和救援措施是磁浮铁路设计中一个很重要的内容。

Maglev lines are basically elevated lines to avoid interference with ground traffic. Vehicles running on the guideway beam are usually more than 7 m above the ground. Maglev trains are different from ordinary trains in that there are no shoulder passages on both sides of the beam for passengers to use in case of emergency. Therefore, safety and rescue measures are very important in the design of maglev railway.

磁浮列车的安全设计在以下 3 个方面进行。

The safety design of maglev train is carried out in the following three aspects.

一、车辆系统的安全设计

6.7.1　Safety Design of Vehicle System

与 TR 磁浮列车一样，HSST 磁浮列车从外侧环抱着轨道梁，从根本上消除了翻车和脱轨的可能。防止列车撞车的措施与地铁或轻轨相似，也是依靠联锁或闭塞系统，只是列车定位采用交叉感应回线，这在国外某些地铁和轻轨系统中也已经投入使用，因此并无特殊性。

Like the TR Maglev train, the HSST Maglev train hugs the track beam from the outside, essentially eliminating the possibility of rollover and derailment. The measures to prevent train collision are similar to those of subway or light rail, which also rely on interlocking or blocking system, but the train positioning uses cross induction loop, which has been put into use in some foreign subway and light rail systems, so there is no particularity.

列车供电采用双路供电，提高了供电系统的安全性，也就提高了列车运行的安全性。列车上安装有备用电源，以保证供电系统发生故障时，维持列车悬浮直到安全停车。列车上的悬浮和驱动等关键部件采用冗余设计，个别部件甚至一部分部件发生故障时，仍可保证列车安全运行。车厢采用阻燃材料设计，以确保旅客在发生火灾情况下的人身安全。

Dual power supply is adopted for train power supply, which improves the safety of power supply system and the safety of train operation. The train is equipped with a standby power supply to ensure that the train is suspended until it stops safely in the event of a power supply system failure. The key components such as suspension and drive on the train adopt redundant design, which can ensure the safe operation of the train when individual components or even some components fail. The carriage is designed with flame retardant materials to ensure the personal safety of passengers in case of fire.

二、留车救援措施

6.7.2　Rescue Measures for Leaving the Vehicle Behide

若列车在运行区间发生异常情况，尽量将车辆行驶至车站，然后让旅客下车疏散。若列车在区间段发生故障无法行驶，可派救援车前往故障地点。在双线并行设计路段，救援车可利用另一条线开往事故车旁对齐车门平行停放，再于两列车之间放置踏板，使乘客撤离至救援车。

If the train has an abnormal condition in the running section, try to drive the train to the station, and then let the passengers get off and evacuate. If the train breaks down in the section and cannot run, the rescue vehicle can be sent to the fault location. In the double-track parallel design section, the rescue vehicle can use the other line to drive to the side of the accident vehicle, align the door and park in parallel, and then place the pedal between the two trains, so that passengers can evacuate to the rescue vehicle.

三、落地救援措施

6.7.3　Landing Rescue Measures

由于 HSST 一般用于城市轨道交通，沿线通常有城市道路，个别地段也因施工等原因需修建辅助道路，这些道路可用于紧急情况下的救援使用。通过救援车辆将乘客转移至地面，乘客利用绳索或滑道直接从车厢降至地面。

As HSST is generally used for urban rail transit, there are usually urban roads along the line, and some sections need to build auxiliary roads due to construction and other reasons. These roads can be used for rescue in case of emergency. Passengers are transferred to the ground by rescue vehicles, and passengers are lowered directly from the carriage to the ground by ropes or slides.

第八节　HSST 与 TR 系统的比较

Section 6.8　Comparison of HSST and TR System

日本 HSST 系统与德国运捷 TR 系统同为磁吸型磁浮铁路技术，但两者在驱动、导向等方面有较大的不同。

Japan's HSST system and Germany's TR system are both magnetic levitation railway technology, but they are quite different in driving and guiding.

一、导向、悬浮特征

6.8.1　Guidance and Suspension Features

HSST 与 TR 系统在悬浮方面的基本原理基本相同，在此不再赘述。

The basic principles of HSST and TR systems in terms of levitation are basically the same and will not be repeated here.

在 HSST 系统中，导向力也是由悬浮磁场的同一闭合磁路而产生的，垂直悬浮力和导向力合二为一，原因是图中气隙内磁通产生的电磁力力图保持图中上下两个铁心的对中位置，即磁阻最小的位置。假如在通过曲线时，由于离心力的作用使车辆横向移动，气隙内磁力线受到扭曲就会形成横向电磁分力。只要设计适当，在列车过弯道时选择合理的线路超高和横向电磁力的大小，导向力就可以与离心力平衡。

In the HSST system, the guiding force is also generated by the same closed magnetic circuit of the levitation magnetic field. The vertical levitation force and the guiding force are combined into one. The reason is that the electromagnetic force generated by the magnetic flux in the air gap in the figure tries to maintain the alignment position of the upper and lower cores in the figure, that is, the position with the minimum reluctance. If the vehicle moves laterally due to the centrifugal force when passing through the curve, the magnetic lines of force in the air gap will be twisted to form a lateral electromagnetic force component. As long as the design is appropriate, the guiding force can be balanced with the centrifugal force by selecting a reasonable line superelevation and lateral electromagnetic force when the train passes through the curve.

这种悬浮与导向力合二为一的系统，可用于中低速磁浮铁路（如日本 HSST 型），不适用于高速磁浮列车，如德国 TR 型。原因是依靠上下两个铁心相对错位而产生横向电磁力，其值毕竟较小；离心力与速度的平方成正比，在高速时，离心力随速度的增加急剧增加，该系统产生的横向电磁力已不能满足要求。因此，德国 TR 型磁浮列车的垂直悬浮力和横向导向力由两个独立系统产生。

This system, which combines suspension and guiding force, can be used for medium and low-speed maglev railway (such as HSST in Japan), but not for high speed maglev trains (such as TR in Germany). The reason is that the transverse electromagnetic force generated by the relative dislocation of the upper and lower iron cores is small after all; the centrifugal force is proportional to the square of the speed, and at high speed, the centrifugal force increases sharply with the increase of speed, and the transverse electromagnetic force generated by the system can not meet the requirements. Therefore, the vertical levitation force and lateral guidance force of the German TR maglev train are generated by two independent systems.

TR 系统在线路两侧垂直地布置有钢板、导向电磁铁，它与线路的钢板形成闭合磁路，电磁铁线圈通电后产生横向导向力，两边横向气隙为 8~10 mm。车辆正好在中心线位置时，两边气隙和横向电磁力相等，而方向相反，互相平衡；通过曲线时，车辆一旦产生横向位移偏差，位移传感器会检测其变化，通过控制系统改变左右两侧电磁铁线圈电流的大小，使气隙小的一侧电流减少，电磁吸力变小，而气隙大的一侧电流增加，电磁吸力增大，合成产生导向恢复力并与列车离心力相平衡。显然，这种独立的导向力系统所产生的导向力远大于 HSST 的导向力。实质上，HSST 导向力的形成是利用磁场的边缘效应，它是垂向悬浮力的切向分力，不会很大。但是 TR 型磁浮列车的独立导向是用专门的电磁铁与线路两侧钢板产生的，车的质量、导向功耗以及线路成本会增加。所以对于中低速磁浮列车，由于离心力不是很大，用不着采用这种独立导向系统，而采用悬浮与导向合二为一的结构是可取的，日本 HSST 和我国正在研制的大部分磁浮铁路就是采用这种结构。

Steel plates and guide electromagnets are vertically arranged on both sides of the line in the TR system, which form a closed magnetic circuit with the steel plates of the line. After the electromagnet coil is energized, a transverse guiding force is generated, and the transverse air gap on both sides is 8-10 mm. When the vehicle is just in the center line position, the air gap and the transverse electromagnetic force on both sides are equal, but in opposite directions, and are balanced with each other; When the vehicle passes through the curve, once the lateral displacement deviation is generated, the displacement sensor will detect its change, and the control system will change the current of the electromagnet coils on the left and right sides, so that the current on the side with a small air gap is reduced and the electromagnetic attraction is reduced, while the current on the side with a large air gap is increased and the electromagnetic attraction is increased, so that the guiding restoring force is synthesized and balanced with the centrifugal force of the train. Obviously, the guiding force produced by this independent guiding force system is much larger than that of HSST. In essence, the formation of the HSST guidance force uses the edge effect of the magnetic field, which is the tangential component of the vertical levitation force and will not be very large. However, the independent guidance of TR maglev train is produced by special electromagnets and steel plates on both sides of the line, which will increase the mass of the train, the power consumption of guidance and the cost of the line. Therefore, for medium and low speed maglev trains, because the centrifugal force is not very large, it is not necessary to use this independent guidance system, and it is desirable to use the structure of combining suspension and guidance, which is used in most of the maglev railways being developed by HSST in Japan and China.

德国 TR 型磁浮列车的垂向悬浮力是由线路的同步电机铁心与车辆上同步电机磁极之间形成气隙磁通产生的，驱动力（纵向牵引力）与垂向悬浮力两个系统合二为一，这也是德国 TR 型磁浮列车优势所在。而日本 HSST 磁浮直线电机产生列车驱动力时，不但不产生有用的垂向悬浮力，而且产生有害的垂向干扰力。

The vertical levitation force of German TR maglev train is generated by the air gap flux formed between the synchronous motor core of the line and the magnetic pole of the synchronous motor on the vehicle. The two systems of driving force (longitudinal traction force) and vertical levitation force are combined into one, which is also the advantage of German TR maglev train. However, when the Japanese HSST maglev linear motor generates the driving force of the train, it not only does not produce useful vertical suspension force, but also produces harmful vertical interference force.

二、驱动特征

6.8.2 Drive Features

用直线电机取代轮轨机车中采用的旋转电机,纵向(列车运行方向)牵引力不受轮轨黏着力限制,这决定了磁浮列车具有牵引力大、爬坡能力强、起动快和速度高等一系列优点。

The linear motor is used to replace the rotating motor used in the wheel-rail locomotive, and the longitudinal (train running direction) traction force is not limited by the wheel-rail adhesion force, which determines that the maglev train has a series of advantages such as large traction force, strong climbing ability, fast starting and high speed.

磁浮铁路采用两种不同形式的直线电机,即短定子直线感应电机(LIM)和长定子直线同步电机(LSM)。

Maglev railway uses two different types of linear motors, namely, short-stator linear induction motor (LIM) and long-stator linear synchronous motor (LSM).

(一)长定子线性同步电机技术特征

6.8.2.1 Technical Characteristics of Long Stator Linear Synchronous Motor

德国 TR 和日本 MLX 磁浮超高速铁路都采用长定子直线同步电机(LSM)驱动,即电机定子三相交流绕组铺设在地面线路两侧,动力电源 VVVF(变频、变压系统)也设在地面变电所内,列车运行控制在地面运行控制中心完成。该技术对同步电机的同步控制精度要求也很高,需要对列车的速度和位置进行精确测控。

German TR and Japanese MLX maglev ultra-high-speed railway are driven by long-stator linear synchronous motor (LSM), that is, the three-phase AC winding of the motor stator is laid on both sides of the ground line, the power supply VVVF (variable frequency and variable voltage system) is also set in the ground substation, and the train operation control is completed in the ground operation control center. This technology also requires high precision of synchronous control of synchronous motor, and needs to measure and control the speed and position of the train accurately.

长定子方案由于沿线铺设电机定子绕组,其造价必然很高。地面同步电机的优点是功率大,功率因数高,适用于高速、超高速磁浮铁路。

The cost of the long stator scheme is bound to be high due to the laying of motor stator windings along the line. The ground synchronous motor has the advantages of high power and high power factor, and is suitable for high-speed and ultra-high-speed maglev railway.

（二）短定子直线感应电机技术特征

6.8.2.2 Technical Characteristics of Short Stator Linear Induction Motor

日本 HSST 磁浮铁路采用短定子直线感应电机（LIM），或称短定子线性异步电机。电机定子三相绕组布置在车辆两侧，而异步电机转子结构简单，仅仅是厚 4 mm 左右的铝板，铺设在线路与车上定子位置相应的两侧。所以，短定子磁浮线路的造价远低于长定子磁浮线路。由于电机绕组在车上，动力电源（VVVF）也必须装在车内，而 VVVF 是从地面供电轨（DC 1 500 V 或 750 V）取得电能，地面与磁浮列车之间必须安装受流器。所以严格地说，这种短定子直线电机铁路不是完全无机械接触的，高速时受流性能恶化。受流器（供电轨）决定了这种磁浮列车的运行速度不能很高，一般在中低速范围内运行比较合适。从目前的技术水平来说，速度超过 200 km/h 时的受流性能很难保证，故在高速范围内，HSST 的技术目前还不成熟。

Short-stator linear induction motor (LIM), or short-stator linear asynchronous motor, is used in HSST maglev railway in Japan. The three-phase windings of the motor stator are arranged on both sides of the vehicle, while the rotor of the asynchronous motor has a simple structure, which is only an aluminum plate with a thickness of about 4 mm, and is laid on both sides of the line corresponding to the position of the stator on the vehicle. Therefore, the cost of short stator maglev line is much lower than that of long stator maglev line. Since the motor winding is on the vehicle, the power supply (VVVF) must also be installed in the vehicle, and the VVVF obtains power from the ground supply rail (DC 1,500 V or 750 V), so a current collector must be installed between the ground and the maglev train. Therefore, strictly speaking, this kind of short stator linear motor is not completely without mechanical contact, and its current collection performance deteriorates at high speed. The collector (supply rail) determines that the running speed of this maglev train can not be very high, and it is generally suitable to run in the range of medium and low speed. From the current technical level, it is difficult to guarantee the current collection performance when the speed exceeds 200 km/h, so the technology of HSST is not mature at present in the high-speed range.

从运行控制方面来说，短定子磁浮列车控制是在车上完成的，相对比较容易。但是，对磁浮直线感应电机控制时，必须使其法向力（垂向力）的影响降至最小。图 6-8 表示直线感应电机牵引力 F_x 和法向力 F_z 与频率 f 的关系曲线。

In terms of operation control, the control of short stator maglev train is completed on the train, which is relatively easy. However, the influence of the normal force (vertical force) must be minimized in the control of the magnetic levitation linear induction motor. Figure 6-8 shows the relationship between the traction force F_x, and the normal force F_z of the linear induction motor and the frequency f.

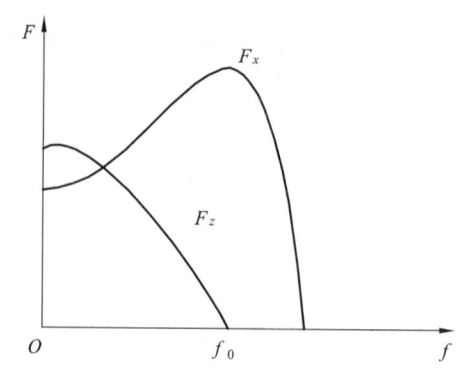

图 6-8 直线感应电机牵引力 F_x 和法向力 F_z 与频率 f 的关系示意图

Fig. 6-8 Schematic diagram of relationship between traction force F_x and normal force F_z of linear induction motor and frequency f

图 6-8 表明，法向力 F_z 的极性在 f 前后是发生变化的，在 $f \leqslant f_0$ 时，法向力 F_z 表现为斥力；而在 $f \geqslant f_0$ 时，则表现为吸力，这种变化对磁浮系统来说是有害的。因为设计磁浮系统时，除了要克服车辆重力以及在运动中所产生的动力作用外，还必须考虑这种由电机而产生的法向干扰力。且分析证明，电机的法向力是很大的，它和电机牵引力有同样的数量级。为了避免这种干扰力，在设计电机和控制系统时，必须使磁浮铁路电机工作在频率 f_0 附近，即 $F_z \approx 0$。这就要求对磁悬浮列车的速度进行精确测量和控制。

Fig. 6-8 show that the polarity of the normal force F_z changes before and after f, and when $f \leqslant f_0$, the normal force F_z exhibits repulsion; When $f \geqslant f_0$, it exhibits suction, which is harmful to the maglev system. When designing a maglev system, in addition to overcoming the vehicle's gravity and the dynamic effects generated during motion, it is also necessary to consider the normal interference force generated by the motor. And analysis has proven that the normal force of the motor is very large, which is of the same order of magnitude as the traction force of the motor. To avoid such interference, when designing motors and control systems, it is necessary to operate the maglev railway motor near the frequency f_0, i.e. $F_z \approx 0$. This requires precise measurement and control of the speed of maglev trains.

三、结 论

6.8.3　Conclusion

表 6-4 列出了日本 HSST 和德国 TR 磁浮铁路的主要技术特征。具体选用何种磁浮交通方式，应根据要求的运行速度及技术经济要求综合考虑确定。

Table 6-4 lists the main technical features of the Japanese HSST and the German TR Maglev Railway. The specific selection of maglev transportation mode should be determined according to the required running speed and technical and economic requirements.

表 6-4 HSST、TR 主要技术特征比较

Table 6-4 Comparison of Main Technical Characteristics of HSST and TR

性　能 Performance	日本 HSST Japan HSST	德国 TR Germany TR
目前最高设计速度/（km/h） Current Maximum DesignSpeed/(km/h)	130	450
直线电机 Linear Motor	短定子直线感应电机（LIM） Short Stator Linear Induction Motor(LIM)	长定子直线同步电机（LSM） Long Stator Linear Synchronous Motor(LSM)
电机定子绕组安装位置 Installation Position of Motor Stator Winding	车上 On the Vehicle	地面线路上 On the Ground Line
导向与悬浮 Steering and Suspension	合并设置 Merge Settings	分别设置 Set separately
导向力 Guiding Force	小 Small	大 Large
直线电机功率 Linear Motor Power	小 Small	大 Large
功率因数 Power Factor	低 Low	≈1
控制难度 Control Difficulty	小 Small	大 Large
线路造价 Line Cost	低 Low	高 High
是否需要受流器/供电轨 Current Collector/Power Rail Required?	需要 Yes	不需要 No
适用场合 Applicable Occasions	城市轨道交通、机场铁路 Urban Rail Transit, Airport Railway	城际铁路、长大干线铁路 Intercity Railway and Long Trunk Railway

复习思考题

Questions for Revision

1. 为什么说日本 HSST 系统不应称作高速地面运输系统，而应称作中低速地面运输系统？

1. Why should the Japanese HSST system be called a medium-low speed ground transportation system instead of a high speed ground transportation system?

2. 简要分析 HSST-200 型系统的主要参数。

2. Briefly analyze the main parameters of HSST-200 system.

3. 简要总结 HSST 系统具有的特征。

3. Briefly summarize the characteristics of the HSST system.

4. 简要分析 HSST 系统的工作原理。

4. Briefly analyze theworking principle of the HSST system.

5. 简要分析 HSST 系统车辆的各部分组成。

5. Briefly analyze the vehicle components of the HSST system.

6. 简要分析 HSST 系统的轨道和供电系统。

6. Briefly analyze the track and power supply system of the HSST system.

7. 简要分析 HSST 系统的安全与救援措施。

7. Briefly analyze the safety and rescue measures of the HSST system.

8. 简要分析 HSST 系统与 TR 系统的异同。

8. Briefly analyze the similarities and differences between the HSST system and the TR system.

第七章　我国磁浮铁路研究、发展及实践

Chapter 7　Research, Development and Practice of Maglev Railway in China

我国政府和有关研究机构比较重视磁浮铁路的研究和开发，目前正大力推进几项磁浮铁路技术的开发及工程项目的建设。世界上第一条超高速磁浮营业线（上海磁浮线）已在上海建成，中国已成为继德国、日本之后第三个掌握高速磁浮铁路技术的国家，中国将为世界高速铁路、磁浮铁路谱写新的篇章。

Chinese government and relevant research institutions pay more attention to the research and development of maglev railway, and are vigorously promoting the development of several maglev railway technologies and the construction of engineering projects. The world's first ultra-high-speed maglev operating line (Shanghai Maglev Line) has been completed in Shanghai. China has become the third country to master high-speed maglev railway technology after Germany and Japan. China will write a new chapter for the world's high-speed railway and maglev railway.

磁浮铁路分为中低速和高速两大类。目前，我国磁浮铁路的研究重点主要放在中低速磁浮铁路技术方面。长沙磁浮快线和北京首条磁浮线路交通示范线 S1 线的相继开通，表明中国已成为日本、韩国之后第三个掌握中低速磁浮技术的国家。在我国，对磁浮列车技术的研究起步较早的有西南交通大学、国防科技大学、中国科学院、中国铁道科学研究院等几家单位。

Maglev railway is divided into two categories: medium and low speed and high speed. At present, the research of maglev railway in China is mainly focused on the technology of medium and low speed maglev railway. The successive opening of Changsha Maglev Express Line and Beijing's first Maglev Traffic Demonstration Line S1 Line shows that China has become the third country to master medium and low speed maglev technology after Japan and ROK. In China, Southwest Jiaotong University, National University of Defense Technology, Chinese Academy of Sciences, China Academy of Railway Sciences and other units started the research of maglev train technology earlier.

本章主要介绍我国磁浮车辆、试验线及线路规划设想等方面的研究、发展及实践情况。

This chapter mainly introduces the research, development and practice of maglev vehicles, test lines and line planning in China.

第一节 磁浮技术在中国的研究及发展概况

Section 7.1 Research and Development of Maglev Technology in China

早在20世纪70年代,我国科技工作者对磁浮交通系统新技术的进展就给予关注。一些大学、研究机构开展了基础性研究,如国防科技大学在20世纪80年代开始研制小型磁浮试验系统,对电磁浮机理进行了理论分析、实验研究。中国科学院电工所在20世纪70年代中期开始了直线感应电机驱动的研究,对直线感应电机端部效应、直线电机的设计及计算方法进行理论研究和实验。西南交通大学和中国铁道科学研究院在20世纪80年代也对磁浮的原理进行了探讨研究。

As early as the 1970s, Chinese scientists and technicians paid attention to the progress of the new technology of maglev transportation system. Some universities and research institutions have carried out basic research, such as the National University of Defense Technology began to develop a small maglev test system in the 1980s, and carried out theoretical analysis and experimental research on the mechanism of electromagnetic levitation. The Institute of Electrical Engineering of the Chinese Academy of Sciences started the research on linear induction motor drive in the mid-1970s, and carried out theoretical research and experiments on the end effect of linear induction motor, the design and calculation method of linear motor. Southwest Jiaotong University and China Academy of Railway Sciences also studied the principle of maglev in the 1980s.

在各单位研究工作的基础上,国家科委在"八五"期间组织了"磁浮列车关键技术"科技攻关。由中国铁道科学研究院牵头,国防科技大学、中国科学院电工所和西南交通大学参加,主要研究对象为低速磁浮列车。通过项目实施,基本掌握了低速电磁吸引式短定子直线感应电机驱动的磁浮列车的悬浮、驱动等关键技术,并研制成国防科技大学的3 m×3 m 可载40人的单转向架磁浮列车系统,西南交通大学的4 t 电气解耦双转向架磁浮实验车,以及铁科院牵头的6 t 单转向架磁浮实验车。6 t 单转向架磁浮试验车的研制成功,为低速常导磁浮列车的研究提供了技术基础,填补了我国在磁浮列车技术领域的空白。

On the basis of the research work of various units, the State Science and Technology Commission organized the scientific and technological research of "Key Technologies of

Maglev Train" during the Eighth Five-Year Plan period. Led by the Chinese Academy of Railway Sciences, with the participation of the National University of Defense Technology, the Institute of Electrical Engineering of the Chinese Academy of Sciences and Southwest Jiaotong University, the main research object is low-speed maglev train. Through the implementation of the project, the key technologies such as suspension and drive of the maglev train driven by the low-speed electromagnetic attraction short-stator linear induction motor have been basically mastered, and the 3 m × 3 m single-bogie maglev train system of National University of Defense Technology, which can carry 40 people, and the 4 t electric decoupling double-bogie maglev experimental vehicle of Southwest Jiaotong University have been developed. As well as the 6 t single bogie maglev experimental vehicle led by the Academy of Railway Sciences. The successful development of the 6 t single bogie maglev test car provides a technical basis for the research of low-speed EMS maglev train and fills in the gaps in the field of maglev train technology in China.

1996年4月，科技部又组织了"九五"国家重大课题"磁浮列车重大技术经济问题研究"；组织了全国有关专家总结消化已有资料，进一步收集了新资料；对"八五"期间低速磁浮列车攻关情况进行考察论证、成果鉴定；多次与国外专家技术交流，并组团考察了日本和德国磁浮列车；对日本超导高速磁浮列车、德国高速磁浮列车和日本中低速HSST磁浮列车做了专题分析研究。结合我国实际，探讨我国发展磁浮列车的可行性和基本思路，进行了沪杭高速磁浮线可行性研究（日本超导方案）。项目组最后完成"磁浮列车重大技术经济问题研究报告""沪杭高速磁浮线可行性研究报告"和一系列的专题技术报告。

In April 1996, the Ministry of Science and Technology organized the "Research on Major Technical and Economic Issues of Maglev Trains", a major national project in the "Ninth Five-Year Plan", organized relevant experts throughout the country to summarize and digest existing data and further collect new data, and carried out investigation, demonstration and achievement appraisal on the research of low-speed maglev trains during the "Eighth Five-Year Plan"; We have communicated with foreign experts for many times, organized a delegation to inspect Japanese and German maglev trains, and made special analysis and research on Japanese superconducting high-speed maglev train, German high-speed maglev train and Japanese medium-low speed HSST maglev train. The feasibility and basic idea of developing maglev train in China are discussed in combination with the actual situation in China, and the feasibility study of Shanghai-Hangzhou high-speed maglev line (Japanese superconducting scheme) is carried out.The project team finally completed the "Research Report on Major Technical and Economic Issues of Maglev Train", "Feasibility Study Report on Shanghai-Hangzhou High-speed Maglev Line" and a series of special technical reports.

1999年年底，科技部又组织了"九五"攻关课题"我国第一条高速磁浮列车试验运行线的可行性研究",进一步消化、吸收了德国 TR 电磁吸引式高速磁浮列车技术,并以引进德国 TR 技术为基础进行了试验运行线选线方案比较,同时提出建设上海磁浮列车示范运营线的建议。

At the end of 1999, the Ministry of Science and Technology organized the "Ninth Five-Year Plan" key project "Feasibility Study of the First High-speed Maglev Train Test Line in China", further digested and absorbed the German TR electromagnetic attraction high-speed maglev train technology, and compared the route selection schemes of the test line based on the introduction of German TR technology. It is suggested that Shanghai Maglev Train Demonstration Line should be constructed.

一、西南交通大学研究情况

7.1.1 Research of Southwest Jiaotong University

(一) 基础研究

7.1.1.1 Basic Research

西南交通大学从 1986 年开始磁浮列车技术的研究,1994 年研制成功了我国第一辆可载人的 4 t 磁浮列车及其试验线,并通过科技成果鉴定。"九五"期间承担了国家重点攻关项目"常导短定子磁浮列车工程关键技术研究"和国家高技术研究发展计划(863)项目"高温超导磁浮列车系统实验装置"。2001 年 1 月 3 日,世界上第一辆载人高温超导磁浮实验车在西南交通大学研制成功。该车采用国产高温超导材料,底部 3 mm 厚的车载薄底液氮低温容器连续工作时间大于 6 h,悬浮净高 23 mm,加速度 6 m/s²,悬浮总质量 530 kg,可载 5 人。

Southwest Jiaotong University started the research of maglev train technology in 1986, and successfully developed the first manned 4 t maglev train and its test line in 1994, which passed the appraisal of scientific and technological achievements. During the Ninth Five-Year Plan period, he undertook the national key research project "Research on Key Technologies of Normal Conductor Short Stator Maglev Train Project" and the National High-tech Research and Development Program (863) project "Experimental Device of High Temperature Superconducting Maglev Train System". In January 3, 2001, the world's first manned high-temperature superconducting maglev experimental vehicle was successfully developed in Southwest Jiaotong University. The vehicle is made of domestic high temperature superconducting materials, and has a thin bottom liquid nitrogen cryogenic vessel with a bottom thickness of 3 mm. The continuous working time is more than 6 hours, the net height of suspension is 23 mm, the acceleration is 6 m/s², the total mass of suspension is 530 kg, and it can carry 5 people.

（二）配套建设

7.1.1.2 Supporting Construction

磁浮列车是一个复杂的交通系统，为便于组织跨学科联合攻关，学校于1996年成立了以电气工程、土木工程和机械工程三个一级学科为基础的"西南交通大学磁浮列车工程研究中心"，中心下设"磁浮列车与磁浮技术研究所"和"磁浮列车与磁力应用工程实验室"，实验室被确定为四川省重点实验室和四川省青年科技创新示范基地。"九五"期间完成了国家"211工程"建设项目"磁浮列车基础研究设备及试验线"，该项目包括磁浮列车电气试验系统、中低速磁浮列车直线电机及悬浮磁铁综合试验台、三磁转向架磁浮车及S形试验线，初步建成中低速磁浮列车基础试验基地。

Maglev is a complex transportation system. In order to facilitate the organization of interdisciplinary joint research, the University established the "Maglev Engineering Research Center of Southwest Jiaotong University" in 1996, which is based on three first-level disciplines of electrical engineering, civil engineering and mechanical engineering. The center consists of "Maglev Train and Maglev Technology Research Institute" and "Maglev Train and Magnetic Application Engineering Laboratory", which has been designated as the key laboratory of Sichuan Province and the Youth Science and Technology Innovation Demonstration Base of Sichuan Province. During the "Ninth Five-Year Plan" period, it completed the national "211 Project" construction project "Basic Research Equipment and Test Line for Maglev Trains", which includes the electrical test system for maglev trains, the linear motor and suspension magnet comprehensive test bed for medium and low speed maglev trains, the three-magnetic bogie maglev train and S-shaped test line, and initially built the basic test base for medium and low speed maglev trains.

（三）应用研究

7.1.1.3 Applied Research

1. 三磁转向架磁浮车及"S"形试验线

1. Maglev Vehicle with Three Magnetic Bogies and "S" Test Line

经过艰苦的努力，1999年9月2日，西南交通大学磁浮列车工程研究中心研制成功采用常导短定子技术的磁浮列车演示模型，它是接近应用水平的三磁转向架的第二代磁浮车，同时建成了28 m"S"形钢筋混凝土线路，工作人员接通电源后，车体便浮起，离开轨道近4 mm，同时在7.2 m长的轨道上快速运动。

After arduous efforts, in September 2, 1999, the Maglev Train Engineering Research Center of Southwest Jiaotong University successfully developed a demonstration model of maglev train with normally conducting short stator technology, which is the second of the three magnetic bogies close to the application level. At the same time, a 28 m "S" shaped reinforced concrete line was built. After the staff connected the power supply, the car body was It floats and leaves the track by nearly 4 mm, while moving rapidly on a 7.2 m long track.

2. 常导磁浮车辆

2. Magnetic Levitation Vehicles with Common Conductor

为了使磁浮列车技术走向实际应用，西南交通大学联合长春客车厂和株洲电力机车研究所成立了产、学、研相结合的磁浮列车研制、生产联合体，同时还与地方多家设计及工程单位合股组建了交大青城磁浮列车工程发展有限公司，负责青城山磁浮列车工程试验示范线的建设与试验。该项目还得到科技部的资助。

In order to put maglev train technology into practical application, Southwest Jiaotong University, together with Changchun Passenger Car Factory and Zhuzhou Electric Locomotive Research Institute, has established a maglev train development and production consortium combining production, learning and research, and has also established Qingcheng Maglev Train Engineering Development Co., Ltd. of Jiaotong University in partnership with several local design and engineering units. Responsible for the construction and test of Qingchengshan Maglev Train Engineering Test Demonstration Line. The project is also funded by the Ministry of Science and Technology.

经过完善与改进，西南交通大学与长春客车厂和株洲电力机车研究所联合试制完成国产磁浮车辆，并于2001年8月14日在长春客车厂竣工下线。

After perfection and improvement, Southwest Jiaotong University, Changchun Passenger Car Factory and Zhuzhou Electric Locomotive Research Institute jointly trial-produced domestic maglev vehicles, which were completed and rolled off the production line in Changchun Passenger Car Factory in August 14, 2001.

这辆磁悬浮车辆为常导吸浮式磁浮车，车辆与轨道间距始终保持8~10 mm的悬浮气隙。它采用短定子直线感应电机驱动，制动系统为电阻制动与液压制动相结合的混合系统，列车采用自动运行控制系统、司机驾驶控制系统，采用交叉感应回线定位、测速和通信，运营速度60 km/h，最高试验速度可达100 km/h。这辆磁浮车长11.2 m，宽2.6 m，自重18 t，载重4 t，座位30个。车体采用铝合金板梁焊接，车体质量轻，自重仅16 t。

The maglev vehicle is a normally conducting, suction and floating maglev vehicle, and the distance between the vehicle and the track always maintains a suspension air gap of 8-10 mm. It is driven by short-stator linear induction motor, the braking system is a hybrid system combining resistance braking and hydraulic braking, the train adopts automatic operation control system, driver driving control system, cross induction loop positioning, speed measurement and communication. The operating speed is 60 km/h and the maximum test speed can reach 100 km/h. The maglev vehicle is 11.2 m long and 2.6 m wide, with a weight of 18 t, a load of 4 t and 30 seats. The car body is welded with aluminum alloy plate beam, which is light and has a dead weight of only 16 t.

3. 青城山磁浮列车工程示范线

3. Qingchengshan Maglev Train Project Demonstration Line

西南交通大学曾经与有关单位合作在青城山风景区建设磁浮旅游试验线项目。青城山磁浮旅游线路位于成都市境内青城山附近，为一条旅游专线，使用西南交通大学的常导短定子磁浮技术。青城山磁浮列车为3辆编组，由两辆带控制室的头车和1辆拖车组成（车辆长11.2 m，宽2.6 m，自重18 t，载重4 t，座位30个，采用短定子异步直线电机牵引，制动系统为电机电阻制动与液压制动相结合的混合系统；列车采用自动运行控制系统、司机驾驶控制系统），可载客80人左右，运营速度60 km/h，最高试验速度100 km/h，线路轨道梁全部采用空心混凝土梁结构，采用交叉感应回线定位、测速和通信。

Southwest Jiaotong University has cooperated with relevant units to build a maglev tourism test line project in Qingcheng Mountain Scenic Area. Qingcheng Mountain Maglev Tourist Line is located near Qingcheng Mountain in Chengdu City, which is a special tourist line, using the normal guide short stator maglev technology of Southwest Jiaotong University. Qingchengshan maglev train is a 3-car train, consisting of two head cars with control room and one trailer (11.2 m in length, 2.6 m in width, 18 t in weight, 4 t in load, 30 seats. It is driven by short-stator asynchronous linear motor. The braking system is a hybrid system combining motor resistance braking and hydraulic braking; The train adopts automatic operation control system and driver driving control system), which can carry about 80 passengers. The operating speed is 60 km/h, and the maximum test speed is 100 km/h. The track beams of the line are all hollow concrete beam structures, and cross induction loop positioning, speed measurement and communication are adopted.

这种常导磁浮铁路适合于城市内的有轨运输和城市到郊区的运输，预计每千米的造价在2亿元左右。

This kind of permanent maglev railway is suitable for rail transportation in cities and transportation from cities to suburbs, with an estimated cost of about 200 million yuan per kilometer.

青城山山门到白鹭度假村线路长425 m，最大坡度20‰，最小曲线半径250 m，线路轨道梁全部采用空心混凝土梁结构。桥梁工程已于2001年4月开工，2001年8月完成。原准备将来在这段线路上先进行有关的试验，如果指标正常，该铁路即可投入商业运营，现该线路遭到破坏。

The route from Qingcheng Mountain Gate to Egret Holiday Village is 425 m long, with a maximum slope of 20‰. The minimum curve radius is 250 m, and all track beams of the line are of hollow concrete beam structure. The bridge project was started in April 2001 and completed in August 2001. It was originally planned to carry out relevant tests on this section of the line in the future. If the indicators are normal, the railway can be put into commercial operation. Now the line has been damaged.

4. 长沙磁浮快线（长沙南站至长沙黄花机场线）开通投入运营

4. Changsha Maglev Express Line (Changsha South Railway Station to Changsha Huanghua Airport Line) has been Put into Operation

2014年5月16日，采用了西南交通大学和国防科技大学磁浮技术的长沙高铁南站至黄花国际机场的磁浮线路正式开工建设，这是我国第一条完全自主研发的商业运营磁浮线。2016年5月6日，长沙磁浮快线载客试运营，现已投产正式运营，乘客从长沙南站至长沙黄花机场T2航站楼仅需20 min。

In May 16, 2014, the maglev line from Changsha South high-speed railway Station to Huanghua International Airport, which adopted the maglev technology of Southwest Jiaotong University and National University of Defense Technology, was officially launched, which is the first commercial maglev line developed by China. In May 6, 2016, Changsha Maglev Express Line was put into trial operation and has been put into operation. It only takes 20 minutes from Changsha South Railway Station to Terminal 2 of Changsha Huanghua Airport.

5. 高温超导磁浮车

5. High temperature superconducting maglev vehicle

1997年初，中德曾合作研制成功20 kg的高温超导磁浮模型车。

At the beginning of 1997, China and Germany successfully developed a 20 kg high temperature superconducting maglev model vehicle.

1997年10月，国家"863"计划立项研究载人高温超导磁浮试验车，由西南交通大学主持，北京有色金属研究总院、西北有色金属研究院、中国科学院电工所参加。

In October 1997, the National "863" Program was established to study the manned high-temperature superconducting maglev test vehicle, which was hosted by Southwest Jiaotong University and participated by Beijing General Research Institute of Nonferrous Metals, Northwest Research Institute of Nonferrous Metals and Institute of Electrical Engineering, Chinese Academy of Sciences.

20世纪的最后一天，历时3年的"高温超导磁浮车"在西南交通大学研制成功，为新世纪献上了一份厚礼。2001年2月，该高温超导磁浮车辆"世纪号"通过国家超导技术专家委员会专家组验收，并参加了在北京举办的"863计划15周年成就展"。

In the last day of the 20th century, the three-year "high-temperature superconducting maglev vehicle" was successfully developed in Southwest Jiaotong University, presenting a great gift for the new century. In February 2001, the high-temperature superconducting maglev vehicle "Century" passed the acceptance of the expert group of the National Superconducting technical specialist Committee, and participated in the "863 Program 15th Anniversary Achievement Exhibition" held in Beijing.

该磁浮轨道上不是使用电磁铁而是使用永磁铁。永磁导轨长 15.5 m，采用双轨结构，车体的运动状态由地面控制系统控制。与目前德国 TR（常导）和日本 ML（低温超导）技术相比，高温超导磁浮在节约能源和操作维护方面更具有竞争力。

The magnetic levitation track does not use an electromagnet but a permanent magnet. The permanent magnet guideway is 15.5 m long and has a double-track structure, and the motion state of the vehicle body is controlled by the ground control system. Compared with the current TR (normal conductor) technology in Germany and ML (cryogenic superconductor) technology in Japan, HTS maglev is more competitive in energy saving and operation and maintenance.

二、国防科技大学研究情况

7.1.2　Research of National University of Defense Technology

（一）研究背景

7.1.2.1　Research Background

国防科技大学的磁浮技术研究工作始于 1980 年，先后研制过几个小型磁浮实验系统。1989 年，集悬浮导向与推进为一体，研制成功重约 80 kg 的小型磁浮模型样车，可在 10 m 长的轨道上往复运行。该系统在长沙和北京进行了展示，接待了国家和政府部门的领导及近万名参观者；1991 年 5 月，国家科委组织立项论证，并于 1992 年正式列入国家"八五"科技攻关计划。

Research on maglev technology in National University of Defense Technology started in 1980, and several small maglev experimental systems were developed. In 1989, a small maglev model prototype weighing about 80 kg was successfully developed, which integrates suspension guidance and propulsion, and can run back and forth on a 10 m long track. The system was demonstrated in Changsha and Beijing, and received leaders of the state and government departments and nearly 10,000 visitors. In May 1991, the State Science and Technology Commission organized a project demonstration, and in 1992, it was formally included in the national "Eighth Five-Year Plan" for tackling key scientific and technological problems.

通过科技攻关，1995 年研制成单转向架磁浮列车系统。磁浮转向架是磁浮列车车辆的最小功能单元，具有独立悬浮、导向、推进与制动等功能。该系统具有4套独立的悬浮控制系统（含8个电磁铁、4套控制器）、一套推进系统（含一对电机）、相应的二次悬挂系统、3 m×3.3 m 的车厢底板，可承载40多人，在10 m 长的轨道上往复平稳运行。目前，正在进行试验的系统就是以该项研究成果为基础的。

Through scientific and technological research, a single-bogie maglev train system was developed in 1995. Maglev bogie is the smallest functional unit of maglev train, which has the functions of independent suspension, guidance, propulsion and braking. The system has four sets of independent suspension control systems (including eight electromagnets and four sets of controllers), a set of propulsion system (including a pair of motors), a corresponding secondary suspension system, and a 3 m×3.3 m carriage floor, which can carry more than 40 people and run smoothly on a 10m long track. The system currently being tested is based on the results of this study.

（二）应用背景

7.1.2.2　Application Background

根据规划，北京至八达岭高速公路通车后，高速公路的出口处建有停车场，停车场到八达岭长城景区距离 2.6 km，必须修建一条旅游连接线将游客运送到长城景区。考虑到磁浮列车具有无污染、噪声低、乘坐平稳舒适等特点，以及国防科技大学在"八五"科技攻关中所取得的进展，北京控股有限公司与国防科技大学共同商定进一步开发中低速磁浮列车技术。

According to the plan, after the Beijing-Badaling Expressway is opened to traffic, a parking lot will be built at the exit of the expressway. The distance between the parking lot and the Badaling Great Wall Scenic Area is 2.6 km. A tourist connection line must be built to transport tourists to the Great Wall Scenic Area. Considering that the maglev train has the characteristics of no pollution, low noise, stable and comfortable ride, and the progress made by the National University of Defense Technology in the "Eighth Five-Year Plan" scientific and technological research, Beijing Holding Co., Ltd. and the National University of Defense Technology have jointly agreed to further develop the technology of medium and low speed maglev train.

（三）长沙中低速磁浮列车中试基地与CMS-03试验车

7.1.2.3　Changsha Medium and Low Speed Maglev Train Pilot Test Base and CMS-03 Test Vehicle

为使国防科大的磁浮技术走向应用，北京控股公司愿意出资支持国防科大建设中试基地，使国防科大的实验室成果能够在接近八达岭应用的环境下试验和改善各项关键技术。中试基地包括一辆试验车（CMS-03型）和一段试验线路。

In order to apply the maglev technology of the National Defense Science and Technology University, the Beijing Holding Company is willing to invest in supporting the National Defense Science and Technology University to build a pilot base, so that the laboratory results of the NUDT can test and improve various key technologies in an environment close to Badaling. The pilot test base includes a test vehicle (CMS-03) and a test line.

2001年4月，中国首条自主开发的常导中低速磁浮列车试验线在位于长沙的国防科技大学建成并开始工程化试验。试验线由第三勘察设计院和国防科技大学磁浮技术研究中心设计。该试验线位于国防科技大学校园内，可以对线路和车辆进行各种试验，包括对磁浮列车转向架、整车、车载电器及车辆控制系统进行全面运行试验和调试。

In April 2001, China's first self-developed test line for normally-guided medium-low speed maglev trains was built in the National Defense of Changsha. The University of Science and Technology was completed and began engineering tests. The test line consists of the Third Survey and Design Institute and the Maglev Technology of the National University of Defense Technology. Research Center Design. Located on the campus of the National University of Defense Technology, the test line can carry out various tests on the line and vehicles. It includes the comprehensive operation test and debugging of the bogie, vehicle, on-board electrical appliances and vehicle control system of the maglev train.

该试验线是设想的北京八达岭长城磁浮列车旅游运营线的前期工程，参照该运营线的弯道及坡度设计，试验线路长204 m、弯道半径100 m、坡度4.0‰，竖曲线半径1 000 m。下路部分于2001年5月建成，从9月初开始系统试验，11月通过专家验收。

The test line is the preliminary project of the envisaged Beijing Badaling Great Wall Maglev Train Tourist Line. It is designed with reference to the curve and slope of the operation line. The test line is 204 m long, with a curve radius of 100 m, a slope of 4.0‰, and a vertical curve radius of 1,000 m. The lower part of the road was completed in May 2001, and the system test began in early September and passed the acceptance of experts in November.

该试验线的导轨结构与日本的HSST导轨结构类似。为了给列车供电，在导轨下方采用一般的钢轨作为供电轨。

The guideway structure of this test line is similar to that of the HSST in Japan. In order to supply power to the train, the general steel rail is used as the power supply rail under the guide rail.

CMS-03型试验车首车长15 m，中间车长14 m、宽3 m，可承载100人左右，车体由4组转向架组成，车体于2001年7月下线。该磁浮车辆采用全新的外形曲线，流线型子弹头前围，设计速度150 km/h，车身采用全铝合金结构，外蒙玻璃钢材料，车内设有空调暖气等装置。该车由北京控股有限公司投资并组织实施，国防科技大学负责系统集成，上海飞机制造厂、株洲机车车辆研究所、常州长江客车集团合作开发。

整车四转向架的悬浮、推进、爬坡、制动、加载等试验已全部完成，各项测试指标达到设计要求。

The CMS-03 test car is 15 m long in the first car, 14 m long in the middle car and 3 m wide. It can carry about 100 people. The car body consists of four sets of bogies. The car body rolled off the production line in July 2001. The maglev vehicle adopts a new shape curve, a streamlined bullet front wall, a design speed of 150 km/h, an all-aluminum alloy structure, an outer glass fiber reinforced plastic material, and air conditioning and heating devices in the vehicle. The vehicle is invested and implemented by Beijing Holding Co., Ltd., the National University of Defense Technology is responsible for system integration, and Shanghai Aircraft Manufacturing Factory, Zhuzhou Locomotive and Rolling Stock Research Institute and Changzhou Changjiang Bus Group cooperate in the development. The suspension, propulsion, climbing, braking, loading and other tests of the four-bogie have been completed, and the test indicators meet the design requirements.

2001年11月25日，北京科学技术委员会在长沙主持召开了北京控股磁浮技术发展有限公司和国防科学技术大学中低速磁浮列车中试系统评审会，该系统通过了评审。

In November 25, 2001, the Beijing Science and Technology Commission hosted a review meeting on the pilot test system of medium and low speed maglev trains of Beijing Holding Maglev Technology Development Co., Ltd. and National University of Defense Technology in Changsha, and the system passed the review.

2014年5月16日，采用了西南交通大学和国防科技大学磁浮技术的长沙高铁南站至黄花国际机场的磁浮线路正式开工建设，这是我国第一条完全自主研发的商业运营磁浮线。2016年5月6日，长沙磁浮快线载客试运营，现已投产正式运营，乘客从长沙南站至长沙黄花机场T2航站楼仅需20 min。

In May 16, 2014, the maglev line from Changsha South high-speed railway Station to Huanghua International Airport, which adopts the maglev technology of Southwest Jiaotong University and National Defense University of Science and Technology, officially started construction, which is the first commercial maglev line developed by China. In May 6, 2016, Changsha Maglev Express Line was put into trial operation and has been put into operation. It takes only 20 minutes for passengers to travel from Changsha South Railway Station to Terminal 2 of Changsha Huanghua Airport.

2015年4月20日，采用了国防科技大学磁浮技术建设的北京第一条中低速磁浮线路开工建设，该线路是我国第二条中低速磁浮列车线路，现已投产运营。

In April 20, 2015, the construction of the first medium and low speed maglev line in Beijing, which adopted the maglev technology of the National University of Defense Technology, was started. This line is the second medium and low speed maglev train line in China and has been put into operation.

三、中国科学院电工所研究情况

7.1.3 Research of Institute of Electrical Engineering, Chinese Academy of Sciences

中国科学院电工所在 20 世纪 70 年代初期，开展了直线电机研究。当时的重点是短定子直线感应电机，对直线感应电机的纵向和横向端部效应、短定子两端空槽效应进行了深入的理论分析和试验研究，提出了计算公式，取得了较满意的成果。此外还对直线感应电机设计计算做了研究，并研制了直线感应电机加速器（100 kV·A、推力 4 820 N、速度 15 m/s），在航空部件试验装置上得到满意应用；还研制了铁路自动编组站推动货车车厢的直线电机(每台推力 1 940 N，同步速度 7.2 m/s，12 台电机串联，组成推车动力单元)。

In the early 1970s, the Institute of Electrical Engineering of the Chinese Academy of Sciences carried out research on linear motors. At that time, the focus was on the short-stator linear induction motor. The longitudinal and transverse end effect of the linear induction motor and the empty slot effect at both ends of the short stator were deeply analyzed theoretically and experimentally, and the calculation formula was put forward, which achieved satisfactory results. A linear induction motor accelerator (100 kV·A, thrust 4,820 N, speed 15 m/s) has been developed, which has been satisfactorily applied in the aeronautical component test device; the linear motors for pushing freight cars in the railway automatic marshalling station are also developed (each motor has a thrust of 1,940 N and a synchronous speed of 7.2 m/s, and 12 motors are connected in series to form a power unit for pushing cars).

在"八五"磁浮列车关键技术科技攻关中，电工所承担了直线电机研制，完成了样机设计和研制，样机功率 93 kW，额定速度 60 km/h，样机安装在铁科院牵头研制的 6 t 磁浮车上。在试验室建立了短定子直线感应电机试验台，并对用于磁浮列车的短定子直线感应电机特性及设计计算进行了理论和实验研究。

In the "Eighth Five-Year Plan" key technology research of maglev train, the Institute of Electrical Engineering undertook the development of linear motor, and completed the design and development of the prototype. The power of the prototype is 93 kW, and the rated speed is 60 km/h. The prototype is installed on the 6 t maglev train led by the Academy of Railway Sciences. A short-stator linear induction motor test-bed is established in the laboratory, and the theoretical and experimental study on the characteristics and design calculation of the short-stator linear induction motor for maglev train is carried out.

对超导推斥式磁浮列车，中国科学院电动所对其复杂的多回路、无铁心的电磁系统进行了理论研究。利用电路回路法，研究了空间磁场，计算了推力、悬浮力和导向力，其结果在第 14 届国际磁浮和驱动技术会议上发表。中国科学院电工所还与浙江大学合作用数值法计算了电磁场和相应推力、悬浮力及导向力。

For the superconducting repulsion maglev train, the Institute of Electric Power of the Chinese Academy of Sciences has developed its complex multi-loop, coreless electromagnetic system. All right, theoretical research. The space magnetic field is studied and the thrust, levitation force and guidance force are calculated by using the circuit loop method. The results were presented at the 14th International Maglev and Drive general technical meeting. The Institute of Electrical Engineering of the Chinese Academy of Sciences has also cooperated with Zhejiang University. The electromagnetic field and the corresponding thrust, levitation force and guidance force are calculated by numerical method.

对于块状高温超导体推斥磁浮，中国科学院电动所与德国布伦瑞克大学电气传动所、中国西北有色金属研究院合作，在1997年研制了高温超导磁浮列车原理模型，模型车自重约7 kg，有效载荷20 kg。环形轨道周长10 m，采用长定子空气芯直线同步电机驱动，分段供电。该试验装置在1997年国际第15届超导磁体技术会议展出。与此同时，对模型的静态、动态特性进行了理论分析和试验研究，对高温超导磁浮的机理进行了分析和研究。

As for the repulsion maglev of bulk high temperature superconductors, the Institute of Electric Power of the Chinese Academy of Sciences, in cooperation with the Institute of Electric Drive of Braunschweig University in Germany and the Northwest Institute of Nonferrous Metals in China, developed the principle model of high temperature superconducting maglev train in 1997. The weight of the model vehicle is about 7 kg, the payload is 20 kg, and the circumference of the circular track is 10 m. The model vehicle is driven by a long stator air core linear synchronous motor and powered by segments. The experimental device was exhibited at the 15th International Superconducting Magnet general technical meeting in 1997. At the same time, the static and dynamic characteristics of the model are theoretically analyzed and experimentally studied, and the mechanism of HTS maglev is analyzed and studied.

四、中国铁道科学研究院研究情况

7.1.4　Research of China Academy of Railway Sciences

中国铁道科学研究院于1998年8月安装调试完成6 t单转向架电磁悬浮铁道试验车辆 CHN-001，并于同年11月通过鉴定。该车采用IGBT现代电力电子斩波器控制车辆的悬浮高度，采用调压调频交-直-交变频器对直线感应电机进行变频调速，使车辆在倒"U"形感应板上行驶。推进电机参数按200 km/h设计，车辆按100 km/h设计。

China Academy of Railway Sciences completed the installation and commissioning of

6 t single bogie electromagnetic levitation railway test car CHN-001 in August 1998, and passed the appraisal in November of the same year. The vehicle adopts IGBT modern power electronic chopper to control the suspension height of the vehicle, and adopts voltage regulating frequency modulation AC-DC-AC frequency converter to carry out variable frequency speed regulation on the linear induction motor, so that the vehicle can run on the inverted "U" shaped induction board. The parameters of the propulsion motor are designed as per 200 km/h, and the vehicle is designed as per 100 km/h.

中国铁道科学研究院还在环形试验基地试验室内修建了 36 m 长的一段线路，并建有室内悬浮试验系统。

China Academy of Railway Sciences has also built a 36 m long section of track in the laboratory of the ring test base and built an indoor suspension test system.

车辆主要参数如下：
Main parameters of the vehicle are as follows:

车辆尺寸：6.3 m × 3 m × 3 m；
Vehicle dimensions: 6.3 m × 3 m × 3 m;

额定悬浮高度：10 mm；
Rated suspension height: 10 mm;

磁铁数量及悬浮质量：8 × 750 kg=6 000 kg；
Magnet number and suspension mass: 8 × 750 kg = 6,000 kg;

直线电机数量及功率：2 × 93 kW=186 kW；
Number and power of linear motor: 2 × 93 kW = 186 kW;

座席数：15 人（含司机）；
Seats: 15 (including the driver);

供电电压：750 V。
Supply voltage: 750 V.

五、国内磁浮发展大事记

7.1.5　Memorabilia of Maglev Development in China

1989 年，国防科技大学研制成中国第一台小型磁浮原理样车。

In 1989, the National University of Defense Technology developed the first small maglev prototype vehicle in China.

1990 年，第一次"磁浮列车、直线电机技术研讨会"在西南交通大学召开。

In 1990, the first "Seminar on Maglev Train and Linear Motor Technology" was held in Southwest Jiaotong University.

1992 年，研制载人磁浮列车被正式列入国家"八五"科技攻关重点项目。

In 1992, the development of manned maglev train was officially listed in the national "Eighth Five-Year Plan" key scientific and technological projects.

1994年，西南交通大学研制成功了中国第一辆可载人常导低速磁浮列车。

In 1994, Southwest Jiaotong University successfully developed the first manned low-speed maglev train in China.

1995年5月11日，中国第一台载人磁浮列车在国防科技大学研制成功，使中国成为继德国、日本、英国、苏联、韩国之后，第六个研制成功磁浮列车的国家。

In May 11, 1995, China's first manned maglev train was successfully developed at the National University of Defense Technology, making China the sixth country to successfully develop a maglev train after Germany, Japan, Britain, the Soviet Union and ROK.

2000年，西南交通大学磁浮列车与磁浮技术研究所研制成功世界首辆高温超导载人磁浮试验车（因受经费限制，从2001年到2011年的10年时间里，高温超导磁浮几乎没有大的应用进展）。

In 2000, the Institute of Maglev Train and Maglev Technology of Southwest Jiaotong University successfully developed the world's first high-temperature superconducting manned maglev test vehicle (due to financial constraints, in the 10 years from 2001 to 2011, the high-temperature superconducting maglev vehicle was There seems to be no major application progress).

2001年1月23日，上海磁浮交通发展有限公司与由德国西门子公司、蒂森快速列车系统公司和磁浮国际公司组成的联合体签署《上海磁浮列车项目供货和服务合同》，合同总金额12.93亿马克；2001年1月26日，与德国线路及轨道梁技术联合体（TGC）签署《磁浮快速列车混凝土复合轨道梁系统技术转让合同》，合同使用德国政府赠款共1亿马克。2001年3月1日工程正式开始，5月专用道路全线贯通，7月轨道梁生产基地投产。

In January 23, 2001, Shanghai Maglev Transportation Development Co., Ltd. signed the Supply and Service Contract for Shanghai Maglev Train Project with a consortium composed of Siemens, Thyssen Rapid Train Systems and Maglev International, with a total contract value of 1.293 billion marks; In January 26, 2001, it signed the "Maglev Express Train Concrete Composite Track Beam System Technology Transfer Contract" with the German Line and Track Beam Technology Consortium (TGC), using a total of 100 million marks of German government grants. The project was officially started on March 1, 2001, the special road was completed in May, and the track beam production base was put into operation in July.

2001年8月14日，由长春客车厂、西南交通大学和株洲电力机车研究所联合研制开发的我国首辆磁浮客车，在长春客车厂竣工下线，从而使我国继德国和日本之后，成为世界上第三个掌握磁浮客车技术的国家。

In August 14, 2001, the first maglev vehicle in China, jointly developed by Changchun

Passenger Car Factory, Southwest Jiaotong University and Zhuzhou Electric Locomotive Research Institute, was completed and rolled off the production line in Changchun Passenger Car Factory, making China the third country in the world to master maglev vehicle technology after Germany and Japan.

2001年11月24日，北控磁浮第一台磁悬浮列车通过中试评审。

In November 24, 2001, the first maglev train of Beikong Maglev passed the pilot test evaluation.

2002年2月28日，上海磁浮列车示范线下部结构工程全线贯通并开始架梁。

In February 28, 2002, the substructure project of Shanghai Maglev Train Demonstration Line was completed and the girder erection began.

2002年12月31日，上海磁浮列车示范线开始试运营。

In December 31, 2002, the Shanghai Maglev Train Demonstration Line began trial operation.

2003年，四川成都青城山磁浮列车线完工，该磁浮试验轨道长420 m，主要针对观光游客。

In 2003, the Qingchengshan Maglev Train Line was completed in Chengdu, Sichuan. The maglev test track is 420 m long and is mainly aimed at tourists.

2005年5月，中国自行研制的"中华06号"吊轨永磁悬浮列车于大连亮相，据称其速度可达400 km/h。

In May 2005, China's self-developed "Zhonghua 06" suspension rail permanent magnet levitation train was unveiled in Dalian, and it is said that its speed can reach 400 km/h.

2005年7月，北控磁浮第二辆磁浮车在北车唐山客车厂下线，并投入试运行。

In July 2005, the second maglev vehicle of Beikong Maglev rolled off the production line in Tangshan Passenger Car Factory of North Railway and was put into trial operation.

2005年9月，中国成都飞机公司开始研制CM1型"海豚"高速磁浮列车，最高速度500 km/h，原本预计会于2006年7月在上海试行。然而，由于技术难题，该车转交国防科技大学继续研制成功，该车在上海同济大学嘉定分校内。

In September 2005, Chengdu Aircraft Corporation of China began developing the CM1 Dolphin high-speed maglev train with a maximum speed of 500 km/h, which was originally expected to be tested in Shanghai in July 2006. However, due to technical difficulties, the vehicle was transferred to the National University of Defense Technology to continue its successful development, and the vehicle was located in Jiading Branch of Tongji University in Shanghai.

2005年，由长春客车厂生产的另一辆高速磁浮车研制成功。

In 2005, another high-speed maglev vehicle produced by Changchun Passenger Car Factory was successfully developed.

2006年4月30日，中国第一辆具有自主知识产权的中低速磁浮列车，在四川成都青城山一个试验基地成功经过室外实地运行联合试验，利用常导电磁悬浮推动。

In April 30, 2006, China's first medium and low speed maglev train with independent intellectual property rights successfully passed the outdoor field operation joint test at a test base in Qingchengshan, Chengdu, Sichuan Province, using normal electromagnetic levitation propulsion.

2008年5月，唐山客车厂建成了一条1.547 km的中低速磁浮列车工程化试验示范线，科技部将其确立为国家科技支撑计划中低速磁浮交通试验基地。

In May 2008, Tangshan Passenger Car Factory completed a 1.547 km engineering test demonstration line of medium and low speed maglev train, and the Ministry of Science and Technology established it as the medium and low speed maglev traffic test base of the National Science and Technology Support Plan.

2009年5月13日，国内首列具有完全自主知识产权的实用型中低速磁浮列车在唐山客车厂完成组装，顺利下线，并随即开始进行列车调试。

In May 13, 2009, the first practical medium and low speed maglev train with completely independent intellectual property rights in China was assembled in Tangshan Passenger Car Factory and successfully rolled off the production line, and then began to debug the train.

2010年4月8日，由成都飞机公司（简称成飞）制造的中国首辆高速磁浮国产化样车在成都实现交付，标志着成飞已具备磁浮车辆国产化设计、整车集成和制造能力。

In April 8, 2010, China's first high-speed maglev localization prototype vehicle manufactured by Chengdu Aircraft Corporation (hereinafter referred to as Chengfei) was delivered in Chengdu, indicating that Chengfei has the capability of maglev vehicle localization design, vehicle integration and manufacturing.

2012年1月20日，一列中低速磁浮列车在株洲电力机车有限公司下线，该磁浮列车采用三节编组，最高运行速度为100 km/h，列车最大载客量约600人。

In January 20, 2012, a medium-low-speed maglev train rolled off the production line at Zhuzhou Electric Locomotive Co., Ltd. The maglev train is composed of three cars, with a maximum running speed of 100 km/h and a maximum passenger capacity of about 600 people.

2014年5月16日，高铁长沙南站至长沙黄花国际机场的长沙磁浮工程正式开工建设。这是我国第一条完全自主研发的商业运营磁浮线。

In May 16, 2014, the construction of Changsha Maglev Project from Changsha South Railway Station to Changsha Huanghua International Airport was officially started high-speed railway. This is the first commercial maglev line developed independently in China.

2014年8月，中国中低速磁浮列车技术在常州实现新突破：西南交通大学牵引动力国家重点实验室与西南交通大学常州轨道交通研究院联手，自主研制出速度可达400 km/h的磁浮列车车架。

In August 2014, China's medium and low speed maglev train technology achieved a new breakthrough in Changzhou: the State Key Laboratory of Traction Power of Southwest Jiaotong University and the Changzhou Rail Transit Research Institute of Southwest Jiaotong University jointly independently developed a train with a speed of up to Maglev train frame at 400 km/h.

2015年4月20日，北京第一条中低速磁浮线路，也是我国第二条中低速磁浮列车线路 S1 线全面开工。

In April 20, 2015, the first medium and low speed maglev line in Beijing was also the second medium and low speed maglev train in China. Train line S1 is fully started.

2015年12月8日，由铁四院设计施工总承包的湖南长沙中低速磁浮铁路工程全线疏散平台铺架完毕。长沙中低速磁浮铁路是中国首条自主研发的磁浮线，西起长沙南站，东至黄花机场，线路全长 18.55 km。

In December 8, 2015, Changsha Medium and Low Speed Maglev Railway Project, Hunan Province, was designed and contracted by the Fourth Railway Institute. The laying and erection of the line evacuation platform is completed. Changsha Medium and Low Speed Maglev Railway is the first independently developed maglev line in China. It starts from Changsha South Railway Station in the west and ends at Huanghua Airport in the east, with a total length of 18.55 km.

2015年12月2日，长沙磁浮列车首次进行全线 18.55 km 的热滑试验，经磁浮榔梨站、抵达磁浮机场站后，顺利返回磁浮车辆段综合基地。

In December 2, 2015, Changsha maglev train carried out the first 18.55 km hot sliding test on the whole line. After arriving at Pear Station and Maglev Airport Station, they returned to the comprehensive base of Maglev Depot smoothly.

2016年5月6日，中国首条具有完全自主知识产权的中低速磁浮商业运营示范线——长沙磁浮快线开通试运营，该线路也是世界上最长的中低速磁浮运营线。

In May 6, 2016, Changsha Maglev Express Line, China's first medium and low speed maglev commercial operation demonstration line with completely independent intellectual property rights, was put into trial operation, which is also the longest medium and low speed maglev operation line in the world.

2017年12月30日，北京中低速磁浮交通示范线 S1 线（以下简称 S1 线）石厂站至金安桥段首班车开通试运营，这是首都地铁路网中的首条磁浮线路。

In December 30, 2017, the first train from Shichang Station to Jin'anqiao Section of Beijing Medium and Low Speed Maglev Transportation Demonstration Line S1 (hereinafter referred to as Line S1) was put into trial operation, which is the first maglev line in the capital metro network.

2018年1月25日，速度 600 km/h 高速磁浮交通系统技术方案在青岛已通过专家评审，今年将研制一节样机，2020年研制出样车并完成 5 km 试验线验证。这标志着由中车四方车辆股份有限公司牵头承担的国家重点研发专项"高速磁浮交通系统关键技术"课题取得重要阶段性成果。

In January 25, 2018, the technical scheme of high-speed maglev transportation system with a speed of 600 km/h has been approved by experts in Qingdao. According to the review, a prototype will be developed this year, and a prototype will be developed in 2020 and verified on the 5 km test line. This marks an important stage achievement of the national key research and development project "Key Technologies of High-speed Maglev Transportation System" led by Zhongche Sifang Vehicle Co., Ltd.

第二节 我国已建成的磁浮铁路线

Section 7.2 Maglev Railway Lines Built in China

除第五章介绍的上海磁浮示范线于 2002 年 12 月 31 日建成并开通商业运营外，长沙磁浮快线 2016 年 5 月 6 日正式开通商业运营，北京首条磁浮线路中低速磁浮交通示范线 S1 线（以下简称 S1 线）石厂站至金安桥段首班车也于 2017 年 12 月 30 日开通试运营，这是首都地铁路网中的首条磁浮线路。目前，全国已经商业运营的三条磁浮铁路上海磁浮示范线、长沙机场线、北京 S1 线运行均良好。

In addition to the Shanghai Maglev Demonstration Line introduced in Chapter 5, which was completed and put into commercial operation in December 31, 2002, Changsha Maglev Express Line was officially put into commercial operation on May 6, 2016. The first train from Shichang Station to Jin'anqiao Section of Line S1 (hereinafter referred to as Line S1), the first low-speed maglev traffic demonstration line in Beijing, was also put into trial operation in December 30, 2017, which is the first maglev line in the capital metro network. At present, there are three maglev railways in commercial operation in China, namely, Shanghai Maglev Demonstration Line, Changsha Airport Line and Beijing S1 Line, which are running well.

值得一提的是，2002 年年底上海引进德国技术建成了国内首条高速磁浮线，至今已 22 年，仍是全球唯一商业运营的高速磁浮线路，而长沙磁浮快线和北京首条磁浮线路中低速磁浮交通示范线则属于磁浮中的另一个类别——中低速磁浮，设计最高速度为 100 km/h。对于长沙和北京中低速磁浮与上海高速磁浮的区别，应该说两者应用领域完全不同，高速磁浮适用于长大干线，如京沪线，对标的是高铁；而低速磁浮则运用于城市轨道、旅游景区等短途线路，对标的是地铁、轻轨。

It is worth mentioning that at the end of 2002, Shanghai introduced German technology to build the first high-speed maglev line in China, which has been the only commercial high-speed maglev line in the world for 22 years, while Changsha Maglev Express Line and Beijing First Maglev Line Medium and Low Speed Maglev Transportation Demonstration Line belong to another category of maglev-medium and low speed maglev. The design maximum speed is 100 km/h. As for the difference between Changsha and Beijing medium-low speed maglev and Shanghai high-speed maglev, it should be said that the application fields of the two are completely different. High-speed maglev is suitable for long trunk lines, such as Beijing-Shanghai line, and the target is high-speed railway; while low-speed maglev is used in urban rail, tourist attractions and other short-distance lines, and the target is subway and light rail.

除中国外，目前世界上商业运营的中低速磁浮线路还有三条，首先是日本名古屋中低速磁浮线路，2005年3月开通，连接名古屋到爱知世博会举办地丰田市，全长约9 km；其次是1998年预算，2010年完工的华盛顿杜勒斯机场地铁，采用德国TR技术，用长定子直线同步电机驱动，由地面控制中心予以控制；再次是韩国，2014年7月，仁川国际机场至龙游站磁浮线路投入运营，全长6.1 km。

In addition to China, there are currently three medium and low speed maglev lines in commercial operation in the world. The first is the Nagoya medium and low speed maglev line in Japan, which was opened in March 2005, connecting Nagoya to Toyota City, the host city of the Aichi World Expo, with a total length of about 9 km; The second is the Washington Dulles Airport Metro, which was budgeted in 1998 and completed in 2010. It uses German TR technology and is driven by long-stator linear synchronous motors and controlled by the ground control center. The third is ROK. In July 2014, the maglev line from Incheon International Airport to Longyou Station was put into operation, with a total length of 6.1 km.

本节重点介绍长沙磁浮快线开通和北京首条磁浮线路中低速磁浮交通示范线（S1线）开通。

This section focuses on the opening of Changsha Maglev Express Line and the opening of Beijing's first medium and low speed maglev traffic demonstration line (Line S1).

一、长沙磁浮快线开通

7.2.1 Opening of Changsha Maglev Express Line

（一）开通情况

7.2.1.1 Opening Status

1980年，国防科技大学、西南交通大学和同济大学等科研机构相继开始常导电磁悬浮技术研究。2000年以来，相继在长沙国防科技大学校内、成都青城山、上海临港、河北唐山客车厂、湖南株洲电力机车厂建设了中低速磁浮中试基地和工程试验线，形成以中车株机公司和中车唐山厂为代表的磁浮车辆总成厂，以株洲电力机车研究所为代表的磁浮交通牵引和供电等核心电气设备制造单位。

In 1980, the National University of Defense Technology, Southwest Jiaotong University, Tongji University and other scientific research institutions began to study the electromagnetic levitation technology. Since 2000, a medium and low speed maglev pilot test base and engineering test line have been built successively in Changsha National Defense University of Science and Technology, Chengdu Qingchengshan, Shanghai Lingang, Hebei Tangshan Passenger Car Factory and Hunan Zhuzhou Electric Locomotive Factory, forming a maglev vehicle assembly plant represented by Zhongche Zhuzhou Locomotive Company and Zhongche Tangshan Factory. Zhuzhou Electric Locomotive Research Institute is the representative of the core electrical equipment manufacturing units such as maglev transportation traction and power supply.

长沙磁浮快线连接长沙火车南站和长沙黄花机场，全长 18.55 km，全线设高铁站、榔梨站和机场站 3 座车站，2014 年 5 月开工建设，2016 年 5 月 6 日载客试运营。湖南磁浮公司统计数据显示，2016 年 5 月 6 日至 2017 年 5 月 5 日，长沙磁浮快线共计开行列车 35 175 列次，累计发送旅客 2 599 762 人次。运行中的长沙磁浮快线列车如图 7-1 所示。

Changsha Maglev Express Line connects Changsha South Railway Station and Changsha Huanghua Airport, with a total length of 18.55 km. There are three stations along the line, namely, high-speed railway station, Langli station and airport station. The construction started in May 2014 and the passenger trial operation started in May 6, 2016. According to the statistics of Hunan Maglev Company, from May 6, 2016 to May 5, 2017, Changsha Maglev Express Line operated 35,175 trains and sent 2,599,762 passengers. Changsha Maglev Express Line trains in operation are shown in Figure 7-1.

图 7-1　运行中的长沙磁浮快线列车

Figure 7-1　Changsha Maglev Express Train in Operation

长沙磁浮工程正式开通商业运营，标志着我国已全面掌握中低速磁浮研发、制造、建设及运营的成套技术，这是中国首条具有完全自主知识产权的中低速磁浮商业运营示范线，也是世界上最长的中低速磁浮运营线。

The Changsha Maglev Project has officially opened for commercial operation, marking that China has fully mastered the complete technology of research and development, manufacturing, construction, and operation of medium and low-speed maglev. This is China's first commercial operation demonstration line for medium and low-speed maglev with completely independent intellectual property rights, and also the world's longest medium and low-speed maglev operation line.

该线路磁浮列车由中国中车株洲电力机车公司与国防科技大学等高校研发制造，设计最高速度100 km/h，每列车最大载客量363人。

The maglev train on the line is developed and manufactured by CRRC Zhuzhou Electric Locomotive Company and National University of Defense Technology, with a maximum design speed of 100 km/h and a maximum passenger capacity of 363 per train.

长沙中低速磁浮列车具有安全、噪声小、转弯半径小、爬坡能力强、运行平稳等特点，多项成果达到国际领先水平。中国也由此成为世界少数几个掌握中低速磁浮列车技术的国家之一。转弯半径小是磁浮列车又一个显著的特点。磁浮列车能通过100 m甚至更小的弯道。而一般轮轨要转弯起码需要300 m。之所以能有爬坡能力强、运行平稳、转弯半径小的特点，都依赖于磁浮列车靠的是脱离轨道的离地运行。

Changsha medium and low speed maglev train has the characteristics of safety, low noise, small turning radius, strong climbing ability and smooth operation, and many achievements have reached the international leading level. As a result, China has become one of the few countries in the world to master the technology of medium and low speed maglev train. Small turning radius is another remarkable feature of maglev train. Maglev trains can pass through 100 m or even smaller curves. Generally, it takes at least 300 m for the wheel-rail to turn, so it has strong climbing ability. The characteristics of smooth operation and small turning radius depend on the maglev train running off the track.

中低速磁浮列车的工作原理：中低速磁浮列车的铁轨本身不带电，而列车底部装有磁铁（见图7-2）。当列车底部与铁轨接近时，磁铁就产生吸力。而磁浮技术的核心就在于通过8 mm的间隙，让吸力始终保持在较为稳定的状态，从而实现列车的平稳悬浮。最后磁浮列车再通过车上装载的直线电机产生的牵引力，实现列车悬浮于轨道上的离地运行。

Working principle of medium and low speed maglev train: the rail of medium and low speed maglev train is not charged, but the bottom of the train is equipped with a magnet (see Figure 7-2). When the bottom of the train is close to the rail, the magnet generates attraction. The core of maglev technology is to keep the suction in a relatively stable state through a gap of 8 mm, so as to realize the smooth suspension of the train. Finally, the maglev train is suspended on the track and runs off the ground through the traction force generated by the linear motor loaded on the train.

图 7-2 长沙中低速磁浮列车

Figure 7-2　Changsha Medium and Low Speed Maglev Train

长沙中低速磁浮列车还具有另外一个特点是，无须大规模拆迁改造地面建筑，线路建设成本低。因为悬浮在铁轨上，没有轮轨接触，所以磁浮列车爬坡时就不会受到车轮的限制。一般的轮轨列车，在 100 m 之内爬不到一层楼高，而磁浮列车至少可以爬到三层楼的高度。较之其他的轮轨列车，磁浮列车可以轻松地穿越地面上的障碍物。同时，因为转弯半径小，磁浮列车在建设时可以少走很多弯路。建设磁浮线路时就不需要对城市已有的地面建筑进行大规模的拆迁改造，也不用在地下挖隧道、架设线路，所以如果在一个城市里修建一条磁浮铁路，成本就很低。长沙的这条中低速磁浮线路，全线投资包括拆迁在内，1 km 的成本只需 2.3 亿元，而长沙的地铁 1 km 成本则要 7 亿元。

Another characteristic of Changsha medium and low speed maglev train is that it does not need large-scale demolition and reconstruction of ground buildings, and the cost of line construction is low. Because it is suspended on the rail, there is no wheel-rail contact, so the maglev train will not be restricted by the wheels when climbing. The general wheel-rail train can not climb to the height of one storey within 100 meters, while the maglev train can climb to the height of at least three storeys. Compared with other wheel-rail trains, maglev trains can easily cross obstacles on the ground. At the same time, because of the small turning radius, the maglev train can avoid many detours in the construction. When building a maglev line, there is no need to carry out large-scale demolition and reconstruction of the existing ground buildings in the city, nor to dig tunnels underground and erect lines, so if a maglev railway is built in a city, the cost is very low. Changsha's medium and low speed maglev line, including demolition, costs only 230 million yuan for 1 km, while Changsha's subway costs 700 million yuan for 1 km.

不过对于磁浮列车，乘客也会有一些担心，在空中悬着，如果突然遭遇停电，乘客会不会有生命危险呢？首先，磁浮列车上装有三组牵引系统、三套电源、一套备用的蓄电池。其次，即使遇到意外，全部部件失灵，列车也不会脱轨。如果突然停电，列车会从 8 mm 的空间落到轨面上，但冲击不会很大。同时，磁浮列车还有"抱轨"设计（见图 7-3），即在磁浮列车的下端，设计了两个钢铁"胳膊"，这两个臂膀将铁轨紧紧搂住，防止磁浮列车发生脱轨和侧翻。

But for the maglev train, passengers will also have some worries, hanging in the air, if there is a sudden power outage, will the lives of passengers be in danger? First of all, the maglev train is equipped with three sets of traction systems, three sets of power supply and one set of standby batteries. Secondly, even if there is an accident and all the parts fail, the train will not derail.If there is a sudden power failure, the train will fall from the 8 mm space to the rail surface, but the impact will not be great.At the same time, the maglev train also has a "rail holding"design (see Figure 7-3), that is, two steel "arms" are designed at the lower end of the maglev train, which hold the rails tightly to prevent derailment and rollover.

近年来，国内有些城市也曾有过建设磁浮线路的规划，但因为公众对磁浮列车辐射和噪声的担忧，让很多建设计划暂时搁浅。磁浮列车的辐射真的很大吗？测试团队来到了距离长沙磁浮快线 5 m 的地方，进行了一次现场测试，仪器记录了列车经过时的辐射最大值，表上显示的是 1.46 μT。测试团队又找了一把电吹风，进行了一次比较测试，电吹风的辐射值是 47.03 μT。电吹风辐射值是磁浮列车的几十倍。

In recent years, some cities in China have had plans to build maglev lines, but because of public concerns about the radiation and noise of maglev trains, many construction plans have been temporarily stranded. Is the radiation of the maglev train really great? Test team Arrived at the place 5 meters away from Changsha Maglev Express Line, a field test was carried out, and the instrument recorded when the train passed. The table shows a maximum of 1.46 μT. The test team found another hair dryer and made a comparison. According to the test, the radiation value of the hair dryer is 47.03 μT. The radiation value of the hair dryer is dozens of times that of the maglev train.

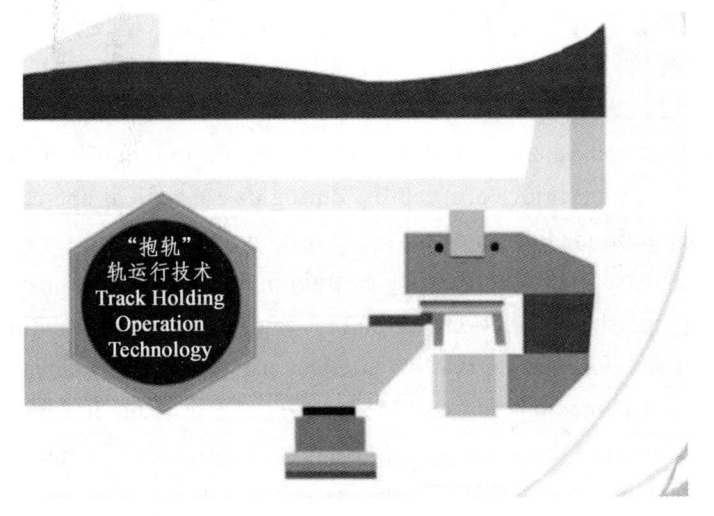

图 7-3 磁浮列车"抱轨"设计

Figure 7-3 Design of "Rail Holding" of Maglev Train

噪声也是公众担心的问题。在车厢里磁浮列车的噪声不大，但是磁浮列车沿途要直接穿过一些生活小区。在楼宇间行驶，它运行时的外部噪声会不会对周边的居民造成很大的影响呢？测试团队又进行了一个噪声的测试，与磁浮列车相距 5 m 的地方，平均 73 dB。噪声测试工程师表示：事实上，这个测试值偏高，原因是正常情况下，我们是不可能站在与磁浮列车相距 5 m 的地方的。随后，测试团队又在一个路口测试了一辆普通汽车经过时的噪声值，这个噪声值远高于磁浮列车从身边经过时产生的噪声。

Noise is also a public concern. The noise of the maglev train is not big in the carriage, but the maglev train has to pass through some residential areas directly along the way. When driving between buildings, will the external noise of its operation have a great impact on the surrounding residents? The test team also conducted a noise test, which was 5 m away from the maglev train, with an average of 73 dB. The noise test engineer said: In fact, this test value is too high, because under normal circumstances, it is impossible for us to stand 5 m away from the maglev train. Subsequently, the test team tested the noise value of an ordinary car passing by at an intersection, which was much higher than the noise generated by the maglev train passing by.

2002 年年底，我国第一条高速磁浮线路在上海正式试运营，运行速度达到 430 km/h。但是上海的高速磁浮快线运营 22 年间，未能实现盈利。在这种情况下，我国为什么还要打造中低速磁浮线路，并将它投入运营呢？通过把城市轨道交通中的地铁、轻轨和磁浮列车从单程运力、速度、建设成本、对周边环境的影响几个方面进行对比。从这个比较中可以看出，地铁的单程运力最高，中低速磁浮列车的运力最低；从速度上看，中低速磁浮列车速度最快，而轻轨的速度最慢；而从对周边环境的影响上看，地铁因为在地下运行，影响最小，而轻轨因为噪声较大，对我们的生活影响比较大；而从建设成本上来看，地铁的成本最高，中低速磁浮远低于地铁，略高于轻轨。综合几种城市轨道交通的优劣，我们发现中低速磁浮列车因为速度快，建设成本低，除了适于在城市间穿行，它还比较适合城际间的交通连线。

At the end of 2002, the first high-speed maglev line in China was put into trial operation in Shanghai, with a running speed of 430 km/h. However, the high-speed maglev express line in Shanghai failed to achieve profitability during its 22 years of operation. In this case, why should China build medium and low speed maglev lines and put them into operation? By comparing the metro, light rail and maglev train in urban rail transit from the aspects of one-way capacity, speed, construction cost and the impact on the surrounding environment. From this comparison, we can see that the one-way capacity of the subway is the highest, and the capacity of the medium and low speed maglev train is the lowest; from the speed point of view, the speed of the medium and low speed maglev train is the fastest, while the speed of the light rail is the slowest; from the impact on the surrounding environment, because the subway runs underground, it has the least impact, while the light rail has a greater impact on our lives because of its noise; From the point of view of construction cost, the cost of subway is the highest, and the medium and low speed maglev is much lower than that of subway and slightly higher than that of light rail. Combining the advantages and disadvantages of several urban rail transit, we find that the medium and low speed maglev train is not only suitable for traveling between cities, but also suitable for inter-city traffic links because of its high speed and low construction cost.

中国工程院院士刘友梅说，一个城市要解决交通出行的问题，地铁、公交、轻轨样样都不能少，各种交通工具都有自己的长处和短处，城市交通的多样性需求决定了各种交通装备不可简单地相互代替。

Liu Youmei, academician of the Chinese Academy of Engineering, said that in order to solve the problem of transportation in a city, subway, bus and light rail are indispensable. All kinds of transportation have their own strengths and weaknesses, which are determined by the diverse needs of urban transportation. All kinds of transportation equipment can not simply replace each other.

中国交通运输系统工程学会一位专家表示，磁浮列车具有环保、快速、安全、舒适、易于修建、维护成本低等优点，尤其中低速磁浮列车特别适用于城市客流不大的快速延伸线，像机场、产业区、郊区间等。

An expert from the China Society of Transportation Systems Engineering said that maglev trains have the advantages of environmental protection, speed, safety, comfort, easy construction and low maintenance cost, especially medium and low speed maglev trains are especially suitable for fast extension lines with small urban passenger flow, such as airports, industrial zones and the space between suburbs.

长沙中低速磁浮示范线是我国完全享有自主知识产权的高科技产品，它的运营标志着我国在相关领域的科研和生产能力获得了突破，走在了世界前列。磁浮交通作为先进轨道交通制造业的一部分，它将带动机械、电气、电子、网络等相关产业的迅速发展，为经济带来新的增长点。

Changsha Medium and Low Speed Maglev Demonstration Line is a high-tech product with independent intellectual property rights in China. Its operation marks a breakthrough in China's scientific research and production capacity in related fields and is in the forefront of the world. As a part of advanced rail transit manufacturing industry, maglev transportation will promote the rapid development of machinery, electrical, electronic, network and other related industries, and bring new growth points for the economy.

作为湖南构建中国中部空铁一体化综合交通枢纽，实现磁浮技术工程化、产业化的重大自主创新项目，长沙磁浮工程采用PPP融资模式，总投资42.9亿元人民币。

As a major independent innovation project for Hunan to build an air-rail integrated transportation hub in central China and realize the engineering and industrialization of maglev technology, Changsha Maglev Project adopts PPP financing mode with a total investment of 4.29 billion yuan.

长沙磁浮快线与高铁的结合情况如下：

The combination of Changsha Maglev Express Line and high-speed railway is as follows:

（1）磁浮高铁站与长沙火车南站"无缝连接"，磁浮-高铁一体化换乘；

(1)"Seamless connection" between Maglev High-speed Railway Station and Changsha South Railway Station, and integrated transfer between Maglev and high-speed railway;

（2）"和谐共存"，线路及电磁环境互不干扰；

(2)"Harmonious coexistence", lines and electromagnetic environment do not interfere with each other;

（3）空铁联运，与长沙黄花机场"无缝连接"，在磁浮高铁站建设城市航站楼。

(3) Air-rail intermodal transport, "seamless connection" with Changsha Huanghua Airport, and the construction of urban terminal at Maglev High-speed Railway Station.

（二）长沙中低速磁浮列车司机操纵台简介

7.2.1.2 Brief Introduction to Driver's Console of Changsha Medium and Low Speed Maglev Train

司机操纵台设备布置如图 7-4、图 7-5 所示。

The equipment layout of driver's console is shown in Fig. 7-4 and Fig. 7-5.

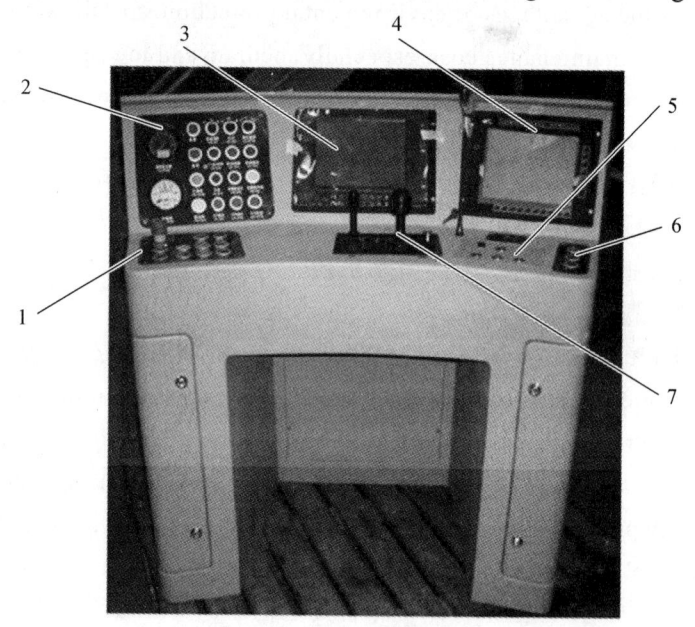

1—按钮面板；2—仪表面板；3—ATC 车载显示屏；4—网络控制显示屏；
5—司机广播控制和刮雨器控制盒；6—右门按钮面板；7—司机控制器。

1—button panel; 2—instrument panel; 3—ATC on-board display screen;
4—network control display screen; 5—driver broadcast control box and wiper control box;
6—right door button panel; 7—driver controller.

图 7-4 司机操纵台布置

Figure 7-4 Layout of Driver's Console

图 7-5 司机操纵台设备示意图

Figure 7-5 Schematic Diagram of Driver Console Equipment

按钮面板和仪表面板配置如图 7-6、图 7-7 所示。

The button panel and instrument panel are configured as shown in Figure 7-6 and Figure 7-7.

部件及代码 Components and Codes	功 能 Function	备 注 Remarks
紧急制动按钮 Emergency Braking Button	触发紧急制动 Trigger Emergency Braking	自锁，复位需旋转 Self-locking, Rotation Required for Reset
起浮按钮 Lifting Button	给出起浮指令 Give Lifting Instruction	自复位，脉冲触发 Self-reset, Pulse Triggered
降落按钮 Landing Button	给出降落指令 Give Landing Instruction	自复位，脉冲触发 Self-reset, Pulse Triggered
空调关按钮 Air Conditioning Off Button	给出关空调指令 Give the Instruction to Turn Off the Air Conditioner	自复位，脉冲触发 Self-reset, Pulse Triggered
空调开按钮 Air Conditioning On Button	给出开空调指令 Give the Instruction to Turn On the Air Conditioner	自复位，脉冲触发 Self-reset, Pulse Triggered

续表

部件及代码 Components and Codes	功 能 Function	备 注 Remarks
合主断按钮 Close Main Circuit Breaker Button	给出合主断指令 Give the Instruction to Close the Main Circuit Breaker	自复位，脉冲触发 Self-reset, Pulse Triggered
分主断按钮 Open Main Circuit Breaker Button	给出分主断指令 Give the Instruction to Open the Main Circuit Breaker	自复位，脉冲触发 Self-reset, Pulse Triggered
关左门按钮 Left Door Closing Button	给出左门关指令 Give the Instruction to Close the Left Door	自复位，脉冲触发 Self-reset, Pulse Triggered
开左门按钮 Left Door Openning Button	给出左门开指令 Give the Instruction to Open the Left Door	自复位，脉冲触发 Self-reset, Pulse Triggered
强泵按钮 Strong Pump Button	给出强泵指令 Give Strong Pump Instruction	自复位，脉冲触发 Self-reset, Pulse Triggered
汽笛按钮 Whistle Button	给出鸣笛指令 Give the Instruction to Whistle	自复位，脉冲触发 Self-reset, Pulse Triggered
再关门按钮 Door Re-closing Button	给出再关门指令 Give Door Re-closing Instruction	自锁，复位需旋转 Self-locking, Rotation Required for Reset
开右门按钮 Right Door Openning Button	给出右门开指令 Give the Instruction to Open the Right Door	自复位，脉冲触发 Self-reset, Pulse Triggered
关右门按钮 Right Door Closing button	给出右门关指令 Give the Instruction to Close the Right Door	自复位，脉冲触发 Self-reset, Pulse Triggered

说明：自复位按钮，脉冲触发操作时不用长按，触发时 $0.5\ s \leqslant t < 1\ s$
Note: self-reset button, no need to press for a long time during pulse triggering operation, during triggering $0.5\ s \leqslant t < 1\ s$

图 7-6　按钮面板配置及功能

Figure 7-6　Configuration and Function of Button Panel

司机控制台仪表面板
Instrument Panel of Driver's Console

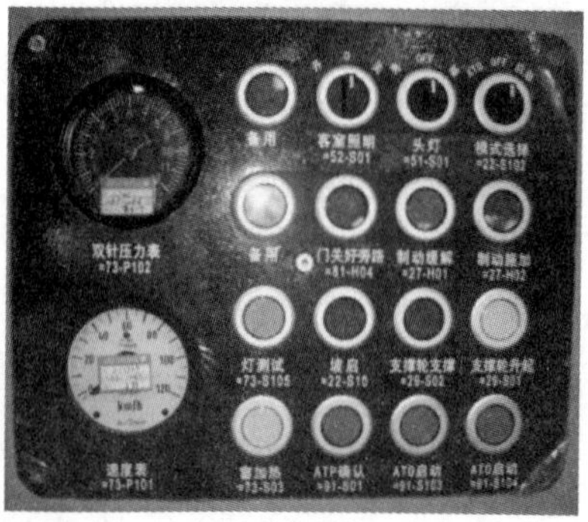

续表

部件及代码 Components and Codes	功　能 Function	备　注 Remarks
客室照明开关 Lighting Switch in Passenger Compartment	开启客室灯和司机室灯 Turn on the Lights in Passenger Compartment and Cab	自复位，脉冲触发 Self-reset, Pulse Triggered
头灯开关 Headlight Switch	开启头灯，有弱光功能 Turn on the Headlights, with Low-light Function	电平式 Level Triggered
模式选择开关 Mode Selection Switch	选择列车运行模式 Select Train Operation Mode	电平式 Level Triggered
门关好旁路指示灯 Bypass Indicator with Door Closed	此灯亮起，门关好已旁路 This Light is On, the Door is Closed and Bypassed	
制动缓解指示灯 Brake Release Indicator	此灯亮起，列车制动已缓解 When This Light is On, theTrain Brake has been Released.	
制动施加指示灯 Brake Application Indicator	此灯亮起，列车制动已施加 When the Light is On, the Train Brake has been Aapplied.	
灯测试按钮 Lamp Test Button	给出灯测试指令 Give Lamp Test Instruction	自复位，脉冲触发 Self-reset, Pulse Triggered
坡起按钮 Hill Start Button	给出坡起指令 Give Hill Start Instruction	自复位，脉冲触发 Self-reset, Pulse Triggered
支撑轮支撑按钮 Supporting Wheel Application Button	给出支撑轮施放指令 Give Instruction to Release the Supporting Wheel	自复位，脉冲触发 Self-reset, Pulse Triggered
支撑轮升起按钮 Supporting Wheel Lifting Button	给出支撑轮收起指令 Give Instruction to Retract the Supporting Wheel	自复位，脉冲触发 Self-reset, Pulse Triggered
窗加热按钮 Window Heating Button	给出窗加热指令 Give the Window Heating Instruction	自复位，脉冲触发 Self-reset, Pulse Triggered
ATP 确认按钮 ATP Confirmation Button	给出 ATP 确认指令 Give ATP Confirmation Instruction	自复位，脉冲触发 Self-reset, Pulse Triggered
ATO 启动按钮 ATO Start Button	给出 ATO 启动指令 Give the ATO Start Instruction	自复位，脉冲触发 Self-reset, Pulse Triggered
ATO 启动按钮 ATO Start Button	给出 ATO 启动指令 Give the ATO Start Instruction	自复位，脉冲触发 Self-reset, Pulse Triggered

说明：自复位按钮，脉冲触发操作时不用长按，触发时 $0.5\ \text{s} \leqslant t < 1\ \text{s}$

Note: self-reset button, no need to press for a long time during pulse triggering operation, during triggering $0.5\ \text{s} \leqslant t < 1\ \text{s}$

图 7-7　仪表面板配置及功能

Figure 7-7　Instrument Panel Configuration and Function

司机控制器结构及功能如图 7-8 所示。

The structure and function of the master controller are shown in Figure 7-8.

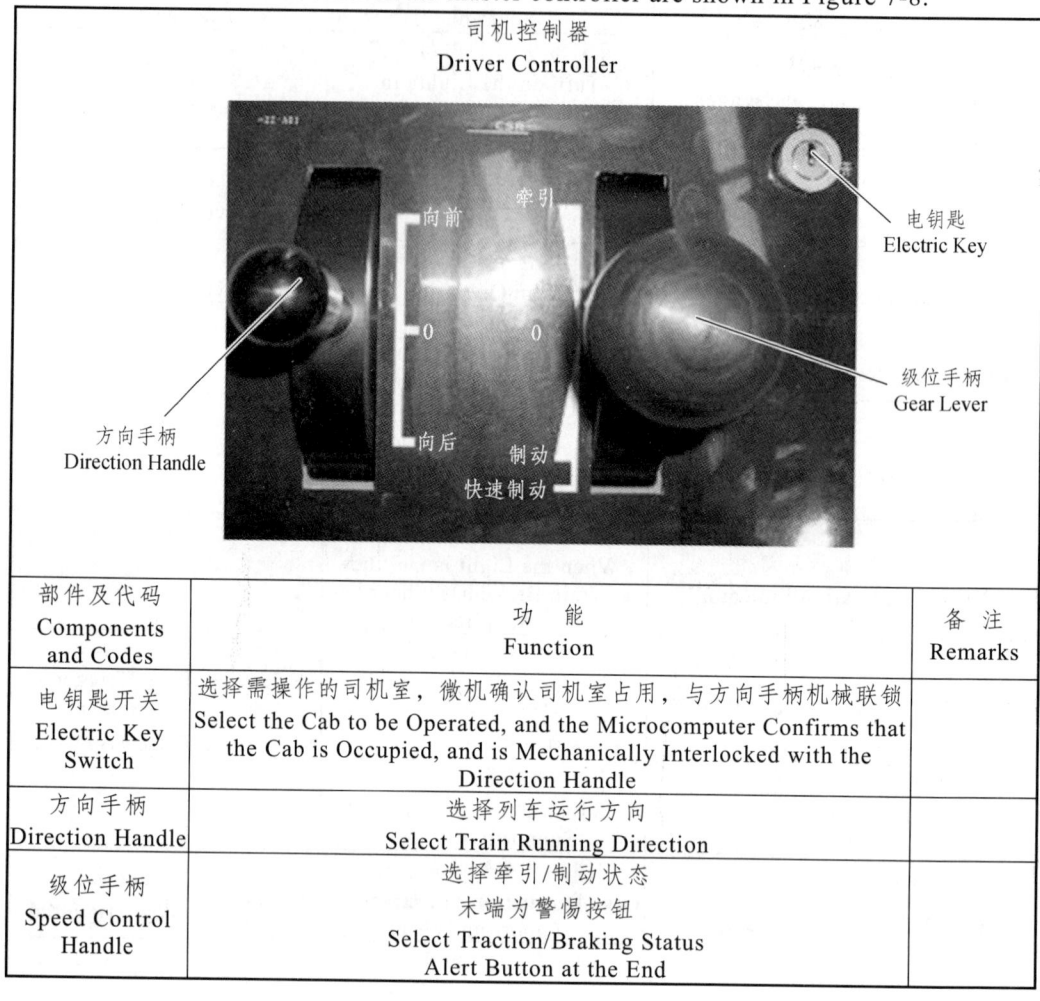

部件及代码 Components and Codes	功 能 Function	备 注 Remarks
电钥匙开关 Electric Key Switch	选择需操作的司机室，微机确认司机室占用，与方向手柄机械联锁 Select the Cab to be Operated, and the Microcomputer Confirms that the Cab is Occupied, and is Mechanically Interlocked with the Direction Handle	
方向手柄 Direction Handle	选择列车运行方向 Select Train Running Direction	
级位手柄 Speed Control Handle	选择牵引/制动状态 末端为警惕按钮 Select Traction/Braking Status Alert Button at the End	

图 7-8 司机控制器结构及功能

Fig. 7-8 Structure and Function of Master Controller

（三）基本开车流程

7.2.1.3 Basic Start-up Process

1. 开车前列车基本检测

1. Basic Inspection of Train before Departure

检查司机室操作台按钮板件在初始位置，检查司机室继电器柜各空气开关处于闭合位，各旋钮按键在初始正常位，110 V 电池电压值在正常范围内。

Make sure the button plate of the cab console is in the initial position, each air switch of the cab relay cabinet is in the closed position, each knob key is in the initial normal position, and the voltage value of the 110 V battery is within the normal range.

2. 列车激活

2. Train Activation

将列车激活旋钮（72-S101）打到合位，然后激活列车，屏幕上电点亮。

Turn the train activation knob (72-S101) to the closed position, then activate the train, and the screen will be on.

3. 模式选择

3. Mode Selection

选择是否 ATC 切除模式（91-S09）。

Select whether ATC removal mode (91-S09).

4. 开车前基本测试操作

4. Basic Test Operation before Start-up

灯测试，汽笛鸣音。

Lamp test, whistle sound.

5. 司机室占有

5. Occupation of Cab

司机室钥匙由关转到开位置，HMI 司机室前端显示占有指示。

The key in the cab is turned from off to on, and the front end of the HMI cab displays the occupancy indication.

6. 检测客室门关闭状态

6. Check the Closing Status of Passenger Compartment Door

确保客室门关闭，检查门关好指示灯亮起（81-S101）。

Make sure that the passenger compartment door is closed, and check that the door closing indicator is on (81-S101).

7. 列车起浮

7. The Train Lifts

按压起浮按钮（25-S101），完成列车起浮。

Press the lifting button (25-S101) to complete the lifting of the train.

8. 合高速断路器

8. Close the High-speed Circuit Breaker

高速断路器（21-S101）合。

High-speed circuit breaker (21-S101) is closed.

9. 方向施加

9. Directional Application

方向手柄向前。

Directional handle forward.

10. 牵引施加

10. Application of Traction

施加警惕（手柄按下即可施加警惕），牵引手柄向前。

Apply vigilance (press the handle to apply vigilance) and pull the handle forward.

注：如果以上步骤正确操作，此时列车将处于启动状态。

Note: If the above steps are operated correctly, the train will be in the starting state.

二、北京首条磁浮线路中低速磁浮交通示范线 S1 线开通

7.2.2 Beijing's First Maglev Line, Medium and Low Speed Maglev Traffic Demonstration Line S1 Opened

2011 年 2 月，经国家发改委批复，经北京市政府批准，同意建设 S1 工程。在规划图纸上，S1 线呈现出"反 Z"形状，西起门头沟石门营站，东至石景山区苹果园站。

In February 2011, the construction of S1 project was approved by the National Development and Reform Commission and the Beijing Municipal Government. On the planning drawings, Line S1 shows an "anti-Z" shape, starting from Shimenying Station in Mentougou in the west and Apple Orchard Station in Shijingshan District in the east.

2017 年 10 月 16 日，在行驶的磁浮列车上，北京市重大项目建设指挥部办公室公布了 S1 线路车站的定名。定名内容显示，北京 S1 线线路全长 10.236 km，设站 8 座，全部为高架站，分别是石厂站、小园站、栗园庄站、上岸站、桥户营站、四道桥站、金安桥站、苹果园站。8 站中，换乘站两座，在金安桥站与地铁 6 号线换乘，在苹果园站与地铁 1 号线、地铁 6 号线换乘。在石厂站北侧设车辆段 1 座，北京 S1 线控制中心接入北京市轨道交通指挥中心。

On the maglev train in Beijing in Oct 16, 2017, the Beijing Major Project Construction Headquarters Office announced the names of stations on the S1 line. According to the naming content, the total length of Beijing S1 Line is 10.236 km with 8 stations, all of which are elevated stations, namely Shichang Station, Xiaoyuan Station, Liyuanzhuang Station, Shangan Station, Qiaohuying Station, Sidaoqiao Station, Jin'anqiao Station and PingGuoyuan Station. Among the eight stations, there are two transfer stations, connecting to subway line 6 at Jinanqiao Station and subway Line 1 and Line 6 at Pingguoyuan Station. One rolling stock depot is set up in the north side of Shichang Station, and the control center of Beijing S1 line is connected to the Beijing Railway Transit Command Center.

2017年12月30日，北京中低速磁浮交通示范线 S1 线石厂站至金安桥段首班车开通试运营，这是首都地铁路网中的首条磁浮线路。全线长 9 km，列车单程运行需用时 16 min。S1 线将和地铁 6 号线西延段、1 号线苹果园站实现换乘。运行中的北京磁浮 S1 线列车及其司机室见图 7-9 和图 7-10。

In December 30, 2017, the first train from Shichang Station to Jin'anqiao Section of Beijing Medium and Low Speed Maglev Transportation Demonstration Line S1 was put into trial operation, which is the first maglev line in the capital metro network. The whole line is 9 km long, and it takes 16 minutes for the train to run one way. Line S1 will transfer with the West Extension Section of Metro Line 6 and Apple Garden Station of Line 1. The Beijing Maglev Line S1 train in operation and its cab are shown in Figure 7-9 and Figure 7-10.

图 7-9　运行中的北京磁浮 S1 线列车

Figure 7-9　Beijing Maglev Line S1 Train in Operation

图 7-10　S1 线首列磁浮列车司机室

Figure 7-10　Cab of the first maglev train of Line S1

磁浮列车的新特点：磁浮列车与轮轨列车最大的区别就是靠电磁系统取代了轮轨系统，没有车轮，车体和轨道不接触，没有摩擦，因此也没有振动，噪声非常小，磁浮系统保证列车与铁轨之间有 8~10 mm 的空隙，车身起落时非常平稳，乘客基本感受不到振动；同时，S1 线列车安装有专门的制动器，保证了列车安全、平稳刹车。目前，S1 线共有 10 辆磁浮列车，其中 5 辆列车投入运营，同时，每辆列车还配有日检、月检和年检，以保证其安全运行。

New features of the maglev train: The biggest difference between the maglev train and the wheel-rail train is that the wheel-rail system is replaced by the electromagnetic system. There is no wheel, no contact between the body and the track, no friction, so there is no vibration, and the noise is very small. The maglev system ensures that there is a gap of 8-10 mm between the train and the track, and the body rises and falls very smoothly. Passengers can hardly feel the vibration; at the same time, the S1 train is equipped with a special brake, which ensures the safe and stable braking of the train. At present, there are 10 maglev trains on Line S1, of which 5 trains are put into operation. At the same time, each train is equipped with daily, monthly and annual inspection to ensure its safe operation.

在磁浮地铁 S1 线正式试运行前，北京地铁公司对列车进行了全方位的检测，确定了磁浮列车可以在雨雪天气正常行驶，同时，十级以下的风，对车辆行驶没有较大影响。

Before the official trial operation of Maglev Metro Line S1, Beijing Metro Corporation carried out a comprehensive inspection of the train, and determined that the maglev train can run normally in rainy and snowy weather, at the same time, the wind below level 10 has no significant impact on the vehicle running.

即使悬浮列车突然没电，列车也不会有危险，因为除了持续供电之外，列车上还配有专门的蓄电池，蓄电池的作用之一就是在线路突然断电的情况下保证车辆能安全落下。根据设计数据，列车上安装的蓄电池，能给车辆供应 2 min 的电；而车辆安全下落的时间只要 20 s，蓄电池的电足够使车辆安全落在轨道上。

Even if the levitation train suddenly runs out of power, the train will not be in danger, because in addition to continuous power supply, the train is also equipped with a special battery, one of the functions of the battery is to ensure that the vehicle can fall safely in the case of sudden power failure on the line. According to the design data, the battery installed on the train can supply 2 minutes of electricity to the vehicle, while the time for the vehicle to fall safely is only 20 seconds, and the battery is enough to make the vehicle fall safely on the track.

北京 S1 线项目国防科技大学技术总工程师、国防科技大学教授接受采访时曾表示，这些没有轮子的车厢安装了电磁铁，和 F 形的轨道通电后产生吸引力，悬浮距离为 8~10 mm。磁浮列车具有很多优越性，它安全可靠，爬坡能力是地铁这些轮轨列车的两倍。关于磁浮交通的安全性，车辆始终抱轨运行，没有脱轨危险。这个坡度是往前走 1 km 可以爬 70 m 的高度，有 20 层楼这么高。

Chief technical engineer of Beijing S1 Line Project and professor of National University of Defense Technology, said in an interview that the carriages without wheels were equipped with electromagnets, which attracted the F-shaped track after electrification, and the suspension distance was 8 to 10 mm. Maglev train has many advantages, it is safe and reliable, and its climbing ability is twice that of the wheel-rail train in the subway. With regard to the safety of maglev traffic, the vehicle always runs on the track without the danger of derailment. The slope is 1 km ahead and you can climb 70 m, which is 20 stories high.

北京 S1 线噪声小、无摩擦、养护成本低，而且还节能。北京地铁供电分公司项目部经理说："节能模块设置了再生系统，当车辆制动的时候，产生的电能可以反馈到电网，然后再次利用，节省电能的消耗。直流系统有直流母线和备用母线，可以保证应急情况下正常供电。"

Beijing S1 line has low noise, no friction, low maintenance cost and energy saving. The project manager of Beijing Metro Power Supply Branch said: "The energy-saving module is equipped with a regeneration system. When the vehicle brakes, the generated electricity can be fed back to the grid and then reused to save the consumption of electricity. The DC system has DC bus and standby bus, which can ensure normal power supply in case of emergency."

对于市民关心的电磁辐射问题，总工程师说："S1 线采用车、轨、梁一体化技术，电磁完全封闭，不会泄漏。"另外，中国科学院电工研究所研究员介绍，电工所曾多次测量 S1 线的电磁辐射，结论是强度远低于国际非电离辐射防护委员会（ICNIRP）公布的国际标准。在距离车辆 1 m 处，辐射已经很弱；在 5～10 m 处，甚至弱于手机辐射。

Regarding the problem of electromagnetic radiation concerned by the public, the chief engineer said: "Line S1 adopts the integrated technology of vehicle, rail and beam, and the electromagnetism is completely closed without leakage." In addition, the researcher of the Institute of Electrical Engineering of the Chinese Academy of Sciences introduced that the Institute of Electrical Engineering had measured the electromagnetic radiation of S1 line many times, and concluded that the intensity was far below the international standard published by the International Commission on Non-ionizing Radiation Protection (ICNIRP). At the distance 1 m from the vehicle, the radiation is already very weak; at 5-10 m, it is even weaker than the mobile phone radiation.

首列磁浮列车上首次使用的高科技还很多。北京地铁机电分公司第二项目部副经理介绍说："消防水系统是地铁首次采用干式消防系统，平时消防水系统水管是不带水的。因为 S1 线属于地上站，冬季的时候管网不会冻裂；当接到报警信号以后，泵排水 5 min 之内把全站的消防管路打满水，末端能提供 10 m 的水柱。"

There are still many high technologies used for the first time on the first maglev train. The deputy manager of the second project department of Beijing Metro Mechanical and Electrical Branch said: "The fire water system is the first time that the dry fire system is used in the subway. Usually, the water pipes of the fire water system do not carry water. Because S1 line belongs to the ground station, the pipe network will not be frozen in winter; after receiving the alarm signal, the pump drainage will fill the fire pipeline of the whole station with water within 5 minutes, and the end can provide 10 m water column."

红外对射装置类似于通常的激光头，在两节车厢之间站台门的上面，装有两个红外对射，在车门关闭的过程中，如果有人挡住红外对射时，会影响安全回路，列车门和站台门都无法关闭，这样保证了乘客不会被夹伤。

The infrared radiation device is similar to the usual laser head. Two infrared radiations are installed on the platform door between two carriages. In the process of closing the door, if someone blocks the infrared radiation, it will affect the safety circuit, and the train door and the platform door can not be closed, so as to ensure that passengers will not be pinched.

最后简要回顾一下北京第一条中低速磁浮梦实现的漫长历程。

Finally, a brief review of the long history of the realization of Beijing's first medium-low speed maglev dream.

（一）八达岭磁浮项目最终搁浅，耗时5年的建设准备工作无果

7.2.2.1 Badaling Maglev Project has Finally Run aground, and Five Years of Preparation for Construction has been Fruitless

北京八达岭长城，中国铁路梦开始的地方，贯穿八达岭的京张铁路是中国自主修建的第一条干线铁路。一个世纪前，詹天佑博士创造性地设计了"人"字形线路，使火车在此处翻山越岭。他的铜像至今竖立在八达岭长城脚下的青龙桥火车站前。鲜有人知的是，八达岭也是中国中低速磁浮梦开始的地方。1999年初，八达岭长城景区外扩，新建停车场在距长城2.6 km外的高速公路出口处，究竟采用怎样的交通方式将游客搭载上行？轻轨、大巴这两种载客模式先后被否决，最新的磁浮技术进入人们的视野。为建造八达岭磁浮，北京磁浮公司（当时名为北控磁浮公司）应运而生。2002年11月，原北京市计委在完成对八达岭示范线前期操作审查后，向北京市政府提交了《关于八达岭旅游示范线立项请示报告》。此时，八达岭磁浮线的选型、可行性研究、办公楼建设等都已完成。但事与愿违，由于方方面面的原因，八达岭磁浮项目最终搁浅，耗时5年的建设准备工作无果。

Beijing Badaling Great Wall, where China's railway dream began, the Beijing-Zhangjiakou Railway, which runs through Badaling, is the first trunk railway built independently by China. A century ago, Dr. Zhan Tianyou creatively designed a "herringbone" line to make trains cross mountains here. His bronze statue is still standing in front of the Qinglongqiao Railway Station at the foot of the Badaling Great Wall. What few people know is that Badaling is also the place where China's low-speed maglev dream began. At the beginning of 1999, the Badaling Great Wall Scenic Area was expanded, and a new parking lot was built at the exit of the expressway 2.6 km away from the Great Wall. What kind of transportation mode was used to carry tourists up? The two passenger modes of light rail and bus have been rejected successively, and the latest maglev technology has entered people's vision. In order to build Badaling Maglev, Beijing Maglev Company (then known as Beikong Maglev Company) came into being. In November 2002, after completing the preliminary operation review of the Badaling Demonstration Line, the former Beijing Municipal Planning Commission submitted to the Beijing Municipal Government the Request Report on the Establishment of the Badaling Tourism Demonstration Line. At this time, the selection, feasibility study and office building construction of Badaling Maglev Line have been completed. However, contrary to expectations, due to various reasons, the Badaling Maglev Project finally ran aground, and the construction preparations that took five years failed.

继八达岭线之后，中国中低速磁浮推广有过多种传言，包括昆明世博园项目、成都青城山项目、北京东直门到首都机场线、沪杭磁浮线等，但都无疾而终。

Following the Badaling Line, there have been many rumors about the promotion of China's medium-low-speed maglev, including the Kunming Expo Park project, Chengdu Qingcheng Mountain project, Beijing Dongzhimen to the Capital Airport line, Shanghai-Hangzhou Maglev line, etc., but all have come to nothing.

（二）北京 S1 线立项，北京的磁浮交通建设得以重新开始并最终建成

7.2.2.2 Beijing S1 Line Project, Beijing's Maglev Transportation Construction Can be Restarted and Finally Completed

直到 2011 年 2 月，由门头沟通往市区的北京 S1 线立项，北京的磁浮交通建设得以重新开始。当年，公司领导在接受媒体采访时展望"两年以后（注：即 2013 年），我国第一条，世界第二条，也将是世界上最长的中低速磁浮交通线，将在首都大地上舞动它的风采。"然而，好事注定多磨，S1 沿线大量复杂的拆迁工作让工期一推再推。此外，2013 年 5 月，国务院将城市轨道交通项目审批权下放到地方，由于审批权下放过程中，两级政府之间存在衔接空当，工期再一次被推后。始料未及的还有，长沙磁浮后来居上，2014 年审批，2015 年建成，2016 年通车，长沙磁浮以迅雷不及掩耳之势夺下了"我国第一""世界上最长"等桂冠。

It was not until February 2011 that the construction of Beijing's S1 line from Mentougou to the city began again. In an interview with the media, the leader of the company predicted that "two years later (note: 2013), the first maglev transportation line in China, the second in the world, and the longest maglev transportation line in the world, will dance its style in the capital." However, good things are bound to take time, and a large number of complex demolition work along S1 has pushed the construction period back and

—299—

forth. In addition, in May 2013, The State Council delegated the approval authority of urban rail transit projects to local governments. Due to the gap between the two levels of government in the process of approval authority delegation, the construction period was once again delayed. What was unexpected was that Changsha Maglev took the lead. It was approved in 2014, completed in 2015, and opened to traffic in 2016. Changsha Maglev quickly won the title of "the first in China" and "the longest in the world".

从 1999 年，北京磁浮公司的八达岭之梦开始，到 2017 年年底 S1 线建成，北京的第一条磁浮线路前后经历了 18 年。十年磨一剑已经不足以描述它的漫长历程。但这 18 年并非虚度，北京磁浮公司标准和知识产权部经理说："在这 18 年里，我们取得多项磁浮技术及工程化应用成果，立项国家标准 1 项，颁布行业标准 9 项，地方行业标准 1 项，企业标准 50 多项。我们建立的标准为国家磁浮发展奠定了基础。"

From 1999, when Beijing Maglev Company's Badaling Dream, to the end of 2017 when Line S1 was completed, Beijing's first maglev line has experienced 18 years. Ten years is not enough to describe its long journey. But these 18 years are not wasted. The manager of Standard and Intellectual Property Department of Beijing Maglev Corporation said, "In these 18 years, we have achieved a number of achievements in maglev technology and engineering application. We have established 1 national standard, promulgated 9 industrial standards, 1 local industrial standard, and more than 50 enterprise standards. The standards we have established have laid the foundation for national maglev development."

除此之外，广东清远磁浮旅游专线和湖南凤凰磁浮观光快线已投入使用。清远磁浮旅游专线列车 2024 年 2 月启动试运营。凤凰磁浮观光快线（Fenghuang Maglev Express），是服务于湖南省湘西土家族苗族自治州凤凰县的一条城市轨道交通线路，是中国首条旅游观光磁浮线路，于 2022 年 5 月 1 日开通运营。

In addition, the Guangdong Qingyuan Maglev Tourism Line and the Hunan Fenghuang Maglev Express have been put into operation. The Qingyuan Maglev Tourism Line started trial operations in February 2024. The Fenghuang Maglev Express, which serves Fenghuang County in the Tujia and Miao Autonomous Prefecture of Xiangxi, Hunan Province, is China's first tourism-oriented maglev line. It began operations in May 1, 2022.

第三节 我国在建或拟建的磁浮铁路线

Section 7.3 Maglev Railway Lines Under Construction or Proposed in China

上一节谈到磁浮沉寂多年后，近年来以长沙磁浮和北京磁浮等为代表的国产中低速磁浮另辟蹊径，呈现燎原之势。应该说，长沙机场线和北京 S1 线具有示范意义：它不仅示范着磁浮的性能优势与应用场景，也示范着磁浮技术在中国的曲折进程。本节主要介绍我国在建或拟建的磁浮铁路线。

As mentioned in the previous section, after many years of silence, in recent years, the domestic medium and low speed maglev represented by Changsha Maglev and Beijing Maglev has opened up a new path, showing a prairie fire. It should be said that Changsha Airport Line and Beijing S1 Line have demonstration significance: they not only demonstrate the performance advantages and application scenarios of maglev, but also demonstrate the tortuous process of maglev technology in China. This section mainly introduces the maglev railway lines under construction or proposed in China.

一、新疆首条磁浮铁路在乌鲁木齐开建

7.3.1　Xinjiang's First Maglev Railway Opens in Urumqi

2016 年 11 月 16 日，新疆首条磁浮铁路在乌鲁木齐开建，预计很快就能完工通车，速度为 100~120 km/h。随着中铁第一勘察设计院承担的乌鲁木齐至南山中低速磁浮铁路测控工作的圆满完成，新疆首条磁浮铁路的建设正式启动。

In November 16, 2016, the first maglev railway in Xinjiang started construction in Urumqi, and is expected to be completed and opened to traffic soon, with a speed of 100-120 km/h. With the successful completion of the measurement and control work of the medium and low speed maglev railway from Urumqi to Nanshan undertaken by the First Survey and Design Institute of China Railway, the construction of the first maglev railway in Xinjiang has been officially launched.

乌鲁木齐至南山中低速磁浮铁路项目起点为高架车站三屯碑站，终点至南山的游客中心站，线路全长 38.07 km，其中高架线长约 36.26 km，地面线长约 1.81 km，全线新设车站 8 座，均为高架站，站均间距 5.4 km。全线设一段一场，车辆段自城南经贸区南站引出，停车场自游客中心站引出。该项目主要服务于乌鲁木齐市区至南山旅游产业基地旅游客流，并兼顾乌鲁木齐城南经贸合作区到南山旅游产业基地的交通需求，速度设定为中低速。

The project of Urumqi to Nanshan Medium-low-speed Maglev Railway starts from Santunbei Station, an elevated station, and ends at Nanshan Tourist Center Station. The total length of the line is 38.07 km, of which the elevated line is about 36.26 km long and the surface line is about 1.81 km long. There are 8 new stations on the whole line, all of which are elevated stations, and the spacing between stations is 5.4 km. Car depot from the South station of Southern Economic and Trade zone, parking lot from the tourist center station.

This project mainly serves the tourist flow from Urumqi urban area to Nanshan Tourism Industrial Base, and takes into account the traffic demand from Urumqi Chengnan Economic and Trade Cooperation Zone to Nanshan tourism Industrial Base, with the speed set at medium and low speed.

据了解，乌鲁木齐中低速磁浮项目由乌鲁木齐市建委牵头，将与北京中铁建集团通过"政府与社会资本合作"模式建设，项目开建后，预计3年左右的工期便能完工，届时从乌鲁木齐市区只需要 20 min 即可抵达南山。

It is understood that Urumqi low-speed Maglev project is led by Urumqi Municipal Construction Committee and will be constructed with Beijing China Railway Construction Group through the mode of "cooperation between government and social capital". After the construction of the project, it is expected to be completed in about 3 years, and it only takes 20 minutes to reach Nanshan from downtown Urumqi.

相比地铁交通，中低速磁浮具有成本低、行驶稳等特点。地铁每千米造价约 8 亿元，而磁浮每千米只要 2 亿元。由于没有轮轨的摩擦振动，磁浮车辆在速度 80 km/h 运行时的噪声仅为 70 dB 左右，可以做到车辆从楼房窗外 10 m 穿过而楼内的人员不易察觉；最小转弯半径只有 50 m，仅为地铁的 1/2，最大限度地避免拆迁；爬坡能力强，可以在 100 m 的距离内爬上 2 层楼的高度，而一般的轮轨交通最大爬坡能力仅为其 1/2。

Compared with subway transportation, the maglev has the characteristics of low cost and stable running. Subways cost about 800 million yuan per kilometer, while maglev floats cost only 200 million yuan per kilometer. Because there is no friction and vibration of wheel and rail, the noise of maglev vehicles is only about 70 dB when they are running at a speed of 80 km/h, which can make the vehicles pass 10 m from the window of the building without being easily detected by people inside the building. The minimum turning radius is only 50 m, only 1/2 of the subway, to avoid demolition to the maximum extent; Climbing ability is strong, can climb the height of 2 stories in the distance of 100 m, while the maximum climbing ability of ordinary wheel-rail traffic is only 1/2 of its.

二、成都中低速磁浮试验线和示范线的选线及建设方案已稳步推进

7.3.2 The Route Selection and Construction Scheme of Chengdu Medium and Low Speed Maglev Test Line and Demonstration Line have been Steadily Promoted

2018 年是成都轨道交通建设开拓创新之年，轨道交通建设将按照全面支撑东进、加密中优线网、发展西控旅游线、稳妥推进北改和南拓轨道交通建设的总体思路，以

实施轨道交通加速成网建设计划为总体目标，加快建设步伐。成都市轨道交通有关中低速磁浮试验线和示范线项目将结合成都市"东进"战略、国内外新型中低速磁浮系统技术和产业本地化发展前景对试验线和示范线的选线及建设方案进一步深入研究，并从政府引导、项目引领、技术整合等层面谋划成都市磁浮轨道交通技术产业中低速—中高速—高速—超高速的发展路径，成都至德阳尤其具有修建优势。

It was a pioneering and innovative year for Chengdu's rail transit construction in 2018. The rail transit construction will speed up the pace of construction with the overall goal of implementing the plan of accelerating the rail transit network construction, in accordance with the overall idea of fully supporting the eastward route, consolidating the China-superior line network, developing the west-controlled tourist line, and steadily promoting the North reform and south expansion of rail transit construction. The selection and construction plan of the test line and demonstration line of Chengdu rail transit will be further studied in combination with Chengdu's "eastward" strategy, domestic and foreign new medium and low speed maglev system technology and industrial localization development prospects. And from the government guidance, project guidance, technology integration and other aspects, plan the development path of Chengdu maglev rail transit technology industry of medium-low-speed, medium-high-speed, high-speed and ultra-high-speed, Chengdu to Deyang is especially advantageous in construction.

三、山东计划开跑磁浮列车

7.3.3　Shandong Plans to Run Maglev Train

山东交通迎来新规划，未来不但能在家门口坐上磁浮列车，还能享受以济南、青岛为中心的"1 h、2 h、3 h"高速铁路交通圈。未来将实现济南至青岛、青岛至周边市、全省相邻各市 1 h 通达，济南与省内各市 2 h 通达。

Shandong traffic ushered in a new plan, the future can not only take the maglev train at home, but also enjoy the "1 h, 2 h, 3 h" high-speed railway traffic circle centered on Jinan and Qingdao. In the future, it will realize 1 h access from Jinan to Qingdao, Qingdao to surrounding cities and neighboring cities in the province, and 2 h access from Jinan to cities in the province.

2021 年，高速磁浮列车已在山东青岛下线，速度 500～600 km/h，已在试验线上试运营，预计会进行推广。

In 2021, the high-speed maglev train has rolled off the production line in Qingdao, Shandong Province, with a speed of 500-600 km/h. It has been put into trial operation on the test line and is expected to be promoted.

四、八达岭磁浮梦有望重启

7.3.4 Badaling Maglev Dream Is Expected to Restart

第三节已谈到八达岭磁浮项目由于种种原因最终搁浅，耗时 5 年的建设准备工作无果。但据有关负责人介绍，八达岭是磁浮梦开始的地方，有关部门和人员正在计划重启这个搁置了十多年的项目，期待圆梦长城脚下。也许古老文明遇见现代科技只是时间问题。

In the third section, it has been mentioned that Badaling Maglev project finally ran aground due to various reasons, and the construction preparation work which took 5 years was fruitless. But according to the person in charge, Badaling is where the maglev dream began, and relevant departments and personnel are planning to restart the project, which has been shelved for more than a decade, looking forward to fulfilling the dream at the foot of the Great Wall. Perhaps it is only a matter of time before ancient civilizations meet modern technology.

除此之外，另据报道，四川成都都在建设中低速磁浮铁路，江苏徐州等城市将于近期开始筹建磁浮铁路。

In addition, it is reported that Chengdu in Sichuan Province are both building medium-low-speed maglev railway, while Xuzhou in Jiangsu Province and other cities will soon start to build maglev railway.

第四节 新型磁浮交通方式的探索

Section 7.4 Exploration of New Maglev Transportation Mode

本节主要介绍新型磁浮交通方式，主要包括磁浮飞机和真空永磁悬浮列车。
This section mainly introduces the new maglev transportation mode, mainly including maglev aircraft and vacuum permanent magnet levitation train.

一、磁浮飞机

7.4.1 Maglev Aircraft

（一）磁浮飞机简介

7.4.1.1 Introduction to Maglev Aircraft

美国麻省理工学院（MIT）从 20 世纪 70 年代开始磁浮飞机（Magplane）概念的

研究。在国家科学基金资助下，完成了一个 1/25 的试验模型，在 100 m 的试验轨道上进行过 5 代车的数百次试验，建立了全尺寸的 6 维仿真模型，对列车的各种性能进行了仿真。

The Massachusetts Institute of Technology (MIT) began to study the concept of Magplane in the 1970s. Under the support of NSFC, a 1/25 test model has been completed, hundreds of tests of five generations of trains have been carried out on a 100 m test track, and a full-scale six-dimensional simulation model has been established to simulate various performances of the train.

磁浮飞机的基本结构特点是轨道和车体下部的断面均呈圆弧形。轨道两侧为导电的铝质材料，中间部分为长定子直线电机的绕组（空心线圈）。车体下部的中间部分是作为直线电机次级的永久磁铁，两侧也是按照一定极性排列的永久磁铁。

The basic structural feature of maglev aircraft is that the sections of the track and the lower part of the vehicle body are arc-shaped.The two sides of the track are made of conductive aluminum material, and the middle part is the winding (hollow coil) of the long stator linear motor.The middle part of the lower part of the vehicle body is a permanent magnet used as the secondary of the linear motor, and the two sides are also permanent magnets arranged according to a certain polarity.

车体开始运行时由车轮支撑，轨道两侧的铝导轨内将产生涡流，从而产生车体的上浮力，当速度达到 20 km/h 以上时，车轮将离开轨道，磁浮飞机的悬浮间隙为 5~15 cm。由于车体下部的磁场呈弧形分布，因此这个磁场同时具有悬浮与导向的功能。长定子直线电机牵引功能与德国 TR 类似，只不过是永磁型同步直线电机，据介绍磁浮飞机的速度可达 400~500 km/h，也可低速运行。低速时，牵引磁场与永久磁铁之间有防滚作用，高速时车体上部的翼面也起防滚作用。

The car body is supported by the wheels at the beginning of operation. Eddy currents will be generated in the aluminum guide rails on both sides of the track, thus generating the buoyancy of the car body. When the speed reaches more than 20 km/h, the wheels will leave the track. The suspension gap of the maglev aircraft is 5-15 cm. Because the magnetic field at the lower part of the car body is distributed in an arc shape, the magnetic field has the functions of suspension and guidance at the same time. The traction function of the long stator linear motor is similar to that of the German TR, except that it is a permanent magnet synchronous linear motor. According to the introduction, the speed of the maglev aircraft can reach 400-500 km/h, and it can also run at low speed. At low speed, there is an anti-rolling effect between the traction magnetic field and the permanent magnet, and at high speed, the wing surface on the upper part of the car body also plays an anti-rolling role.

磁浮飞机的道岔没有机械移动部件，主要依靠牵引磁场的导向力。

The turnout of maglev aircraft has no mechanical moving parts and mainly depends on the guiding force of the traction magnetic field.

磁浮飞机的概念是从低温超导悬浮结构概念发展而来的。早期的磁浮飞机车体下部两侧不是永久磁铁，而是低温超导线圈，20世纪70年代的试验模型就是用超导悬浮系统实现的。近年来，稀土合金的永磁材料大幅度降价，磁浮飞机改用永磁材料取代超导部分，形成现在的概念。之所以称之为磁浮飞机，因为它有三大特点：一是磁浮飞机运行中离开轨道的高度比磁浮列车更高，距离有80~150 mm，如同在轨道上"飞行"；二是其运行速度非常高，可达550 km/h；三是具有许多飞机的特点，如列车两侧有"牙翼"，有点像飞机的翅膀，尾部还有起平衡作用的"尾翼"，这样保证了磁浮飞机在运行时，无论前、后、左、右所坐的乘客质量是否相近，都能保持它的平衡性和稳定性，其自动控制系统、方向舵、车厢、卫星定位系统等设备都是按飞机标准设定的，具有无机械噪声、无污染、速度快、节约能源等优点。磁浮飞机的概念结构非常简单，很有特色。但目前尚未进行工程试验，其商业运用尚需时日。

The maglev aircraft concept was developed from the cryogenic superconducting levitation structure concept. Early maglev aircraft did not have permanent magnets on both sides of the lower body, but cryogenic superconducting coils, and the test model in the 1970s was realized by superconducting levitation system. In recent years, the price of rare earth alloy permanent magnet materials has been greatly reduced, and the magnetic levitation aircraft has replaced the superconducting part with permanent magnet materials, forming the current concept. The reason why it is called maglev aircraft is that it has three major characteristics: one is that the height of the maglev aircraft leaving the track is higher than that of the maglev train, the distance is 80-150 mm, just like "flying" on the track, the other is that its running speed is very high, up to 550 km/h; Third, it has many characteristics of aircraft, such as "tooth wings" on both sides of the train, a bit like the wings of an aircraft, and "tail wings" at the tail, which ensure that the maglev aircraft can maintain its balance and stability when it is running, regardless of the quality of passengers sitting in front, back, left and right. Its automatic control system, rudder, carriage, satellite positioning system and other equipment are set according to aircraft standards, which has the advantages of no mechanical noise, no pollution, high speed and energy saving. The conceptual structure of maglev aircraft is very simple and distinctive. However, engineering tests have not yet been carried out, and its commercial application still needs time.

（二）我国的研究与探索情况

7.4.1.2　Research and Exploration in China

据媒体报道，继国产磁浮车辆在西南交通大学完成各项性能试验后，磁浮飞机项目也将落户成都。该项目的投资方之一的成飞集团公司负责人说，磁浮飞机项目是中美双方共同合作的项目，2001年9月26日已在四川成都正式签署了项目合同。中美两国的 5 家公司将共同出资组建成都飞美合资有限公司，利用美国的技术，建立"磁浮飞机"研制生产基地。

According to media reports, following the completion of various performance tests of domestic maglev vehicles at Southwest Jiaotong University, the maglev aircraft project will also be settled in Chengdu. A person in charge of Chengdu Aircraft Corporation, one of the investors of the project, said that the maglev aircraft project is a joint project between China and the United States, and the project contract was formally signed in Chengdu, Sichuan, in September 26, 2001. Five companies from China and the United States will jointly invest in the establishment of Chengdu Feimei Joint Venture Co., Ltd. to use American technology to establish a "maglev aircraft" development and production base.

这种美式磁浮飞机是一种新型的陆上有轨高速交通运输工具。它实际上是磁浮列车，用永磁铁替代超导磁铁。最高的"飞行"速度可达 500 km/h，从成都到北京只需 4 个多小时，城内速度最高可达 120 km/h，而票价定位将在空调大巴和出租车之间。磁浮飞机可容纳 100 余名乘客，将适用于 20 km 以上的运距，对西部地区高密度人口城市之间的交通将起极大的作用。比如成都至重庆，如果建设磁浮飞机，1 个半小时可以到达。而且磁浮飞机还具有结构简单、造价低、噪声小等特点，其造价也远低于日式、德式磁浮列车。

This American maglev aircraft is a new type of land rail high-speed transportation. It's actually a maglev train, with permanent magnets instead of superconducting magnets. The highest "flight" speed can reach 500 km/h, from Chengdu to Beijing only takes more than four hours, the highest speed in the city can reach 120 km/h, and the fare will be positioned between air-conditioned buses and taxis. The maglev aircraft can accommodate more than 100 passengers and will be suitable for transportation distances of more than 20 km, which will play a great role in the transportation between cities with high population density in the western region. For example, from Chengdu to Chongqing, if a maglev aircraft is built, it can be reached in one and a half hours. Moreover, maglev aircraft has the characteristics of simple structure, low cost and low noise, and its cost is far lower than that of Japanese and German maglev trains.

目前，中美双方就磁浮飞机项目仅初步达成意向性合作，最终还要通过中美双方政府的认定。如果合作成功的话，将在成都建立一个磁浮飞机生产基地，整个生产线都将建立在轨道上。

At present, China and the United States have only preliminarily reached an intentional cooperation on the maglev aircraft project, which will eventually be approved by the Chinese and American governments. If the cooperation is successful, a maglev aircraft production base will be set up in Chengdu and the entire production line will be set up in orbit.

二、真空永磁悬浮列车

7.4.2 Vacuum Permanent Magnet Suspension Train

在 2002 年 9 月举行的乌鲁木齐经济贸易洽谈会上，乌鲁木齐磁谷科技有限公司展示的磁浮原理车吸引了众多宾客的目光。

At the Urumqi Economic and Trade Fair held in September 2002, the maglev principle vehicle displayed by Urumqi Magnetic Valley Technology Co., Ltd. attracted the attention of many guests.

磁谷科技有限公司首席执行官介绍说，目前他们正在研发的课题被称作"中华 06 号磁浮列车之概念设计"，设计出的一套真空磁浮管道输送系统已获成功。经有关专家论证，根据"中华 06 号磁悬浮列车的概念设计"制作出的原理车，在实验室内运行成功。其中，吊轨式磁浮结构在国际上尚无先例，与德国 TR 系列、日本 ML 系列相比，在关键技术上，如吊轨系列、永磁补偿悬浮等具有创新性。

The CEO of Magnetic Valley Technology Co., Ltd. said that the project they are currently developing is called "Conceptual Design of China 06 Maglev Train", and a set of vacuum maglev pipeline transportation system has been successfully designed. According to the demonstration of relevant experts, the principle vehicle produced according to the "conceptual design of China 06 maglev train" has been successfully operated in the laboratory. Among them, the suspension rail maglev structure has no precedent in the world. Compared with German TR series and Japanese ML series, it is innovative in key technologies, such as suspension rail series and permanent magnet compensation suspension.

据有关媒体介绍，中国正在研制超级磁浮列车，采用真空钢管设计，未来的速度可达到 2 000 km/h。

According to relevant media, China is developing a super maglev train, which is designed with vacuum steel tubes and can reach a speed of 2,000 km/h in the future.

最早提出真空管道磁浮运输概念的，是美国兰德咨询公司和麻省理工学院的专家。真正将这一运输方式落实为图纸的，是美国佛罗里达州机械工程师戴睿·奥斯特（Daryl Oster），经过多年的研究与设计，戴睿于 1999 年在美申请获得真空管道运输（ETT）系统发明专利。

The concept of vacuum pipeline maglev transportation was first put forward by experts from Rand Consulting Company and Massachusetts Institute of Technology. It was Daryl Oster, a mechanical engineer in Florida, USA, who really implemented this mode of transportation as a drawing. After years of research and design, Daryl applied for a patent for the invention of vacuum tube transportation (ETT) system in the United States in 1999.

复习思考题

Questions for Revision

1. 中国是什么时候开始研究磁浮技术的？

1. When did China begin to study maglev technology?

2. 中国研究磁浮技术的单位有哪几家？各自研究情况如何？

2. What are the units that study maglev technology in China? What is the status of their respective research?

3. 简要介绍长沙磁浮快线及其特点。

3. Briefly introduce Changsha Maglev Express Line and its characteristics.

4. 简要介绍北京首条磁浮线路 S1 线及其特点。

4. Briefly introduce the first maglev line S1 in Beijing and its characteristics.

5. 我国在建或拟建磁浮线路有哪些？

5. What are the maglev lines under construction or proposed in China?

6. 新型磁浮交通方式有哪些？各自有何特点？

6. What are the new modes of maglev transportation? What are the characteristics of each?

参考文献

References

[1] 叶云岳. 直线电机及其控制[M]. 杭州：浙江大学出版社，1989.

[1] Ye Yunyue.Linear motor and its control [M]. Hangzhou: Zhejiang University Press, 1989.

[2] 刘华清. 德国磁悬浮列车 Transrapid [M]. 成都：电子科技大学出版社，1995.

[2] Liu Huaqing.German Maglev Transrapid [M]. Chengdu: University of Electronic Science and Technology Press, 1995.

[3] 吴祥明. 磁浮列车[M]. 上海：上海科学技术出版社，2003.

[3] Wu Xiangming.Maglev Train [M]. Shanghai: Shanghai Science and Technology Press, 2003.

[4] 连级三. 磁浮列车原理及技术特征[J]. 电力机车与城轨车辆，2001, 24(3): 23-26.

[4] Lian Jisan. Principle and technical characteristics of maglev train[J]. Electric Locomotive and Urban Rail Vehicles, 2001, 24 (3): 23-26.

[5] 魏庆朝，孔永健. 磁悬浮铁路系统与技术[M]. 北京：中国科学技术出版社，2003.

[5] Wei Qingchao, Kong Yongjian. Maglev Railway System and Technology [M]. Beijing: China Science and Technology Press, 2003.

附录　学习资源

Appendix　Learning Resources

关于磁浮技术的视频资料和课件，可扫描下方二维码查看：
Video materials and courseware about maglev technology can be viewed by scanning the QR code below:

科技之光——上海磁悬浮列车（视频）
Light of Science and Technology—Shanghai Maglev Train (Video)

电磁悬浮系统原理演示（视频）
Principle Demonstration of Electromagnetic Levitation System (video)

神秘列车——真空管道磁悬浮列车（视频）
Mysterious Train—Vacuum Tube Maglev Train (Video)

磁悬浮列车原理、特点、应用（课件）
Principle, Characteristics, Application of Maglev Train (PPT)

真空管道超高速地面轨道交通（课件）
Vacuum Tube Ultra-high-speed Ground Track Transportation (PPT)